ENTREPRENEUR FOR EQUALITY

ENTREPRENEUR FOR EQUALITY

Governor Rufus Bullock, Commerce, and Race in Post–Civil War Georgia

❧ RUSSELL DUNCAN

THE UNIVERSITY OF GEORGIA PRESS / ATHENS AND LONDON

© 1994 by the University of Georgia Press
Athens, Georgia 30602
All rights reserved
Designed by Louise OFarrell
Set in 10/13 Sabon by Tseng Information Systems, Inc.
Printed and bound by Thomson-Shore, Inc.
The paper in this book meets the guidelines for permanence
and durability of the Committee on Production Guidelines
for Book Longevity of the Council on Library Resources.

Printed in the United States of America

98 97 96 95 94   C   5 4 3 2 1

Library of Congress Cataloging in Publication Data
Duncan, Russell.
Entrepreneur for equality : Governor Rufus Bullock, commerce,
and race in post–Civil War Georgia / Russell Duncan.
p.   cm.
Includes bibliographical references and index.
ISBN 0–8203–1557–5 (alk. paper)
1. Bullock, Rufus B. (Rufus Brown), 1834–1907.   2. Governors—
Georgia—Biography.   3. Reconstruction—Georgia.   4. Georgia—
Politics and government—1865–1950.   5. Georgia—Race relations.
I. Title.
F291.B93 D86   1994
975.8'03—dc20   93–4163
British Library Cataloging in Publication Data available

Title page: Rufus Bullock, in a portrait by Mathew Brady
(Library of Congress)

For Emory, who guaranteed it

Contents

Preface

THE YEARS OF Reconstruction and the New South were about hope and expansion, but they also were filled with corruption and racism—two realities that so coexisted and fed upon each other that they are difficult to distinguish. For years novelists, newspaper writers, and historians recanted a depiction of Reconstruction as "a blackout of honest government." Tales of corruption pointed fingers at Republican officeholders, white and black.

In Georgia, even though acquitted of gubernatorial wrongdoing and prominent in New South circles, Rufus Brown Bullock was a "carpetbag beast man"—part carpetbagger and part scalawag—who for over one hundred years remained the symbol of military-Negro-Yankee rule. Critics insisted that Bullock was corrupt and hailed the return and redemption of planter control. The resultant disfranchisement of half the state's male population reflected the degree to which white Southerners would not recognize the real meaning of corruption as a denial of the American creed.

Many have written of the Gilded Age in terms of robber barons and the runaway graft of Boss Tweed, Grant's men, the Philadelphia Ring, and the corruption of Reconstruction governments. Although it is unnecessary further to demonstrate the ubiquity of collusive boodle rings and individual looters, it would be of benefit to find a definition of corruption which goes beyond graft and self-aggrandizing politicians to discover why Reconstruction failed to meet the promise of equality of opportunity and justice inherent and overt in the American creed. Our Declaration of Independence, Constitution, and Statue of Liberty, to say nothing of our idea of manifest destiny, scream our mottoes of equality to the world, and yet the reality of American history is the story of failing to live up to our professed ideals.

As governor of Georgia when three amendments to the Constitution—the Thirteenth, Fourteenth, and Fifteenth—and the still smoldering specter of civil war marked out the path for reforming the real to the creed, Bullock stood out manfully for change. When forced to decide if his own political and economic career mattered more than racial justice, Bullock opted for the latter. For so doing, he was vilified by a racist press that sought to keep blacks in their place. Thereafter, his every action was scrutinized and labeled corrupt by the partisan minions of reactionary conservatism.

Bullock is of prime importance to Georgia history because around him revolves the myth of the Lost Cause with its need to keep blacks in their place. Many historians accepted the Lost Cause myth, the charges of monetary corruption, or both and portrayed the governor as a self-serving opportunist. This study attempts to revise that judgment by looking at Bullock's life from his early days as a New York schoolboy, past his Confederate activities, through his gubernatorial difficulties, and into his prominent position near the head of New South circles. I hope this biography will help illuminate the often misunderstood eras of Reconstruction and Gilded Age Georgia while it attempts to demonstrate that, when considering forms of corruption, stealing money is a minor blip compared to the degradation of a people by a people who insist they are devoted to a higher creed.

I would like to thank all those who involved themselves in this project. Many people behind the scenes who remain invisible to me were nonetheless the sine qua non of formulations, research, writing, rewriting, editing, evaluation, and publishing that made this book possible. A few of the more visible people who guided me along the way must be named here.

Numan V. Bartley influenced my interpretations of history in many ways for which I must blame, praise, and never forgive him. Others who studied with him and, in particular, who took his 1983 seminar in historiography at the University of Georgia had their minds forced open by his intense interrogations. That he suggested this biography of Bullock only implicates him further. But because he will cringe at some of my conclusions, proofs, and intellectual voids, I reluctantly admit that any gaps in argument are mine and mine alone.

Other friends and teachers who helped me survive the rigors of graduate school and directed my advance include Michael Cassity, Joe and Ann Berrigan, Tom Ganschow, Fran Thomas, Alf Heggoy, Bennett and Neva Wall, Mary McFeely, Kirk and Libby Willis, Gilbert Fite, Lester Stephens, Phinizy Spalding, and William Leary. Special thanks to Bill McFeely, Bob

Pratt, and Jean Friedman for serving on my reading committee. Bill's continuing advice and friendship challenge and support all my trajectories.

Graduate student mates helped ease and increase the load at O'Malley's Tavern and elsewhere. Thank you and damn you Terri Blair (and John), Brian Wills, Christopher Phillips (and Dulcie), Winfield Myers (and Deena), Tom Richey, Randy Patton, Mick Jagger (honorary), Glenn Eskew, Sharon Flanagan, Michael Justus, LeAnn Grabavoy, Stan Deaton, Jennifer Lund, Jon Bryant, Kevin Pittard, and Glenna Schroeder-Lein for all the times that still hold us close and far.

The librarians at all the repositories were very professional. Those at the University of Georgia's main library, the Swan Library in Albion, New York, the Georgia Historical Society in Savannah, the National Archives, Library of Congress, and Atlanta Historical Society went beyond the required to give me extraordinary help. Georgia's Larry Gulley, Nelson Morgan, and Joe Cote deserve special mention. Virginia Shadron at the Georgia Department of Archives and History introduced me to a wealth of informative materials. Local historians Neil Johnson and Bill Lattin of Albion, New York, opened their homes and files and showed me along the paths of Bullock's youth.

Director Malcolm Call and the staff of the University of Georgia Press provided more encouragement than criticism in turning this manuscript into a book. Talented copyeditor Trudie Calvert spent days of hours bettering my work. Matt Brook and Karen Orchard especially kept up my spirits with their positive advice and good humor. Press readers Edmund L. Drago and Eric Foner offered professional critiques that strengthened my understanding and prose; their earlier works on overlapping topics provided direction from the start. They are not responsible for suggestions I failed to heed.

Mary McGeary of John Carroll University unselfishly transformed computer formats. Arts and Sciences Dean Frederick Travis, Graduate School Dean Sally H. Wertheim, History Department Chair David Robson, and the Faculty Development Committee provided funding in support of this project. A Phelps-Stokes Fellowship contributed greatly to my ability to complete the manuscript.

Psychological and other support also came from my family. Love and thanks to my mother, Joan, and to J. W., Mary Ella, Pete, and Betty. Holly and Bonnie Katherine not only survived the comic tragedy of my being in graduate school but always stood ready to give me more than smiles and hugs. That they continue to do so is a special godsend.

Emory Thomas has sustained me in ways that only he can relate. He directed my intellectual growth after I climbed from the cockpit of a reconnaissance aircraft in 1982, threw down my flight suit, and approached him with a wide-eyed naïveté about wanting to study the Civil War. He made order where I had none, listened to deep confidences, persuaded others that I could make it, and pulled me along with his gracious patience. This book is his.

ENTREPRENEUR FOR EQUALITY

Chapter 1 ✣ Yankee Schoolboy to Confederate Lieutenant Colonel

Be Just and Fear Not
—*Orleans Republican*, February 5, 1845

Principles, Not Men
—*Orleans Republican*, March 7, 1849

SITTING ONSTAGE just behind the speaker, the distinguished master of ceremonies, Rufus Brown Bullock, listened to Booker T. Washington give the speech of his life. The audience enthusiastically applauded the black man's words that his race was an economic ally, not the enemy, of Southern white society. "In all things that are purely social, we can be as separate as the fingers, yet one as the hand in all things essential to mutual progress. There is no defence or security for any of us, except in the highest intelligence and development of all."[1]

Washington accommodated too much; this was his chance to speak for black people to a nationwide audience, and he told white people only what they wanted to hear. But Bullock must have thrilled to watch a former slave give a keynote address opening the 1895 Atlanta Cotton States and International Exposition. Like Washington, Bullock at that time advocated equal but separate coexistence for blacks and whites in the South. Like Washington, Bullock was a principled but practical man.

A quarter of a century earlier, Bullock, Georgia's only Republican governor, had joined black leaders Henry M. Turner, James M. Simms, and Tunis G. Campbell to promote full equality and equal citizenship for all Americans. Eventually, he came to realize that most white Georgians, and white Americans generally, were incapable of living out their expressed creed that "all men are created equal." So Bullock made the best of the times. He supported Washington's call for separate but equal as the expedient to save black lives and help black people advance at the most deliberate speed. He came to this accommodation as a result of a long career in the business world, where the marketplace promoted compromise, and after sixty-one years of reconciling what ought to be with what was possible.

Born in Bethlehem, New York, on March 28, 1834, Bullock moved with his family to Albion when he was six years old. His father, Volkert Veeder Bullock, was interested in the business opportunities of this Orleans County village, halfway between Rochester and Buffalo. By routing the Erie Canal through this country place, engineers and promoters assured Albion's rise.[2]

Volkert's father, Joseph, immigrated to New York from Yorkshire, England, sometime before the American Revolution. He bought a large amount of land in the Hudson Valley, locating near an immigrant of Dutch origins, Peter Veeder. Later, Joseph married Veeder's daughter Margaret. The Bullocks raised four children; Volkert was born in 1806. In 1830 Volkert married Jane Eliza Brown, thereby joining large agricultural interests with the city mercantile interests of her father, Rufus Brown. Volkert and Jane Eliza had three children, Rufus, Cornelia (named after Jane's mother, Cornelia McClellan), and Freeman Clarke.[3]

Resettling from Albany to the town of Barre in 1840, the Bullocks paid $800 for land and a house in the village of Albion. For the next twenty-six years, they increased their income by purchasing real estate, some of it at courthouse sales, and selling it later at a profit. In 1841 they bought and moved into a house on a half-acre plot on Liberty Street near the center of Albion; there they remained until their deaths forty years later.[4]

The Erie Canal opened in 1825, linking New York City through Albany to the West. From Albany to Buffalo the forty-foot-wide, twenty-eight-foot-deep canal stretched 363 miles. The canal, plus dominance in the Southern cotton trade, combined to make New York the nation's leading commercial center. Trade flowed through Albion, which was located on the canal. The small village grew rapidly and offered chances for enterprising Yankees to grab a handful of their own particular American Dream. Journalist and poet Philip Freneau wrote quatrains to promote the canal:

With such gigantic works of old
This proud *Canal* may be enrolled,
Which to our use no tyrant gave
Nor owes its grandeur to one Slave,

. . . .

See Commerce *here* expand her sail,
And distant shores these waters hail,
As wafting to Manhattan's coast
The products that new regions boast.

One enthusiastic Albionite added: "Prosperity came in on every hand; the mud dried up, and the musketoes and the ague, and the fever, and the bears, left the country."[5]

Still, Orleans County, located on the south shore of Lake Ontario, remained primarily agricultural. The principal crops included barley, oats, corn, beans, potatoes, apples, peaches, cherries, and plums. Shippers sent thousands of barrels of produce yearly to eastern buyers. Later, lumber, cattle, and sheep were conspicuous among the commodities headed to market. Albion became the county seat as stores and businesses made way for manufacturing interests. Prominent, or soon to be, business leaders included banker and communications entrepreneur Freeman Clarke and industrialist George M. Pullman.

Clarke rose from a position as bank cashier to become director and president of many New York banks, railroads, and telegraph and trust companies. Politically a Whig, then a Republican, who had been vice-president of the 1850 Whig National Convention, he served six years in Congress, two years as a Lincoln-appointed comptroller of the currency, and as a delegate to the New York State constitutional convention of 1867.

During his life in Albion, George Pullman built a steam factory to make cabinets, furniture, and coffins. In an early advertisement he offered to rent hearses and carriages for funerals "on the most reasonable terms." Both Clarke and Pullman served as examples for aspiring young entrepreneurs growing up in Albion. The paths of Freeman Clarke and Rufus Bullock crossed there in the 1850s, in Augusta in the 1860s, and in Atlanta in the 1880s.[6]

Supported by kinship ties to Freeman Clarke and with the help of his father-in-law, longtime Albany merchant Rufus Brown, Volkert Bullock plunged into the community's business affairs. He established a stove foundry and operated it for nine years. Bullock joined Clarke and others to organize the House Printing Telegraph Company. An early promoter and operator of the telegraph, he supervised the construction of lines between Albany and Buffalo and remained active in the telegraph business for a decade. In the 1850s, he sat on the board of directors of the Bank of Orleans. After 1859, he promoted the implementation of gas lighting and became treasurer, then superintendent and one of the largest stockholders in the Albion Gas Light Company. One local newspaper wrote of his natural mechanical inclination and called him well-read, "skillful, prompt, methodical, industrious and economical, and [a man who] knew the value of time, and [who paid] constant attention . . . to the minutest details." He grew up in a business-oriented family, married a merchant's daughter, and earned a reputation as a solid worker and leader in community business development. His efforts also facilitated communication, trade, and conveniences for people in western New York.[7]

Bullock also played important roles in Albion society and politics. A church officer for over forty years, he served as the senior elder in the Presbyterian church, Albion's oldest and largest denomination. Peers believed him to be a "sincere and consistent Christian." Jane Eliza lent strong support to her husband's faith and was described by a contemporary as "a zealous and active Christian worker." Another friend remembered her as particularly charitable, "gifted with refinement, education, rare conversational talent and a peculiarly winning and attractive temperament." In 1848, the Bullocks helped form the Albion Temperance Society. Holding meetings in the basement of the Presbyterian church, members advocated "an entire abstinence from all intoxicating drinks." Volkert also stood in the vanguard of those Albionites who advocated and supported a system of free schools. For over twenty years, he served as a school commissioner. He believed in the principles of social overhead capital, considering projects for the public good to be more important than selfish private interest. In politics, Bullock always voted with the Whig, then Republican, party and firmly believed their principles would most benefit the welfare and growth of America. He passed these beliefs on to his son Rufus. In 1856, as proof of his belief in service, Bullock ran for and was elected to a four-year term as justice of the peace.[8]

Bullock's activities as businessman, community booster, and education advocate fit squarely and easily within the confines of Eric Foner's exposition of the "free soil, free labor, free men" ideology of the Republican party. Northerners viewed their own society as a model, rooted in the American creed and dream. Free labor meant having choices in selecting a job and, ultimately, the chance to leave the wage-earning class for economic self-sufficiency. Important to this view was a belief in equality of opportunity and social mobility and the identification of farmers, craftsmen, and businessmen as independent entrepreneurs. Internal improvements such as telegraphs, railroads, and bridges were as vitally important to social and economic advancement as education and religion. As Foner observed, "Material and moral developments were but two sides of the same coin." Clearly, Volkert Bullock's life was directed at improving the material and moral development of himself, his family, and his community.[9]

Jane Eliza's family stressed education. Her three brothers benefited from their parents' ability to send them to good schools: one became a doctor, one a lawyer and a judge, and one, Joseph B. Brown, gained a commission as a general in the Union army.[10]

Shortly after their arrival in Albion in 1840, the Bullocks enrolled Rufus in school. He probably first went to the common school and, in 1844, entered the newly capitalized Albion Academy. A first-year catalog announced that the academy would prepare students for college as well as inculcate them with business skills. Young men enrolled in the senior English course could expect preparation to enter "with success and honor the various professions, and for adorning the numerous situations of profit and responsibility. . . . Peculiar attention is paid to Practical Mathematics . . . to secure lucrative and prominent places [for the graduates]." Teachers expected students to master Latin, Greek, English, and French and to pay strict attention to elocution. Other courses included philosophy, chemistry, astronomy, bookkeeping, moral science, geology, botany, surveying, algebra, and rhetoric. The academic year consisted of two semesters of twenty-two weeks each, which by 1843 had become three quarters of fifteen weeks each. To calm parental fears about licentious behavior, the catalog announced: "The Government of the school is to be strictly paternal." Albion Academy joined Phipps Union Female Seminary and a common school to make Albion a center of learning.[11]

The academy held its first classes in February 1838 in the Baptist church with thirty-six students working under Edwin R. Reynolds, who had studied at Brown University. Reynolds served as teacher until December 1846, when he began a law practice in Albion. As an instructor, he maintained strict discipline, punishing those who broke his rules by pinching them "severely" on the shoulders. One student remembered Reynolds as strongly oriented to helping disadvantaged people who were trying but failing to make it on their own. An early supporter of the Republican party, Reynolds was elected in 1860 to the United States Congress. He consistently opposed any extension of slavery and introduced, unsuccessfully, a bill to abolish slavery in the District of Columbia.[12]

In 1840, classes moved to the new, but yet unfinished, academic building. When completed, the building rose three stories high above a basement and stretched forty by sixty feet. It contained a well-stocked chemistry laboratory and a good library. On the third floor were ten rooms which students leased for $1.00 to $1.50 per term. In 1843, thirty students, two to four in each room, lived there in rooms "furnished with a stove, French bed stead, bed and pillows, table, three chairs, pail, washstand, bowl and pitcher." As an alternative, students could board with village families for $1.25 to $1.50 a week. After the addition of an elementary school, the academy grew rapidly to 170 pupils in 1843, 258 by 1846, and 395 seven years later. By the time Rufus enrolled, the academy had opened its doors to female students.[13]

Teachers at Albion Academy stressed good conduct and character, and the academy advertised: "Special regard will be paid to the manners, habits, and morals of the students." Many of the teachers were, or would become, preachers, missionaries, or social workers. From 1841 to 1848, Reverend J. W. French, a graduate of Middlebury College and the Andover Theological Seminary, taught in the academy. At least three instructors actively involved themselves with the abolitionist crusade. The academy's teachers bravely protested the slave system, providing a waypoint on the underground railroad where "poor refugees found concealment, food and drink in retired rooms in the old Academy, that they might be put upon the night train for . . . liberty." From 1841 to 1865 and 1874 to 1875, Abel Stilson taught there. Upon his death in 1899, a friend described him as a "thorough going republican" who took "an active and influential part in the exciting discussions of the great anti-slavery struggle, from the Free Soil movement in 1848 . . . down to 1863 when slavery was abolished." Stilson believed "in the party and its principles, Free Soil, Free Speech, and Free Men."[14]

Taught by men who shared Stilson's and Reynolds's moral and political convictions, students at Albion Academy learned moral lessons in the equality of man far beyond what normal classical studies offered. The teachers and the lessons had an impact on the young Bullock.

When he entered the academy in 1844, Bullock joined one of the two literary societies and a debating club. He made friends with several boys, including George Pullman's younger brother Jim. Yet the student who had the most impact on "Rufe" was an escaped slave, Jimmy Little, who became the protégé of community leader Thomas C. Fanning. Fanning ran a dry goods and drugstore in town and served as an elder in the Albion Presbyterian Church where Bullock worshiped. Consistent with his egalitarian beliefs, Fanning placed Jimmy in the academy. Fifty years later, Jimmy Little and integrated classrooms were Bullock's most important memory of the academy.[15]

Bullock grew up in the two-story house on the corner of Liberty and Park streets. From his front yard, he could throw a rock to the east across Liberty Street and hit the Episcopal parsonage, or to the south across Park and hit the Baptist church or parsonage on the corner. Three blocks to the northwest was Albion Academy; his walk to school took Rufus by the home of E. R. Reynolds. Three blocks north, the Erie Canal gave a northern boundary to the main business district, which stretched out along the canal and for two blocks perpendicularly down the village's main avenue, Batavia Street. The north side of the canal was the towing path so the village grew southward. Phipps Union Female Seminary, the courthouse, clerk's office, jail, and Presbyterian church stood one block east of Bullock's home, visual reminders of the message of village life in the mid-nineteenth century: education, justice, law, morality, and salvation.[16]

His father's religious and business activities, Albion's location on the canal, his mother's interest in education, the academy's offerings in classical and practical studies, as well as the teachers' egalitarian and abolitionist concerns had an enormous influence on Bullock's growth. Additionally, Albion was a part of the "burned-over district," so named because of the evangelistic fever that swept over the area between Rochester and Buffalo in the late 1820s. Charles G. Finney struck a spark of religious fire by attacking John Calvin's ideas of predestination and promoting instead the idea of individual responsibility for salvation. Finney's efforts pulled thousands into church pews. Coincidentally, this evangelical crusade swept many believers into the antislavery movement.[17]

The influence of nearby Rochester, a center of abolitionist activity and fulcrum for Frederick Douglass's efforts, must have had some impact on Bullock, if only as echoes filtered through local abolitionists and teachers such as Stilson and Reynolds. Travelers who daily arrived and departed on the canal increased the residents' knowledge of national news and gave Albion a more cosmopolitan air than its twelve hundred residents justified. In short, Albion contained just about every influence that promoted a free labor system and ideology. Bullock watched, listened, and lived his teenage years in this environment of education, business, expanding communication and transportation, and moral abolitionism.

After graduating from Albion Academy in 1850 at age sixteen, Bullock worked for a year as a clerk in a general store. The next year, he became interested in telegraphy and, with his father's influence, secured a job with the local company. The telegraph, a new development in rapid communication, was just seven years old when Rufus began his career. In 1844, Samuel F. B. Morse built the first electric telegraph in the United States, and during the next decade new companies rapidly strung wire throughout New York State. By 1849, with the aid of Freeman Clarke, the New York, Albany, and Buffalo Telegraph Company linked Albany to Buffalo along the old stagecoach road. Bullock's father bought stock in the nascent company and worked for some time as an operator in the Albion office. Naturally he promoted his son's career, but young Bullock's abilities were noteworthy. Historians of the telegraph James Reid and George Prescott cite Bullock among the vanguard of the profession and name him as the first person able to interpret signals by sound instead of looking at the printer. In 1880, one telegrapher remembered that of the "bright young men who were attracted toward our profession in the earliest days of the telegraph, there was none that became a more efficient working operator than Rufus B. Bullock." The writer remembered Bullock's "wonderful proficiency" and the "unceasing energy, the indomitable courage, and the love of fair play." [18]

Bullock's father made a $1,000 yearly salary, which he earned by deciding where to locate new routes and repairing lines and procuring poles. To cut costs and accommodate two lines instead of one, he suggested the company buy taller poles. With an eye to more efficient management, Volkert challenged the policy of hiring operators and then leaving them to conduct the affairs of their particular offices as they saw fit. In a letter to Freeman Clarke, he suggested adoption of the Morse method of giving a "competent operator" full authority over all other operators so as to expedite problems and provide better service. He recommended Utica as the base and asked that Rufus "be appointed in that capacity." [19]

But Clarke did not appoint Rufus to the position, and by August 1855 the situation had created tension between the two men. Volkert would not let the matter rest and wrote Clarke two more letters suggesting his son's promotion on merit and on the "ground of old associations, etc."[20]

Rufus wrote Clarke apologizing for his father's letters and restating his qualifications. He admitted that many operators supported another person for the job. Rufus explained that when the other operators claimed not to like his "officiousness," they were simply resentful of his efficiency. Then he confessed: "I do not perhaps stand as well as I should owing to some lackness on my part in not rendering minute items of expenditure." But in the "actual working & management of the wires," Bullock considered himself top of the heap.[21]

As his letter suggested, Bullock seemed inclined to pay more attention to efficiency than to bookkeeping, a flaw on which his enemies would pounce in later, more turbulent years. In 1855, after Clarke again refused to promote him, Bullock looked elsewhere and was soon employed by the newly incorporated American Telegraph Company. As manager of the Philadelphia office, he helped establish operations between Philadelphia and New York in competition with the Magnetic Line. He collaborated with Professor David Hughes to invent a faster printing machine to function over longer circuits. Soon their Hughes Printing Telegraph vaulted the American Telegraph Company to the forefront of the business.[22]

By 1859, the company merged with its competitors and Bullock's was one of the known names in the industry. William B. Dinsmore, president of the Adams Express Company, took special note of Bullock's "remarkable success" and exploited the timing of the merger to hire the young wizard away from the American Telegraph Company. He sent Bullock south, to Augusta, Georgia, to help expand lines and business in a new, yet unstable, market.[23]

Arriving in Augusta in 1859, Bullock must have been reassured by the many Northerners among the city's population. At least twelve of the Adams Express Company's seventeen employees in Augusta were northern-born. Like Albion, this city on the Savannah River had a canal, completed between 1845 and 1852. Industrialists harnessed the power generated by the canal and the river, and Augusta led Georgia in manufacturing interests, with more than a million dollars invested in cotton, flour, and paper mills, an iron foundry, and a porcelain works. By 1860, six of Georgia's twenty-five banks transacted business there.[24]

Yet Augusta at that time must have seemed a foreign culture to the young Northerner. Unlike Albion, which had only two blacks in 1850, African-Americans made up almost one-third of the population. Of 12,493 residents in 1860, 3,663 were slaves of white masters, and 386 free blacks lived in that anomalous status in which race bound them as securely as class. Bullock adapted. He had to if he wanted to expand his business opportunities. He met Benjamin Conley and Foster Blodgett, men who ranked high in Augusta society as mayor and city councilman, respectively. The three soon became fast friends and lifetime associates.[25]

Bullock boarded in the Planters' Hotel before moving to 172 Greene Street, in the most fashionable residential area in downtown Augusta. The move coincided with his marriage in 1860 to Marie Elizabeth Salisbury, daughter of a Pawtucket, Rhode Island, pilot. The Bullocks joined and were active members of St. Paul's Episcopal Church. His change from the Presbyterian church may be explained as adopting his wife's preference or perhaps because St. Paul's membership stood higher socially. Bullock served as a vestryman from 1864 to 1868, and Marie was baptized into the church and confirmed by Bishop Stephen Elliot in May 1864. The couple's three children, Volkert Veeder, born December 8, 1862, Rufus (Rufie) Brown, born August 6, 1864, and Cornelia, born April 22, 1866, were all baptized at St. Paul's. Almost no information has survived about Bullock's home life. He was so involved with business that he had little time for anything else. At this juncture in his life, Bullock was hard-pressed to keep pace with his boss, who seemed to work twenty-four hours a day.[26]

A Connecticut Yankee, Henry Bradley Plant, ran the Southern division of the Adams Express Company. In Augusta in 1854, the year of the company's charter, Plant supervised 24,412 miles of rail, 886 wagons, and 6,808 men. He lived with his wife in the Eagle and Phoenix Hotel until the outbreak of the war, when he moved to 303 Broad Street, the Planters' Hotel. He obviously considered himself a transient and probably feared investing in property during the war. At any rate, for this workaholic, convenience to the office was his prime concern. The Augusta office of the Adams Express was two blocks away at 179 Broad Street.[27]

In 1861 Adams Express Company officials fretted that their Southern interests might be confiscated by the Confederacy. To prevent this, the company sold its Southern operations to Southern stockholders who elected Plant president of the now Southern Express Company. In reality, the new company still transacted business with its parent organization throughout the war. Capitalists had simply protected their investment by dividing it to prevent disunion and war from interfering with business.[28]

Bullock had been in Augusta barely a year when the war came. In such volatile times, when Southerners suspected the intentions of every man of Northern birth, Bullock felt the need to prove that he sympathized with the South. Motivated by business more than anything else, Bullock's Southern "loyalty" stemmed from the chance to make money. He had opposed secession, joining Plant and other Republicans who sought to hold the nation together. Bullock wrote letters home to Albion expressing hope for peace even while realizing that the political situation foreshadowed the worst. Augusta was not rabidly secessionist; moderate leaders Charles J. Jenkins, John P. King, and Foster Blodgett opposed disunion. But with Abraham Lincoln's election, local firebrands stirred up support for a Confederate nation and succeeded in electing their candidates to the 1861 secession convention. In December 1860, Southern nationalists lifted a banner at the Savannah River border with South Carolina. It read: "Side by Side, We Will Secede." [29]

South Carolina left the Union on December 20, 1860. Georgia followed on January 19, 1861. Five days later, under orders from Georgia governor Joseph E. Brown, one thousand men mustered and demanded the surrender of the United States arsenal in Augusta. Brown personally led the men to the arsenal and seized without a fight twenty-two thousand muskets and rifles, a battery of howitzers, some powder and shot, and two cannons. Bullock stood among the ninety-man Oglethorpe Infantry when the arsenal capitulated. A newspaper article later noted that when Governor Brown addressed the successful troops "in the mud and rain drenched to the skin and shivering in the cold winds of winter, stood private Rufus B. Bullock, with gun in hand, applauding, and cheering Brown's . . . utterances." It would have been bad business for Bullock to have done anything else.[30]

With the establishment of the Southern Express Company, Bullock became superintendent of eastern operations. Working as an adjunct to the Confederate Quartermaster Bureau, the Southern Express Company built telegraph lines and transported packages throughout the South. As Northern and Southern armies moved along the battle front, Bullock's company cooperated with the Adams Express at various points to keep packages and freight flowing across the hostile border. Telegraph lines and wagons went back and forth between the companies with minimal confusion. The express companies augmented the postal service and facilitated communication between soldiers and their loved ones.[31]

Many people on both sides believed the express more reliable than the post office, and they were right. The Confederate government in 1861 designated the Southern Express as the official carrier of all Confederate monies, including soldiers' pay. Secretary of the Treasury Christopher G. Memminger exempted Southern Express workers from service in the Confederate army because of their critical duties as civilian contractors. Bullock, who was exempt, wrote Memminger on December 2, 1861, imploring him to intervene with governors, in particular the governor of Tennessee, who did not want to exempt telegraph employees. Bullock termed exemption a "necessity for preventing the disorganization of our present trustworthy corps of employees." [32]

On January 1, 1863, Bullock again wrote Memminger, enclosing a list of an additional ninety employees in North Carolina, South Carolina, and Georgia who were subject to conscription but whom he deemed indispensable to the agency; twenty-three of them resided in Augusta. The Confederate government paid the Southern Express for its services, and beginning in 1862 it also paid $200 monthly to rent fifty-nine rooms of a large, express-owned building in Augusta for use as a hospital for wounded soldiers. [33]

Although Bullock had plenty to do managing his business affairs, he also contributed to the growth and development of enterprise in Augusta as the city became a center of war industry in Georgia. The city's factories produced many items for the Confederate army. A huge mill, the largest in the world, made powder for the Ordnance Bureau. Wounded soldiers convalesced in Augusta's hospitals. Two major textile mills made cotton and woolen goods for the Quartermaster Bureau. The *Augusta Chronicle* singled out Bullock for praise when he purchased some equipment to speed the manufacturing of shoes and clothing for the Southern army. In particular, Bullock bought from Leeds, England, a "labor and time saving machine" that could "cut through five thicknesses of sole leather and sixty thicknesses of grey Confederate cloth, for soldiers coats and pants." With the machine, "one man can do the work of fifty." [34]

Bullock also participated in the Confederate government's management of Southern transport and communications. In December 1862, a convention of railroad managers met in Augusta to discuss the government's decision to control all Southern railroads. Under the plan, the Confederacy would coordinate the use of all lines to transport men and goods but would neither nationalize the roads nor attempt to operate them from Richmond. The railroad men agreed to work with the government in return for higher rates. Thus, as Mary DeCredico points out in her study of

Georgia entrepreneurs, railroad managers dropped some of their parochial activities and worked with other roads in an industrywide focus and plan. The railroaders saw the government's role as one of "aid, not control."[35]

Bullock hardly could have helped becoming involved in this activity. After all, the Southern Express Company had to keep abreast of all railroad activities to conduct its business. Furthermore, Bullock's job entailed establishing telegraph lines throughout the Southern interior and furnishing supplies and payrolls to General R. E. Lee's army. During the war the Confederate government increasingly controlled and aided business development. Bullock would use the experience and ideas gained during that time to implement similar expansion during the postwar years.

Not everyone praised the Southern Express Company. Critics complained about high rates and false patriotism. Reporting that letters from the New York office of the Adams Express regularly arrived at Plant's Augusta office, some newspapers accused the Southern Express of treasonable activities. Of course, Plant called this nonsense and discounted the letters as forgeries. He reaffirmed the independence of the Southern Express and pointed out that Southerners held all the company's stock. Plant explained that his company had had to stop allowing citizens to send freight free of charge to soldiers in the field because of the enormous costs involved: "We support the cause but cannot be expected to bear the expense." At various times during the war, the company did donate horses, wagons, and free service to help the Confederate cause. One editor responded by praising the company as "indispensible to the public good. . . . [It] is a powerful auxiliary to the Government and of incalculable benefit to the soldiers in the field, and to commerce generally." And after the company resumed the practice of sending private parcels to the troops at no charge, the editor crowed: "The recent action of the Southern Express Company in engaging to forward packages of food and clothing free of charge to the soldiers is worthy of all praise." Still, the company operated first for profits and second to help the Confederacy.[36]

During the war, Bullock alternated his time between Richmond and Augusta. Until 1863 he worked under the direction of Plant. In that year Plant went to Europe and left Bullock in charge of operations. Bullock's main job included directing the construction of telegraph lines so that the Richmond government could stay in contact with its troops. His major project was the construction of lines from Richmond to Atlanta. Naturally, such work also promised profits for the company because it sold telegrams from soldiers to civilians and vice versa. The express side of the company also profited from the shipment of packages by rail or wagon throughout the Confederacy. His most interesting single job was probably his last major task for the Confederacy. In the winter of 1865, while General William T. Sherman burned Columbia, Bullock took charge of $1.5 million in Confederate gold, loaded it into six wagons, and transported it from the South Carolina capital to Augusta. To preserve secrecy, Bullock and a group of express teamsters made the trip without a military escort. In Augusta, Bullock deposited the money in the Mechanic's Bank. When the gold later disappeared, Bullock insisted he had done his duty and knew nothing of it.[37]

While the express service profited from the war, Bullock prospered too. By 1864, he reported a total property value of $22,000 to Richmond County tax officers. Tax digests show that he owned seven slaves. The ownership of human beings by a man with Bullock's background and beliefs is inconsistent with his training by abolitionists and his membership in the Republican party as well as with his actions in later life. From 1867 until his death in 1907, Bullock championed equal rights; in fact, that issue cost him a final year in the gubernatorial chair and forty years of public and private abuse. Perhaps Bullock was following the precedent set by his superior, Henry Plant, who had purchased a slave, Dennis Dorsey, to help with work at the company. There is some evidence that Dorsey asked Plant to buy him to keep him from being sold away from Augusta. It is likely that when Plant left for Europe in 1863, Bullock "inherited" the company's slaves; that is, maybe they were listed as his property because he managed the company. Bullock idealized Plant, calling him "persistent . . . industrious . . . friendly, frank, and appreciative . . . a good manager." Perhaps Plant told him the good of the company came before his conscience regarding slavery. Maybe Bullock believed this on his own. Maybe he simply acquiesced to the way of life in this part of the country and convinced himself that someone had to own black people and he would be a kinder owner than most. In any case, Bullock never explained why but did admit to having owned black people during the war.[38]

During the war's final days, Bullock directed the acquisition and transport of private packages and public supplies to Lee's tired army. As an acting lieutenant colonel in the Confederate Quartermaster Bureau, charged with railroad transportation, Bullock surrendered with the Army of Northern Virginia at Appomattox Courthouse in April 1865. On parole, he did not go directly back to Augusta but stayed in northern Virginia. Still working with the Southern Express Company, he supplied Secretary of War Edwin M. Stanton and General Henry W. Halleck with information in the investigation of Lincoln's assassination. Bullock told Stanton that on April 11 a trunk of letters belonging to George N. Sanders had been stored in the cellar of one of the company's agents in Lynchburg, Virginia. Stanton gave Bullock a confidential letter to deliver to Halleck in Richmond which ordered confiscation of the trunk and arrest of Sanders's wife and daughter. Halleck waited for Bullock before complying with the task and beginning a search of houses in Richmond.[39]

Bullock's association with Stanton so soon after the war's end, the nature of his wartime activities, and the link between the Southern and Adams Express companies opened Bullock to charges of having been a federal spy. In April 1868, one Georgia editor claimed that Union general William S. Rosecrans had confirmed that Bullock had furnished "information to the enemies of the South." The *Savannah Morning News* concluded: "He was a spy." Four months later the *Augusta Chronicle* called him the "former Express Agent and reputed Federal spy." If these charges could be proved, Bullock's wartime activities in control of a telegraph system and supply line would be interpreted as invaluable to the federal effort. But no proof has yet been found. These reports remain unsubstantiated Democratic assaults on his character. Bullock's actions in association with Stanton seem consistent with what any Northern man might do who thought he had information concerning the murder of a president. After doing whatever he did in the war's immediate aftermath, Bullock returned home to Augusta to resume his business career.[40]

Bullock's life thus far had been one of steady progress toward wealth and status. Rather than interrupting his advance, the war opened doors of opportunity by crushing the slave system and promising to replace it with the Northern way of work. If ever the chance to become an entrepreneur existed, surely it was now in a South desperate for cash and development. Bullock had been schooled in the ideology of free labor, hammered home to him by his father's business and moral teachings. He would use all his knowledge and connections with the Northern way of life to expand the material prosperity of Georgia—and to fill his own pocketbook.

Chapter 2 ❧ Augusta Entrepreneur

Let not pride, prejudice, and folly blind us and lead
us stumbling backward over a wilderness of graves.
—Osborne A. Lochrane, 1865

WITH THE WAR'S END, the South became a land of opportunity for anyone with money. The fight had settled the question of what kind of labor
system every state would have. The South could no longer use slave labor.
In the devastation of war and poverty, the chance opened for people with
vision to remake the land in a Northern mold. Historian Larry Powell
has described the vast numbers of Northerners who came South after the
war to take advantage of the chance to gain their American dream. Some
succeeded; many failed.[1]

Bullock returned to Augusta to take advantage of peacetime business
opportunities. The city escaped the devastation many Georgia cities experienced from Sherman's destructive war and continued as an active trade
center. As early as 1866 writer John R. Dennett noted Augusta's rising
business climate and surmised that Northern capital flowed into the city.
A scant five years after Appomattox, a visitor remarked that "anything can
be bought there." These descriptions conflict with the usual depiction of
the postwar South as a place where no money existed to buy anything and
there was nothing to buy. Certainly, Augusta was an exception to the extreme deprivation experienced in most areas. Entrepreneurs such as Henry
Plant, John King, and Rufus Bullock helped bring Northern monies to a
capital-poor region.[2]

Although Henry Plant had returned from Europe, Bullock retained his
office as superintendent in charge of the daily management of the South-

ern Express Company. The express business grew as Southerners sought to recapture their lives and locate loved ones. Northerners used the express to transport their belongings and as a supply line for Northern goods. Of course, transplanted Yankees also used the telegraph lines to maintain contact with friends and businesses up north. To expand business, Plant bought a steamer and operated it between Augusta and Savannah, started a semi-weekly wagon line to Orangeburg, South Carolina, and, under Bullock's direction, installed a telegraph line to Atlanta. To speed the dissemination of information and provide a public service, Bullock offered free transmittal of newsworthy events over this wire. The *Augusta Chronicle* hailed his offer as "perfectly characteristic" of the public-spirited executive. More than simply providing a community service, however, newsworthy items originating in Augusta would certainly expand knowledge of that city, advertising it as a business center and drawing investors to the area. Because of the dearth of money in the postwar South, city boosters needed all the advertising they could get. Bullock's actions were good for business, and Augustans appreciated them. *Chronicle* editor Ambrose Wright praised Bullock as a "first rate business and administrative talent, [with] thorough knowledge of the express business in all its details." Bullock combined moneymaking efforts in his own behalf with money-raising efforts in support of Augusta.[3]

As early as May 4, 1865, the day he met with Stanton to share information about the Lincoln conspirators, Bullock wrote a letter to Freeman Clarke from his room in Willard's Hotel in Washington, D.C. He had obtained half a million dollars from Northern friends to organize a national bank at Augusta. He wrote with pride of his success and requested Clarke to use his influence as comptroller of currency to charter the Augusta bank. He advised Clarke of the opportunities for banks in thirteen Southern cities in five states from Alabama to Virginia. Clarke recognized Bullock's foresight and joined the Augusta enterprise. Within days, the National Bank of Augusta had a charter and Bullock was its president.[4]

Although he simultaneously held jobs with the Southern Express Company and the National Bank of Augusta, Bullock sought even more projects. Diversifying his interests, he became president of the Southern Porcelain Manufacturing Company. The factory, located across the river in Kaolin, South Carolina, had to be rebuilt after a fire destroyed it on October 15, 1864. In Bullock's hands, the factory had completely recovered two years later. Seventy to eighty workers skillfully molded clay into household crockery. It is unclear who had the money to buy shares in the company, but Charles J. Jenkins, an Augusta attorney worth $87,000 in 1860 who had been elected governor of Georgia in 1865, purchased ten shares at $100 per share. Clearly the war had not destroyed all Southern wealth.[5]

In March 1867, Radical Republicans in the United States Congress took charge of Reconstruction. Until then, President Andrew Johnson's conservative policies had relinquished war gains by allowing the rebellious states to reenter the Union without changing their ways or their leaders. Indeed, Johnson assisted in returning the Southern elite to political power by rapidly pardoning nearly twenty thousand planters. Southern legislatures responded to presidential magnanimity by returning Confederate leaders to the Congress. Georgians, for example, sent Alexander H. Stephens and Herschel V. Johnson to the Senate. Several states passed a series of restrictive laws, known as black codes, to limit freedmen's opportunities and mock the Thirteenth Amendment. Southern state legislatures, except in Tennessee, refused to ratify the Fourteenth Amendment, which granted citizenship to freedmen. Radical Republicans, with bloody flag in hand, responded to this Southern attempt at restoration by insisting on a genuine reconstruction. On March 2 and 23 and July 19, Congress passed three acts over Johnson's vetoes.

These acts divided the South into five military districts, each under the control of federal troops. Further, the new laws required Southerners to register all qualified voters, to elect delegates to conventions to write new constitutions in compliance with the national Constitution, to elect state governments, and to ratify the Fourteenth Amendment. Major-General John Pope, who had commanded the Army of the Potomac at Second Manassas against Robert E. Lee, took command of the Third Military District—Georgia, Alabama, and Florida.

Pope quickly assigned boards of registrars for each of Georgia's election districts. To ensure black participation, one-third of the registrars were black. In spring 1867, he named Augustan and Southern Express agent Edward C. Hulbert as state chief of registration. Hulbert had come south from Connecticut in 1854 as a messenger with the Adams Express. With the formation of the Southern Express in 1861, Henry Plant named him superintendent of the company's central division. A postwar promoter of the Republican party, Hulbert actively directed registration and voting. He would be an important factor in getting out the vote for the convention and, later, for the 1868 Republican candidate for governor.[6]

Initially, Bullock believed that business was more important than black suffrage; he did not associate economic development and profits with the black vote. That position changed dramatically. Bullock soon realized that with the old political elite disfranchised, new leaders could move rapidly to restore Georgia into the Union firmly in accord with Radical goals— and thereby help business. Late in life, Bullock explained that the congressional plan inspired support among "those of our people who were more interested in economic questions and in material affairs than in Constitutional theories." Military government was disruptive because people who had fought four years against blue-clad soldiers resented having them in their midst. Bullock wanted to expand business and saw the old leaders and the military government blocking the way. If black suffrage helped create solid gains toward business profits, then Bullock wanted black suffrage. Besides, an expansion of the franchise to all men fit his belief in a free labor system wherein people advanced according to ability in an environment of equal opportunity.[7]

In Augusta and elsewhere, the boom times just after the war proved to be temporary. Business languished as the flow of Northern capital into the South slowed to a trickle because of the uncertain economic and political climate. Bullock and other businessmen resented the stagnation of business and blamed intransigent Southern politicians for their problems. The March 2, 1867, act of Congress, commonly called the Sherman Bill, established military control over the South and seemed to threaten many more tumultuous years. Something had to be done. Perhaps if business interests could control the government and write the new state constitution, stability and increased north-south trade and investment would help expand profits.

Bullock understood the political climate. He knew that without representation in Congress, Georgia would suffer because investors were reluctant to risk money in a state that yet stood outside the Union. He saw that the failure of Georgia's legislators to ratify the Fourteenth Amendment and their tirades about states' rights further complicated any solution. Democratic leaders fought back and slung epithets against any new Reconstruction plan. In such circumstances, it seemed, business would continue to languish. Taking matters into his own hands, Bullock wrote on March 7 to former Whig, then Constitutional Unionist and prewar congressman Joshua Hill of "the very general disposition among our business men to cut loose from old wartime political leaders & act at once for a full &

final settlement of our political troubles by hearty acquiescence in & action under the Sherman bill." Bullock believed that the "prostration of all business & enterprise" would continue until someone the people trusted told them that the only Georgians disfranchised by the Sherman Act would be "Governors, Members of the Legislature & Judges, in addition to those who have held office under the General Govt or as MCs [members of Congress] . . . until pardoned by Congress." [8]

Bullock wanted broad enfranchisement; only those in the highest prewar positions would be disqualified. He also wanted to protect Union men such as Blodgett and Conley—mayors, councilmen, sheriffs, city judges—who had sworn allegiance to the United States government and then aided and comforted the Confederacy. Unlike the "die-hards" who opposed any federal action in local affairs, these men were "reconciliationists" who wanted to comply with the victor's demands and get on with business. Many of them were old Henry Clay Whigs who supported a national bank, tariffs, internal improvements, and sectional peace. In July 1865, Macon judge Osborne A. Lochrane, whom Bullock appointed to the Georgia Supreme Court in 1871, made a speech in Augusta warning that the war represented a "chasm which separates the old South from the new." He called for an "improved and enlightened civilization" and exhorted: "We must be men, not monuments. . . . Let not pride, prejudice, and folly blind us and lead us stumbling backward over a wilderness of graves." Bullock could not have agreed more.[9]

General Pope used his power to appoint mayors and councilmen in cities where the incumbents' terms expired or where they flagrantly opposed congressional policies. He received many pleas for help to stabilize conditions in various localities. From Darien, voter registrar Tunis Campbell, a former Freedmen's Bureau agent who was one of Georgia's first black state senators, asked Pope to regulate or remove the city government officials and judges. Campbell accused those judges of carrying out "unjust & partial administration of the civil laws . . . [whereby] citizens are *discriminately* arrested, for less than nothing, (the discrimination is based on color) and with a mocking for a trial are heavily fined, imprisoned or *sold* to labor for the highest bidder for the term of sentence." [10]

In Augusta the mayor's and councilmen's terms ended on the second anniversary of Appomattox, April 9, 1867. Republicans accused these city leaders of violating Congress's will by refusing to allow freedmen to register and thereby preventing them from voting. Pope received a flurry of letters from men applying directly for those offices or supporting favorites. Former council members and mayors Benjamin Conley and Foster Blodgett were prominent among those seeking office in Augusta.[11]

Though born in Newark, New Jersey, Conley had lived in Augusta since 1830; Blodgett was a native of the city. Conley served two terms as mayor in 1857–58, and Blodgett succeeded him in 1859–60. For four years, 1867–71, Blodgett served as Georgia chairman of the Union Republican party. He had been appointed postmaster of Augusta and then removed by President Johnson. Because of that removal, which Congress viewed as illegal under the Tenure of Office Act, Blodgett was a prosecution witness in the impeachment trial of Johnson. In 1871, Conley was governor of Georgia. Both were former Whigs and Constitutional Unionist supporters of John Bell for president in 1860. That year, the credit-tracking firm of R. G. Dun recorded that Blodgett "has some bitter enemies," probably because he chaired the Bell campaign in Augusta. When they lost to the immediate secessionists, the two friends adopted different courses. Conley refused to fight against the Union; Blodgett acquiesced to the new reality and even raised a company of volunteers in 1861. Both were businessmen and, coincidentally, each owned a shoe store in Augusta.[12]

Both had worked hard to establish the Republican party in Augusta, and either would have been a logical choice for mayor. One Augustan supported them both, writing that Blodgett "was in the army from force of circumstances. He made a good mayor, is competent . . . [and] is a popular man with the colored people." After writing that former governor Joseph Brown knew Blodgett, the writer reported: "Mr. Benjamin Conley is a good man and has *never been anything but Union*. . . . He and Mr. Blodget are friends." Probably the decisive letter in Blodgett's favor came from Chief Registrar Hulbert and Union League President Henry P. Farrow: "We regard him . . . as a man who will go full length in wielding all the influence he possesses for the support of the Federal Government and proper men and measures."[13]

On April 30, Pope appointed Blodgett mayor and Conley to the city council. He named Rufus Bullock as one of the other eleven councilmen. For a while, Bullock would play disciple to Blodgett.

Three days after their appointments, Blodgett and the new councilmen took office. Blodgett made a speech in which he called for a new devotion to the public welfare and a "rigid economy in all departments . . . dispensing with all unnecessary objects of expenditure." With the grand total of

$10 in the treasury and a city debt between $112,000 and $124,000, Blodgett's policies of public relief and administrative thriftiness could not be achieved at the same time.[14]

Energetic as always, councilman Bullock sat on the committees of finance, printing, cemeteries, riverbanks, and wharves. Ever concerned with business interests, he persuaded the council to abolish foot tolls on the Savannah River Bridge and authorize police to arrest drummers and peddlers who posed any "interference with trade or business." He helped eliminate the old 10:00 P.M. curfew for freedmen and supported a medical dispensary for the poor. When one of Augusta's fire companies, Citizen No. 8, applied for a new engine, Bullock presented a resolution requiring that the company raise half the cost and the city provide the rest. In a similar case, he suggested that the city issue $6,000 in bonds to enable the Georgia Independent Fire Company to buy a steam fire engine. The company would then repay interest and principal over a ten-year period with the lien secured by the company's property. The Augusta council also issued bonds in lieu of capital to support the Macon and Augusta Railroad. Convinced that the city's growth depended on transportation, the council proposed a $125,000 bond issue as security until the money could be raised. Bullock had spent fifteen years in a transportation and communication business and had grown up watching the influence of the Erie Canal on Albion. Now he learned how to build roads without money, and the lesson was not lost on him.[15]

Augusta leaders needed a railroad between their city and Macon, and they had already made progress toward its construction. The track would pass through the state capital at Milledgeville and then west to Macon to connect with the Macon and Western Railroad. Georgia Railroad president John P. King of Augusta controlled many shares in the project, but the city held a majority. Mayor Blodgett collaborated with King in naming Bullock as president of the line. King supported Bullock over others because "the affairs of the road were in a desperate condition. I thought that Bullock would help the company and had him made President." He believed that Bullock's ties to the Southern Express Company would ensure an influx of money for the project. When money failed to flow in, Bullock went to New York looking for capital. His friends there told him that affairs in Georgia made them nervous so any present investment was dangerous. Bullock returned home resolved to make Georgia more attractive to capitalists.[16]

In later years he explained that the New York trip in November 1867 convinced him of the link between politics and economic development. He remembered the words of reluctant Northern investors: "Mr. Bullock, if you want to run a railroad in the Indian territory or anywhere else we will be glad to hear of the project. But under a military government, it means that one man can dictate policy in a way that is not conducive to the best interests of speculation and investment." They encouraged him to work to generate a stable business climate in Georgia. Bullock understood their argument and saw "the intimate relation of government to business." He resolved to "act at once" on the suggestion.[17]

He already understood the practical power of politics. As a councilman in Augusta, he participated in making rules that controlled taxes, bond issues, and community projects. He learned the power of patronage when he joined the small group of councilmen who had the power to appoint more than thirty city officers, including city clerk, police chief, police lieutenants, jailor, lamplighter, and bridge keeper. Undoubtedly, he also had influence with the mayor, who controlled nearly sixty more positions, including those of assessor, policeman, and fire warden. He knew that a business-government alliance would improve opportunities for profits. He recognized his personal stake in the future course of Georgia's politics. He deemed order and the free labor system to be necessary to procure and protect investments.[18]

In the summer of 1867, Bullock worried about the prudence of becoming directly involved in politics. Newspaper editors might attack his principles and infuriate customers, who could refuse to deal with any merchant who disagreed with their views. Already, such local pressure had forced two Augusta councilmen to resign to protect themselves against public ostracism and retaliation for their association with Blodgett, Conley, and Bullock. Membership in a strong Republican party and compliance with Congressional Reconstruction exacted a price many would not pay. Realizing the pressure a community could bring to bear on individuals, Blodgett advised General Pope that "the efforts of the Anti-Conventionists to make any person representing the Government, or who is favorable to reconstruction upon the Congressional basis, odious in this community, or to ruin his business, are succeeding." Blodgett contended that the community was "in a ferment" and that those "people who are honestly anxious to restore the country to a state of peace and prosperity" had been victimized by withdrawal of consumer patronage.[19]

Throughout July and August, Bullock wavered between the political arena and his business interests. He wrote a note to the very conservative *Augusta Chronicle* denying that his personal views represented those of the Southern Express Company. He said the company had given neither money nor verbal support to the Republican party or any individual and its business was unrelated to his politics. Unconvinced, the *Chronicle* vowed to continue attacking those "who use their influence for the inculcation of Radical ideas and principles."[20]

Bullock also wrote to his old friend Edward Hulbert and expressed his fears of alienating friends and customers. He knew that Hulbert, who as chief of registration located at the headquarters of the Third Military District in Atlanta, had Pope's ear. Hulbert added his unqualified endorsement of Bullock's position and forwarded the letter to the head of the Bureau of Civil Affairs, Colonel J. F. Meline. Bullock's opening words offer clues of his dilemma. He hoped that the federal government would come to the aid of its Southern supporters: "As you know I am not a politician, or am I at this time particularly interested except to see that men who are loyal to the Govt . . . shall not be put down." Bullock told of the loss of patronage and social position suffered by anyone associating with Union men. He called for the government to support "its friends" before "no one will be found" brave enough "to admit that they support the Govt & all will *boast* of their sympathetic affection for & brilliant achievements in the *Confederate* cause."[21]

Clearly, Bullock wanted the federal government to accelerate Reconstruction by supporting the reconciliationists. He also desired the military to remove those who opposed government policy and replace them with men who favored the congressional plan. Bullock's final sentences to Hulbert reveal his understanding of what the lack of resolve by congressional Republicans and military leaders would bring. He feared that Georgia Republicans, lacking support and under pressure from without to match and overcome the internal pressure to conform, would deny their party and claim that their fealty had always been with the Democrats. Bullock's statement that "all will *boast* of their sympathetic affection for & brilliant achievements in the *Confederate* cause" was an obvious appeal to the "bloody shirt." It was also true.

During the next thirty days Bullock thrust himself into politics, working for the election of Republican delegates and for calling a constitutional convention. He supported the establishment of a Radical newspaper in

Augusta, the *National Republican,* edited by E. H. Pughe. Writing on *National Republican* letterhead, Bullock demanded tougher voter qualifications and asked Hulbert to suggest to General Pope that *all* men who had served in the Confederate military be ordered to take the parole. "There are many who have shirked even that mild punishment & are charging around the country damning the Govt & all who befriend it." Bullock cited Robert Toombs's comment that "if anybody in Washn [Washington, Georgia] dared to vote the 'Radical' ticket, bullets would fly around thicker than they did during the war." Bullock complained that Toombs's intent was to intimidate blacks into not voting. Meanwhile, Toombs "is practicing law without even being a *citizen.*"[22]

Under the March 23 Reconstruction Act, the parole, or amnesty oath, was required of all who had engaged in the rebellion and wanted to regain their right to vote or hold office. Bullock was correct in calling the requirement "mild," for President Johnson had removed any necessity of taking it before military officers, allowing county clerks to administer it. Imagine the levity with which the oath must often have been issued and taken. Bullock added that all military orders sent to the *Atlanta New Era,* the most prominent Radical paper in the state, "should be sent here to the Republican so that they can appear in each simultaneously. It costs too much to have them telegraphed." If state Republicans hoped to succeed, they must be kept informed by reliable presses free from Democratic control.[23]

The Congressional Reconstruction plan required each state to hold a referendum and select delegates to a convention to write a new constitution. Bullock made his decision about political involvement and announced himself a candidate for a seat as delegate to the convention. His position in the community as a business leader and city councilman made Bullock a prominent man, and he won election with ease. Other local delegates included Benjamin Conley, Foster Blodgett, John E. Bryant, and Simeon W. Beard. Bryant had been born and educated in Maine and in the war commanded black troops on the Georgia and South Carolina sea islands. He returned to Georgia as an agent with the Bureau of Refugees, Freedmen, and Abandoned Lands. In 1866, he organized the Georgia Equal Rights Association and, the next year, actively participated in the formation of the Georgia Republican party. He was a leading voice at the convention and from his seat on the state central committee of the Republican party later promoted Bullock for governor.[24]

Little is known about African Methodist Episcopal minister Simeon

Beard. Born in South Carolina, Beard, a mulatto, was somehow educated
and by 1867 established himself as a leader among Augusta blacks and
became closely allied with Blodgett, Bullock, and other Republican leaders.

Under the 1867 Reconstruction Acts, 95,214 whites and 93,433 blacks
registered to vote. Those numbers make obvious the revolution that was
Reconstruction. More than half of the potential voters were from the lower
class—the majority black. Any chance the Republican party had of electing its delegates and gaining a constitutional convention rested with the
votes of these freedmen. On August 12, chairman of the Republican party
in Georgia and one of its founders Foster Blodgett spoke before a Union
Club organizing meeting in Augusta and urged Southerners to "let the
past go." He promoted "the rapid restoration of our State to a condition
of peace" and acceptance of the "Congressional scheme." Blodgett spoke
of the advantages of a free labor system: "Hereafter Labor will hold its
proper station. . . . Slavery tended to degrade labor. . . . Now the honest
and hard-working citizen . . . can compete for any of the prizes the world
has for honorable conduct, and will no more be dragged downward by the
humiliating reflection that he occupies an inferior position." [25]

Blodgett's statement about opportunities for free labor open to all citizens showed his acceptance of the new order and awareness that black
and white workingmen would play a key role in the Republican party. No
doubt, the speech inflamed the old leaders and their Lost Cause allies.

For four days, October 29 to November 2, Georgians cast ballots for
or against holding a constitutional convention. They also elected delegates
to attend the convention in case the vote favored one. Most Democrats
adopted the strategy advocated by Benjamin H. Hill to stay away from
the polls. By refusing to vote in the referendum on the convention and
in the election of delegates, Hill and other Democratic leaders hoped to
keep a majority of the registered voters from voting and thereby thwart
any possible convention. Georgia law required that for any referendum
to be valid, a majority of registered voters must cast ballots. Newspapers
hoped that conservative white Georgians, "by inaction alone, can defeat
a Convention and give more time to popular reaction." In a slight varia-
tion of this strategy, the *Augusta Chronicle* advised Democrats to vote for
delegates but to abstain from voting on the convention. That strategy, if followed statewide, probably would have given conservatives a majority in the
convention. Most Democrats abstained from voting in a referendum they
believed illegal and corrupt. After all, they reasoned, Georgia had already

complied with President Johnson's plan by reconstituting its government in 1865, ratifying the Thirteenth Amendment, repudiating its war debt, and electing representatives to Congress. Republicans agreed that Georgia had done all that. Yet Georgia's new constitution barely differed from the 1861 constitution. Radicals argued that because Georgia's senators had not been allowed to take their seats, the state had not yet reentered the Union and remained subject to national demands. In short, Georgia needed more reconstruction. Hill's strategy succeeded in keeping approximately 60,000 whites from the polls, but it ultimately failed when Georgians cast 12,087 votes more than necessary to validate the referendum.[26]

No one worked harder to ensure a Republican victory than Edward Hulbert. Just before the vote, he published a notice in many newspapers which set forth Republican strategy: "Let the motto of the Reconstruction Party be 'Convention and Relief.' . . . The Convention is now our only hope. Let the platform of all reconstruction candidates for the Convention be 'Reconstruction and Relief,' and we will sweep the state by thousands." During the five days of the referendum, Hulbert closely monitored the vote. Pope had promised Congress that he would "get out the full colored vote"; undoubtedly he expected his appointee Hulbert to fulfill this promise. Worried that the number of voters might fall short of the majority necessary to validate the referendum, Hulbert sent a flurry of telegrams to election managers statewide. He advised Savannah manager S. D. Dickson to send workers to Bryan and Effingham counties to "get voters to the polls." He implored all election managers to do their utmost to get people to vote and sent messages such as this one to Quitman, Georgia: "Why is it that you are voting so slow? We must have a majority of voters in your county. Send out runners and get the voters in." He urged Republicans to "work with a will." Most of the telegrams appear to be legitimate attempts to get the most complete vote possible. The message to A. N. Wilson in Savannah, however, indicates corruption. Hulbert suggested that Wilson trick voters into coming to the polls: "Put one or two leading anti-Bradley Negroes on your white [Democratic] ticket and get out a full vote. We must have the colored vote." Hulbert knew that Savannah freedmen adored Aaron Alpeoria Bradley, black organizer of the Republican party in the low country. Thus to get his supporters to the polls, Hulbert suggested lying about his opponents by putting bogus, anti-Bradley blacks on the ballot. This ploy probably had little influence and seems tame compared with the intimidation and violence used by the Democrats.[27]

Of Georgia's 188,647 registered voters, 102,283 voted for a convention, as opposed to 4,127 against. Approximately 10,500 whites could not vote because they were disfranchised under the Sherman Act for having sworn allegiance to the United States before 1861 and then participating in the rebellion or for holding civil office under the Confederacy. Additionally, nearly 8,500 whites failed to register and thus could not vote. Hulbert's analysis of those voting for the convention revealed that approximately 32,000 whites had joined 70,283 blacks in support of a new constitution. Thus 71 percent of eligible blacks and 31 percent of eligible whites voted in favor of Congressional Reconstruction.[28]

The whites voting for the convention probably were Union League members. During the Civil War the nascent Union League expanded from North to South enrolling Southerners disaffected with the war and planter leadership. By 1867, it made up a prominent wing of the Georgia Republican party with 117 chapters in 132 counties. Georgia Union League President Henry P. Farrow claimed that at the time of the referendum, the organization had 27,830 white members and almost 53,000 black members.[29]

Although Democrats did not vote, they did participate in the election. Besides withdrawing patronage from those who supported the Republicans, Democrats used economic intimidation to discourage the freedmen. General Pope received many requests for military support and letters detailing acts of intimidation. Sparta freedmen wrote of being "driven off by their imployers for cuming to the Election. In vain we have tride the civil athority." In Atlanta, freedman Munday Johnson filed suit for wages lost when "his imployer . . . did on the 31st day of October 1867 discharge [him] . . . from his employ and would not settle with him because . . . Munday Johnson came to town to vote." In Thomasville, George Alexander, Tom Turner, Israel Bacon, and Wade Philip defied their employer, voted, and found themselves out of work. The situation was much the same throughout the state. Undoubtedly, the black vote would have been even greater had not many employers used economic coercion to intimidate their workers.[30]

Even after Radicals carried the referendum, conservatives increased their attacks on Republicans, especially delegates to the convention. The *Milledgeville Southern Recorder* referred to the convention as "a miserable mulatto concern—the bastard of Abolition policy, begotten of negro ignorance and prejudice." When Milledgeville hotel owners threatened to refuse to rent rooms to black delegates, Pope ordered that the convention be held in Atlanta. On December 9, amid the storm of slander, the delegates assembled to construct a constitution that would restore Georgia to the Union. Republicans held a majority of seats, but they failed to achieve consensus as members split into Radical and moderate groups. Of the 170 delegates, approximately 85 were native Georgians. Fifty more came from other Southern states, especially South Carolina. There were 29 of Northern birth, 2 from Scotland, and 2 from Ireland. There were 46 uncompromising Democrats, 59 moderate Republicans, and 65 Radicals. The presence of 37 black Georgians made the constitutional convention of 1867–68 the most democratic body ever to assemble in the state.[31]

On the opening day, George W. Ashburn of Columbus called the convention to order in the Atlanta City Hall. For purposes of organization, he nominated the leading Republican in the state, Foster Blodgett, as temporary chairman. The next day, Blodgett established the tone of the convention. He spoke to the delegates' task in the context of Republican free labor ideology and stressed a platform of reconstruction, equal rights, justice, education, relief, and homestead exemptions on which Georgia Republicans had agreed at their July 4 party convention in Atlanta. Blodgett rejoiced that "a new era has dawned. . . . The principles of the Declaration of Independence have, at length, been vindicated." Slaves were free, but too many Southerners still "cling to the ruins of a structure that now belongs in the past." Himself a former slaveowner, he called black freedom "just" and spoke of "the complete overthrow of that monstrous system which held millions of human beings in a bondage that required a national convulsion to destroy." He addressed the issue of debt relief for all Georgians, insisting that "relief must be had." Planters "oppressed with debts" needed help, he said, because agricultural prosperity would create better conditions for everyone. But more than that, Blodgett cried that "the condition of our people, of all classes, demands from this body some measures of relief." He asked the convention to establish a system of public schools so that "the waters of life should be open to all." Blodgett told the delegates not to worry about the slander from those unable to "emancipate themselves from their prejudices" but to work for all Georgians. In conclusion, he stated: "It is all-important that the two races shall live in harmony. . . . There must be no conflict between capital and labor. . . . They must strive to advance the interests of each other." Clearly, Blodgett sought to reassure planters that

their interests were important and that they would continue to have reliable
laborers. He called for peace and prosperity under a new system. Blodgett
invited planters to join the free labor system and the Republican party.[32]

But the old leaders resisted change and refused to accept Blodgett's call.
When delegates elected Josiah R. Parrott as president of the convention,
conservatives responded with more slander. The ultraconservative *Rome
Weekly Courier* smirked:

> Parrott in the chair, Monkey on the floor,
> Scattered round the hall, five and twenty more,
> Hundred odd of white skunks, mean as they can be
> That's the *tout ensemble* of this Menagerie.
> Way off in the corner is the keeper of the show,
> A-balancin' accounts. Name is Snaky Joe.[33]

Former governor Joseph E. Brown did not have delegate status, but
he should have. He had been one of the first Democrats, and by far the
most prominent, to counsel acceptance of Congressional Reconstruction.
As early as March 4, 1867, two days after Congress passed the Sherman
Bill, Brown made a speech in Atlanta asking Georgians to accept the law
and the freedmen's right to vote. Many historians have tried to decipher
Brown's actions in shifting from Democratic wartime governor to Reconstruction Republican and chief justice of the Georgia Supreme Court to
redeemer United States senator. Most historians agree with C. Mildred
Thompson's assessment that he was a political chameleon: "He was first
in secession, first in reconstruction, and very nearly first in the restoration
of Democratic home rule."[34]

Although Thompson is probably correct, an 1867 letter from Tennessee
governor William G. Brownlow to Brown amplifies the judgment: "You
and those who act with you may be abused for a time, but you will finally be
sustained. And all who wish to avoid the horrors of confiscation had better
act with you." With rumors of land confiscation and distribution to the
freedmen rampant, worried property owners might have seen acceptance
of Congress's wishes as a way to forestall extreme action. Confiscation
threatened to unite poor whites with blacks, as one white tenant farmer
told Englishman John Trowbridge in 1865: "We should tuk the land, as we
did the niggers, and split it, a[nd] giv part to the niggers and part to me
and t'other Union fellers." In light of such suggestions, it was no wonder

property holders fretted. But whether or not he changed sides primarily
to protect his property, Joe Brown's defection gave him immense power
among Republicans anxious to have him on their side. Even though conservative papers and speakers lambasted Brown as the worst scalawag of
all, his influence remained strong among Georgia voters, especially in the
state's northwest corner. "Snaky" or not, Brown was a man to be reck-
oned with.[35]

Even though Democratic papers like the *Atlanta Opinion* reviled them
as "men, possessing neither education, character, natural ability nor political experience," the delegates wrote a very good constitution. The liberal
document ended imprisonment for debt, gave suffrage to black men, and
provided a public school system for all children. Bullock was prominent
in the convention. His place at the head of the committee of seven which
communicated convention resolutions to General Pope made him visible to
other delegates. When Bullock reported Pope's pleasure with the progress
toward reconstruction, he seemed to be a spokesman for the military. His
close ties to the powerful Blodgett and new association with the military
commander advanced Bullock's standing among Republican leaders. On
December 12, he offered an ordinance asking relief for all Georgia debtors.
The 1865 convention had nullified the Confederate debt so it made sense
to cancel all individual debts contracted during the war. Bullock argued
that the convention definitely would act on this question, and a timely
ordinance would save property from sheriffs' sales. Bullock's ordinance
passed without amendment. Four days later, Parrott appointed Bullock to
the committee on relief.[36]

Every state convention in the South Atlantic states incorporated relief
measures into its new constitution. Intertwined with relief was the issue
of the homestead, that is, how much real and personal property would
be exempt from the grasp of creditors. Small property owners required
protection from foreclosure. The amounts to be exempted needed to be
large enough to protect small landholders but not so large as to protect
planters. Many people of all classes had contracted debts during the war
which creditors now wanted to collect. In the depressed economy of the
South and the extreme poverty all around, it made some sense to void individual debts and start again. Bullock led the vanguard of those insisting on
relief of debtors and supporting a liberal homestead allowance. Delegate
W. L. Goodwin of Cartersville also favored relief for debtors, arguing that

without it, "the entire landed estates of Georgia will pass into the hands of a few extremely wealthy men. . . . This is a strife between capital and labor; between the wealthy aristocrats and the great mass of the people."[37]

The committee on relief made its first report to the convention on January 9, 1868. The majority report, with which Bullock agreed, recommended canceling all debts and denying jurisdiction of any court for all obligations contracted before June 1, 1865. Committee members felt that forced payment of debts would "result in bankruptcy and utter ruin of the great masses, and concentrate into the hands of a few the little remaining." Four days later, Amos T. Akerman and Thomas Saffold presented a minority report saying, "It is an abuse of the language to apply the term 'Relief' to a measure that takes from one and gives to another." Realizing that some exceptions might be necessary, Bullock offered a substitute that would allow courts to decide cases in which the debt grew out of a trust or money was due to a charitable institution. Courts could also decide suits by laborers demanding wages due them for services rendered, cases in which property had been sold but less than one-third of the purchase money had been paid, or instances when the General Assembly voted by a two-thirds majority to allow a judgment. Akerman still disagreed with any relief provision because it "impairs the obligation of any contract, or denies the right of the citizen to sue and enforce his rights therein . . . and therefore [is] *null and void*" under the nation's Constitution. Finally, after much maneuvering and debate, delegates adopted Bullock's substitute to the majority report.[38]

On the matter of the homestead exemption, Blodgett wanted to exempt from any court action $2,500 in land and $2,000 in personal property. Augustan John Bryant favored $1,000/$500 and persuaded moderate Republicans and Democrats to vote for those amounts. But in a revote the next day, Radicals and non-black-belt Democrats raised it to $2,000/$1,000 and Blodgett successfully added a provision applying the homestead exemption to no more than 250 acres of land. Bullock voted with the majority on every provision relating to debt relief. Radicals, led by the Augusta delegation, got upcountry support for debtor relief and homestead laws.[39]

Repudiation of debts and homestead exemptions were volatile issues. On one side were people like Peter Reynolds from Covington who wrote General George G. Meade about advocates of debt relief decrying "bankers, corporations, stockholders, merchants, and those that have been speculating . . . and now want to hold on to all they have and let their creditors suffer the loss." If Reynolds was right, debt relief measures primarily served the rich. More evidence for this view came from a citizen who wrote Benjamin Conley after the convention passed relief measures: "Two months ago verry many people were standing . . . uppon the brink of ruin, the sherif was beginning to sell out the lands . . . and leave the defendant pennyless with a heavy debt hanging over him. Some estates were sold . . . but the convention came to the rescue." Obviously, debt repudiation helped landholders retain their properties.[40]

Without such relief, banks and creditors would foreclose on poor farmers. With relief, small landholders gained, or thought they did. The debt issue became crucial to the Republican campaign in 1868, and many whites voted to ratify the constitution on the basis of this plank. Groaning about that vote, the *Milledgeville Southern Recorder* reported: "Many, very many, who desired relief from their debts eagerly seized hold of the Relief presented in the Constitution." Other Democratic papers called relief a "flimsy pretext . . . the Shibboleth of the Nigger Bullock Party." Perhaps there is no answer to the question of who benefited most from the relief issue, yet it seems that the rich stood to gain the most. Freedmen, without land or debts, gained nothing from repudiation; theoretically, in the future, they would gain from the homestead exemption. Banks, corporations, individual planters, and merchants gained because their wartime speculations were absolved. The debt issue was further confused because the 1865 constitutional convention had been forced under presidential Reconstruction to repudiate the Confederate debt as prerequisite to rejoining the Union. The delegates had voted 135 to 117 to repudiate. Most of the negative votes came from nabobs in the richest counties—those in the black belt—while favorable votes came from the poorer counties. Because the Southern states did not pay money owed by the Confederacy to planters and merchants, those groups hoped to recoup their losses by collecting money owed them by their poorer brothers. Debt repudiation would hurt those chances. Yet planters who owed money surely must have welcomed relief. Thus this issue apparently helped all groups. The poor farmers universally gained and planters gained or lost on an individual basis according to whether they owed or were owed money.[41]

Very little debate surrounded the issue of black suffrage and the conclusion that blacks had obtained the vote. Delegates discussed prescribing an education qualification for voting but decided against reducing the number of voters in that way. The central questions were whether former Confederates would be allowed to vote and the necessity for placing a specific clause regarding black officeholding in the constitution. Bullock and Bryant wanted to exclude large numbers of former Confederates from voting, but the convention voted 116 to 15 against large-scale disfranchisement. That vote makes it obvious that although Radicals held powerful positions, they could not impose their programs at will. The Augusta leadership divided over Bryant's proposal to include a specific provision granting blacks the right to hold office. Democrats threatened to walk out of the convention if such a clause prevailed. Bullock, Blodgett, Conley, and every black delegate voted against inclusion of any such provision. The Fourteenth Amendment already guaranteed it and specific mention of it tended to break down the premise the Republican party invoked whenever possible: "All men are created equal." Additionally, because Republicans wanted to present voters with a constitution they would ratify, it was better to be ambiguous than stupid. Thus in a strange alignment of Democrats with Radicals, the convention decided 126 to 12 against a clause regarding black officeholding.[42]

The convention finished its work in early March and voted 118 to 13 in favor of the constitution. Delegates were rightfully proud of their work. Years later Bullock bragged, "If this was accomplished in spite of a public condition which rendered impossible a calm and fair discussion of vital issues, what might it not have been if we had cultivated that 'grain of common sense'?" In spite of the rancor the document provoked, it protected all citizens' rights: "The social status of the citizen shall never be the subject of legislation." It prohibited whipping as punishment and ended imprisonment for debt. It guaranteed property rights for married women, authorized government support for economic development—including aid to railroads—granted relief and exempted homesteads, called for the first General Assembly under the new constitution to establish a common school system for all children, provided for black suffrage, and promised equal justice for all.[43]

Republicans in the convention sought to protect their ascendancy by providing that "all the civil officers of the State are only provisional until this State is represented in Congress." Hoping for a Republican victory in the upcoming election for governor, they changed the executive's term from two to four years. Article Ten of the constitution moved the capital from Milledgeville to Atlanta, which was a railroad center, headquarters of the Third Military District, and a stronger Republican base than Milledgeville. Republican delegates accomplished one more task before they returned home; they selected Bullock as their gubernatorial candidate for the April general election.[44]

The cause of Bullock's advancement to the forefront of Republican ranks remains somewhat obscure. Clearly his friendship with Blodgett had much to do with his rapid rise. As early as November 5, 1867, in a letter to General Pope, Blodgett expressed hope that he would remove all state officers opposed to Congressional Reconstruction and replace them with men loyal to the Union. He did not ask to be made governor but wrote: "I do desire that you will give us an earnest, honest, and competent man. . . . I am convinced that a better man than Col. Rufus B. Bullock for Governor cannot be found." Because his problems with Governor Jenkins were increasing, Pope might have considered Blodgett's suggestion. He never got the chance.[45]

Just three weeks after the convention opened, President Johnson sent General George G. Meade to replace Pope, who had been too supportive of Radical interests for Johnson's taste. The probable cause of Johnson's dissatisfaction was Pope's August 19 order that all jurors "will hereafter be taken exclusively from the lists of voters, without discrimination, registered by the boards of registration." Many prominent Georgians resented this incline toward equality; Johnson responded in their favor. Meade immediately became involved in the squabble Pope had had with Governor Jenkins. Jenkins refused to honor Pope's order and the convention's request that he authorize the state treasurer to pay the delegates $40,000 for their total per diem expenses. When Meade ordered compliance, Jenkins again refused. On January 13, 1868, Meade removed him and replaced him with a provisional military governor, General Thomas Ruger. Jenkins left office and left the state, taking with him the total state treasury of $400,000 and the state seal.[46]

Just as Pope's problems with Jenkins reached their height, Augusta delegate John H. Caldwell motioned the convention to petition the general "to restore loyalty, harmony, and tranquility . . . and to secure for our State her proper place in the Union." The motion petitioned Pope to appoint a provisional governor and recommended Bullock for the post. Clearly, Bullock stood high among the Radicals and among all Republicans at the convention.[47]

Of course, not all delegates favored him or desired the removal of Jenkins. They voted 95 to 59 to remove Jenkins and 81 to 59 to replace him with Bullock. The vote indicates that at least fourteen delegates preferred someone other than Bullock. Pope did not act on the request before Meade took command. Meade preferred to appoint a military man to the post until the general election produced a governor. Still, the fact that Bullock had won the first and only "straw" vote put him in good position for a future nomination. His ubiquitous efforts at the convention kept him in the public eye, and one pundit, in 1871, claimed that the 1868 constitution was "largely due to his efforts." [48]

Ten years later, a friend of Bullock's recalled the effect the convention had on him: "[He] never dreamt of going into politics when he agreed to run for the Convention. He was strictly a business man. He enjoyed the confidence of the whole community. . . . He believed, however, that the State had best reconstruct itself quickly and finally." The same man remembered that Bullock believed the best men should ensure the enactment of good laws. Bullock expected to retire from politics when the convention ended. But soon "the newspapers, after expressing surprise that no respectable man should go into the 'nigger convention,' began to abuse him." Then the convention rewarded his efforts by petitioning Pope to make him governor. "Here, in my opinion, is where he determined to go regularly into politics. He withdrew from his business and devoted himself to the canvass. His ambition was awakened and his resentment stimulated." [49]

This interpretation of Bullock's entry into politics appears to be the best analysis of his actions. It is consistent with his own statements about his efforts in raising capital in the North and the interdependence of government and business. Manifestly an entrepreneur, Bullock probably itched for the power a governor could bring to bear in favor of business. He recognized that if he could help promote business interests at the convention, what might he be able to do as governor? But that was not all. In the future, he would speak and write at length about his "good name" and the abuse his political convictions brought him. Human beings usually respond to lies and slander about themselves by attempting to clear the record. Some may be able to turn the other cheek; most would rather laugh last. Bullock would get his chance.

The central committee of Georgia's Republican party had announced a nominating convention for February 19, only to cancel that call on the last day of January. Many observers readily understood what the change meant. The same day, the *Albany Tri-Weekly News* warned that an "Augusta clique had organized to elect Brown and Blodgett for the United States

Senate, and Bullock for Governor. . . . This combination is gotten up for two purposes . . . to monopolize the offices . . . and secondly, to defeat Farrow." [50]

On March 2, guided by Blodgett and Bryant, the party's central committee decided that instead of calling for districts to vote for new delegates, it made sense simply to have the Republicans in the constitutional convention reconvene as a nominating convention five days hence. Blodgett explained the decision as pragmatic because the constitutional convention was largely Republican and the delegates to it would surely be reelected. Thus the Augusta men controlled the party's nomination; the candidate certainly would be Rufus Brown Bullock. And the Albany paper's prediction came true in later months when Bullock promoted Blodgett and Brown for the U.S. Senate.[51]

Bullock's was not the only name mentioned for the Republican nomination. Henry P. Farrow made a strong bid. Explaining his failure, he wrote: "When Blodgett saw that I would get the nomination over Bullock he withdrew the call and resolved the constitutional convention into a nominating body." Georgia Supreme Court judge Dawson A. Walker hoped he might get the nomination; he had Joe Brown's support. But Brown was outmaneuvered and knew it: "Colonel Farrow's friends used the Leagues; some of us used other methods. We all did the best we could. Colonel Bullock's friends outplayed us a little, and I think we should all acquiesce with a good grace, and give him our active support." [52]

Many people supported Blodgett for the state's highest office, but he declined in favor of Bullock. Blodgett reiterated the state's need for careful management of its finances and affirmed that "Col. Bullock possesses the business capacity and practical ability necessary for such an emergency and . . . every financial and commercial interest of the State could be safely confided to his care." Blodgett added that the next governor should be thoroughly familiar with all aspects of the new constitution and supportive of its provisions. An intimate knowledge of the constitution would help, but Blodgett was clearly campaigning against Farrow and Walker, neither of whom served as delegates. Because he controlled the central committee and the constitutional convention, Blodgett picked the candidate.[53]

On Saturday afternoon, March 7, Blodgett took the podium in the Atlanta City Hall to nominate his friend for governor. The delegates declared unanimously in his favor before any further nominations could be made. In response, Bullock said simply, "I plant myself squarely on the

Constitution, which we have just framed, and the principles of the Union Republican Party of Georgia." That night a large meeting of Republicans in the Atlanta City Hall began the campaign. Many made speeches. Joe Brown promoted Bullock as "a gentleman of ability, of unimpeachable character, of industry and energy, of first-rate business habits, and strong common sense." Convention delegate and future Georgia Supreme Court justice Henry K. McCay called Bullock "a man whom I have uniformly regarded as the very embodiment of our principles, a gentleman of fine capacity, and one whom, if he were not present, I would call one of the very best looking men in the South." After four days of protesting the convention's action, Henry Farrow announced that the Union League would back the candidate, proclaimed his "unqualified and earnest support," and agreed to "stump the state" for Bullock and the constitution. At that moment, Republicans in Georgia were as united as they would ever be during Reconstruction. It was good that they were. Bullock needed all the help he could muster for the bitter and dangerous campaign that followed.[54]

Chapter 3 ❧ Bullock Is Our Man

GEORGIA'S REPUBLICAN LEADERS wasted no time producing campaign tracts and stumping the state for the candidate. They knew that this election would be different from the contest over whether to hold a constitutional convention because white Democrats intended to vote. Even before the constitutional convention met in 1867, Republican delegate A. L. Harris of Savannah anticipated the struggle and informed Radical Ohio senator John Sherman: "The white people of Georgia have thrown off their 'masterly inactivity' . . . and are going to work in earnest to *defeat the constitution, whatever it may be!*" Harris went so far as to suggest that Congress ratify the constitution without letting Georgians vote on it. He

feared that large numbers of freedmen who voted for a constitutional convention would not vote in the upcoming election and reasoned that "having
'seen the elephant' and [having] failed to get their 'land and mules,' which
large numbers, without doubt, expected to get, [it] will be difficult to persuade [them] to come out to vote." Obviously, Republicans understood
that their campaign depended on the black vote and a strong congressional
commitment to a real reconstruction. By "white people," Harris surely
meant the old antebellum leadership. This election and referendum faced
a new Democratic strategy based on getting out the vote, intimidation of
Union men, and active involvement in the campaign. The old strategy of
nonparticipation had failed to stop the convention from meeting. Democrats pledged themselves to defeating the Radical Bullock and electing their
own candidate.[1]

Throughout the state, orators and newspaper editors echoed Democratic
party resolutions against the "unconstitutionality and injustice of the Reconstruction Acts of Congress." They chastised the recent convention as
an "effort to establish the supremacy of the negro race in the south, and
to place the destinies of [the state] . . . in the hands of adventurers and
irresponsible persons." Democrats asked all "our friends to participate in
the election . . . to the end that the best and wisest men—men perma-
nently identified with Georgia, and who will administer her government
in the interests of the people and not for the purposes of plunder—may
be chosen." From the beginning, the old conservative leadership conjured
the specter of black and carpetbag misrule, while hailing themselves as
"the best and the wisest." Anyone who stood in their way would feel the
wrath of slander, intimidation, or murder. But first, they had to select a
candidate.[2]

In March, the Democratic executive committee nominated Augustus
Reese for governor, but General George G. Meade declared him ineligible
under the provisions of the Fourteenth Amendment. The Democrats' second choice, David Irwin, met the same prohibition by Meade. Clearly
conservatives had no intention of following the spirit of Reconstruction.
They hoped to elect their old leaders, including those obviously ineligible. Finally, with Meade's prearranged approval, the Democratic committee named former Confederate major-general John B. Gordon as their
standard-bearer.[3]

Strictly speaking, Gordon was eligible because he had not held any prewar office. His nomination indicates the depth of the resistance to Reconstruction and the commitment of most white Georgians to past leaders and

war heroes for positions of power. These "captains" were prewar politicians, planters, and high-ranking Confederate warriors. Gordon grew up
in a privileged family, the son of a Baptist minister, planter, and coal mine
owner. He spent a year at the University of Georgia before withdrawing
to study law and become an Atlanta attorney and north Georgia coal mine
operator. He had favored secession, served with Lee's army throughout the
war, and survived more than five wounds at the battle of Antietam.[4]

A good soldier, Gordon rose quickly in rank and commanded rear-
guard actions for the Army of Northern Virginia when it stumbled from
Gettysburg and fell at Appomattox. In 1865, he resumed his law practice
in Atlanta and became outspoken in his resistance to Congressional Reconstruction. He was Georgia's premier war hero, a good speaker, and
leader of the state's Ku Klux Klan. With Gordon as the nominee, Benjamin
Harvey Hill flinging philippics at the Radicals, and unreconstructed Rebel
Robert Toombs directing the campaign, the Democrats were formidable
indeed. But to win, they would need to outmaneuver the most experienced
and well-known politician in the state.[5]

Former governor Joe Brown led the Bullock campaign and drew strength
from white yeoman farmers of north Georgia. Years later, Bullock acknowledged that he would not have been elected without the support of those
upcountry whites; the black vote was not large enough. Brown proved to be
an indefatigable campaigner for Bullock and Reconstruction. Just ten days
after Bullock's nomination, Brown took the political stump in Marietta
and called him a "strong relief man" and a "strong Union man." Assuring
yeoman whites that the new constitution did not specifically allow blacks
the right to hold office, he cited Bullock's leadership of the constitutional
convention and stated: "If elected he will move off smoothly and harmo-
niously, in accord with the Federal Government, which will be infinitely
better than the election of a man who may not be regarded its friend. . . .
As we are now seeking peace, I think it is best that we do not irritate."[6]

Brown's message of reconciliation and relief pulled many into the Republican camp. Pointing to the depressed Southern economy, Brown compared
the business abilities of the candidates to show that Bullock could better
manage the state's financial affairs. After all, he said, had Bullock been "an
ordinary business man," neither the Southern Express Company nor the
Macon and Augusta Railroad would have sought his management services.
Brown was so successful that Georgians clamored for printed copies of his
speeches.[7]

In response, Bullock wrote Brown asking him to "print pamphlets at

once, at my expense, and give them wide circulation throughout the state."
Bullock added that he felt they would win and gave credit to the faith-
fulness of the "union men of the mountains." The next day, confident of
victory for the constitution and for Bullock, Brown wrote a friend: "The
Constitution is a good one and Bullock will make a good governor. He has
been in Georgia long enough to be twice naturalized. He is a good business
man and a very sensible one."[8]

Republicans campaigned for new directions under new leadership. They
printed ballots headed: "Bullock, Relief and Reconstruction. For the
Constitution." Their campaign fliers announced: "Reconstruction Express
Train. Clear the Tracks." True to his word, Henry Farrow canvassed twenty-
five north Georgia counties for Bullock and coordinated the printing and
distribution of campaign materials. Among the 108,500 published pamphlets were 15,000 copies of Brown's Marietta speech. Republicans promoted Bullock as the workingman's champion and trumpeted his efforts
to gain relief for debtors.[9]

In March 1868, the *Atlanta Daily New Era* drew the lines for the class
nature of the campaign in terms that closely resembled the prewar conflict between a bourgeois North and an aristocratic South: "Bullock is a
friend of the working man, and the working men are for Bullock. Ben Hill
is opposed to the Homestead Bill. Bullock is for it, and so are the people.
Ben Hill is down on the 'Poor Masses.' Bullock is for them. Ben Hill is
opposed to relief. Bullock is for it. . . . The mechanics and working men
are all declaring for Bullock." A Radical handbill further stirred up class
antagonisms: "Be a man! Let the slaveholding aristocracy no longer rule
you. Vote for a Constitution which educates your children free of charge;
relieves the poor debtor from his rich creditor; allows a liberal homestead
for your families; and more than all, places you on a level with those who
used to boast that for every slave they were entitled to three-fifths of a vote
in congressional representation."[10]

Not only was it good political strategy to align the poor whites with the
freed people in an economic struggle, it was a move toward equality of
opportunity and a restructuring of Southern society to the free labor mold
of the North. Clearly, Republicans were concerned with keeping the freed
people free, not just from black codes but in the marketplace, at the voting
booth, and in thought and speech. Radical John E. Bryant emphasized "the
principles we advocate" as Congressional Reconstruction, "equal political
and legal rights of all citizens," a common school system, the dignity of

labor, "and the passage of such laws as will protect the toiling masses of society in their just and legal rights." [11]

Equating a vote for the constitution and Bullock with an affirmation of the principles of the American creed, Bryant stressed longtime values of law, justice, civil rights, education, and equality of opportunity. He also wanted to punish the prewar Southern leadership, calling members of the old elite "felons" and seeking to deny them the vote. This was consistent with his unsuccessful efforts in the convention to place a liberal disfranchising clause in the new constitution. Of course, such a clause also would have helped the Republican party maintain its strength by disfranchising a large and powerful bloc of Democratic ballots.

Blodgett joined those who expressed the struggle in class terms. He warned Senator Sherman that if Georgia elected Democrats, "the poor Negroes will have no rights and . . . will not be allowed even to exist except as the nominal slaves of the landed aristocracy of this section." Of course, his choice of words conformed to Charles Sumner's views, but they also accurately prophesied the real world of post-Reconstruction sharecropping, intimidation, and disfranchisement. Blodgett extolled the elevation of labor. Obviously supporting a biracial coalition, he reached out to lower-class whites and asked them to compare their old position under planter rule with the vision he professed. As early as August 1867, Blodgett evoked an image of ground-down poor whites held in contempt by their planter neighbors. Blodgett said Reconstruction offered each "honest and hardworking citizen . . . the opportunity to elevate himself." A worker "will no more be dragged downward by the humiliating reflection that he occupies an inferior position." Common to Blodgett's speeches—stated or implied—was his appeal to Georgians to accept the free soil, free labor ideology as manifested by Congressional Reconstruction. He upheld the Republican party as a guarantor of "the grand principle that labor and capital are equal," and he envisioned the birth of a new society, not the restoration of conservative white rule.[12]

In ways similar to the Populist revolt in the 1880s and 1890s, the Republican organizers struggled to maintain the tenuous coalition of white yeoman farmers and blacks. Republicans were well aware that to win they must gain the votes of mountain whites and the state's entire black vote. In late March 1868, hoping for the white vote, Bullock wrote Brown: "All our men are wide awake for the great necessity of bringing out the black vote & nothing is more sure to secure it than the fact that colored men are on the county tickets." In counties with black majorities, Republicans promoted black candidates for the legislature and local offices. They knew they had to seize every advantage if they were to have a chance against the tactics of terror employed by the Democrats. They used what Eric Foner has described as a "two-faced strategy" of nominating blacks for office in black-belt counties while telling north Georgia whites that blacks could not hold office under the new constitution. That strategy worked for the 1868 election, but, in Steven Hahn's words, "Reconstruction . . . foundered on the rocks of class and racial tensions" as Blodgett, Bullock, and others were unable to maintain the coalition they forged in this initial election.[13]

Bullock seems to have been less active in the campaign than his supporters. His one campaign tour took him from Atlanta to Rome and then north to Dalton. He knew that he must gain the votes in these antisecession, antiplanter counties to have any chance of winning the election. Accompanied by Joe Brown and others, Bullock made "short but plain and practical" speeches. Newspapers published only one address he made during the entire campaign. In it, Bullock accepted the nomination and stressed the party platform. Bullock maintained that he had been virtually drafted from business into politics and his purpose was "to be of service to the whole people." He promised to help the state "in building up her waste places and in reviving her prostrated industrial and commercial system." He stood before the people "fully committed to the new Constitution and [with] an earnest desire to vitalize those great measures—the 'Relief' and the 'Homestead.'" In closing, Bullock said, "I have the honor to be your fellow citizen."[14]

His opening remarks reflected the difficult decision he made in entering politics and his view that politics represented a call to service. Bullock worshiped at the altar of internal improvements and strongly believed that expansion of business would bring good times. In support of the construction of a railroad to tie Atlanta to Washington and Philadelphia, he said, "It is only from an industrious and judicious development of our internal resources, that we can look for general and progressive prosperity." He viewed state aid to railroads as necessary for "the products of the mine, the factory, and of the farm [to] find ready sale." The state would profit by increased tax revenues from more valuable properties and from the opening up of previously untapped lands and resources; consumers would gain because of lower shipping costs.[15]

Historian Mark Summers aptly described this campaign optimism which linked economic and industrial growth with free labor ideology as the "gospel of prosperity." Clearly Bullock preached that gospel. Although he was promoted as a champion of working-class debtors and believed that he had been "called" to help the state, Bullock was still a businessman who would rely on business methods to improve the state's economic position. His final statement was intended to throw off any opprobrium that he was a "carpetbagger," "outside speculator," or anything other than a common citizen of Georgia.[16]

In appearance, Bullock had few peers. Atlanta native, Democrat, and historian Lucian Lamar Knight knew him and described him as "politically and personally a commanding figure, handsome, tall, and well-built." The *Atlanta Daily New Era* characterized him as "a gentleman of fine personal appearance—an elegant picture of good health, portly, courteous, sociable and always appearing in a good humor with everyone." A contemporary called him "splendid looking, being tall and large, with dark hair." He had a distinguished forehead and brow, the prominence of which increased over the years as his hairline receded. His nose was prominent, and he wore a thick mustache and beard, cropped at the chin so the beard's two extending ends seemed to flow from the mustache. He habitually wore a three-piece suit and top hat and carried an umbrella, all of which made him even more impressive in size and bearing. In 1871, writer John Wilson described Bullock as a pleasant, barrel-chested bear of a man, "stoutly built, and his whole physique indicates great solidity of body united with a mental breadth and firmness. . . . In manners he is pleasant and accessible; in business prompt, liberal, and, offhand, being, apparently, a man of few words."[17]

Before Bullock became involved in politics, no one questioned his integrity or loyalty or hinted that he was not a Georgian. That changed when he became a candidate and opponents made wild accusations and claims accompanied by racial slurs. Some insisted that Bullock was a mulatto from Massachusetts; others claimed that to secure the nomination he had danced with "negro wenches." Gordon used the latter rumor to fire racists against Bullock. Gordon claimed that Bullock habitually attended black dances to campaign for votes and "to be introduced to the colored ladies!" He condemned any man who would seek the governor's office by flirting with black women.[18]

Others called Bullock alternately and simultaneously "carpetbagger," "scalawag," "Yankee adventurer," and "interloper" as white Democrats associated him with Yankee triumph and emancipation. In 1936, Margaret

Mitchell captured the feeling many had toward Bullock when Melanie scolded Scarlett for inviting Bullock to a party:

> But, oh, Scarlett! . . . Can you forget what these people did to us? Can you forget darling Charlie dead and Ashley's health ruined and Twelve Oaks burned? Oh, Scarlett, you can't forget that terrible man you shot with your mother's sewing box in his hands! You can't forget Sherman's men at Tara and how they even stole our underwear! And tried to burn the place down and actually handled my father's sword! Oh, Scarlett, it was these same people who robbed us and tortured us and left us to starve that you invited to your party! The same people who have set the darkies up to lord it over us, who are robbing us and keeping our men from voting! I can't forget. I won't forget.[19]

Democrats denounced him for his politics and called him many names in many papers. They also set their pens against those who cooperated with him or his free labor ideas and lashed out at Joe Brown. Almost seven decades later, Margaret Mitchell described the fury of white conservatives: "The hate that enveloped the Bullock regime enveloped her too. . . . Whatever her birth and family connections, [Scarlett] . . . was now . . . a turncoat, a nigger lover, a traitor, a Republican—and a Scallawag." In 1868, with only four papers statewide supporting Bullock, the Democrats held an unquestionable advantage in advertising and slander.[20]

Conservatives expanded their obloquy of Bullock to assault the constitution and equate Republicans with Negro rule and robbery. Benjamin Hill led the way, denouncing all Union men as thieves "whose only object is to plunder." He wrote the editor of the *Macon Telegraph* that Bullock expected to be elected "by deluded negroes and designing robbers. His supporters will not embrace one-hundredth part of the intelligence, property, or interests of the State! Nay, they embrace only the ignorance, pauperism and crime in the State." Similar articles charged that "if the Government fall into their hands, they will bankrupt Georgia in less than twelve months. . . . Their only object is to PLUNDER a people with whom they are in no way identified."[21]

Stressing pillage by Republican usurpers, Democrats saw the campaign as a class struggle of intelligence and wealth against ignorance and poverty. Thus both parties emphasized the battle for political control between the planter elite and the underclasses. While Joe Brown and others attempted to form a coalition of white yeomen and freedmen, Democrats invoked provincialism and used the race issue to pry the white lower class from the Republican fold. Many editors preyed on white fears of race mixing. The *Augusta Constitutionalist* warned that "niggers are in haste to vote always, run for every office, sue their old masters and marry their masters' daughters. . . . We are threatened with a season of robbery. . . . Then, on the heel of this is to come the woe and horror of miscegenation." When slander and race-baiting failed to secure victory, Democratic leaders resorted to violence.[22]

An hour or two past midnight on March 31, a mob of thirty to forty men that included at least one U.S. soldier masked or blackened their faces, entered a boardinghouse in Columbus, and killed George W. Ashburn. Ashburn, a white man, had been an early organizer of Columbus freedmen. He was outspoken in wanting to prohibit former Rebels from holding office, and he was a candidate for the Georgia Senate. He had been a delegate to the 1868 constitutional convention and sat as temporary chairman of the initial session. An open friend of blacks, Ashburn boarded in the home of Hannah Flourney, a black woman. Whites hated him for that, and they resented his electioneering among the freedmen and his support of the new constitution. Commenting on his murder, the *Columbus Sun* explained: "The man was thoroughly detested; every white man had the most profound contempt for him, socially and politically." In light of the long history of abuse of freedmen by Columbus city officials, neither this newspaper comment nor the verdict by a local white jury that Ashburn had been murdered by "unknown persons" was surprising.[23]

Ashburn's murder was the first reported outrage committed by the Ku Klux Klan in Georgia, and it focused national attention on the state. The appearance of this terrorist organization coincided with the March 11 visit of former Confederate general Nathan Bedford Forrest to Atlanta. The organization quickly infected the state and spread to Columbus just one week before the killing. Judge John H. Caldwell of LaGrange, a supporter of Bullock and a convention delegate, had been with Ashburn just two days before his death and remembered seeing Klan warnings depicting "Ashburn lying in his coffin; his name was on it, and it also had the emblems of death, with a warning that he should die."[24]

On April 2, from the nation's capital, General Ulysses S. Grant ordered Meade to investigate the crime and punish the offenders. The fiasco of the local jury's verdict caused Meade to retry the case in a military court. In a letter to Brown, Bullock expressed his concern and emphasized the importance of a quick, firm response to the murder: "The outrages in Columbus should be dealt with severely and promptly or our voters will be intimidated." The military trial became a showcase of resolve and competing interests that revealed how far the United States government would go to protect its citizens and the lengths to which the Rebels would go to resist. The military seemed to take a strong stand in the case and quickly arrested and jailed nine of the twenty-three accused men. But after the April election, interest waned. Meade confessed to Joseph Brown his belief that a trial, not a conviction, was the important thing. One of Meade's friends said that the general had been "impatient for the legislature to convene so that he could suspend the trial." Finally, on June 29, the long-delayed trial began with Joe Brown prosecuting and Alexander Stephens and six others defending the prisoners. The trial continued almost a month before Meade returned jurisdiction to local courts, a move that corresponded with the impending readmission of Georgia to the Union. Of course, that act effectively ended the case, and no one was ever convicted for Ashburn's murder. Judge Caldwell expressed the common knowledge that community planters planned and participated in the murder. The effect of the failed effort to convict the murderers undoubtedly made the Klan bolder. Its activities increased wildly between 1868 and 1871, and Georgia members murdered hundreds of Republicans. The Ashburn murder and later Klan actions were major factors in the failure of Reconstruction in Georgia.[25]

As the campaign continued, Republicans and Democrats urged their people to register and vote. Edward Hulbert still acted as chief registrar, and his bias in favor of Reconstruction and Bullock was important to the success of both. Hulbert still worked for the Southern Express Company and supported the business interests expressed by the Republican party. He conveniently located the Bureau of Registration adjacent to the Atlanta office of the Southern Express so that he could easily attend to his duties as superintendent of the company as well as facilitate communication with county registrars and election managers. Hulbert received letters detailing abuses against blacks who had voted Republican in the last election or who might do so in the next, and he made suggestions about troop deployment so as to maintain order during the election. He ensured that the registrars had ample copies of the test oath and oversaw the publication and dissemination of election notices. These notices informed people of the election and of Meade's orders that any violence or threat aimed at keeping people from voting would not be tolerated, that laborers were not bound to vote as their employers asked, and that people could vote whether or not they had paid their taxes. Of course, those who planned violence and believed military rule illegitimate paid no heed to Meade's orders. And once the election was past, many employers did discharge workers who voted for Bullock.[26]

The election spanned four days, April 20 to 23, and drew over 75 percent of the 201,758 eligible voters. Hulbert was active, instructing managers to open more ballot boxes and to get out the vote. He wrote a LaGrange election manager and warned him to stop intimidating voters by questioning them on their politics and opening their ballots: "Let them vote as they please." According to the official count, voters ratified the constitution by 88,172 to 70,200 and elected Bullock over Gordon 83,527 to 76,356.[27]

Both sides immediately screamed fraud. Democrats claimed that in tallying the vote Hulbert had counted Bullock in when actually Gordon had won. There is no proof of that assertion, and considering the number of registered freedmen (98,507) and support from the 30,000 to 40,000 mostly upcountry whites who voted Republican, the results are probably accurate. It is more likely that any discrepancy between what the count should have been and what it was most likely resulted from intimidation of voters by Democrats. If anything, the count for ratification and for Bullock should have been greater.[28]

Republicans also challenged the results and cited widespread violence and intimidation of voters. From Cuthbert, W. B. Dixon wrote: "Our men were forced to vote against their will. . . . The police were against us. Wealth and intellect were also used to the extreme." Lawyer and future United States attorney general Amos T. Akerman explained the Democratic victory in Elberton: "During the election there was a reign of lawlessness. . . . Ballots were snatched from their hands and democratic ballots substituted. . . . Pistols were drawn on negroes. . . . Hundreds of others abstained from voting altogether. . . . Even the few U.S. soldiers here took an active part in electioneering with negroes for the Democratic ticket. . . . The negroes were utterly cowed."[29]

Akerman's revelations were indicative of the intimidation that occurred throughout the state. The military commander received at least 118 letters from officers and civilians complaining about threats and irregularities at the polls. In a region and among a people who were mostly illiterate, this is a staggering number of complaints. Akerman's letter shows how the politics of fear—a sword of Damocles tactic—can keep qualified candidates from running for office and force people to vote against their will or abstain. Nor did the presence of the federal army guarantee fair elections or Republican victories. Far from aiding the freedmen, the soldiers often supported the conservatives. Akerman had requested and obtained five soldiers to oversee elections in Elberton, but they helped the Democrats.[30]

David Cotting reported that in Robert Toombs's hometown of Washington the conservatives used bribes: "The soldiers sent here have been bought. . . . They are distributing Democratic tickets & in other ways are helping them. I believe it would be better to be without them." Surely, freedmen who saw the military helping former masters would have considerable difficulty deciding who their friends were in later elections. Yet there was no apparent solution to the problem. If Republicans did not get military help to deter violence, they were certain to lose; if the troops were sent, they often aided the Democrats. Amid confusion, threats, and violence, the people of Georgia voted their future.[31]

As it happened, Georgians elected the most representative biracial legislature ever in the state's history. There were three black senators—Aaron Bradley, Tunis Campbell, and George Wallace—and twenty-nine black representatives. Republicans held a majority in the senate, but historians still disagree over the proportional composition of each party in the lower house. Meade's figures are often cited. His May 8 report listed ninety-five Republicans, seventy-four Democrats, and six unknown, but his April 29 and July 6 letters to Grant announced a Democratic majority. One week after the election, the *Savannah Morning News* rejoiced that the legislature was Democratic.[32]

Historian W. E. B. Du Bois gave Democrats the slight majority, eighty-eight to eighty-two; C. Mildred Thompson agreed that there were eighty-eight "Conservative Democrats" in the house. The figures of Du Bois and Thompson agree with Atlanta Republican Volney Spalding's note to Republican national secretary William Chandler that Democrats held a majority in the house and John H. Caldwell's report to Republican national chairman William Claflin: "We have in our Senate a good working majority of Republicans, and all the Senate officers elected are Republicans. In the House the two parties are nearly equal. We succeeded, however, in electing a Republican Speaker." Republicans barely succeeded in electing the Speaker, and only the late arrival of some legislators made it possible. Bullock acknowledged that on July 4, the first day of the session, Republicans had a slim majority with which to elect the Speaker, seventy-six to seventy-four to one; but on the following Monday, Democrats held the edge. The July 18 *New York Times* agreed and reported a Democratic majority of six. Perhaps historian Numan Bartley comes closest to the real count: Radicals, sixty-seven; moderate Republicans, twenty-six; Democrats, eighty. Bartley's breakdown accounts for the Radicals' failure to elect their choices to the U.S. Senate because moderates joined with Democrats. His figures also help explain the early vote on eligibility and the later expulsion of black legislators. "Moderate" may be another way of saying for Union, not black equality. Because any truly Radical program was destined to fail, Bullock would have difficulty working with the legislature. After reviewing Georgia's constitution and election results, the U.S. Congress passed the act of June 25, commonly referred to as the Omnibus Act, allowing Georgia and five other Southern states to reenter the Union. All would have to organize legislatures and ratify the Fourteenth Amendment. In addition, Georgia had to nullify sections of its constitution which granted relief from debts because Congress meant to uphold contracts at all costs.[33]

On July 4, Meade replaced General Ruger with Governor-elect Bullock. For the next eighteen days, Bullock complained to Meade that approximately thirty of the newly elected legislators were ineligible. Under the third section of the Fourteenth Amendment as enforced by the Omnibus Act, no one was eligible to hold civil office who had previously sworn to uphold the Constitution of the United States and then participated in the rebellion or had given "aid or comfort" to the enemy. Bullock contended that the legislature was invalid, "organized in violation of the law," and he wrote Meade on July 8 that even though the General Assembly said it was organized, "a number of the members . . . are not eligible to their seats."[34]

Meade immediately responded that "neither House is organized legally until they have complied with . . . Article 14." Preferring not to interfere because he believed "each House is undoubtedly the judge of the qualifications of its members," Meade maintained that he had authority over the provisional legislature. Bullock relayed Meade's position to the lawmakers, but after investigating their members, both houses claimed all were eligible. Bullock protested and used the house majority and senate minority reports to show that many were ineligible. But Meade seemed convinced that he had done enough and wrote Bullock that he no longer opposed the legislature and considered it "legally organized." Meade informed Grant that "I performed my duty when I called their attention to the law and required action to be taken under it. I do not feel myself confident to overrule the deliberate action of a legislative body." Meade's failure to act in accordance with the will of Congress deserves censure. Grant sustained Meade's actions and so in the initial struggle between Bullock and the legislature, the military supported the Democrats.[35]

Bullock would later refer to this as "the sham of July 1868," chide Meade for his failure to enforce the law, and argue that "a fundamental idea of the whole reconstruction policy" revolved around seating only eligible officeholders. "And it is trifling with that whole policy to permit . . . the first Legislature, before reconstruction is complete, and while the military jurisdiction is still paramount to be organized in defiance of that policy." Bullock scoffed at the "vain hope" that the legislature would "purge itself of its ineligible members." He ridiculed the efficacy of the eligibility oath as "simply absurd."[36]

Bullock blamed Meade's inaction for the subsequent defeat of the Radical Senate ticket and for the expulsion of blacks from the legislature. If ever there was a time when the government needed to prove its resolve and support the new Reconstruction and Republican administration in Georgia, it was then. But the beginning was inauspicious. Bullock's actions in favor of strict compliance with Radical wishes made him many enemies in both parties, but he had proven himself to be a man of principle and a believer in the federal and state constitutions. He would always endeavor to uphold the laws of Congress.[37]

The organization of the General Assembly was approved on July 20, and the legislators quickly complied with the Omnibus Act by ratifying the Fourteenth Amendment. At noon on July 22 they inaugurated the new governor in the assembly chamber. In his address, Bullock spoke of the "fostering care and protection of our General Government" and previous "erroneous opinions" about slavery and secession. He blamed Andrew Johnson for failing to act in accordance with the "will of the people." Expressing hopes for "peaceful progressive prosperity," Bullock praised the restoration of self-government under a new constitution that promised to educate even the poorest children and to protect the "equal, political and social rights" of all Georgians. He spoke of the "wisdom" and "justice of enfranchising the freedmen." Bullock recited the gospel of prosperity and asked for "united efforts in the enforcement of civil law, securing to every one the lawful expression of their political opinions, and the enjoyment of the results of their labor."[38]

Obviously, Bullock believed in the law and would rely on the new constitution to uphold it. As always, he stressed education, equality, justice, and economic development. He praised the freedmen and appealed to whites to overcome their prejudices. He hoped that Georgians would obey the laws, tolerate alternative political opinions, treat labor with respect, and thereby encourage investors and workers to send their capital or bring their skills to the state. He promised to fulfill his duties "by a strict adherence to the provisions of the Constitution." A man of integrity, Bullock intended to keep his pledge.

Following Bullock's address, General Meade and a packed house watched U.S. Circuit judge John Erskine administer the oath of office. President of the senate Benjamin Conley smiled at his friend and proclaimed him the new governor to serve for four years. Conley capped his proclamation: "God save the governor and the commonwealth of Georgia." Perhaps Conley would have done better to evoke the name of Congress instead of God, for Congress had it in its power to demand a true Reconstruction. In the end, however, neither God nor Congress would save the governor or the commonwealth.[39]

On July 24, Bullock addressed the General Assembly. He applauded the constitutional provisions that outlawed imprisonment for debt and changed the judicial system from a court in each county to a district system. He cited a letter from former military governor Ruger that work remained to be done in the area of criminal justice. The penitentiary owed $10,000 and too many inmates had cruel or lengthy sentences—the punishment for burglary in the night was death. Two convicts were serving life sentences for stealing cornmeal and molasses. Bullock wanted action to correct the iniquity of the system. Further, he told the legislators that the poll tax for education established by the constitution was good and "within the ability of all" but emphasized that they should impose no other poll tax. He spoke to the issue of relief, canceled by act of the U.S. Congress, and expressed the hope that they would find new measures to help Georgia debtors. He also enjoined them to provide for an adequate homestead law to protect the property of small landholders and encouraged them to get their own communities to help the indigent poor.[40]

Bullock called for the people to recognize the equality of all men: "It is too late now to argue, that a native American has no rights because his complexion is not that of the majority. . . . All civilized men are citizens." He asked the legislature to establish quickly a system of common schools to educate every child in Georgia. He paid homage to the benefits the free labor market would bring in replacing "the old system of labor, which was a continual oppression to the owner as well as the owned." Blacks would work hard and were "the most efficient and reliable class of agricultural laborers to be found." Bullock proposed a "wise use of the State credit" to promote railroads that would link buyers and sellers, increase population, and accelerate the "demand for our lands."[41]

Bullock asked the legislators to revise *Irwin's Code,* Georgia's basic book of statute law, to reflect the changes made by the new constitution. He also called for approval to establish a state capitol suitable to the needs of the government and suggested that the General Assembly consider plans to occupy the largest and newest building in Atlanta. All in all, Bullock put forth the constitution as the basic law, called for development of Georgia's resources under a system of state aid and free labor, extolled the virtue of the American creed on the equality of all men, and initiated the hunt for new physical facilities necessary for the transfer of state government from the old capitol at Milledgeville to the new center of a new Georgia.[42]

Bullock had a clear plan for the people, white and black, under Congressional Reconstruction and within the union of states. He continued to praise the benefits of free labor, equality, and progress, but not everyone agreed. The future remained uncertain. Democrats increased the violence and slander they had begun in Columbus and elsewhere as they worked to keep the hated symbol of Northern victory, "Unconditional Surrender" Grant, from carrying Georgia in the upcoming presidential election.

On the day after Bullock's inaugural, Democrats held a mass rally in Atlanta with fifteen to twenty thousand people attending and protesting the new government. The politicking for Horatio Seymour and Francis P. Blair had started. Bullock remembered that his enemies called for wives to leave their husbands and sons to disown their fathers if they voted Republican. Robert Toombs, Howell Cobb, and Benjamin Hill remained in character by joining the chorus making incendiary speeches against Congressional Reconstruction. Toombs had earlier declared: "I regret nothing in the past but the dead and the failure; and I am ready today to use the best means I can command to establish the principles for which I fought." He must have been extremely proud of his son-in-law Dudley M. DuBose, chief recruiter and organizer for the Ku Klux Klan in Georgia. Howell Cobb had returned to his plantations after the war only to become "thoroughly disgusted" with free negro labor. Hill had stated that "slavery is the only civilizer of the negro."[43]

Standing below the bush arbor on Alabama Street in 1868, this reaction-ary triumverate damned the rule of "Bullock and a nigger government." Speaking first, Toombs cursed the Republicans as "a mass of floating putrescence which rises as it rots and rots as it rises." Cobb followed with a more moderate speech but added that "we are now passing through a purgatory" in which illiterate "negroes fill up the ballot box." Hill spoke last and announced that "white blood is superior" and traitors who joined the Radical call for the equality of the races became themselves Negroes. He appealed to God, Southern honor, and the Lost Cause:

> Ye generation of vipers, how will you escape the damnation of hell? That's what is coming. Oh, it's coming; thank God it's coming—coming to the cheer of patriots and the dismay of traitors. Yes, I tell you victory is coming. We have suffered, and suffered much. Our comrades are sleeping. Ah, sleep-ing! many of them by the streams and in the valleys of Georgia. They are sleeping on the banks of the deep-rolling Mississippi; they are sleeping all over Virginia. . . . Spirit of our departed braves, we are not dishonored yet! and though the vile, the low, the corrupt, and the perjured are seeking to be our rulers, and have seized upon our high places, the noble, the valiant, and the true are still left to us, and through all our borders are taking courage and hymning the notes of coming triumph. Ye miserable spawns of political accidency, hatched by the putrid growth of revolutionary corruption into an ephemeral existence—renegades from every law of God and violators of every right of man—we serve you with notice this day that this victory is coming.[44]

This triumverate of Democratic leaders resolved never to surrender until the state had been returned to its "natural" leadership—planter leader-ship. They had won the tests of strength in Columbus and on the eligibility question; now the fight was about who would represent Georgia in the United States Senate, whether blacks could or could not hold office, and the national election of a president. They put so much pressure on anyone who associated with Radical rule that many changed sides. Bullock fought them every step of the way.

Chapter 4 ❧ A Vital Question

Reconstruction was war not finished,
in bellum non cessante.
—Senator John Scott, 1871

A week before Scarlett and Rhett announced their
engagement, an election for governor had been held.
The Southern Democrats had General John B. Gordon,
one of Georgia's best loved and most honored citizens,
as their candidate. Opposing him was a Republican
named Bullock. . . . Bullock had won. If the capture of
Georgia by Sherman had caused bitterness, the final
capture of the state's capitol by the Carpetbaggers,
Yankees, and negroes caused an intensity of bitterness
such as the state had never known before. Atlanta and
Georgia seethed and raged. And Rhett Butler was a
friend of the hated Bullock!
—Margaret Mitchell, *Gone with the Wind*

THE STRUGGLE to secure a place for blacks in postwar Georgia began before Bullock became governor. In 1867, after Milledgeville hostelers threatened not to rent rooms to black delegates attending the constitutional convention, Atlanta served as a ready alternative. The delegates responded to
Atlanta's kindness and Milledgeville's snub by using their authority to relocate the seat of government. Article Ten of the new constitution formally
made Atlanta the capital. City councilman Richard Peters was influential
in getting the city of Atlanta to provide, for a ten-year period, suitable

buildings to house the state government. On February 26, 1868, the council approved the plan; the next day the constitutional convention accepted. When the legislators met in the city hall, which had been renovated to accommodate them, they found it inadequate and persuaded the city to seek an alternative. Peters suggested either expanding the city hall or acquiring the new Opera House, which was owned by Hannibal I. Kimball.[1]

Kimball was an entrepreneur par excellence who shared Bullock's vision of a free labor South dominated by business interests. Born and educated in Maine, Kimball worked as a carriage maker and mine superintendent during the Civil War. In 1866, former Albionite George Pullman hired him and sent him south to investigate and develop a market for Pullman sleeping cars. Calling Atlanta "the place where things would naturally congregate," Kimball quickly established the Pullman, Kimball, and Ramsey Sleeping Car Company. He turned his profits from that company into ventures in railroad building and hotel construction. In 1868, R. G. Dun and Company believed Kimball to be "making a fortune & are every way worthy of cr[edit]." "Good for all contracts, worth over 200,000$," Dun's agent reported in 1869. When Kimball realized that the constitutional convention might change Georgia's capital, he promoted that move as best he could. He paid $31,370 to buy the financially plagued and still unfinished Opera House and then spent an additional $100,000 to complete construction. After the Georgia legislature decided that the Opera House offered the better option as a capitol, the City Council agreed to pay Kimball $6,000 a year for five years to rent the building.[2]

Symbolically, moving the capital was important as a break from the old Georgia, which had seceded at Milledgeville, to a new Georgia raised from the ashes left by a conquering army. During the war, Sherman's army burned nearly five thousand Atlanta houses and business establishments and, according to one contemporary Atlantan, "left a scene of charred and desolate ruins, the home of half-starved and half-wild dogs, and of carrion fowls feeding upon refuse and the decaying carcasses of animals." The city's importance as a railroad center combined with chance to make certain that Georgians would quickly rebuild after the war. During Reconstruction, General John Pope established his headquarters in the city and built McPherson Barracks on its western edge as quarters for his six hundred men. Those men spent money in Atlanta which helped the city recover, and the troops provided visible evidence that the federal government expected Georgians to comply with the Reconstruction Acts.[3]

Around the time of his inauguration in July 1868, Bullock relocated his wife and three children from their Augusta residence and settled them into a house on Peachtree Street in the heart of downtown Atlanta. Nearby neighbors included William M. Lowry and his son Robert, two of the city's wealthiest men. Financier William Markham and other upper-class residents made Peachtree a center for Atlanta's social life. In 1870, the state spent $100,000 to purchase the Peachtree residence of banker John James and convert it into the governor's mansion. The new executive residence was a three-story brick building with a sixty-foot tower, one-and-a-half-acre lawn, carriage house, and brick stables. Bullock was the first governor to occupy the mansion, which remained the official home for Georgia chief executives until 1921.[4]

The Atlanta to which Bullock and the legislature relocated was a city only twenty-five years old. Always directed toward business interests, Atlanta was established in the early 1840s as terminus and distribution center for the state-owned Western and Atlantic Railroad. The Civil War increased prosperity and doubled the prewar population as Atlanta became an important Confederate military transportation and hospital hub. In the immediate aftermath of the war, more than three hundred new commercial firms opened their doors in the city. Non-Southerners influenced Atlanta's growth from the beginning and composed one-fourth of the city's economic elite in 1848 and one-third by 1860. In manufacturing, Atlantans followed a Northern Moses—Pennsylvanian Moses Formwalt—who established the city's first factory and became the first mayor. Joseph and Isaac Winship, from Massachusetts, fired iron in Atlanta's maiden foundry. During the seven years preceding the Civil War, Connecticut Yankee William Markham financed the construction of nearly ninety buildings, including the Atlanta Rolling Mill, which he operated. Markham became mayor in 1854 on the Whig ticket, participated in Republican politics after the war, and helped resurrect the city by constructing nearly fifty more buildings— including one of the finest hotels in the South, the Markham House. Pennsylvanian Richard Peters came to Atlanta via Augusta in 1845 as superintendent of the Georgia Railroad. Soon Peters became Atlanta's largest landowner and real estate broker and added to his fortune by operating one of the largest flour mills in the South and raising huge flocks of sheep. With all his business interests, it is easy to see why Peters wanted Atlanta to be the new capital in 1868.[5]

Perhaps all these business-oriented, transplanted Northerners gave Atlanta an open upper class, not dominated by planters. In his study of Georgia, Numan Bartley referred to this group as the "Uptown"—indigenous only to this one city in Georgia. Commercial and industrial business leaders dominated the city leadership and believed local business interests were more important than all other issues. They supported Bullock's goals of economic development even if they did not support his politics.[6]

Even though European writer F. Barham Zincke traveled throughout the former Confederacy in early 1868 and reported Atlanta as "the most flourishing place in the South," postwar conditions were bad. Atlantan Kate Massey remembered: "People lived in anything they could find. Some families were housed in old freight cars. Some used discarded army tents. . . . Others were sheltered by scraps of old tin roofing nailed to a slight framework of timber." Educator Elizabeth Sterchi agreed that "Atlanta is . . . crowded with poor people piled the one upon the other, perfect heathen in a civilized country with the most savage tastes, fighting, murdering, stealing, quarreling, begging, swearing, drinking and possessing the most abject ideas of life."[7]

In 1867, a Freedmen's Bureau officer reported that twenty-two hundred whites and twelve hundred blacks were destitute in the city. By 1871, one Atlanta newspaper lamented: "We build railroads, fair grounds, Kimball houses [hotels], depots that astonish the natives, capitol buildings, etc., while our poor die in the streets." The industrializing South had adapted to the Northern way of building impressive structures while neglecting the primary needs of most of the working class. George Fitzhugh, James Henry Hammond, and others who had warned of the brutality of the free labor system watched and nodded knowingly as Atlanta grew in the Northern mold.[8]

Federal and private organizations and individuals tried to respond to the people's needs. The Freedmen's Bureau hospital operated until 1868 and although a city almshouse helped to fill the void after it closed, Atlanta desperately needed a hospital. In September 1870, while Democratic and moderate city leaders turned deaf ears, blind eyes, and stone hearts to these dire straits, Bullock and other Radicals led those subscribing to build a hospital and soup kitchen: "The beneficiaries . . . will be the homeless sick of Atlanta, such invalid persons as have no fit shelter and are destitute of the means of procuring food, necessary attention, and medical treatment." But when the Radical government fell in October 1871, the effort lost its main supporters and failed. Atlanta went without a hospital until 1880, when a facility for whites only opened; blacks finally got a hospital in 1892. The *Atlanta Herald* deftly summarized the problem of getting a hospital as owing to "city rulers . . . [who] have been more interested in . . . increasing the value of their landed property." One Atlanta historian concluded that those Atlantans who "sickened, suffered and died were victims to the inhumanity of their rulers," but another argued that Atlanta elites were more committed to order than justice. Protestant churches, believing that the city's overall health depended on orderliness, "helped conserve the pattern of segregation and white supremacy." Dominated by men of wealth, these "churches were not for the poor and outcast." The rich and their churches helped little; instead of achieving social justice, they closed their doors to the less fortunate and clung to the past.[9]

Black Georgians not only required relief, they needed to be educated. Georgia had made a commitment to public education, for whites only, in the late 1850s under Governor Joseph Brown. By 1867, Atlantans maintained seventy-five schools for white children, but few conservatives seemed to care about educating the freed people or their children. Article Six of the 1868 constitution promised that "the General Assembly, at its first session after the adoption of this constitution, shall provide a thorough system of general education, to be forever free to all children of the State." Nevertheless, the General Assembly failed or was unable to act until it finally settled on its own membership in 1870. Throughout that period Bullock answered letters from Georgians wanting schools by explaining that he had "no control whatever of the matter except to urge upon the members personally and officially the necessity of passing a school bill without delay." Bullock consistently and continually asked the legislature to act.[10]

On August 15, 1870, Bullock tried to persuade the legislators to refit the old capitol and executive mansion in Milledgeville as a state university for black students. The governor told the legislators: "Justice to a very large portion of our citizens as well as good policy require, that early provision be made . . . so that separate facilities shall be afforded to colored students, equal in kind and character, to those now furnished to white students." He wanted an endowment for this new university equal to that given to the University of Georgia. Apparently, two years of frustration with no general system of education caused him to conclude that whites would not allow blacks in the University of Georgia. So he tried the next best thing and asked for a state-funded black university.[11]

Black state representative Henry M. Turner of Macon supported the governor: "We would never bother Franklin University [University of Georgia] if the State would make an equal appropriation to our University." The legislature compromised between the plans of Bullock and Turner, refusing the governor's suggestion to refit the old capitol but appropriating $8,000 yearly to Atlanta University. It also passed a school bill and provided for equal but separate schools for black and white children. Considering the emotional climate in the state, the legislators would have been unrealistic to try anything more egalitarian and, with Bullock, they settled on the equal but separate approach as better than nothing.[12]

Bullock stressed the Radical goal of education as a necessary component to advancement and equality in a free labor system, and he looked for proof that children were attending schools. As governor, he offered free railroad passes to anyone who established schools or taught the freed people anywhere in the state. Even before his inauguration, Bullock wrote the American Missionary Association for information concerning the work in Georgia of Northern missionaries and received a reply that the schools were good and the former slaves were progressing. The association's superintendent for middle Georgia, John Rockwell, expressed the belief many held in the recuperative value of educating the freedmen: "We think the future must look hopeful. We must temporarily be overshadowed and put out of sight by the local money and hostile powers but so far as we are entering the true leaven into the body politic it must work and in time—shall it be twenty or forty years—a complete revolution."[13]

American Missionary Association teachers Frederick and Elizabeth Ayer had been teaching black Atlantans since 1865 and by 1866 operated three primary schools for seven hundred children. That year, Edmund Ware took charge and increased enrollment to fifteen hundred. Ware also purchased sixty acres of land in the western part of the city and, after the Freedmen's Bureau donated $50,000, began construction of Atlanta University in 1869. Bullock joined Freedmen's Bureau inspector of schools and black leader John Mercer Langston and others at the cornerstone-laying ceremony on June 1. Bullock voiced his approval of Langston's speech to the crowd: "It is necessary that the white and black races should be educated together to accustom themselves in childhood to their new relations; to destroy the spirit of servility and fear in the one and arrogance in the other. . . . As for social equality no legislation should or could regulate that."[14]

A century later, Martin Luther King, Jr., a graduate of Morehouse College, one of the schools in the Atlanta University group, expressed the same sentiment and insisted that integration was necessary to dissipate the clouds of inferiority formed by segregation in the mental sky of black children. In the fall of 1870, Atlanta University opened, committed itself to racial equality, and taught the classics to eighty-nine students, black and white, male and female. Bullock was among the university's most active supporters, donating money, sitting on the board of directors, giving speeches, attending every commencement ceremony possible, and writing letters on behalf of the institution.[15]

Bullock knew that all citizens needed to be educated so that they could better protect themselves against those who would take advantage of their ignorance. He told Freedmen's Bureau school superintendent J. W. Alvord that schools "help all our institutions; our political prosperity must be based upon intelligence; the Freedmen will be on the right side if they are well instructed." He promised to do everything he could to establish a state-wide system of general education. Bullock spoke with enthusiasm about the promise of education, but he was realistic and knew that conservative white Georgians were not ready to sustain black schools and would fight any attempt to establish such a system. Revealing that the average white attitude toward black education had changed little one decade later, Joel Chandler Harris spun an Uncle Remus yarn in the *Atlanta Constitution* with the moral that book learning "spoiled a good Nigger" because blacks were "unfit for education" and those that "got learning" got "sassy." [16]

The reason no rudimentary school system had been established even though the constitution called for one lay in the disruptive power struggle Bullock was having with the legislature. Just one week after becoming governor, Bullock lost the first real test of strength. At issue was the election of the state's two United States senators. Bullock supported the two leading Republicans in the state, men to whom he owed his success in the last election, Joseph E. Brown and Foster Blodgett. Of course, it was a payback for their efforts, but they were well qualified and would give the best new look to Georgia's efforts to rejoin the Union. Democrats would have to get the support of moderate Republicans to have any chance of winning, for if the vote split entirely along party lines, Bullock's men would prevail 120 to 97 in the combined house and senate vote. Because Radicals held 84 seats to the Democrats' 94, the votes of the 36 moderate Republicans were the key to the election. Democrats initially supported Alexander Stephens and Horace Virgil Milton Miller but agreed to drop Stephens in favor of the moderate choice, Joshua Hill, who had run for governor in 1863 as a

Unionist candidate opposing Governor Brown. On July 29, this coalition of moderates and Democrats elected Hill over Brown, 110 to 94, and Miller over Blodgett, 120 to 72. Bullock claimed that if Meade had dismissed the legislators who were ineligible under the test oath, Reconstruction in Georgia would have worked and the Radical candidates for the Senate would have won. Emboldened by their successes, Democrats made a daring move to unseat blacks from the legislature.[17]

Democrats abhorred the presence of blacks in the statehouse and had wanted to expel them since the opening session. The rewards of doing so were considerable for it would raise the stock of Democrats among white Georgians and mock the "equality" of the hated Thirteenth and Fourteenth Amendments. Moreover, Georgia law required that the expelled members be replaced with men who had received the second-highest number of votes in the election—all Democrats—which would strengthen and reinstall the old conservative leadership in power. Then, no matter what the "stupid express agent" attempted, they could override him.

As early as the fourth day of the session, July 8, Democrats asserted that blacks were ineligible under the state constitution. Less than three weeks later, on July 26, state senator Milton Candler of Washington repeated the claim and threw Joe Brown's Marietta speech in the face of the Radicals. Calling Brown "one of the ablest lawyers of the Republican party of Georgia," Candler reiterated Brown's campaign platform in north Georgia that the constitution did not entitle blacks to hold office. Thus the blacks now seated were obviously ineligible and should be removed.[18]

The Republican-led senate decided not to consider the resolution and laid it on the table. In the house, Democrats surveyed the issue and waited for evidence that the moderates would support them and the military would not obstruct them. After the vote for U.S. Senate seats went their way, the coalition of Democrats and moderates was a reality. Bullock's administration and goals were in trouble.

On September 3, members of the Georgia House voted to expel all twenty-nine black legislators on the grounds that they were ineligible on condition of race under the constitution and the Georgia Code. When Speaker of the House Richard McWhorter, a moderate Republican, ruled that the black legislators could not vote on their own eligibility, he ensured expulsion. Many Republicans failed to vote on the question; they were either resigned to the reality that their votes would not matter or in fear of being branded "nigger lover" and targeted by the Klan as Ashburn had been. When Bullock testified later before the Joint Committee on Reconstruction, he explained that many Republicans failed to vote after receiving "letters advising them to prepare to meet their Maker, &c., if they dared to vote to keep negroes in their seats." The final vote to expel was eighty-three to twenty-three. The senate followed suit and on September 12, by a vote of twenty-one to eleven, expelled its two black senators, Tunis Campbell and George Wallace. The votes clearly show that on the question of racial equality, only thirty-four white Republicans were committed to the Radical program. The moderates agreed with the Democrats that freedom was enough; to make former slaves their political equals went too far.[19]

Blacks did not acquiesce quietly to their removal. Senator Campbell vehemently protested the action as "illegal, unconstitutional, unjust and oppressive." The most prominent black leader in the house, Henry M. Turner, saw the expulsion as paradoxical: "Cases may be found where men have been deprived of their rights for crimes and misdemeanors; but it has remained for the State of Georgia . . . to call a man before the bar, and there charge him with an act for which he is no more responsible than for the head which he carries upon his shoulders. . . . It is very strange, if a white man can occupy on this floor *a seat created by colored votes, and a black man cannot do it.*"[20]

In an effort to regain their seats, the expelled legislators sent Campbell and his son to Washington, D.C., to lobby for congressional interference into Georgia affairs. For five weeks the Campbells pleaded with Senators Charles Sumner, E. D. Morgan, and others for some protection in their rights as citizens. Georgia's thirty-four white Radical legislators joined their expelled colleagues in petitioning Congress to intervene. More than a year would pass before Congress returned them to their seats.[21]

Bullock reluctantly did his duty and submitted the names of the Democrats who had finished second in the late election to take the seats of the expelled Republicans. The house was then overwhelmingly aligned against any Republican program. Bullock's loud objection to the General Assembly's action stimulated even more political animus. He reminded the legislators of his "solemn oath" to uphold the constitution and his intention to do so. He declared that he would not be "a silent spectator" to their prejudiced actions in excluding "electors who are not of Anglo-Saxon blood from the right of representing the voters by whom they were legally and constitutionally elected." Bullock tried to disarm the ridiculous assertion that a constitution had to grant specific rights to citizens by countering,

"It might with more propriety be argued that a Constitution framed by delegates who were voted for by 85,000 black men and 25,000 white men and ratified by the votes of 70,000 black men and 25,000 white men, did not carry with it that privilege to the white elector because it was not affirmatively stated."[22]

Bullock reminded the legislators that during the constitutional convention Democratic delegate James Waddell's motion that "white men only shall be eligible to office . . . in this State" was defeated overwhelmingly, 113 to 19. Bullock said that since "the framers of the Constitution made no distinction between electors, or citizens, on account of race or color . . . neither can you without violating it." He chided the legislators for their failure to live up to republican ideals. Bullock cited sections of the Georgia law, *Irwin's Code*, which granted all citizens the right to hold office, "unless specifically prohibited by law." He concluded by pleading with them "to pause in the suicidal course upon which you have entered."[23]

His words fell upon unsympathetic, but not deaf, ears. There were signs that even Bullock might be removed if he pursued his denunciation of the legislature. Indeed, as early as August 24, Savannah Republican Charles H. Hopkins told him of the impending expulsion of black legislators and warned: "You will be impeached . . . your enemies have all their plans well laid to destroy you." Democratic senate leader Milton Candler rebuked the governor for his "interference" in legislative matters and told him to mind his own business. The Democratic press used Bullock's stance to inflame whites: "Bullock is . . . a sincere and consistent advocate of negro supremacy in the South. He hates the white people . . . so intensely that he would prefer to see all the offices in the State filled by the most ignorant and corrupt of the black race."[24]

Labeling the expulsion "the great wrong," Bullock reached a crisis that became a turning point in his political and personal life. A close friend remembered that Bullock had to decide "a vital question." He could turn his back on those who risked everything to elect him or "he had to take sides with the negroes in their contest with the white people. . . . He was bound to do the latter, and after that decision it was a bitter and deadly fight. There was no compromise possible. It was war."[25]

Bullock realized that to control Georgia's economic development he must maintain political power. He had been a reluctant politician, but once in office, he threw himself into his job. And yet his defense of black rights went deeper than just an attempt to remain in power. Forced to examine his fundamental beliefs, Bullock realized, maybe consciously for the first time, that justice required equal rights for all men. He believed in the Union, in the Constitution, and in obedience to law. He believed in progress and the advancement of the nation under its original revolutionary creed. He came to see the injustice of racial arrogance. In a time and section where everything was increasingly defined in terms of black or white, Bullock went against the current to support the freed people and the Constitution. He remained steadfast even though admitting, "Earnest appeals were made to me by frightened and discouraged Republicans to acquiesce in this outrage." With his sense of propriety bruised and his insistence on doing what was right, Bullock could not retreat to a "whatever is good for business and damn the rest" philosophy.[26]

Psychologist Robert Kegan explained in his 1982 study of human development, *The Evolving Self*, that humans are meaning-making organisms, that is, they are organisms that organize experience into meaning. The activity of meaning is irreducible; Kegan explains it as "the primary human motion"—it is what a human is, not something he or she does. During this process of being human—and thereby of making meaning—a person comes down to moral decision making and asks, "Do I or don't I make a stand for something?" Kegan explains that while making a moral decision, most people are bound to the group they associate with; but some people can move beyond that "loyalty" to something else, "toward something that looks more like the human community."[27]

Bullock was able to see a broader duty beyond the narrow interests of self or party. From this point, when he supported the rights of black men to hold office in Georgia, supporting the principles for which Republicans stood, Bullock set a course he would have to defend the rest of his life. He became the black man's friend and devoted his time in the governor's chair to achieving as much as possible for blacks and for business. But his path was hazardous.[28]

The presidential campaign of 1868 only intensified the vituperation of Democratic legislators and widened the split among Georgia Republicans. But incidents during the campaign led Congress to reevaluate Georgia's relationship with the Union and thus worked in Bullock's favor. Just one week after the Georgia Senate completed the removal of blacks from the General Assembly, some white men in the south Georgia town of Camilla killed and wounded nearly forty Republicans. Known thereafter as the Camilla Massacre or the Camilla Riot, according to one's perspective, the

violence of September 19 awakened Northern consciousness while simultaneously warning all Georgians that participation in Republican politics
imperiled life and property.

As part of the presidential campaign, Republican organizers planned a
rally in Camilla and spread word among the neighboring plantations and
towns. The day of the meeting, nearly three hundred African-Americans
left their homes and made the long walk to Camilla. A few carried fire-
arms. Mitchell County sheriff M. S. Poore intercepted the walkers near
the outskirts of town and told them not to enter town with the weapons.
The blacks responded that they were going to a political meeting and did
not intend to breach the peace. Unhappy with the answer, the sheriff raced
back to town, organized a posse, and met the people as they entered the
town. Somebody fired a shot. There was a general exchange of gunfire, and
then the freedmen broke and ran out of town back toward their homes.
The sheriff and townsmen pursued and shot down the black Republicans
wherever they found them. In the immediate aftermath of the slaughter,
local Freedmen's Bureau officers counted twelve freedmen floating in a
pond two miles from town, five more dead in other places, and fifteen
wounded. Other reports varied the count between seven and seventeen
dead and twenty-five to forty wounded. Only six white attackers sustained
wounds, all of them slight.[29]

Two days later Bullock communicated the news to the General Assembly
that "the right of the people to peaceful assembly has been violently and
barbariously impaired and that the civil officers . . . of Mitchell [County],
are wholly unable to protect the rights of citizens." In Camilla, townsmen
responded that they had only protected themselves against an armed band
of black men who were obviously in violation of Bullock's proclamation
of September 14, which outlawed armed meetings of any kind. Camillans
did not distinguish between armed meetings and meetings at which a few
men had arms. They ignored another of Bullock's proclamations that asked
Georgians to stop all acts of violence against people and their constitutional rights. Newspapers throughout the state came to the aid of the white
Camilla Democrats who met the "armed invasion." The *Augusta Chronicle*
reported: "Bullock is himself the chief cause of the Camilla tragedy. . . .
He is today the true murderer of the Camilla victims." That paper called
Bullock "an insurrectionist—he desires war and blood and rapine." With
battle lines drawn for more violence, a few lies and innuendos seemed
harmless. French statesman and historian Georges Clemenceau analyzed

this Southern violence and the response of the Southern press: "In all events of this kind, the remarkable feature is that according to telegraphic reports, there is always a band of heavily armed negroes attacking a handful of harmless whites. Then when it comes to counting the dead, a few negroes are always down, but of white men, not a trace."[30]

To prevent further violence, Bullock asked General Meade for troops to protect the loyal people of Camilla. Meade queried Grant for instructions and after receiving an answer told Bullock that local sheriffs had to apply directly to the president before the military would act. Meade admitted that this process did not promise the quick action required for a situation like that in Camilla and acknowledged that had his troops been in Camilla at the time of the riot they would have faced a conundrum because they were "instructed to obey [the civil officer] . . . the very one who is apparently most guilty." Then Meade told Bullock that if blacks retaliated against whites, he would immediately send troops to restore order. Here was a double standard at work. Clearly, Meade had the authority to decide when and where to intervene in civil affairs; his supposed dependence on Grant was a dodge.[31]

Meade decried his small number of troops and his difficulty deciding when and where to use them. The number of soldiers in Georgia had dwindled from the September 1865 high of 15,779, when twenty-one of the twenty-five regiments were black, to 983, with no black regiments, in October 1868. These 983 men might have made some difference if commanded by a general determined to protect lives and follow the Reconstruction plan, but under Meade the military contingent was barely credible. Additionally, in confrontations between Republicans and Democrats, the troops often sided with the Democrats. Writing from Talbotton in 1868, schoolteacher Edwin Higbee described the request for aid and the soldier-Democrat alliance: "'Tis said the frogs demanded a king and a serpent was sent to them."[32]

Meade never had his heart in the work of Reconstruction and was by no means sympathetic toward blacks. After President Johnson sent him to replace General Pope, Blodgett wrote Senator Sherman: "The rebels are rejoicing over it and are now bragging that Reconstruction is a failure." As early as March 27, 1868, Bullock complained that Meade was overly concerned with being liked and worried that "his excessive impartiality will lean him a little the wrong way." During the 1868 gubernatorial canvass, Meade dismissed any registrar who made political speeches in favor of Reconstruction and, in Bullock's words, "made no secret of his desire that the constitution should be ratified and that General Gordon should be elected." On March 27, 1868, former Third District commander General John Pope advised Joe Brown that Meade would not lend "aid or sympathy" to the Republicans and added, "I never supposed he would take much interest in reconstruction." Freedmen Robert Crumley of Warrenton and Philip Joiner of Albany analyzed Meade's inaction: "General Meade was afraid of being called a 'despot.' If such charge was ever made against him he has refuted it, but the refutation has cost the lives of hundreds of colored and loyal white people." Perhaps Meade was reluctant to use military force as a substitute for civil due process—sheriffs, grand juries, courts, and such. If so, his failure to sustain the Reconstruction Acts was compounded by his inability to understand what the situation required.[33]

To ensure a fair election in November 1868, Bullock requested that soldiers be posted in numerous Georgia towns. Meade said he did not consider these requests urgent. The sheriff of Warren County requested troops to forestall certain violence on election day; he received none. Meade explained to Bullock: "We are all aware that the reported condition of affairs in Warren County is not exceptional." Meade said that if Bullock expected him to preserve the peace everyplace civil officers could not, "I shall be compelled to send troops not only into every county in this State, but in all the five Sates [States] comprising this Department." Bullock believed the national government should protect loyal citizens and looked on Meade's response as an evasion of responsibility.[34]

Bullock wrote Secretary of War John M. Schofield complaining of Meade's attitude and protesting that Congress had made rules to establish the civil government of Georgia and that that government by necessity relied on the physical support of the United States government in times of emergency. He argued that no government "in its infancy—not having been yet one year in existence—[can] be left to rise or fall, independent of the sustaining power of the authority which conceived and established it." He concluded his letter with a cry for help: "I have no means of obtaining this necessary support except from the Government of the United States."[35]

Bullock could not turn to a state militia for help because Congress prohibited the formation of militia units in Southern states. And who knows what might have happened had there been a state militia. Democrats were already murdering Republicans. Had Bullock issued to the three hundred freedmen in Savannah the military charter they requested in August 1868, and other militia charters throughout the state, Georgia might have seen a real race war. No, if help were to come, it must come through federal military intervention. But the president refused to help, and whites murdered Republicans while the army watched. Meanwhile, the campaign for president continued.[36]

Democrats had reason to believe that they could win the national election; if so, Bullock would lose even symbolic support, and Reconstruction would fail. State Democrats readily endorsed the national Democratic platform, which contained such planks as "immediate restoration of all the states to their rights in the Union," "amnesty," "abolishment of the Freedmen's Bureau," and "subordination of the military to the civil power to the end that the usurpations of Congress and the despotism of the sword may cease." The Democratic platform concluded with an assault on the Republican party "for its disregard of right and unparalleled oppression and tyranny." Democrats charged that the Union went unrestored while "military despotism and negro supremacy . . . corruption and extravagance have exceeded anything known in history." Finally, the platform called Congressional Reconstruction "unconstitutional, revolutionary and void."[37]

Clearly Democrats wanted to restore their way of life while restoring— not reconstructing—the Union. In Georgia, Democrats vowed to win the November election and embarked on a campaign of enticement and intimidation.

To prove their friendship to the freedmen, Democrats held huge barbecues and political rallies. They reminded blacks of their common interests and heritage in the South and told them that they were better off with those who knew them than with Radicals, who only used them. Democrats soon realized that this tactic would not work and if they hoped to win, they had to do more than lie to the freedmen, who ate their food without accepting their message.

Increasingly, Georgia Democrats advocated white supremacy and relied on violence, intimidation, and trickery to defeat Grant. The leaders of the Democratic party were men of wealth who also led the Ku Klux Klan, and Klan activities became an integral component of the Democratic campaign. One man later remembered that the South "was fighting for life and the preservation of the white race. To the Ku Klux Klan it owes its final salvation." Grand Dragon of Georgia John B. Gordon explained his entry into the Klan and its constituency: "I was approached by some of the very best citizens of the State—some of the most peaceable, law-abiding men, men of large property, who had large interests in the State." Gordon summarized the group as simply "a brotherhood of property-holders. . . . It was purely a peace police." [38]

Years later, the enigmatic Tom Watson captured the mood of white Southerners toward Reconstruction: "Who dreamed of the horrors of Reconstruction? Who dreamed of the deliberate, vindictive crusade against Southern civilization? What prophet warned us of Loyal Leagues and carpet-bag hosts bearing down upon us to destroy the white man's pride and purity of race and system to plant upon its ruins the foulest negro domination? We had been duped, betrayed . . . but we were not remediless." [39] The Klan rose under John Gordon, supported by the pen of Ben Hill. Murders, threats, and lies followed. The Camilla Massacre was only the most publicized of innumerable outrages perpetrated on Republicans in Georgia.

Since July, Republicans had been busy organizing clubs throughout the state to inspire enthusiasm for Grant's election and a fraternal spirit to withstand Democratic threats. Many clubs failed in both regards. Bullock received letters from organizers statewide detailing their troubles with local officials and the Ku Klux Klan. The Camilla Massacre was representative of the Democratic response to Grant club organizations. There were many less violent, but equally effective, examples of what would happen if freedmen persisted in meeting to support Grant. On August 15, one month before the Camilla Massacre, Hugh Dean, an educated black organizer of Grant clubs, met with seventy-six freedmen in Dooly County to discuss politics. Soon the county sheriff and nearly four hundred armed white men broke up the meeting and arrested Dean. County judge and Democrat Shep Rodgers directed the arrest and declared: "The colored men should not raise no such clubs." Further, an enraged Rodgers declared that "his party would kill every negro in the Southern States" if necessary to prevent the election of Grant. Freedmen's Bureau agent Daniel Losey investigated the incident and reported that whites claimed blacks caused the problem by marching with guns to the meeting and the whites had responded with force to protect themselves. Losey concluded that the whites were lying to stop any Republican clubs from forming in their county. As the law in Dooly, kingpin Rodgers wrote Losey that he was not afraid of him or his superiors. Calling Losey a "negro worshipper and scalawag," Rodgers ridiculed his call for armed assistance: "Bullock has not any to give you. General Meade can't send them without violating his orders." Daring Losey to raise a black militia group, Rodgers laughingly replied, "We don't fear your negro brigade." [40]

Democrats clearly understood Bullock's helplessness and Meade's unwillingness to respond to their campaign of violence and intimidation and seemed to welcome the outbreak of a race war. Republicans, lacking committed military support, responded as best they could.

Republicans implored Congress and the national Republican party to do something. From Dalton, L. P. Gudger challenged Republican national secretary William E. Chandler to act: "If the Government of the United States intend to see & have the loyal White & Colored peoperl Butchered up after they have sacrafised 300,000 lives of good men, and spent 4 Billion Dollars, it is time they should say so by open declarations." He begged for help before "we are Butchered up and Law & Constitution trampled under foot." [41]

Blodgett wrote Chandler speculating that in a fair election Grant would win Georgia by at least twenty thousand votes. He predicted that blacks would be forced to vote Democratic against their will or not "be allowed to vote in many counties." Citing Southern dedication to the old order, Blodgett insisted that "the rebellious spirit is more intense and bitter now than in 1860 & 1861. Negroes are killed almost every day while white Republicans are threatened, abused and maltreated." Blodgett suggested that Congress initiate a provisional government with Bullock at its head and "six regiments of infantry and one of cavalry to sustain him." He also asked for acts forbidding the seating of Georgia's senators and representatives and excluding Georgia's electoral vote on grounds of noncompliance with the Reconstruction Acts. Joe Brown also wrote Chandler that Democrats had instituted "a reign of terror" and would keep blacks from voting in November. Less astute Georgia Republicans, particularly John Bryant and J. H. Caldwell, sent Chandler conflicting information: "We have well grounded hopes that we can carry the State for Grant . . . by 10,000." Chandler responded to these sanguine predictions and, in the face of Blodgett's request not to waste precious funds in Georgia, sent $1,500 more to help Grant's campaign. Obviously, Bryant, Caldwell, and Chandler dreamed a fool's dream. [42]

While the letter-writing campaign proceeded, Bullock responded to the violence as best he could. He had no militia, and if he had, to use it might have precipitated open revolution and mass killings. Bullock certainly did not want to give whites another excuse for killing Republicans. His appeals for military intervention had no effect on an unresponsive Meade. His only recourse seemed to be to offer rewards for murderers and issue official proclamations in favor of black rights. The records of the Georgia Executive Department are filled with Bullock's orders offering reward money to anyone who would arrest murderers. The rewards were usually between $250 and $1,000, but Bullock did offer $5,000 for the arrest of the man who killed Augusta sheriff Albert Ruffin on the night of the election. In addition to offering rewards to deter violence, he ordered all sheriffs, policemen, and other civil officers "to see to it that the lives and property of all citizens, and the peace of the community are preserved." Bullock wrote personal letters to sheriffs and pleaded with them to enforce the law. When he learned that blacks might be kept from voting for nonpayment of poll taxes required under the new constitution, Bullock issued a proclamation suspending all poll taxes for the 1868 election. But his proclamations had little effect because Democrats ignored them and Republicans were afraid to enforce them. White election officials turned away from the polls many thousands of freedmen for nonpayment of taxes, unless, of course, they held Democratic ballots.[43]

For Bullock the stakes in the election were clear. To lose meant economic retardation because Democrats would certainly fail to implement the free labor system. For state politics, Grant's defeat would put the Democrats firmly back into power and destroy the Republican party by making it even more dangerous, economically and personally, to be a Republican. Bullock received many letters like the one from Francis Kirby, who hoped for the success of Bullock's administration and feared that "with defeat there would be no safe place for us here." One month before the election, Bullock told a Republican meeting in his hometown of Albion, New York, that "a Democratic success at the polls will very properly be construed by the malcontents at the South and the Copperheads at the North as an endorsement by the American people that the 'lost cause' has been regained, and that war was a failure."[44]

Bullock believed that Congress must take control and rectify Meade's errors in letting the legislators "decide for themselves" their own eligibility. In addition, Congress must ascertain whether Georgia had complied with the Reconstruction Acts and remove from office those who could not take the test oath. Bullock said that if Congress would act on his suggestions and if the people put Grant in the White House "we will be safe."[45]

Meanwhile, Georgia Democrats accelerated their campaign of economic pressure and violence. Planters in Irwinton told freedmen who share-cropped their land that they would not get their full shares unless they voted for Seymour. In LaGrange, a white man, Jim Woodruff, rode up to freed-man Harry Kidd and asked him if he was a Radical. When Kidd answered "yes," Woodruff yelled that he would die a Radical and murdered him on the spot. In Perry, Democrats set fire to the house of freedman carpenter Jack Ballard, boycotted his work, and leaned sticks, emblazoned with the word "Death," against his door. In Irwinsville, a black man named Joshua killed two white men after they shot his dog, broke down his door, and entered his house. The sheriff arrested him and put him in jail. That night white citizens burned down the jail with Joshua in it. From Jackson County, Freedmen's Bureau agent Howell Flourney reported that blacks and whites were arming themselves. Whites claimed that blacks intended "to murder all the whites at a certain time not particularly specified." Blacks said all they wanted was to be left alone, but "large bodies of armed white citizens are roving through the district . . . halting and hailing every colored man they see and compelling them with threats of violence and draw weapons upon them" to force them to vote the Democratic ticket. Flourney said that no Radical would be allowed to vote unless he voted for Seymour. Even as Flourney wrote for help, Democrats killed the leading Republican in the county, Peleg Cornell, and a black friend for being Radicals. On September 23, after Ben Hill and John Gordon spoke to a Democratic rally in Covington, about fifty Ku Klux Klan members rampaged the town's black neighborhood, breaking into houses and threatening to kill those who voted in November. Bullock was inundated with pleas for help and information about Klan outrages.[46]

One of the most illustrative letters came from Justice of the Peace F. J. Robinson of Lexington. He told how on Friday night, September 25, for two hours after midnight, thirty men "with masks and fancy dresses" in-flicted themselves upon an "old and inoffensive" black man, Jonathon Hooper:

> He was seized, carried to his horse lot and then and their choked & beat & dragged over the stony ground, until he was well nigh killed—only saving his life . . . by saying that he would vote a Democratic ticket. . . . Is the Gov-ernment we live under & which we have been sworn to support to leave us to Ku Klux Klans & midnight thieves & assassins any longer? . . . Every sort

of intimidation is being used . . . not only to colored men but to fine white men, and the culmination will be a war, not of races exactly, but a war to the knife & the knife to the hilt. Legislators may lounge . . . & talk soft nonsense . . . until the continued outrages and villanries of so called Democracy will inaugurate a war. . . . I tell you sir the mine awaits but the spark, and anarchy rules supreme! I hope Gen. Meade understands the situation and will promptly aid you in protecting our people. . . . Every murderer escapes with an alibi or some other subterfuge of the Ku Klux lawyers.[47]

From across the state letter after letter came to the governor asking for help that he could not give. With no one to stop them, Democrats and their terrorist wing intimidated, beat, and murdered with immunity.

From January 1 to December 31, the Freedmen's Bureau received complaints of 407 "Outrages Committed Upon Freedmen in the State of Georgia." This list included only murders and assaults and battery. The bureau reported incidents of violence in at least fifty-nine different counties that undoubtedly represented only a small number of the actual incidents that occurred. Most abuses went unreported. It is impossible to determine the true number of victims who experienced death, beatings, threats, economic pressure, and other forms of intimidation or who changed their stance from fear that something might happen to them. Henry Turner, one of the expelled legislators, testified before the 1871 congressional committee investigating the Klan that between fifteen and sixteen hundred blacks had been murdered in Georgia and approximately twenty thousand in the entire South. Bullock's secretary of state, David G. Cotting, sadly informed the governor that: "no human being will ever know the number of murders committed in Georgia. . . . The murderers and buzzards only can give a guess." Klan terror in Georgia accomplished its goals of controlling the freedmen and subverting Reconstruction. Bullock fought but lost the battle.[48]

When the votes were counted in Georgia in November 1868, Seymour defeated Grant by 102,822 to 57,134. An estimated 54,000 freedmen were intimidated into not voting or coerced into voting for the opposition's candidate. Obviously the Klan had done its work very well. Bullock carried 62 counties in April; Grant won only 17 of 132 in November. Pointing to the racial nature of this election, Grant won only 4 counties (all in extreme north Georgia) where whites outnumbered blacks, while Democrats took the other 74. Indicating the amount of intimidation that occurred, Democrats won 41 of 54 counties where blacks outnumbered whites. Election returns recorded no votes for Grant in 11 counties where 4,065 blacks and 4,840 whites were registered; in those same counties Seymour polled 4,126 votes (see Table 1). Additionally, only seventeen votes went for Grant in 5 counties where 4,718 blacks outregistered 3,039 whites (see Table 2).[49]

Registrar Romulus Moore explained that in Columbia, Lincoln, and Wilkes counties, armed whites prevented blacks from voting for Grant. Lieutenant Murray Hoag reported that during the election in Savannah, Democrats killed a few men at the polls and, to deceive the freedmen, "the Democratic ticket, headed with pictures of Grant & Colfax were freely used." The situation was much the same everywhere as Democrats grabbed Republican ballots from freedmen, substituted Democratic ones, and then forced them to vote. The violence did not end with the election. After all, Grant was in the White House and the hated Bullock was still governor. Clarke County papers seethed with anger over the election: "Is it right to

Table 1. November 1868 Election Returns for Eleven Counties with No Republican Votes

County	Registered Voters		Vote	
	White	Black	Grant	Seymour
Appling	456	94	0	336
Bulloch	553	238	0	425
Coffee	354	93	0	160
Early	467	799	0	548
Irwin	196	37	0	145
Jones	1,073	1,559	0	423
Lincoln	297	590	0	824
Montgomery	338	158	0	220
Miller	272	185	0	302
Tatnall	478	146	0	452
Telfair	356	166	0	291
	4,840	4,065	0	4,126

Source: Georgia, Comptroller.General's Office, Report of Madison Bell, Comptroller General of the State of Georgia. From August 11, 1868 to January 1, 1869 (Atlanta: Samuel Bard, 1869), Table A. Nine of the eleven counties are located on the lower side of the black belt; only Lincoln and Jones are north of the fall line.

nurse vipers in our bosom. Then give no employment to any barber, black-
smith, or any other negro mechanic who voted the Radical ticket. They are
the open and avowed enemies of the white race." [50]

Bullock's first hundred days as governor would have destroyed a lesser
man. He had little support from the legislature, the military, or the Congress. He had been unsuccessful on the eligibility question, on the expulsion
of black legislators, and in his efforts to stem Klan violence. His frustration
might have led him to accept defeat and turn the government over to the
Democrats, but he did not.

Bullock realized that the state still might be saved if he could keep Georgia affairs before the Northern press. Democrats accused him of manufacturing outrages, but Klan violence was rising, and there was little need
for anything but the truth. The expulsion, violence, and vote for Seymour
helped him convince Congress that Georgia needed more reconstruction.
The events of those days also provoked Bullock to reconsider a fundamental question: Should blacks have an equal chance in American life? Once
he concluded that they should, he became a champion of equal treatment
without regard to race. Even if it meant destroying the party in Georgia,
Bullock would not retreat from his program of change.

As he faced the job of running the state, his immediate problem was to
gain control over the legislature. Only Congress could help him with that.

Table 2. November 1868 Election Returns for Five Counties with
Seventeen Republican Votes

County	Registered Voters		Vote	
	White	Black	Grant	Seymour
Chattahoochee	463	569	3	533
Columbia	669	1,854	1	1,120
Jasper	696	988	5	873
Randolph	954	1,193	1	969
Wilcox	257	114	7	237
	3,039	4,718	17	3,732

Source: Georgia, Comptroller General's Office, *Report of Madison Bell, Comptroller
General of the State of Georgia. From August 11, 1868 to January 1, 1869* (Atlanta: Samuel
Bard, 1869), Table A.

Chapter 5 ❧ An Expressive Sense of Justice

A moral principle cannot be compromised.
—Charles Sumner, 1867

But far and above their anger at the waste and mismanagement and graft was the resentment of the people
at the bad light in which the governor represented them
in the North. When Georgia howled against corruption,
the governor hastily went North, appeared before
Congress and told of white outrages against negroes, of
Georgia's preparation for another rebellion and the need
for a stern military rule in the state. No Georgian wanted
trouble. . . . All Georgia wanted was to be left alone so
the state could recuperate. But with the operation of what
came to be known as the governor's "slander mill," the
North saw only a rebellious state that needed a
heavy hand.
—Margaret Mitchell, *Gone with the Wind*

THE DEMOCRATIC VICTORY at the polls in 1868 with its attendant violence and intimidation brought Bullock to a crisis point. Just four months
into his four-year term as governor, he confronted recalcitrant and reactionary whites who proved that they would do anything necessary to
deny a reconstruction of the state. In the interests of business, the Republican party, and justice to the freedmen, Bullock took action. He determined
that, as governor, he would govern; if that meant sidestepping what he
believed to be an illegal legislature, then so be it. If it meant bringing

more slander upon himself, he was braced for the onslaught. His foremost concern was to reorganize the state legislature.

During the next sixteen months Bullock became preoccupied with efforts to restore the expelled legislators to their rightful seats and expel those white Democrats who were ineligible. Under the test oath provisions of the July 2, 1862, statute as incorporated into the March 23, 1867, Reconstruction Act and the Fourteenth Amendment, no person who once had sworn to uphold the Constitution and then had supported the South by arms or aid could be elected to public office unless the disability was removed by a two-thirds vote of Congress. Bullock sought congressional interference to uphold the so-called test oath that members had to take, swearing that they were eligible under the law. In this effort he was not alone.[1]

Soon after their expulsion, black leaders met in convention in Macon where Henry M. Turner urged them to be alert for Republican "vipers" who voted alongside Democrats. Turner and other black leaders spent much of the next year in Washington, D.C., imploring Congress to support Bullock, whom they trusted more than any other white man in the state. Their faith in him was well placed. The issue of black officeholding demonstrated that he was different from Brown, Bryant, and the majority of white Republicans. After black Georgians lost faith in other white party leaders, they continued to believe in Bullock. Committed to a true Reconstruction, the governor sought to reinstate blacks even if it meant alienating white members of his party.[2]

And it did just that. Many white Republicans feared that further congressional interference in Georgia affairs, even if necessary to protect freedmen's rights and Republican lives, would be a major political blunder. Joseph Brown understood that Democrats could impose economic and personal intimidation upon freedmen. He wrote Bullock that the success of the Republican party no longer depended solely on the black vote but also upon a divided white vote. He observed that planters "will always control tenants and laborers" and concluded that Congress should "act cautiously" and "take no step backward" to "undo what has been done." Brown explained that peace and the future of the party were at stake. Congressional interference, he predicted, "would raise such a storm and so embitter the feelings of our people" that the Republican party would be cast out at the next election.[3]

Bullock thanked Brown for expressing his views but proceeded along his own course. Had he followed Brown's advice and courted white Georgians at the expense of the freedmen, the state's Republican party might have remained viable in the post-Reconstruction years. But what would that matter if equality was abandoned? Thirty years later, an admirer recalled Bullock's course of action: "Undaunted by obloquy and although deserted by some of his best friends, Governor Bullock stood out conscientiously and manfully for the rights of the negro representatives in the legislature." He had become an entrepreneur for equality.[4]

Although some Republicans compromised to retain power, Bullock stuck to his beliefs. Historian of Reconstruction Michael Perman, using the terminology of political scientists, has written that after 1868 the Republican party moved from being an "expressive" party to become a "competitive" party. An expressive party, he explained, maintains its consistency and ideological principle above all other issues, including broadening its membership and winning elections. An expressive party would rather lose an election than compromise a moral stance. Conversely, a competitive party maintains flexibility and constantly adjusts its stance to try to appeal to a broader constituency; winning elections is the goal; everything else is of secondary importance. The national Republican party increasingly became dominated by non-Radicals, headed by Ulysses S. Grant, and thus made the transition from expressive to competitive.[5]

In Georgia, Joseph Brown led the competitive wing—those willing to compromise on equality to remain in power. He wrote President Grant about the Radicals' failure to compromise and shared his fears with Massachusetts senator Henry Wilson: "I respectfully say that a few extreme men, mostly, popularly called carpetbaggers are not the best judges of what will promote our interests or the interest of the government." Brown hoped that most Georgians eventually would settle to the center—or Centrist position—equidistant from the extremes of Klan violence and Radical egalitarianism.[6]

The Centrists joined Democrats to put competitivists in the U.S. Senate and expel the black legislators. Increasingly, as Bullock continued to insist that Georgians follow the Reconstruction Acts, borderline Radicals drifted to the center or became Democrats. Bullock understood the consequences and recalled that his action in defending the political rights of blacks "was intensely unpopular at the time, and . . . large numbers of white men who had accepted the reconstruction policy, condemned my course in behalf of the colored men and withdrew from the party."[7]

Some Republicans fumed over the way Bullock's forces had commandeered his nomination at the constitutional convention. Others who were not rewarded with patronage positions abandoned Bullock. Some feared that his attempts to gain congressional interference would precipitate open rebellion within the state. Many left for other reasons. As more Georgia Republicans moved to the center, they split the party and ensured Democratic victories.[8]

Bullock did not join the defection to the competitivists but retained his expressive views. Because he stuck to his principles, many of his friends and fellow Republicans accused him of destroying the party in Georgia. Historians have used the testimony of these defectors to place the blame on Bullock. Yet if others had persisted in the promise of Reconstruction as a precious opportunity to realize the American creed that all indeed are equal, the Republican party might have remained viable in the South. Radical U.S. senator Samuel C. Pomeroy of Kansas agreed with Bullock that if the party abandoned its principles, "the party itself would not be worth preserving. The strength of the Republican party consists in its adherence to principle, and to that embodiment of its principles, equality of rights among men."[9]

In Georgia, the party splintered and failed because of Centrists such as Brown, John Bryant, and John Caldwell, who placed their own political futures over the principles of the party. Bryant and Caldwell had campaigned vigorously for Bullock, but when he failed to provide them with patronage plums, they split the party by maligning Bullock and Blodgett in an attempt to seize power themselves. Observing their defection from principle, one member of the Georgia General Assembly informed Massachusetts representative Benjamin F. Butler that Bryant, Caldwell, and others acted solely for their own aggrandizement and called the intimacy between them and the Democrats "marked." In 1870, Freedmen's Bureau school superintendent J. W. Alvord wrote bureau commissioner O. O. Howard of the change in Bryant: "One old friend of ours seems to be foolishly selling himself and his party, if he can, to the opposition. Not a colored member goes with him in either House." Bryant told Alvord that he would "rather the whole Republican party in Georgia should be a failure than Bullock should triumph." Alvord insisted that "no true Republican here stands by him."[10]

Bullock and black Georgians continued to oppose Bryant and other Centrists. But because the Centrists conformed to the tendency of the national party to move toward a competitive position, they soon took control.

Less than a week after Brown counseled him not to seek congressional intervention, Bullock went to Washington. He reminded the legislators that under a section of the 1867 Reconstruction Acts, Georgia was to remain in provisional status until Congress allowed the state's representatives to sit. Although the House had admitted the representatives from Georgia, the Senate had not yet seated Joshua Hill and H. V. M. Miller; thus Georgia remained in limbo. Bullock informed Congress that Georgia's legislature had not been "organized in accordance with the Reconstruction acts" because the test oath had been ignored. He asserted that the legislature had compounded this iniquity by expelling its black members. Bullock asked Congress to assert its authority over Georgia by reseating the rightful members and requiring all legislators to take the test oath.[11]

Joe Brown, leading the opposition to Bullock's plan, stated his case in a letter to Joshua Hill. Although he conceded that some of Georgia's state legislators sat illegally, Brown believed that the governor's "proposition to declare that all that has been done in Georgia illegal and remand the state back under military government" was unwise. Brown feared that "our people will lose all patience and become desperate under the belief that we are never to have stability." He told Hill that, in his opinion, "the reconstruction acts no where require us to give the negroes the right to hold office." Brown gave Hill permission to use the letter as he saw fit to prevent Congress from acquiescing to Bullock's requests. Other Georgia Republicans of the Centrist stripe joined Democratic letter writers to oppose the Radical plan. With such conflicting counsel, members of Congress had a difficult time deciding what to do.[12]

Bullock remained in Washington and joined eight other Georgia Republicans who testified on conditions in the state before the Joint Committee on Reconstruction. On December 19, Bullock repeated his criticism of Meade's failure to require legislators to take a valid test oath and charged that there were "not less than 40 in the House and 15 or 18 in the senate" who were unable to take the oath. Responding to a question from committee chair George Boutwell, who asked for suggestions about what should be done in Georgia, Bullock answered only that the nation "carry out the laws literally, and to admit to the legislature only those who could take the oath required by law. By these means the colored members who were expelled will be reinstated."[13]

Bullock wanted Congress to execute the law by having the military commander reassemble the original 1868 legislature and then investigate each member's right to be seated. He questioned the efficacy of the oath but still hoped it would serve as the vehicle to effect a true Reconstruction. He opposed "any new legislation to bring about results which would have been accomplished by the legislation already had." Democrats had proven beyond a doubt that they intended to use all methods available—intimidation, obloquy, election fraud, perjury, judicial corruption, lawless sheriffs, assault, murder, and collusion of all sorts—to hold onto old ways. Bullock understood their resistance. But the Civil War mandated change; progress would not come unless Radical Republicans sat in the state legislature. Clearly, Bullock's insistence on the oath was a partisan effort that would result in more "loyal Union men" gaining office, but they had rightful claims to those offices. By supporting the oath, Bullock acknowledged the primacy of law.[14]

Eight other Georgians answered questions before the Joint Committee. James Simms of Savannah, an expelled member of the legislature, spoke about the intimidation and violence toward black voters and the fact that powerful Democrats condoned such action, if only by their silence. In obvious reference to the Camilla Massacre, Henry Turner told of freedmen's political meetings, which were enthusiastic yet controlled: "At no meeting did the colored people ever inaugurate strife or collision with the whites." Amos Akerman trumpeted Simms's analysis, saying that "there are two and only two very disturbing elements in our southern society": Democratic politicians and sons of wealthy men who saw their "easy lives" threatened by the results of the war. John E. Bryant disagreed with Simms and Akerman and testified that he thought the leading Democrats did not control their constituents and could not prevent violence in the state. He argued that Georgia's constitution gave blacks the right to hold office but contended that further congressional interference would "stir up the people." The other four Georgians focused their remarks on the violence and fraud that attended the 1868 presidential election. The Joint Committee accepted into evidence documents, memorials, petitions, and letters, some assembled by the Georgia Republican party, from other Georgians, military officers, and Freedmen's Bureau agents. The testimony and documents present a sordid portrait of a recalcitrant Georgia where Republican lives and votes had little value.[15]

Congressman Nelson Tift from Albany, Georgia, presented the most effective argument for the Democrats and Centrists, and undoubtedly his efforts confused the issue and created further indecision in Congress. Tift,

a lifelong Democrat, represented Georgia's Second Congressional District;
he probably was one of those fraudulently elected because even though
his twenty-two-county district had a black majority of over 8,100 votes,
he "won" the election by 2,500 votes. He labeled Bullock a "traitor" who
used "false pretexts and false testimony" to persuade Congress. Democratic newspapers followed Tift's lead and filled their columns with fustian
innuendo of a "slander mill" originated and operated by the governor.
The *Augusta Chronicle* fumed: "Outrages of the most horrible description, and murders [of] the most cold-blooded [kind] were manufactured in
Atlanta . . . and sent Northward . . . for Congressional consumption." [16]

To counter Republican testimony and documentation, Tift distributed a
questionnaire among "the best citizens of the state" asking whether they
believed that all citizens, black and white, Republican and Democrat, had
equal protection and security in Georgia. In a private letter, Tift held up
the specter of "the dictatorship of a provisional governor, with the army
and navy of the United States to enforce his edicts." Predictably, respondents almost uniformly answered that no violence or even discrimination
existed in Georgia; indeed, Georgians did not resist the laws of Congress
and had good government under the existing legislature. Joseph E. Brown,
however, dissented.[17]

Brown wrote to Nelson Tift that in the last election "a great deal of lawlessness and crime . . . has gone unpunished." Brown blamed the situation
on election excitement, "bitter and vindictive" leaders, and local law officers who "yielded to the strength of the current, and neglected to discharge
their duties with firmness and strict impartiality." Brown forthrightly stated
his opinion that "the whole mass of the people are controlled by passion or
prejudice . . . beyond the corrective power of congressional legislation or
military dictatorship." Brown argued against a re-Reconstruction but believed that Congress had the power to reseat the black legislators and expel
illegal members of the Georgia legislature. Anything further would give
Democrats a "cause" and hurt Republican chances to split them. Although
Brown's response acknowledged the turbulence in Georgia, Tift used it to
bolster his case that Congress should recognize Reconstruction as complete
and enact no further legislation.[18]

In a long letter to the Joint Committee, Bullock refuted Tift's repre-
sentations and denied that he wanted a resumption of military rule. He
admonished Congress "to carry out the laws literally." He claimed, "My
only object . . . is to secure the establishment of a loyal civil government in

this State." Bullock challenged Tift's argument that Georgia had complied with every particular of the Reconstruction Acts: "If this statement can be true, it must be admitted that the laws of Congress, instead of accomplishing reconstruction, have effectively secured the destruction of the hopes, expectations, and prayers of the loyal men, who have suffered ostracism, outrage, and, in many instances, death." [19]

Bullock emphasized that blacks were citizens who had been deprived of their right to hold office. He denounced the validity of Tift's questionnaires and said that of those judges, mayors, ordinaries, and others who answered, only six were Republicans. Some respondents wrote entirely against Tift and some were misrepresented. Bullock cited the "evidence" of ordinary Lewis Jackson of McIntosh County, a freedman, who supposedly agreed with Tift but "denies, on oath, ever having made any reply whatever to the interrogations of Mr. Tift . . . and pronounces . . . [his questionnaire] a forgery." [20]

After listening to the evidence, two of the nation's most powerful and consistent Radicals, Senator Charles Sumner and Representative Benjamin Butler, presented bills in the Senate and House supporting Bullock's request for another Reconstruction in Georgia. But a full year would pass before Congress came to a decision. [21]

On January 13, 1869, Bullock presented his annual message to the General Assembly. He began by reading the letter he wrote to Congress asking for a literal interpretation of the Reconstruction Acts. Then he scolded the legislators for expelling black members and called for them to "take the initiative" and reseat those members. Referring to the murders of freedmen in Camilla and to the recent New Orleans race riot, when thirty-four blacks were killed and two hundred injured against four whites killed and ten wounded, Bullock demanded that the government tighten officeholding and voting requirements for former Confederates: "With me, no more amnesty or removal of disabilities till the life of the humblest individual who walks on God's foot-stool, be he black or white, is as sacred in Camilla, Georgia, or in New Orleans, Louisiana, as it is in . . . Amesburg in Massachusetts." [22]

Bullock promised the lawmakers that if they would recognize their former slaves as equal citizens of Georgia, he would support removal of all political disabilities. He warned them that if the state refused to act, the national government surely would intervene.

Despite this forceful plea, the General Assembly failed to act and Congress dallied. Perhaps Congress's failure to act was in part because Johnson was a lame-duck president and Republicans preferred to wait for Grant. During this period of obstinate inaction, state Republicans wrote many letters supporting the Sumner and Butler bills and pleading for action. In his letter, J. L. Dunning blamed Meade: "The curse of present troubles grew out of shirking a plain duty by neglecting to apply the 14th Article or Amendment when the Legislature was first organized." Bullock told Butler that many feared Grant might refuse to support intervention and hoped that Congress would take the chance that Johnson might sign the bill. Bullock suggested disfranchising "all the rebs who still persist in their opposition to Congress" and pointed out that enfranchising them had led to violent opposition to Reconstruction. Bullock felt confident that "prompt action will save many lives & make a loyal state." Clearly, he had given up hope that Georgia Democrats would do justice.[23]

Savannah Republican Charles H. Hopkins wrote Butler in support of Bullock and praised the governor as "the champion of the weak and op-pressed in this State." Hopkins predicted: "Should your bill fail in Congress their [the black legislators] last hope will have expired." Expelled legislator Henry Turner explained his impatience with a Congress that moved too slowly: "If it is a fact that the party for whome we have sacrificed every thing is going to desert us . . . then it is high time we knew it." Turner mentioned the murders, imprisonments, burned churches and schools, and bragging Democrats. Then in a flurry that must have bruised Butler's ego and moved him to action, Turner ended his letter: "Thousands have already declared that the Republican party have led us into the wilderness and de-serted [us]. And the democrats are daily taunting us with it, by saying, *Now where is your damned Radical party. Why don't Beast Butler, and old Sumner come to your aid etc.*"[24]

While Congress deliberated, the Georgia House and Senate supported a resolution that a test case be tried before the state supreme court to de-cide if black men were eligible to hold office. The legislators believed that this would show good faith and keep the federal government deadlocked. Legislators also hoped that the chief justice would sway the court in their favor and declare blacks ineligible. After all, only one year earlier, that chief justice had told north Georgia whites that black men were ineligible to hold office. Joseph Brown was now Georgia's top jurist, and Democrats must have delighted to see him squirm.[25]

Bullock believed that Democrats had adopted the resolution for a trial case "without any intention on their part to abide by such decision." He vetoed the resolution and returned it with the explanation that the original organization of the legislature without application of the test oath was the main issue. Thus, he continued, "evil results" had followed. Bullock then went into a long and tightly reasoned argument to show why the legislature was unlawfully constituted.[26]

Since the Georgia House in July had responded through him to General Meade that "all persons now in their seats are eligible," the subsequent decision to remove blacks was obviously based on racism. As proof of black eligibility, Bullock cited the Fourteenth Amendment, the test oath, and the Georgia constitution, as well as the fundamental principle that individuals in a democracy can elect whoever they want to represent them. He conceded that in due judicial time a case then pending in Savannah would reach Georgia's highest court, which would decide the eligibility question. But until then he asked them to proceed quickly to do what was right.[27]

With the governor and the legislature at an impasse and before the Savannah case reached Georgia's supreme court, Congress sent the Fifteenth Amendment to the states for ratification. That amendment specifically granted the right to vote regardless of "race, color, or previous condition of servitude." Surely, with the fight in Georgia raging over black rights, Democrats in both houses of the Georgia legislature would refuse to support the amendment. But when Georgia voted not to ratify, it was Bullock, not the Democrats, who defeated the amendment. Bullock knew that Democrats would support ratification, for to oppose it would risk further intervention by a Congress that seemed willing to acquiesce to their seizure of the state legislature.

On March 10, Bullock transmitted the amendment to the General Assembly with the warning that ratification without reorganization and reseating could not be taken seriously. He argued that for democracy to work, blacks must participate in the government and hold seats so that "their voices may be heard in your halls and their votes recorded on public measures." He emphasized: "This Amendment is specifically designed to secure political privileges to the colored man." Bullock told the legislators that he cherished the amendment because it embodied the spirit of the American creed that "all men are created equal" as "the very foundation of Republican Government." He reminded them that the "colored race is free" and this last step would complete the transition from slavery to citizenship.[28]

Bullock's message to the Georgia legislators followed the resolution of the March 5 Republican convention held in Atlanta. Led by Chairman Foster Blodgett, 238 delegates from 104 counties sent a resolution to Congress claiming that the loyal men of Georgia had been denied representation by the usurping legislature. The delegates cited their fears of terrorism and murder but declared themselves "totally opposed to the remanding of our State to military government and only ask such interference . . . as may be necessary to a thorough and Moral execution of that portion of the Reconstruction acts which should control the organization of the General Assembly." They praised the Fifteenth Amendment as "a measure of right and justice and [we] shall recommend its adoption when we have a legislature that will, in good faith, provide for its enforcement." Blodgett and Bullock held the upper hand. For if the General Assembly did not reorganize itself, Radicals in the state senate could defeat the Fifteenth Amendment. Because Northern Republicans viewed the amendment as a way to consolidate party strength in the North, they would surely intervene in Georgia affairs if the amendment were defeated.[29]

The General Assembly refused to reorganize itself, apply the test oath, and reseat its black members as Bullock requested. The legislators probably would have defeated the amendment had not the threat of a return to military rule been imminent. So Democrats decided to support the amendment—they could always disregard it as they were ignoring the Fourteenth. On March 11 the Democrat-controlled Georgia House voted sixty-seven to fifty-nine to pass the amendment and sent it to the senate, where it failed thirteen to sixteen with fifteen abstentions. Seven senate Radicals voted to defeat the amendment, and nine more failed to vote on the question. Bullock explained by letter to Congress why "ardent Republicans and hearty friends" of the amendment refused to vote or voted against ratification. He reiterated that the Georgia legislature was an illegally constituted body of men who evaded the law and that true Republicans could not now support the amendment while these villians were "cooly trampling" on the Fourteenth Amendment, *"which they had only a few months before made a pretense to ratifying."*[30]

On April 9, 1869, the fourth anniversary of the surrender at Appomattox, Indiana senator Oliver P. Morton introduced a bill requiring Virginia, Mississippi, Texas, and Georgia to ratify the Fifteenth Amendment as a precondition to reentering the Union. Bullock returned to Washington to lobby for the bill and was so active that the *New York World* credited him with authorship. The Senate passed the bill 40 to 9. In the House, Butler presented a similar bill, which passed 121 to 51. One newspaperman commented that "Governor Bullock seemed, in fact, to be managing the bill in the house. He was on the floor all day, and was consulted by Butler at every stage. His presence was . . . the boldest piece of lobbying ever witnessed in Congress." The reporter misstated the situation; Bullock's presence or absence made no difference. The overwhelming vote for the bill indicated that Butler little needed Bullock to lobby for passage.[31]

While Congress debated freedmen's rights under law, Democratic violence and murders continued in Georgia, undoubtedly encouraged by congressional inaction. In April, in the town of Lexington, near Athens, whites threatened black schoolteacher Frank Coley and burned his school. Lexington resident F. J. Robinson angrily asked Bullock: "Are we to be run over roughshod by the Ku Klux Klans?" With no relief by September and after the murder of four freedmen and one white sympathizer, Robinson again wrote Bullock: "I am getting more and more convinced every day that the only remedy we can succeed with is a Provisional Government and Military Rule with *Garrisons* at every county seat in this part of the state. 'Bluecoats and Bayonets' can only stay this state of things."[32]

From Waynesboro, a similar incident led black minister and teacher Adam Palmer to write the governor that the local law enforcement officers "will not or cannot" aid blacks. "Must we thus endure and see our people murdered and slain and sacrifice our own lives and all we have to the malice and hatred of lawless and unGodly men or else become exhiles in our own country. Is there no power to give us protection?"[33]

Expelled member of the Georgia legislature Eli Barnes pleaded for help after Klansmen killed three freedmen and beat thirteen others in Hancock County. William Wilson's letter from Sparta, which included a petition of sixteen names, expressed particular distress:

> Gov R B Bullock Sir I drop you a fue linds [few lines] to let you know that
> we as a Race ar in a bad condistion hear in hancock county[.] the white peple
> ar kiling us like trouts[.] thar has ben three colard men kild hear in the lenth
> of a week[.] we as a Peple do bedge you for sum pertection in this county
> and hear today they are going taking up colared men and brining them to
> jile by great gangs and what for we cannot tell at this time[.] Dear Sir we as
> a clase has has sind they pertetion to you for some pertection to you once
> would be truly glad for your attention in this occation.[34]

The intimidation and violence were not only directed against blacks. In Social Circle, twenty to thirty men in disguises severely whipped Martha Spencer because her father had not "'fought for his country' he having never been in the Confederate Army." On New Year's Day 1869, Benjamin Ayer of Jefferson County joined nine other white Republican state legislators to write a letter to Congress explaining that they were refugees in Atlanta, unable to return to their homes because of threats on their lives. They cited the folly of thinking any justice could be had from their persecutors because Democrats dominated local grand juries. Less than four months later, Ayer was killed by Klansmen for going to Washington with Bullock to appeal for a true Reconstruction. On May 10, Senator Joseph Adkins of Warren County paid the same price for the same sin. Even though Bullock sent Georgia attorney general Henry Farrow to investigate, posted a $5,000 reward, and persuaded General Alfred Terry, commander of the Department of the South, to send troops to investigate the murders, no one was ever sentenced. Common knowledge held the Klan responsible. The *New York Times* announced that "Republicans who desire legal reconstruction in Georgia are rapidly 'perishing by the wayside.' " [35]

The ubiquitous violence led many to question the hesitancy of Congress. In a letter to Benjamin Conley concerning the murder of Adkins, Augusta Republican A. L. Harris summarized Republican bewilderment with congressional hesitation: "Four years of bloody war to prove *wrong* was *right,* and still they are trying to do the same thing by assassination. How long must such things be? . . . We expect Gov. B's return tomorrow if he is not killed on the way." [36]

Meanwhile, a test case challenging the right of blacks to hold office reached the Georgia Supreme Court. After freedman Richard W. White of Savannah had been elected clerk of the superior court of Chatham County, William J. Clements, a white who had finished second in the voting, filed suit questioning White's eligibility. The case came to trial in Savannah on March 4. Amos T. Akerman, whom Grant would appoint attorney general in 1870, argued White's case before the court.

Akerman was born in New Hampshire but had lived in Georgia since 1850 and sided with the South during the war. Then he accepted the verdict of that contest, became a Republican, and served in the 1867–68 constitutional convention. Explaining his switch in allegiance, Akerman wrote that once the South lost, it was a citizen's duty to "let Confederate ideas rule us no longer . . . [and] to discard the doctrines of state rights and slavery. Regarding the subjugation of one race by the other as an appurtenance of slavery, we were content that it should go to the grave in which slavery had been buried." [37]

Akerman argued before the court that blacks had the right to hold office and referred to the vote in the constitutional convention on the clause that would have specifically granted black officeholding. Akerman insisted that the delegates had refused to include a specific statement in the constitution because it would be "superfluous" and certainly "negroes would be eligible to office even though that section were stricken out." Akerman failed to influence the jury, which decided that White was "a person of color" and therefore ineligible for office. After Judge William Schley named Clements the rightful winner, White appealed the case to the Georgia Supreme Court.[38]

In June, Georgia Supreme Court justices Joseph Brown, Henry McCay, and Hiram Warner heard the case. Undoubtedly, they had already come to their own conclusions. In the gubernatorial race in 1868 and in his letter to Joshua Hill, Chief Justice Brown had denied that blacks had the right to hold office. If he maintained that position, White would lose. But Brown's January letter to Nelson Tift, which had been introduced into evidence before the Joint Committee on Reconstruction, argued for reseating the black legislators and asked for no new Reconstruction. Brown had to decide in White's favor because to do otherwise might spur Congress to intrude further in Georgia affairs.

Hiram Warner, a Democrat, rigidly opposed black officeholding. Warner had been demoted from his position as chief justice when Bullock named Brown to that position. Bullock did not remove him entirely because of Bullock's desire to appease the Democrats by not removing all officials from their appointed positions.[39]

Justice Henry Kent McCay was a delegate to the constitutional convention of 1867–68 and therefore well knew the intentions of the convention on the question of black officeholding. He had supported Bullock for governor and agreed with Congressional Reconstruction. In writing the principal opinion for *White* v. *Clements*, McCay agreed that the 1868 constitution had not specifically granted blacks the right to hold office, but it did not need to. McCay ridiculed the racist assumption that whites got their rights from God but blacks had to be granted rights by the state. He wrote that blacks "form a portion of the body politic" and therefore had the right to hold office. He stated that blacks contributed at least three-fourths of the vote that ratified the constitution and thereby had "made" the constitution. It was ludicrous to think that they would vote for a basic law that denied their right to representation by a man of their choosing. Brown concurred with McCay; Warner dissented. By the vote of two to one, the high court decided that White and, by implication, all blacks could hold office in Georgia. This decision brought the action of the legislature in expelling its black members into an even harsher light.[40]

After the decision, Bullock refused to call a special session of the legislature so that it could debate and possibly reseat the expelled legislators. He wanted to let Congress settle the matter. Besides, as the *Augusta Chronicle* reported, another factor compelled him to wait: "The expelled negroes are not now members, and any call which he could lawfully make would apply to those who were *actual* members at the time of the last adjournment. To call that body together as it was constituted, would expose Bullock to almost certain hazard of *impeachment*." For months the Democrats had been proposing just that. Bullock read the papers, understood the Democratic temper, and realized that men who killed and intimidated might well impeach an unpopular governor. So he preferred to wait for Congress to act and refused to convene the hostile legislature.[41]

A month earlier, after hearing of the Adkins and Ayer murders, Massachusetts senator Henry Wilson wrote to Grant about the continuing bloodbath: "Can nothing be done to stop these outrages in Georgia? These political murders should cease. . . . Martial law is this day needed in that, the worst of all the States." Grant forwarded the letter to William T. Sherman, who, in turn, sent it to the army commander in the South, General Alfred H. Terry.[42]

By early July, Terry had investigated conditions in Georgia. He told Bullock that it would be "fruitless" to prosecute anyone who had previously committed outrages upon Republicans because the local machinery of sheriffs, marshals, and community leaders was Democratic. Bullock wrote Ben Butler that Terry had decided to recommend a return of military rule for Georgia. He hoped Grant would send in the army so that the blacks would gain their constitutional rights, Republicans would be protected, and Georgia would be saved "from the political control of the Rebel Democracy."[43]

Clearly, Bullock wanted a military overseer; he did not necessarily want military government. He realized that Terry's opinion might convince Congress to act, and so he supported it. In December, Bullock explained to the *New York Times* that "the time has come when Congress must go backward or forward." He emphasized that he did not want harsh terms, "nor do we desire military government. . . . All we ask or desire is that congress shall provide for the enforcement of its laws." Others asked for stronger action. In a letter to Butler, Blodgett reluctantly acquiesced to military intervention "until the lawless and rebellious spirit . . . shall be eradicated." After a year of waiting, Bullock and Blodgett would accept anything as an improvement over the status quo.[44]

By mid-August, Terry completed and filed his report. He described Georgia as a lawless region where killings were frequent and local magistrates and government leaders failed to carry out their responsibilities under the laws. Those civil officers who were not participating members or spiritual allies of the Ku Klux Klan were so intimidated by robed night riders as to be ineffective. Terry described Bullock as a governor who would "gladly interpose" to protect all citizens, but "he has power neither to act directly in bringing offenders to justice nor to compel subordinate officers to do their duty." Terry supported a reorganization of the Georgia legislature as Bullock suggested. He stopped short of openly blaming Meade for the current legislature but wrote that Meade could have demanded a formal oath-taking day, which "would have been a *proper* method of ascertaining the facts."[45]

Bullock anxiously awaited the next session of Congress. In late November he wrote Georgia representative Wesley Shropshire: "I profoundly hope and trust that there may be backbone and nerve enough . . . to give our Georgia rebels back seats."[46]

On December 6, 1869, the president made his only real contribution to Congressional Reconstruction. Undoubtedly, he came to this decision reluctantly and after weighing a great deal of conflicting information as to the true situation in Georgia. One letter from elected, but as yet unseated, Senator Joshua Hill of Georgia described violence in the state as "occasional" and insisted that "men are taking the advice of Webster to his farmer John Taylor [to] talk of oxen and horses and deep plowing instead of politics." Eventually Grant came to believe the opposite, and in a message to Congress, he recommended: "It would be wise to pass a law without delay for the Georgia Governor to convene the original members of the legislature and require each to take the oath prescribed in the reconstruction acts"— exactly what Bullock had asked Meade to do in 1868.[47]

Grant's decision supporting the return of Georgia to military supervision also secured the deciding vote necessary to ratify the Fifteenth Amendment. Bullock and Blodgett's plan to have the Radicals defeat the amendment had succeeded. For had those Radicals voted for an amendment which they really wanted, Grant and other Centrists would not have needed one more state to ratify. Because they needed Georgia's vote to secure the Fifteenth Amendment and to consolidate their position in the North, national Republican Centrists joined Radicals in remanding Georgia to military rule. For their part, Radicals were most interested in protecting Southern blacks.[48]

Three days before Christmas, Congress acted on Grant's suggestions and required Georgia to reconvene the original 1868 legislature, reorganize under the test oath, and ratify the Fifteenth Amendment. Many Georgians played key roles in that decision but none more than Governor Bullock. Following heated debates over states' versus national rights, the Senate voted 45 to 9 and the House concurred 121 to 51 to reimpose military rule.[49]

That night, Bullock held a dinner in the Cafe Française to celebrate his triumph. Newspaper reporters, peers, and later historians criticized Bullock for what they termed a "Bacchanalian feast"; but how could he have done less? After struggling for a year and a half with an illegal legislature, seeing friends and supporters killed or intimidated while he stood by unable to protect them, and having been the object of the most abusive slander imaginable, Bullock savored his victory. On Christmas Eve, Bullock met with Grant to thank him for his influence and to watch him sign the bill into law.[50]

Georgia Radicals hailed the governor for his tireless efforts. Congressman Charles H. Prince of Augusta, a Republican who served in the 1868 constitutional convention, wrote to Benjamin Conley lauding Bullock as "deserving of great praise from our party in Ga. on account of his untiring energy. . . . The more I see of him the more I am led to admire him." [51]

Democrats were beside themselves. Newspapers throughout Georgia howled against Bullock as the architect of renewed Reconstruction. Klansman and editor Isaac W. Avery of the *Atlanta Constitution* lamented: "Today is seen the sad, piteous, shameful spectacle of her Executive conspiring with her enemies for the overthrow of her liberties. Plotting, scheming, bribing, truckling, maligning, toiling for her injury and abasement . . . the government of a million virtuous people is demolished by the act, and anarchy and the rule of ignorance substituted thereof." Avery finished his philippic by charging that Bullock cared little for the state's dignity, wanted only self-aggrandizement, and governed "for plunder and despotic control." [52]

Avery and other white supremacists would never understand Bullock's belief that the Civil War had mandated a free labor system in which all races should be treated fairly. For Avery, the "public weal" did not include the rights of half the state's population, those who were now free of slavery's bonds. Bullock did indeed take a partisan stand in favor of Radical Reconstruction; his enemies gave him little option. In fact, collusive Democratic polemicists wounded Bullock's sense of honor and fair play and so drove him ever closer to men who seemed to agree with him. Thus Bullock clung to others who were being abused, tended to disregard all criticism of them as fabrication, and had a difficult time—even a blind spot—in distinguishing the honest and dishonest motives of these friends. A few of the men who gained Bullock's trust did not deserve it, but Avery overstated when he charged that all the Radicals sought was self-aggrandizement.

The same day Grant signed "An Act to Promote the Reconstruction of Georgia," Bullock issued a call for the legislators who were elected in June 1868 to convene in Atlanta on January 10, 1870. Bullock also urged Grant and Sherman, the latter as general of the army, to appoint his friend General Terry as the on-site commander to oversee Reconstruction. On Christmas Eve, Grant gave Bullock the present he wanted.[53]

On January 10, the members of Georgia's original 1868 legislature met in Atlanta. With Terry's approval, Bullock appointed J. G. W. Mills to direct the reorganization of the senate and A. L. Harris to preside in the house. These clerks pro tem called the name of each elected member to come forward and take the oath. This procedure depended on the honesty of the oath takers; it soon became clear that that was not enough. Democrats who were not eligible took the oath as if they were. Senator Campbell stood and protested the seating of seven senators and later asked Bullock and Terry to purge those who were unqualified. In the house, John Bryant complained that Harris had no authority to judge a member's qualifications because he was not himself a member. When Harris ignored him, Bryant maneuvered to name his friend John Caldwell to replace Harris. Those efforts failed when Terry upheld Harris.[54]

Because of the acrimonious sessions in the General Assembly and complaints of false swearing, Terry decided to take matters into his own hands. Terry was more decisive than Meade had been in 1868 and intended to make Georgians comply with the law. On January 13, he appointed a three-man board of military officers, Major General Thomas H. Ruger, Brigadier General T. J. Haines, and Major Henry Goodfellow, to investigate and report on the eligibility of the legislators. Bullock actively pursued the expulsion of those who were ineligible by sending Terry a list of sixteen house members who had sworn to uphold the Constitution and then participated in the rebellion. In accordance with Georgia precedence and instead of calling for new elections, Bullock advocated replacing legislators found ineligible with those who finished second in the April 1868 election. Unsure of what to do, Terry wrote Sherman for advice and then accepted Bullock's plan—a decision that would have important ramifications. Bullock wrote Ohio congressman William Lawrence that Democrats had perjured themselves and evidently believed that no one had the authority to expel them. Clearly no Georgia jury would convict them. Bullock supported Terry's board and understated when he said, "The situation here is critical." Democratic newspapers resonated with accusations against Terry and Bullock. The *Augusta Chronicle* screaked about "plunder," called Bullock a "consumate ass, robber and villain," and referred to Georgia Radicals as a "gang of crawling scum." In the end, Terry's board found nineteen representatives and five senators ineligible to take the oath.[55]

Terry purged the twenty-four Democrats and replaced them with the Republican runners-up in the 1868 election. That, in addition to the re-seating of thirty-one black legislators, gave Bullock a working majority in both houses of the General Assembly. On February 1, nineteen months after Bullock's original protests to Meade that some legislators sat illegally, seventeen months after the expulsion of the black legislators, Georgia had a General Assembly organized in accordance with the 1867 Reconstruction Acts. Bullock could be proud of his efforts on behalf of equality and justice for black Georgians, but his determined stance in their favor rent the Republican party in favor of the Centrists. In Congress, many competitivists protested Terry's actions, denied that the act of December 22 gave any authority for a purge, and questioned the seating of the 1868 runners-up instead of requiring new elections. When the Senate Judiciary Committee began to investigate, Bullock defended Terry's reorganization and, revealing his own polarized political view, asserted that no one disapproved except "the rebel democracy and four recreant republicans whom they have purchased."[56]

The day following the reorganization of the legislature, February 2, Bullock addressed the General Assembly. He described the long struggle as a battle between those who supported Reconstruction and those who opposed it. He called his party "the party of peace" and welcomed everyone who supported "equal rights and republican liberty." Bullock sounded the themes of free labor, stressed the importance of the workingman, supported free public education, and insisted that "a citizen's worth, shall be determined by his own efforts and his own character, neither advanced nor retarded by his birth, his color, his religion or his politics."[57]

Bullock assured Georgians and the nation that laws and agreements made by the late legislature were valid and businesses and railroads should continue to invest in Georgia bonds. The legislature quickly ratified the Fifteenth Amendment and, to show that the ratification of the Fourteenth Amendment had been effected by an illegal legislature, reratified it. But Georgia would not be released from military supervision and become an equal state until July 1870. As the Georgia imbroglio continued, Bullock remained at the center of controversy.[58]

Chapter 6 ❧ Development and Scandal

And this same man, Rufus Behemoth, surnamed the
Bullock, was lavish with the gold and the greenbacks that
came into the public treasury.
—Rabbi Ben-Ansel, *Books of the Chronicles of the
State of Georgia*

Completely surrounding the state capitol was a host of
promoters, speculators, seekers after contracts and others
hoping to profit from the orgy of spending, and many
were growing shamelessly rich. They had no difficulty at
all in obtaining the state's money for building railroads
that were never built, for buying cars and engines that
were never bought. . . . Bonds were issued running into
the millions. Most of them were illegal and fraudulent but
they were issued just the same. . . . It was a glorious spree
for the gang which had Georgia by the throat.
—Margaret Mitchell, *Gone with the Wind*

BULLOCK'S SUPPORT of the black legislators and his successful efforts
at getting Congress to reinstitute military rule were manifestations of his
sense of equality and belief in the Republican party. But even before he
embraced equality and the party he envisioned a business climate built on
the Northern mold. Generally, Radicals believed economic development
to be as crucial as black equality and they wanted to expand the free labor
system nationwide. After the Civil War freed the slaves, many saw the
South as virgin territory prime for expansion, with labor readily available.

These visionaries attempted to redirect the South from staple crop production to agricultural and industrial diversification as part of the effort
to turn the United States into an independent world power, a "core" state
equal to Great Britain and no longer Britain's economic colony. Republicans preached a gospel of prosperity and, when possible, obtained state
funds, usually in the form of bonds, to help finance progress.[1]

Many of these Republicans in the South were young men, rising in their
careers, highly mobile, optimistic, and not bound to the provincialism that
often infected Southern communities. They saw the outcome of the war
as part of the country's manifest destiny, expanding across the Indian and
Southern frontiers, bringing capitalism, moral advancement, and modernization. Eric Foner concluded that Republican ideology and the expansion
of the free labor system depended on equal access to work and education. Historian Richard Abbott further explained that Republican ideology
included "the superiority of free labor, the desirability of a diversified economy, including a significant industrial component, an emphasis on tech-
nological innovation, a commitment to public education, and a belief that
government had a role to play in promoting economic growth." Bullock
embraced this egalitarian, progressive ideology and did what he could to
make it a reality in Georgia.[2]

Although Bullock spent the vast majority of his time and energy during
his first two years in office trying to reseat the black legislators and reorganize the General Assembly, he also promoted a program of internal improvements. Just two days after his inauguration, Bullock told the General
Assembly: "The foundation of all prosperity is the successful development
of our internal resources." In his understanding of things economic, the
interests of labor, capital, and landholders merged; development helped
them all. When capitalists built railroads and factories, land values rose,
which in turn generated more work and income for the laboring class, if
only in the increased job opportunities which transportation and industry provided for workers. As the region developed, prosperity would fuel
itself.[3]

Constructing railroads and rebuilding Atlanta topped Bullock's list of
projects, but lack of money and the factor of time worked against him. Because the state still suffered from the enormous costs of the war, he had to
rely on state bond issues and creative financing to obtain the large amount
of capital necessary for his projects.

Bullock and other Republicans knew the importance of speed. They had to convert Georgians to the gospel of prosperity and "sell" themselves by generating instant growth. Otherwise they would lose the political power required to forge change. Bullock succeeded in many of these ventures, failed in others, and nearly always stretched his schemes to the limits of propriety. Advocates believed he was helping Georgia, and particularly Atlanta, into the future; critics hissed about corruption, extravagance, and illegalities. Conservatives insisted that there were frauds involving the state capitol, railroads, bonds, pardons, and the penitentiary system, as well as general extravagance in running the government. Several General Assembly committees investigated Bullock's official conduct, and in 1878 Bullock stood trial for "cheating and swindling" and "robbing the State of millions."[4]

After Bullock and the Radicals lost power, most Georgians proudly pointed to the economic gains of the period and New South advocates adopted the Republican economic program. Yet, even then, conservatives denigrated Bullock for extravagance and for advocating equality for the freedmen.

Others shared Bullock's vision and cooperated with him to forge a new Georgia. First among them was Hannibal Ingalls Kimball, the entrepreneur who refurbished and rented his Opera House for use as the state capitol. Contemporaries described Kimball as "a steam engine in breeches" or as a man with such a persuasive personality that "the only way to resist him was to refuse to see him." Kimball's biographer concludes that his intentions were good but his "overly ambitious imagination" and schemes outran his finances. Adjudging his credit and operating skills, R. G. Dun correctly reported that Kimball "operates considerably on borrowed cash. He will either make a large fortune or a large failure." He "engages in large schemes," Dun continued. "Some fear he will break." Still, Kimball did much to develop the state and exhorted Georgians to "*encourage the men* who strike out in enterprise, that invite capital to build up the State, whether it be in building railroads, canals, or working your soil or your mines." His 1870 Kimball House hotel, Atlanta's finest, cost $600,000 to build, stood six stories high, had 317 rooms and twenty-one stores, employed one hundred workers, and became the city's business and social center. He helped finance the Union Passenger Depot, built many railroads, and in later years became president of Atlanta's first cotton factory, built another hotel, promoted a cotton exposition and a commercial convention, and in 1880 missed becoming mayor of Atlanta by only fifty-four votes. It is easy to understand why Bullock and Kimball became friends and worked together to develop the state.[5]

Kimball was a Republican but not a Radical. He did not openly support black equality and for more than a decade shied away from politics as detrimental to business. Nevertheless, his association with Bullock provoked Democrats to heap abuse upon him. Some even claimed that Kimball was the brains behind the governor or that Georgia had a "dual executive." Alexander Stephens's brother Linton called them "unprincipled adventurers, hunting in couple, to plunder the public." In reality, Bullock worked with Kimball for the interests of state development; neither realized much financial gain. Both seemed to revel in the attention lavished on them by Northern investors and Southern businessmen. Both men wanted to be known as builders and entrepreneurs. In this age of enterprise, they most wanted a reputation as men of progress, which they knew they could achieve only by expanding the physical assets of the state.[6]

Certainly both men wanted to be rich, but they settled for socializing with rich people and manipulating the power of capital. George Pullman told R. G. Dun & Company that Kimball's assets amounted to at least three-quarters of a million dollars, but "his deeply embedded Spirit of emulation might cause him to jeopardize his wealth." Instead of increasing their own fortunes, Bullock and Kimball invested their energy and money in growth. Perhaps the constant Democratic charges of aggrandizement and fraud prompted them to prove they were primarily interested in the public welfare. Whatever the motivation, neither man put financial gain over public progress nor did either "plunder the public." Slander in the press and Democratic "evidence" convinced most white Georgians and many historians to believe they had.[7]

In 1868, the city of Atlanta agreed to furnish the state legislature with more suitable quarters than the city hall provided, and city fathers rented Kimball's Opera House for use as the state capitol. The state was responsible for supplying heating, lighting, and furniture. Before the legislature allocated funds for that purpose, Bullock advanced Kimball $54,500 in state funds to cover those costs. When a scandal erupted and the governor's right to use state funds in this manner was questioned, Bullock explained that his actions were necessary to ensure that the legislators had heat, seats in which to sit, and light by which to work. He cited an act passed during the 1868 session which gave him authority to make loans and to pay "other expenses of this General Assembly." Bullock maintained that if he had failed to provide for furniture and utilities "I would have been clearly derelict. . . . The use, on my part, of the public money and the public credit for the general welfare of the State, and for public purpose, is fully sustained by a long line of precedents." State attorney general Henry P. Farrow concurred with Bullock's actions in preparing the statehouse as "prompted by high and honorable motives, looking to the interest and dignity of the state, and the convenience and comfort of the legislature." None of these explanations satisfied Bullock's critics.[8]

In 1870, the state legislature and the city of Atlanta maneuvered to purchase the Opera House from Kimball for $130,000 in city bonds and $250,000 in twenty-year 7 percent state bonds. Bullock supported the purchase, but he stood aside while legislators, city officers, and Kimball bargained and completed arrangements. Kimball agreed to the sale and, as part of the deal, repaid the $54,500 in state funds originally advanced. After they discovered that Kimball had failed to mention an outstanding $60,000 mortgage, Democrats screamed fraud, charged that Bullock was financially involved with Kimball, and pronounced the total price excessive. There is evidence that Kimball intended to pay off that mortgage, which if accomplished would have alleviated the charges of fraud, but his subsequent business failure and bankruptcy passed the mortgage debt on to the city. Bullock insisted that he had known nothing of that mortgage but said that the city of Atlanta made a private agreement with Kimball in which he was paid $45,000 less in city bonds than promised. Bullock denounced this affair as a "sharp business transaction" that should be investigated.[9]

The city complied in this deception to keep the capital in Atlanta; failure to support the effort to procure a suitable building might have prompted the legislature to move the capital elsewhere in the belief that city fathers had acted in bad faith. Kimball's bankruptcy exposed the secret deal and forced the city to pay the mortgage.

In the end, Georgians had a new capitol which one newspaper described as "this magnificent building, beyond controversy the finest in the State of Georgia." Its five stories housed the executive offices, supreme court, senate and house, committee rooms, state library, caucus rooms, and dormitories for state officials. And despite Democratic assertions to the contrary, the purchase price of $380,000, even with the mortgage, was reasonable. By comparison, fifteen years earlier, the Milledgeville capitol and governor's mansion cost $500,000. The 1889 capitol cost Georgians $862,756.75.[10]

Public aid to railroads was not a new idea. In antebellum Georgia, city and state support reached nearly $13 million, and in 1836 the state established the first state-owned, state-built railroad in America. The Western and Atlantic Railroad stretched from Atlanta to Chattanooga and joined private roads linking it to Augusta, Macon, Savannah, Charleston, and Birmingham. Always staffed through political patronage, the state road had been a cumbersome expense for its first twenty years, and as early as the 1840s, proposals to sell or lease it were often put forth. In the gubernatorial contest of 1857, Joseph Brown, who favored state ownership of the road, defeated Ben Hill, who advocated selling the "White Elephant." The 1870 legislature would authorize the governor to lease the Western and Atlantic; but before that happened, the 1868–70 legislatures authorized state bond issues to build nearly forty railroads.[11]

Railroad construction, an essential part of Bullock's economic vitalization program, had bipartisan support. Both Democrats and Republicans realized the importance of developing efficient lines of transportation and communication so as to sell products nationwide. During the Civil War, Congress had subsidized two intercontinental railroads under the 1862 Union Pacific and 1864 Northern Pacific acts. After the war, the South had to be linked to the system, and most Southerners were only too happy to support this form of economic modernization. Railroads were essential to industrial expansion. An Augusta newspaper exulted: "We live in an age of enterprise and progress . . . ; we must move along with the spirit." In the two-year period after Appomattox, Georgia's Democratic government granted ten charters to new railroads but only gave state aid to one, a $10,000-a-mile bond endorsement for the Macon and Brunswick line. Community leaders scrambled to get new railroads routed close to their homes. Politicians, who were often the ones most likely to be able to invest in railroad stock, voted local and state bonds to encourage building these iron roads and thereby benefited financially and politically. Georgians joined the railroad-building mania orchestrated by industrialists determined to integrate the nation into a marketplace financed primarily by northeastern capitalists.[12]

Georgians did more than provide money to lure railroads into the state; they supplied labor to build them. Many of those workers were prisoners who labored against their will. Georgians' long-standing desire to make the penitentiary system self-supporting combined with the state's poverty during Reconstruction to force accommodation to a convict-lease system. In December 1866, the legislature authorized the governor to rent out state convicts to private companies. Seventeen months later, military governor Thomas Ruger became the first executive to use that authority and leased one hundred prisoners at $25 each for one year to William A. Fort and his Georgia and Alabama Railroad Company. Fort agreed to supply guards, provide food, shelter, and clothing, and "treat with humanity the convicts committed to his charge, to work them by daylight only, and at no period of the year, to require more than eleven hours labor in the day, giving the usual rest upon the Sabbath." On July 2, Fort leased an additional hundred convicts from Ruger to work on the Selma, Rome, and Dalton Railroad. Everyone understood that if any prisoners died or escaped, the state would replace them.[13]

Bullock supported the system of working convicts outside the penitentiary as a way to save money, further public works, and build railroads to expand the state's commercial interests. Shortly after taking office in 1868, he told the General Assembly: "It is a matter of much importance that the Penitentiary should be as little expense as possible, if it can not be made a source of Revenue to the State." He ordered the warden of the state prison at Milledgeville to work prisoners on the lands and buildings belonging to the state lunatic asylum and in other places in the city of Milledgeville. Bullock also authorized the employment of prisoners in the state library. But he was most interested in building railroads, and prisoners could function as a labor subsidy to encourage construction.[14]

On November 8, 1868, Bullock contracted with John Thomas Grant, pioneer builder of Georgia railroads and lifelong Democrat, to provide 100 to 500 prisoners at $10 each per year to Grant, Alexander, and Company to work on the Macon and Brunswick Railroad. By year's end, 113 convicts labored on that line. After the prison warden reported that Fort treated his charges inhumanely and that some had died, Bullock decided not to renew that contract. After the legislature passed an "Act to Provide for farming out the Penitentiary of the State," Bullock complied and on June 28, 1869, leased all convicts to Grant, Alexander, and Company. By New Year's Day, 393 convicts worked on Grant's several railroads. Under the new two-year lease, that company took possession of the state penitentiary and agreed "to humanely treat each one of said convicts, and to securely keep and manage them." The state specifically forbade the company "to inflict . . . corporal punishment upon the convicts unless absolutely necessary to secure discipline." Grant further agreed to pay all expenses involved in "receiving, control and management, and discharge." Although the lessee did not pay the state for these laborers, he relieved the state of the costs of guarding, feeding, and clothing them. The state still paid the warden, whose duty now was to oversee the lease and report on compliance and violations. As a token effort to compensate the prisoners for their labor, Bullock stipulated in the contract that upon release the company would furnish each convict with a new suit of clothes and $10 cash.[15]

Bullock wanted the railroads built, but he insisted that Grant's company not mistreat the prisoners. Before he signed the contract, Bullock sought advice to make sure that Grant and Alexander would not abuse the prisoners. Edward Hulbert convinced him that "the firm was all right; thought they would be too lenient, if they erred in any way." Bullock got the army to help him oversee the lease. Milledgeville resident Archibald McKinley recorded that on July 10, "a company of Yankee Soldiers arrived this afternoon, to prevent Alexander, lessee of the Penitentiary, from making distinction in treatment of white & black convicts." In May 1870, an eight-man committee of the legislature, which included black Representatives Henry Turner, James Simms, and Senator George Wallace, examined the condition of the state's prisoners and reported them well-clothed, fed, and medically attended. They found that most punishment was within bounds but suggested limitations and condemned whipping of women prisoners in the nude in front of males. They cited the need for improved moral instruction and a better record-keeping system and called upon the governor to address these problems.[16]

Bullock quickly appointed one white and one black chaplain to preach every Sunday and to report monthly on the condition and treatment of each convict. He instructed the chaplains to ensure that the treatment of prisoners was "proper for persons in their condition in life." He informed Grant that he must make weekly reports, list convicts by name, description, and place worked, comply immediately with executive pardons, and report without delay on all new prisoners received directly from county authorities. Grant followed Bullock's orders, decreased the number of whippings, and submitted reports on time. Upon renegotiating the lease in July 1871, Bullock commended Grant for his "humane treatment" of the convicts. Bullock cited the success of the program in building railroads and bragged that the penitentiary, for the first time in the history of the state, was "self-sustaining, and the convicts transformed from consumers to producers."[17]

Bullock was shortsighted and did not see the iniquity of such a system. Perhaps he believed that by taking the precautions and providing the supervision of the prison warden and state chaplains, he had decreased the evil. His use of prisoners in state buildings and to build transportation lines suggests that he viewed their employment in works for the public good as a just punishment for their crimes. He did not lease prisoners to work on the lands and in the mines of private individuals who were not engaged in building for public use.

Later, Redeemers would lease convicts to political bosses John Gordon and Joe Brown, who used them to increase their own profits with no social benefit or prisoner redemption. The employment of prisoners by private leaseholders was an abhorrent practice. Convicts are still used in Georgia in road gangs, not by private persons. Whether Bullock saw the difference is unknown; but his actions providing supervision of convict lease indicate his sensitivity to the treatment of prisoners.

Bullock had been associated with railroads for nearly twenty years. His background in telegraphy and his work with the Southern Express Company were inseparably joined with railroad interests. During the war he worked with the Confederate Quartermaster Bureau and oversaw railway transportation. After the war, Bullock became president of the Macon and Augusta Railroad, but after he became governor he surrendered that position to his Augusta ally Benjamin Conley. Georgia's top railroad promoter and builder, John P. King of Augusta, built the Western and Atlantic Railroad and headed the extensive Georgia Railroad. King had appointed Bullock to the presidency of the Macon and Augusta line. His vast experience and close association with railroad men helped him to understand the enormous costs involved in railroad construction and prompted him to support state aid in the form of convict labor and bond issues.

Of course, railroads sought investment wherever they could obtain it, particularly from Northern banks. State support offered another avenue. Bullock's predecessor, Governor Charles Jenkins, had vetoed three of the four legislative proposals for state aid; many hoped that Bullock's administration would support expansion. Macon resident James A. Nisbet wrote Conley suggesting the "State should give its credit not only to this [Macon and Milledgeville Railroad], but all valuable Roads, to the end that money may be scattered amongst our people and their productive industry stimulated." [18]

Bullock kept a close eye on railroad matters. He believed that the state's economic progress hinged on its transportation system. He promoted the "rapid construction" of all lines and said, "Railway communication is the key which must be forged to unlock and reach the wealth that now lies dormant in the sparsely populated sections of our state." As his accomplishments in this area increased, he crowed: "These new railroads opened up to usefulness and traffic wide sections of timber, mineral and agricultural lands, which, before these roads were built, had no market or taxable value." Bullock insisted that the promise and delivery of state aid was the sine qua non of railroad construction.[19]

To encourage the development of the lands through which the railroads passed, Bullock sponsored several excursions for the press and potential investors. In August 1869, Bullock accompanied a trainload of newspapermen from Atlanta to Chattanooga and promoted industrial mining of north Georgia coal and iron deposits. On another occasion, Bullock arranged for thirty-three Southern railroads to offer a special two-cent-per-mile "prospecting rate" for capitalists who sought investment opportunities in Georgia. In January 1870, while Bullock assisted General Terry in reorganizing the legislature, the engine *Governor Bullock* brought to Atlanta nearly 250 businessmen from Kentucky, Tennessee, and Ohio. The purpose of this "Green Line Excursion" was to promote trade and encourage businessmen to relocate in Atlanta.[20]

During Bullock's administration, the state legislature passed thirty-eight bills authorizing nearly $8 million in state bond support for railroads. To qualify for these bonds, railroads had to complete a twenty-mile section of track before the state would give aid in amounts up to one-third of the total construction costs. After the legislature approved the aid, it was Bullock's duty to ensure that railroads conformed to the law before bonds were signed over. He issued bonds to only seven railroads. Still, he did not always follow proper procedure and sometimes railroads got aid before completing the required mileage. Bullock advanced bonds to those that had started construction if he believed the builders were acting in good faith. Since railroad construction cost at least $20,000 per mile, Bullock understood that costs sometimes overran construction mileage, and he earnestly believed the state should help companies succeed if they honestly tried to live up to their agreements.[21]

As president of seven Georgia railroads, Hannibal Kimball was among the first to receive state aid. By 1871, he completed 160 miles of track and graded another 100 miles. He also surveyed nearly every mile of ground to be developed for railroads over the next twenty years. His expenses were enormous because he employed nearly three thousand workers and spent nearly $25,000 per month on supplies. When Kimball failed financially, the Democratic press charged him with using the bonds for ventures other than railroad building. Whether Kimball was in the wrong cannot be determined by the evidence, although his guilt seems unlikely. Bankrupt and tired, Kimball left Georgia in 1871 with a debt of $5 million owed primarily to New York banks and under a cloud of accusations that he had not only misdirected railroad bonds but had used Opera House bonds illegally as well. The next year, a state investigating committee charged him with conspiring with Bullock to swindle the state. The committee also claimed that the superintendent of the state road had paid him $30,000 for fifty railroad cars from his Tennessee Car Company that he never delivered. Actually, Kimball did deliver forty-four cars on time and there was a dispute, because of bad record-keeping, over whether he delivered the other six as well.[22]

In 1874, Kimball returned to Georgia, denied that Bullock and he were partners, dared anyone to prove he had done anything illegal, and declared: "The broad, sweeping charges against me . . . are not only without foundation in fact, but [are] utterly false." He blamed a "powerful and unprincipled opposition" for misleading the people. After prominent Atlanta businessmen, Democrats and Republicans, joined to welcome him back, even the *Atlanta Constitution,* which had issued the most scathing of many scurrilous charges, proclaimed Kimball's innocence: "He did not make them [bonds] a stepping stone to advance his own fortune by pocketing them, but used the proceeds in building up Georgia enterprises." The *Constitution* followed that reversal by completely taking Kimball's side and satirically challenging his "trumpet-tongued accusers and remorseless denunciators": "Tis strange that a man who, as it is alleged, robbed the State of millions, bribed her legislators, corrupted her people, swindled her citizens, impoverished her taxpayers, and drove her to the terrible alternative of repudiation, should have been permitted again to enter her borders."[23]

There was no evidence with which to indict Kimball of any illegal activity, even after two years of the most searching investigation by the state legislature and by independent investigator Linton Stephens. The charge that Kimball conspired with Bullock to swindle the state was unfounded.

Undoubtedly, Bullock's desire for railroad construction sometimes led him to circumvent the letter of the law, but he intended no fraud. Bullock conceded that he trusted too much in Kimball's ability—was a bit blind to this entrepreneurial dynamo—but argued, "That is not a crime. . . . The evidences of his financial ability were visible on every side and on almost every street. . . . His credit was almost unlimited. He enjoyed the fullest confidence of Bankers and Capitalists everywhere." Bullock added that Kimball had done more to promote Georgia's prosperity "than any one man or set of men had done for fifty years before." Believing that, it is little wonder that he relied on Kimball to forward his program of change.[24]

Kimball admitted that he had received some bonds before complying with the mileage requirement but insisted that he used the funds to speed construction. Whenever Bullock granted aid before railroads met state requirements, he closely monitored the progress of those lines. In June 1870, he wrote Georgia Air Line president A. S. Buford to say the report on his railroad was "not satisfactory." Believing the project to be in the state's best interest, however, Bullock explained: "I have reluctantly endorsed the credit of the State upon $240,000 worth of your bonds. . . . I shall not be willing to approve of bonds for the next section of twenty miles unless the law is fully complied with."[25]

The state legislature approved this aid in September 1868, but, after Bullock delivered the bonds, the Air Line returned them because the company had made other arrangements. In 1870 Bullock felt justified in extending bonds to the company again because it had completed some track. Others who experienced financial problems sometimes convinced the governor to regard the "excess value in the road over the amount in the Mortgage Bonds sufficient security to justify" more bonds. When Bullock complied, he did so to speed development, not to defraud the public.[26]

Bullock usually endorsed state aid when the legislature approved it, but he vetoed acts that did not specify clearly enough the route to be constructed, and he refused to assist companies that demonstrated no real progress in completing the required twenty-mile section. He did not refuse aid on the basis of partisan politics. Bullock wanted railroads built rapidly, and it mattered little to him that most of those incorporating railroads and receiving state aid were Democrats. He called for courage in the face of "some few timid and cautious persons in the state who fear that we are 'going to everlasting ruin' by authorizing . . . 'state aid.'" Bullock explained that after the General Assembly granted a charter, "gentlemen of intelligence and responsibility form themselves together as a company, and they prepare by careful survey, examinations, and estimates, to build a railroad."[27]

Bullock further explained that once these men recognized the feasibility of a railroad enterprise, they invested their money, built the required section, and received state aid. Bullock wanted the companies and the state to be partners, committed to what he called "united action" for the benefit of both. The state's interests were safe because the state held a first lien on railroad property. Georgia also benefited by an increase in taxable property. The railroad gained because state aid not only made it possible to build roads but state endorsement increased bond values because investors felt secure and thus more willing to buy state bonds. Bullock was undoubtedly correct about this because Georgia's bonds sold at higher rates than those of any other Southern state. Obviously, investors accepted the Republican state aid program.[28]

Bullock urged the builders to speed their work. After being told that one road would be "constructed promptly" and then waiting a year without its completion, Bullock told the builders: "I feel a deep interest in the rapid construction and early completion of the Brunswick and Albany RR so that the middle section of the lower part of our State may be afforded railroad facilities." He further warned that if they slowed progress or failed to stay financially solvent, they should "surrender the charter to parties who are able to finish the road promptly." Eventually, Bullock seized this railroad and at least one other line for failing to meet their obligations. Overall, state aid to railroads during Reconstruction was a success, increasing railroad mileage in Georgia by nearly six hundred miles. Democrats were heavily involved from the beginning and generally supported railroad construction; only later did they claim corruption in railroad bonds as a way to attack Republican rule in Georgia.[29]

After the Redeemer legislature took control of Georgia in 1871, Democrats repudiated $6,709,000 in railroad bonds, mostly held by Kimball, and $2,000,000 in gold and currency bonds, which the state had negotiated to pay off old debts, buy a new capitol, pay the legislature, and pay other expenses of state government. Democrats labeled these "wrongful debts" and charged that Bullock had issued bonds fraudulently. A legislative committee investigated Bullock's official conduct and concluded, in dramatic charges designed for political effect, that Bullock and Kimball were financial partners and boodlers of state money. The 1877 constitutional convention made certain that Georgia would never find it necessary to pay its bonded debt by refusing to allow bondholders to sue the state.[30]

The repudiation issue was discussed in the national press for over thirty years. Many investigations and appeals to out-of-state courts by bondholders gained them nothing because Georgia insisted that the bonds were illegal. Wall Street financier Henry Clews, who acted as a state agent for Georgia bonds, lost over $2 million when the state repudiated the "Bullock Bonds." Clews sought help from New York courts to recover his money, but Georgia refused to honor the subsequent judgment that the bonds were valid. As a result, Georgia got railroads and loans without having to pay for them. There would be future costs, measured in the state's inability to negotiate further loans with New York banks and from investors still angry over repudiation; in 1882 the New York legislature prohibited banks from investing in any Georgia bonds.[31]

Bullock denounced repudiation, denied any partnership with Kimball, and defended the validity of his acts, saying, "Every bond was issued [and recorded] in accordance with law." He had negotiated bonds only after the state legislature approved them to authorized railroad lines or to satisfy state expenses. The public debt increased by $11,483,400 from $6,256,635 on July 4, 1868, when he took office. Of the increase, $4,800,000 went for state expenses; railroad bond endorsements made up the rest. In 1870, a reporter for the New York Times wrote, in slightly exaggerated terms, that although Georgia's public debt was larger than ever, "her resources now are as ample to meet it as they ever before were to meet her obligations and to maintain her credit unimpaired. . . . Georgia, in fact, considering her resources and the great railroad she owns, is perhaps in better financial condition than any state in the Union."[32]

Bullock concurred with the repudiation of all lithographed or currency bonds still unaccounted for; those had been temporary issues to be returned once they were replaced by gold bonds. When Bullock discovered that Kimball continued to use the $250,000 in temporary bonds he had obtained for the Opera House, he agreed that was illegal but denied state culpability. Even though Bullock learned of Kimball's actions after the fact, he was negligent for not ensuring that Kimball return the temporary bonds. All others who held the temporary issue returned them soon after receiving the gold bonds.[33]

Except for Kimball's misuse of the temporary bonds, all bond issues and use seem legitimate. In their clamor about unrestrained plundering the Democrats neglected to notice that Bullock could have used an additional $1 million of bonds authorized by the act of September 15, 1870. No one questioned their charges or asked why he canceled bonds he could have endorsed. Bullock insisted that the only fraudulent aspect of the bond question was "in the Democratic opinion that everything done by Republicans under the reconstruction acts is illegal and that the whole system of government which admits 'niggers' to participation in it is a 'fraud,' 'unconstitutional and void.'" He also chastised the 1877 constitutional convention for its refusal to let the courts decide the validity of claims against the state: "To make sure their repudiation should not be exposed, they denied the courts the right to hear and determine the legality of their action." Centrist leader Joe Brown called the bonds "*bona fide*" and identified the real source of the problem as "a political question . . . and the bitterest prejudices of the people have been appealed to and aroused against those who issued these bonds." Democratic leader Alexander H. Stephens refused to join other Democrats and came out against repudiation of the bonds: "In my opinion a refusal to pay them is nothing short of public swindling, not less infamous than the obtainment of money by an individual upon false pretenses and representations." The state of Georgia never did admit that the bonds were legal nor did investors reclaim one lost dollar.[34]

In October 1870, after approving its last state aid bill to railroads, the General Assembly took up a proposition to lease the Western and Atlantic Railroad to a private company. The road sent profits to the state treasury only five out of the thirty years since its laying, although the state received uncountable profits in increased property values, taxes, transportation, and commerce for its citizens. Governors had always used the road to pay off loyal supporters and recognized that promises of a job there could influence, in Joe Brown's words, "1,000 to 1,500 votes in an election."[35]

In 1868, Bullock appointed Edward Hulbert, former chief of voter registration for Georgia, as superintendent of the state railroad. Hulbert's experience as a supervisor with the Southern Express Company prepared him for the managerial duties required. His friendship with Bullock made him a logical choice. With Hulbert in control, the Western and Atlantic deposited $20,000 in the state treasury in August and $25,000 each month thereafter until September 1869. In an effort to lower costs, Hulbert reduced the number of workers from 566 to 415 in one month's time, probably by purging workers who were too avidly Democratic. In January 1870, Bullock replaced Hulbert for openly disagreeing with him over the rights of blacks to hold office. Bullock appointed his longtime ally Foster Blodgett, who had been serving as treasurer of the road since July, as its head. During his first two months as superintendent, Blodgett sent $45,000 to the state treasury. Thereafter, the road operated at a loss.[36]

In May and September 1870, in response to Blodgett's failure to send money to the treasurer, two committees of the state legislature investigated the condition, finances, and management of the Western and Atlantic. Blodgett testified that when he had taken over the job of superintendent, the road had outstanding debts of $106,328.34. He explained that although Hulbert paid the state treasury $150,000 from April to September 1869, this presented a false picture of the road's condition because actual net earnings for that period were $88,673.97. Comparing the expenditures for 1869 against those for 1870, Hulbert spent $985,633.80 to Blodgett's $2,043,293.87. Blodgett accused Hulbert of saving money by laying off workers, letting the road deteriorate, and not paying bills promptly. Blodgett claimed that after he had taken the job, "almost the entire earnings of the road have been expended in payment of contracts for material and stock . . . and in the purchase of new iron, rolling stock, motive power and equipment." [37]

Josiah R. Parrott affirmed Blodgett's testimony about the road's condition in late 1869, when he investigated it for the governor: "One-tenth of the cross-ties were rotten . . . causing the track to spread and many accidents to occur." Parrott said that Bullock and Blodgett acted on his recommendation to double the work force, "and work at once begun to put the road in proper condition." The investigative committees commended Blodgett's management and his reinvestment of earnings to improve the track. Neither committee found Blodgett guilty of mismanagement. Another committee in 1872 would conclude just the opposite.[38]

One other reason existed for the failure of the Western and Atlantic to pay money into the state treasury. Bullock ordered Blodgett to keep every cent possible in the railroad's account, thereby denying the state treasurer control over it. Bullock had been feuding with treasurer Nedom L. Angier since late 1868. Angier, a Centrist Republican, owed his appointment to the 1868 legislature, not to Bullock; thus Bullock could not remove him. Angier opposed Bullock's efforts to reseat black legislators, to purge whites ineligible under the test oath, and to return Georgia to military supervision. Angier disapproved when Bullock advanced Kimball $54,500 to furnish the Opera House without waiting for legislative approval, and he charged the governor with illegal use of state funds. Bullock called the charges unfounded and politically motivated.[39]

Upon investigation by the state legislature (during the time Bullock censured it for expelling blacks) the house adopted the minority report charging that the governor had misspent state money in a "reckless extravagant" way. The majority report held that Bullock had overstepped his authority but cited many precedents for doing so and concluded: "What he did was in good faith, believing . . . it was in the best interests of the State." These state officials seemed to overlook the fact that the Opera House could not have functioned as a capitol if Bullock had not furnished and heated the building. In 1870, another legislative committee reinvestigated the matter and affirmed that Bullock had acted in the state's best interests; in 1872, Redeemer committees charged him with conspiracy to defraud the state. The matter would remain unresolved until a Fulton County court tried Bullock on the matter in 1878.[40]

Angier also began to interfere with railroad promotions by writing New York banks and financiers telling them not to use state bonds without his approval and not to allow the governor to draw money on state accounts. Bullock correctly and easily overrode the treasurer by explaining to Northern bankers and investors that state law gave the governor the right to draw money and that Angier was not an overseer of bonds because "authority for their negotiation rests *entirely* with myself." Bullock further denounced Angier as one of "a small clique of political tricksters [who] are attempting to make capital for themselves with the rebel-democracy." Angier later admitted that he had been elected to the 1868 constitutional convention as a Republican, even though he supported the Democratic view that the freedmen were inferior to whites and should neither hold office nor sit on juries.[41]

Angier became increasingly hostile toward the governor when Bullock took "special pains to restrict the amount of money in the treasurer's hands." Bullock simply circumvented Angier by making the state railroad a subtreasury for his warrants. Blodgett, as railroad superintendent, paid some state bills, governor's warrants, and interest on state bonds. But Bullock instructed him only to cover those expenses if he could do so without injuring the railroad. Still, he encouraged Blodgett to honor his warrants: "The good of the public service requires that they be cashed." Among its expenditures, the subtreasury advanced $6,000 to keep the deaf and dumb asylum operating. Although certainly extralegal, these were not fraudulent actions aimed at lining anyone's pockets. Believing he had the authority to spend the money, and to prove that everything was aboveboard, Bullock opened the state's books to the Democratic editor of the *Atlanta Constitution*. Further, he instructed Blodgett to investigate any irregularity by railroad employees. Beyond that, Bullock kept out of affairs of the road. He gave Blodgett full charge and trusted him to do what was right, explaining that the duties of his office "were onerous and absorbing" and that he had no time "to interfere and intermeddle with the internal management of the State Road." Bullock insisted that he had confidence "in the ability and integrity of the Superintendent."[42]

Certainly, even in "normal" times, a governor has difficulty keeping track of the activities of every department of state government and must depend on trusted subordinates. During Reconstruction, when much of his time was committed to fighting the Klan and protecting black rights, Bullock had to lean heavily on his appointees. Because he had to fight Angier at every step, for every dollar, Bullock found an alternative source of funding. Blodgett managed the road in such a way as to free funds to cover bond issues and other expenses. Thus it appeared that Blodgett was stealing state funds for his own use. But no evidence of theft ever surfaced, only charges by Democrats, hostile newspapers, and Republican Centrists. Although no concrete evidence implicated Blodgett in any boodle, many Democrats wanted to believe that the head of the Georgia Republican party's Central Committee robbed the state. Democratic leaders fed that belief to encourage voters in future elections.[43]

By October 1870, Georgians agreed that something must be done to take the state road out of politics. Republicans hoped a successful lease would defuse the daily criticism of mismanagement and patronage. A lease might also perpetuate the jobs of many present road workers who owed their positions to Republican patronage and help them maintain their jobs when Democrats regained power. Many Democrats supported the lease to eliminate a bloc of Republican ballots by taking the road out of politics; of course, they still could trumpet allegations of corruption as a campaign issue and claim that the state had lost money because of the Republican administration.

Both sides agreed that the road needed major repairs, which the state could not afford; Blodgett put the figure at half a million dollars. Both sides hoped that leasing would put money into the treasury and provide profits without the problems involved in state ownership. By October 11, the legislature considered three options concerning the Western and Atlantic Railroad: make the repairs and retain it, lease it, or sell it.[44]

On October 24, the legislature passed a bill written by Joseph Brown which authorized the governor to lease the road for twenty years to the highest bidder. The state imposed several requirements on companies interested in obtaining the lease. To retain local control, a majority of lease-holders must be citizens of Georgia with at least five years' residency. To secure the road financially and to protect the state's interests, lessees must be worth half a million dollars over indebtedness and give an $8 million bond, $5 million of which had to be located within the state. Finally, the legislature set the minimum bid at $25,000 a month. Two days after the legislature authorized the lease, Bullock gave public notice inviting propos-als, stating the requirements for bidding, and establishing Christmas 1870 as the deadline for bids.[45]

Three companies formed to obtain the road. Joseph Brown headed one group, which included H. I. Kimball, Alexander H. Stephens, John P. King, and Henry B. Plant. A second company included Benjamin H. Hill, Atlanta capitalist and convict lessee John T. Grant, Pennsylvania Railroad presi-dent Thomas A. Scott, United States senator and former secretary of war Simon B. Cameron, and John S. Delano, son of the secretary of the in-terior. The third company of Atlanta businessmen, usually called the Seago group, did not boast the luminaries of its rivals. It did manage to add Fos-ter Blodgett to its party and offered Bullock stock in an effort to sway the governor.[46]

Certainly Bullock had a difficult time awarding the lease. He did not want to alienate any of these powerful men. Reflecting on his position, he knew that he owed his election to the political influence of Blodgett and Brown. His friendships with Kimball and Plant surely played on his mind. Yet he had to consider the prominent capitalists and national politicians.

In an effort to conciliate as many interests as possible, Bullock suggested that Brown and Hill consolidate their companies, and he threatened to refuse all bids and to reopen the bidding if they did not adopt his sug-gestion. Fearing they might lose the lease, the two groups unified and bid $25,000 a month—a move Reconstruction historian Alan Conway called "a pocketbook alignment of prominent political figures." Certainly, Hill seemed among strangers considering his earlier invective against Brown and Kimball. The Seago company bid $36,500 a month, an amount worth $2,760,000 more to the state over the twenty-year lease period; but be-cause it did not meet the bond requirements specified by the legislature to secure the contract, Bullock could not accept the bid. That left one bidder.[47]

On December 27, Bullock awarded the lease to the Brown-Hill combi-nation, a company one Atlanta stockholder called "the strongest ever in the South & . . . [whose] security embraces every road from here to St. Louis & every road in Georgia." In a letter to a member in Blodgett's company who failed to get the lease, Bullock justified his decision as harmonizing "all conflicting interests" and in "both the letter and spirit of the law . . . [as] best for the whole people of the state."[48]

Further, to avoid any possible conflict of interest in granting the lease, Bullock accepted Brown's resignation from the state's highest judicial office. Clearly Bullock was happy with the combination that won; surely, he thought, no one could accuse him of partisanship. He was wrong.[49]

Robert Toombs claimed that Bullock must be a secret shareholder in the company and denounced the lease as a scheme "gotten up solely to defraud the people of the state out of the road." Many Georgians believed Toombs. In 1872, 1876, and 1880, legislative committees investigated the propriety of the lease but found no evidence of any wrongdoing, although the 1872 committee's majority opinion stated: "We think that H. I. Kimball . . . manipulated Governor Bullock in procuring the lease." The minority judgment concluded that Bullock had acted correctly considering the securities restriction. Brown denied that Bullock had any interest in the lease. Ben Hill testified that Bullock "positively" was not involved personally except to insist that only a company representing all the state's political and business interests should get the lease. After each investigation, the state legislature voted to sustain the lease. In 1890, the legislature renewed the lease contract and thus vindicated Bullock's action, which removed the road from politics and guaranteed the state an income of $6 million over the twenty-year lease period. Perhaps Georgia might have reaped greater profits by retaining the road and managing it prudently, but the reality of political patronage reduced the chances and made the lease decision the most pragmatic choice. Most Georgians agreed with the decision.[50]

Most of the charges against Bullock came from Democratic leaders and their presses, labeled by journalist Hodding Carter in his 1969 exposition on the Southern press as a "journalistic judiciary," whose editors "used their type font as bullets, their newsprint as musket wadding, their ink as gunpowder, and their words as tinder." Carter described the Southern press as "a child of sectionalism and hate and fear begotten of bitterness, and defender of borders, which are defensible, and a morality, a slave morality, which is not." In 1871, Atlantan John Wilson wrote that the "partisan press" was hurling "reckless anathemas" against Bullock for "selfish and party purposes." The *Atlanta Constitution* and the *Augusta Chronicle* were two of the most bombastic, libelous papers in Reconstruction Georgia. The *Constitution*'s first issue, June 16, 1868, announced that its purpose was to counter Radical programs and unite Southerners against Reconstruction. But in many ways, the *Augusta Chronicle* led the way in slander and falsehood.[51]

In early 1871, future U.S. senator Thomas M. Norwood, under the pen name "Nemesis," used the columns of the *Chronicle* to ridicule and slander Bullock. Selected quotations from his four articles if strung together compose what became the myth-history of Reconstruction as developed in later years by Thomas Dixon, Margaret Mitchell, Claude Bowers, and other Southern apologists. Nemesis spoke directly to Bullock, calling him a "Satanic Majesty" who "confederated with brutal negroes and every thieving adventurer" to "force your way by the bayonet" on "a noble people, mourning under your wicked rule." Nemesis wondered why much of the world's evil came from men whose names began with the letter "B," among them Belshazzar, Bacchus, Barabbas, Borgia, Bluebeard, Blodgett, Beelzebub, Butler, and Bullock. The source of Nemesis's resentment can be found in his third obloquy: "Your efforts, born of fury and hate, to raise the negro to the station and dignity of the Southern white race, are as silly and futile as the attempt of Xerxes to bind the ocean with an iron chain."[52]

Bullock's efforts to develop the state's commercial and industrial capacity would have placed him in good stead had it not been for his insistence on black equality and right to hold office. Most white Georgians could not overcome their prejudices or abandon a way of life that depended on racial caste. Bullock understood why he was the object of scorn; his program of free labor represented the Northern victory which white Southerners could not accept. Bullock explained the slander and charges of corruption:

> The great issue has been and still is the question of reconstruction. Lifting the negro from slavery to citizenship and establishing governments with the colored man as a voter has aroused the dying hate of the kuklux democracy. . . . Had I seen fit, as I was earnestly urged to do, to pander to their prejudices, by betraying the principles of the republican party and shutting my eyes to a palpable violation of the laws and the wrong and injustice done by their expulsion of the colored members of the legislature . . . I would not only have escaped this ordeal, but these persons would have been as loud and intemperate in their praise, as they now are in their denunciation of me.[53]

But understanding the nature of the slander did not stop it. Democrats decried his use of executive pardons and claimed that a system of pardon brokerage existed that allowed criminals to buy their way out of the penitentiary. Bullock did make extensive use of the pardoning power and released people in approximately 400 of the 523 cases he evaluated. The *Savannah Morning News* interpreted his pardons as a way to ingratiate black voters and to incite whites to commit violent acts against pardoned freedmen. Without explaining his meaning, the editor of the *Augusta Chronicle* assailed Bullock's pardons as stemming from "corrupt motives and for the accomplishment of corrupt purposes." Benjamin H. Hill disagreed with his fellow Democrats: "I believe his action was based upon kindness of heart, more than upon any disposition to shield criminals from the punishment which was their due." Even Nedom Angier conceded that Bullock's pardons were not political because he pardoned as many Democrats as Republicans.[54]

Bullock insisted that his use of executive clemency met "the ends of justice on the one hand, and answered the claims of humanity on the other." He asked for others' opinions on the pardons of specific persons, listened to appeals from communities, and usually responded to requests from legislators, judges, and prosecutors about people wrongly convicted in their districts. Although newspapers claimed that he issued pardons on partisan grounds, Bullock explained that he made "a careful and conscientious examination" of each case. He insisted: "My action is the result of . . . purposes to do right." Bullock believed that if he were at fault it was because "I erred in judgment, and listened too easily to the promptings of mercy."[55]

Many of those pardoned had been indicted and imprisoned before or during the war, and witnesses for and against them had died. During the 1868 constitutional convention, Bullock supported a resolution that persons were being held in the state penitentiary "contrary to the reasonable demands of justice . . . and punishment inflicted on persons unmercifully, for minor offences" and should be released. Once he had the power of the pardon, he used it to free those who had been punished enough. Henry M. Turner recalled that Bullock "was very generous, and would listen to reason and proper appeals, and in many instances, where he knew persons had been penitentiared maliciously, he would pardon them. There are scores at liberty today who would have been in the penitentiary but for him."[56]

Bullock pardoned those whose punishment did not fit their crime. He granted clemency to Robert Garvin, who had committed petty larceny at age thirteen. He pardoned white females Jinsey Rawson and Jane McMasters, convicted in different cases for "living in a state of fornication with a negro." During the period from July 4, 1868, to July 4, 1871, Bullock ordered nineteen prisoners released who had served time for adultery, bigamy, fornication, miscegenation, and seduction. He released Daniel Newton after Newton served two months of a four-year sentence for being near the home of a man who thought he might steal his horse. Bullock ordered R. W. Chaffin released after learning that Chaffin had been pardoned by Governor Jenkins in 1866 but was still in jail. He released many prisoners such as Henry Jasper, who had served his time but could not pay the additional sentence of $25 in reparations because he was too poor. Samuel Gray, A. O. Garrard, and others were pardoned because they had served considerable portions of their time and were too ill or old to remain in jail or on convict lease. Referring to Garrard, Bullock commented that death was not the punishment contemplated. The governor granted clemency to Martha Mullins after she had served a year and a half of a life sentence for stealing a "small quantity of molasses from an out-house." Similarly, he released Jim Jones after one year of a life sentence for trying to reach through the floor of a general store to steal one dollar's worth of candy. He pardoned many others who had served four years or longer after the legislature reduced the punishment for burglary in the night from death to life imprisonment. In response to appeals from people in their communities stressing self-defense or improper evidence, Bullock also released forty-one alleged murderers and twenty-four who served time for voluntary manslaughter. Thirty others got pardons after doing time for vagrancy or using opprobrious words. All in all, Bullock's pardons interposed justice to those who had been, in Turner's words, "penitentiared maliciously."[57]

Of all the charges against Bullock, that of extravagance permeated every issue. Critics claimed that the state's money poured through his fingers and into the sewers or into the coffers of his friends. They howled against the number of bond issues, legislative costs—of course, had only one cent gone to what they considered an illegal legislature forced upon them by bayonets, they would have yelled corruption—excessive pardons, expenses for the capitol, rewards, and printing costs. In many ways they were right; Bullock could have done more to reduce the costs of state government. His problem was that he extolled a gospel of prosperity and held up the Republican party as the harbinger of unlimited growth and economic advancement. If he pinched pennies, he would not be able to create this impression of resurgent progress.

Still, the money he spent did bring physical growth in the form of a new capitol, governor's mansion, other public buildings, and over six hundred miles of railroads. The state's bonded debt did rise, but evidence of public improvements was all around. Over a million dollars had to be spent to pay off antebellum bonds. He did pay a lot of reward money, and the state's costs for printing legislative proceedings and his proclamations were $98,000—all printing was required by law. Certainly, governors used printing as a patronage device by naming the papers the state would pay to print those proclamations and proceedings. Undoubtedly, Bullock was as guilty as anyone in that type of favoritism. An act of June 20, 1874, discontinued state patronage of newspapers, but it also had the negative effect of reducing information on government proceedings to the people.[58]

In 1871, the two Radical newspapers in the state, the *Atlanta Daily New Era* and the *Savannah Republican,* existed only because of official patronage. Bullock knew the importance to the party of keeping these papers alive in Georgia's two largest cities. He ensured that printers got paid only for work actually produced, and he monitored their account books to be sure charges were fair. He might have cut costs by limiting the number of official proclamations, but because local officials were not enforcing the laws, he resorted to the only option he had to get his message out and to maintain a Republican viewpoint. With the conservative press overwhelmingly in control, Bullock's efforts were feeble and useless. In that sense he did throw money away.[59]

Bullock noted that the "outs" always scream extravagance, and he justified the costs because of "numerous ku klux outrages and murders . . . [which] made them necessary in order to uphold the law, protect life and property and if possible lead to the detection of the guilty parties." Joe Brown agreed that large awards led to "more frequent" arrests. From his own experience in the governor's chair, Brown attested, "I frequently offered rewards. . . . I think the large rewards offered by the governor have secured more arrests . . . [and are] the most efficient means the governor can use."[60]

While the charges and slander rocked the state, Bullock pursued economic development. The legislative elections of 1870 approached, Klan violence continued, and Bullock again sought help from Congress to protect lives in Georgia and to continue Republican rule. By 1871, the calumny, threats, and a hostile legislature forced Bullock to an extraordinary decision.

Chapter 7 ❧ Failure and Vindication

He certainly deserves to be impeached. He has committed
a hundred offenses, any one of which is sufficient to
convict him.
—Robert Toombs, 1871

The absolute supremacy of his power and his cool disdain
of trammels for three years constitute a picture of bold,
evil rule not often seen, and admirable in its malicious
and tyrannical consistency. The man made and unmade
Legislatures, toyed with the State's sacred sovereignty like
a worthless bauble, swayed the judiciary, and scattered
the people's money with the lavish liberality of a prince,
and the reckless caprice of a munificent madman.
—*Atlanta Constitution*, 1872

BULLOCK'S SUCCESS in getting Grant and Congress to remand Georgia
to military rule in February 1870 gave him a majority of Republicans in
both houses of the General Assembly. Through six of the next nine months
the Georgia legislature stayed in session and attempted to implement the
governor's program of economic development and black equality. Bullock
believed that if he remained in control and gained support, he might be
able to strengthen the Republican constituency and make Georgia a viable
two-party state.

Democratic charges of his administration's extravagance and fraud
brought the Democrats closer together and drove wedges among Republicans. While Georgia's Republican party increasingly fragmented under

pressure from white supremacists from without and the defection of Centrists from within, Bullock and his allies tried to persuade Congress to prolong the current legislature. He argued that legal representatives had been expelled from their seats for fifteen months and were entitled to sit for a full two-year term. If he could convince Congress of this, Bullock would maintain control for two more years. The outcome of this controversy portended the future of Bullock and Georgia's Republican party.

The legislature of 1870 passed bills for railroad aid at an unprecedented rate, and the working majority of Republicans also supported educational and voting reforms. The solons organized a statewide system of public schools for white and black children, which Bullock had tried unsuccessfully to get the previous legislature to do. The 1868 Democratic legislature provided for citywide elections for Atlanta councilmen; the new legislature ordered elections by wards. As a result, voters elected two black and two white Radicals to the Atlanta City Council. Black legislators initiated reforms in the penitentiary system which led to better treatment of convicts and a more accurate reporting system. Henry Turner proposed two measures that were too radical even for this legislature and consequently lost: he asked that women be enfranchised and that the state establish its own police force. Those reforms would have made Georgia a leader in sexual equality and provide a means to protect citizens when local law enforcement officials would or could not.[1]

If Congress supported prolonging the legislature, those representative and egalitarian-minded men might forge a new, progressive Georgia. Bullock and the black legislators did everything they could to persuade Congress to act. In so doing, they widened the rift in the party and pushed those Bullock called false Republicans into the enemy camp.

After ratifying the Fourteenth and Fifteenth Amendments, the legislature held an election for United States senators. The Republican majority believed Joshua Hill and H. V. M. Miller should be replaced because they had been elected by the illegal 1868 legislature. Because most Democrats refused to vote, Republicans quickly and easily elected Henry P. Farrow for the term ending March 4, 1873, and Richard Whiteley for the term ending March 4, 1871. After they chose Foster Blodgett to replace Whiteley in 1871, the gap in the Republican ranks widened.[2]

Bullock continued to fight Centrists and pretend Republicans—those opposed to black equality and Congressional Reconstruction. The feud with state treasurer Angier, whom Numan Bartley described as "the opportunistic and none-too-scrupulous state treasurer and Republican moderate," undoubtedly increased speculation that Bullock was plundering the state. Joe Brown did not believe that, but he withdrew his support from Bullock after the governor insisted on a third Reconstruction. John Bryant and John Caldwell were disappointed at not being appointed to high offices, and they increasingly castigated Blodgett and Bullock.[3]

On January 14, Bryant consummated his defection when he organized and led a meeting of Democrats and Centrists in Atlanta and called for Republicans to break from Bullock. Two weeks later, on January 26, Bryant was the Democratic and Republican Centrist candidate for Speaker of the House, but he lost to Richard McWhorter, the candidate backed by Bullock, Blodgett, and every black legislator. The next week, Bryant joined Caldwell and deposed senators Miller and Hill (who still claimed their seats) in Washington to lobby against Georgia's reorganization. Obviously, they were holders and seekers of office who saw their only chance to retain or gain power in compromising with the Democrats. They sought federal patronage because Bullock refused them state patronage. They appealed to a Congress growing weary of Georgia affairs. Denouncing Bryant's faction as self-serving, black Georgians continued to support Bullock. Even reactionary Democrat Robert Toombs was a bit startled by his new association with Bryant, Caldwell, and Brown and remarked: "Politics does make us acquainted with strange bedfellows."[4]

For the next six months, Congress wrestled with Georgia affairs as various committees and individuals investigated Terry's reorganization of the state legislature and listened to arguments for and against prolonging it. Democrats and Centrists protested Terry's actions in replacing illegal legislators with those who finished second in the 1868 elections.

In Congress, Benjamin Butler continued to be Bullock's ablest supporter. He introduced a bill for the readmission of Georgia to the Union which included prolonging the term of the new legislature for two years from the day Georgia gained readmission. Countering that move, Republican moderate John Bingham of Ohio sponsored an amendment to the Butler bill which deleted the proposal prolonging the legislature. In the Senate, Charles Sumner supported Bullock and denounced Bingham's amendment as "an engine of Rebel power." Conservative newspapers in Georgia applauded Bingham. The *Macon Telegraph* exulted that "Reconstruction, like the apples of Sodom, has turned to ashes."[5]

Bullock traveled to Washington whenever possible to urge members of Congress to support his plan. Altogether, in the first half of 1870 he consulted with legislators for over a month of days. Bryant was equally active and knew that if he could defeat Bullock, he would wrest control of the party in Georgia away from the Radicals and enhance his position among national Republicans. It was a bitter struggle.

Bullock argued that Georgia's legislature had never been organized correctly and Congress knew it; otherwise the passage of the act of December 22, 1869, authorizing General Terry's reorganization, was wrong. Because that act was valid, the old legislature was illegal and had no right to elect United States senators. The newly elected senators should be seated in their stead. Bullock called the other laws, acts, and orders of that legislature legal because they consisted of the ordinary business of the state and not its status within the Union. He cited the precedent of the March 1867 Reconstruction Acts, which allowed 1865–66 legislative acts to stand despite the words, "No legal State governments exist in the rebel States." Bullock insisted that he did not want Congress to "extend any officer's official term" but asserted that the legislators be permitted to serve "the constitutional term for which they were elected." He demanded that they uphold the moral position they had assumed "so that when the regular legal time for the election shall have arrived, it will be a free and fair expression of political preferment on the part of the voter, whether he be poor, ignorant, and black, or rich, arrogant, and white. Whether he be Republican or Democrat, Radical or Ku-Klux."[6]

To prove his commitment to principle, Bullock stated that if President Grant or General Terry thought the state could benefit "in the least degree by my retirement, it will be a pleasure for me to yield the office." He claimed that he was losing money that could be regained only if he reentered the business world. He complained of losing sleep because of threats to his life. If national leaders thought it necessary for the good of the party, Bullock would resign immediately. But, he added, "Rebel faultfinding and abuse . . . will never accomplish that result." To those who claimed he acted only for personal gain, Bullock answered that since taking the governor's chair he had endured "assassination" threats and "the most villanous slanders . . . charging corruption in office, personal immorality, and in every way impeaching my character as a man and an officer." Then, revealing pride and the shame he felt by having his name dragged through the slime, he lamented, "Fortunate . . . is he who saves his life even though he lose that which to every man should be dearer than life, dearer than pecuniary advancement—his good name and fame." Bullock was a man of moral conviction who sought recognition on the side of progress. He would not sell out.[7]

Bullock claimed that those Republicans who stood against him sought personal gain instead of public benefit. He called them "disappointed aspirants for position," friends of Joshua Hill, or persons who feared an investigation into their past. Among those he named were Bryant, Caldwell, Angier, and John Bowles. The first three were well-known Bullock haters. Bowles was the son-in-law of Joshua Hill and had recently been removed by Grant from his position as federal tax collector in Augusta and replaced by, in Bullock's words, "a worthy colored man." These and other Centrists fought a desperate political battle to gain control of the party in Georgia.[8]

Bryant and others wrote letters, made public statements, and published slanderous articles depicting Bullock as a charlatan who sought pecuniary gain, a man capable of doing anything to further his personal position. In an open letter to Charles Sumner, Bryant claimed he had "fully trusted" Bullock until Bullock slighted those who had helped elect him by appointing many former Rebels and Democrats to office when there were Republicans desiring those positions.[9]

Bullock appointed people to positions as judges, justices of the peace, notaries, and other high positions within his control on the basis of qualifications, not party affiliation. He did not appoint capriciously or unnecessarily, once explaining to the General Assembly: "The multiplying of official positions is not generally deemed desirable nor advantageous except by those who may aspire to such positions." Many Republicans, who saw political victories in terms of patronage, questioned this policy. H. L. Carroll of Blairsville wanted to know why Bullock made appointments "from the ranks of our enemies" and not from "our own party." Carroll complained that the Democrats would give few jobs to Republicans because "Democrats love office like the Tiger."[10]

In truth, both Democrats and Republicans craved office "like the Tiger." Bullock did use the state railroad to political advantage, but he referred letters asking for jobs there to the superintendent of the road, either Hulbert or Blodgett, and deferred to their decisions in hiring. As chairman of the Republican party in Georgia, Blodgett undoubtedly took advantage of his position to influence appointments. It is most likely that Bullock focused on business and let Blodgett distribute the bulk of the patronage.

Continuing his assault, Bryant asserted that Bullock was not interested in helping the party or the freedmen but wanted only to prolong the legislature so "that he might cover up financial operations, and elect Foster Blodgett to the United States Senate." Bryant wrote an open letter to Sumner saying that Georgia's black legislators who supported Bullock—and all but two of them did—were "selfish . . . [and] ignorant" men who did not truly represent the freedmen. He contended that black Georgians no longer wanted black representatives in office. Bryant announced that he represented the true voice of Georgia blacks, even though admitting, "I was denounced by their pimps as an enemy of the colored race." Insisting that "this is not a contest for or against colored men's rights," he asked Sumner to vote for the Bingham amendment. But Sumner and other Radicals knew who befriended black rights. They sided with Bullock.[11]

A ten-man delegation of black Georgia legislators, including Simeon Beard, Tunis Campbell, and his son Tunis, Jr., George Wallace, and Romulus Moore, met with congressmen and with President Grant to oppose the Bingham amendment. They asked that Georgia blacks be allowed to retain what gains they had made, and they denounced Bryant for not representing black interests. Bryant paid them little heed and continued along his course.[12]

Bryant attacked the *Washington Chronicle*, the Republican organ in the nation's capital, for joining Bullock in misrepresenting conditions in Georgia. Bryant stopped short of accusing editor John Forney of accepting bribes, but he did assert that Forney readily published Bullock's and Blodgett's dispatches against the Bingham amendment. Bullock admitted paying the *Chronicle* to print pamphlets and speeches which illustrated his views on the Butler bill and Bingham amendment, but he denied fabricating tales of terrorism or paying bribe money. Not one charge of bribery was ever proven. Bryant implored the congressmen to disregard reports in the *Chronicle* and to support Bingham. He claimed that Bullock controlled several of Georgia's Democratic newspapers, which published "violent anti-reconstruction articles, to abuse President Grant, a Republican Congress, and even Governor Bullock himself, when necessary for the accomplishment of his purposes." [13]

In reality, the Democratic press overwhelmingly supported Bryant's efforts. The *Atlanta Constitution* printed the following bit of political reverse psychology aimed at ridiculing the governor and creating the impression that his stories of Klan violence were false:

Wanted—Ku Klux Outrages

Wanted a liberal supply of Ku-Klux Outrages in Georgia. They must be as ferocious and bloodthirsty as possible. No regard need be paid to truth. Parties furnishing, must be precise and circumstantial. They must be supplied during the next ten days to influence the Georgia Bill in the House. Accounts of Democrats giving the devil to Republicans are preferred. A hash of Negroes murdered by Ku-Klux will be acceptable. . . . The highest cash paid. Apply to R. B. Bullock, or the Slander Mill, Atlanta, Ga, and to Forney's Chronicle, Benjamin F. Butler, or the Reconstruction Committee, Washington, D.C. Georgia Railroad Bonds traded for this commodity.[14]

Conservative papers outside the state joined the attack. The *New York World* reached the nadir of irresponsible journalism with its report that Bullock had resorted to "the use of the female body in connection with the Georgia business." Probing all available avenues, Bryant wrote one of Bullock's former associates with the Adams Express Company asking for any information that might indicate bad character, but James Thompson responded that he knew "nothing against Gov. Bullock's character" and had "never heard anyone speak ill of him. Always understood him to be a high-toned gentleman."[15]

After Bryant claimed that "any amount of corruption could be proved against Bullock," Bullock asked the Senate Judiciary Committee to make him show evidence to back the charges. Bryant's evidence consisted of innuendo and hearsay. The committee investigated the charges of improper lobbying of senators and of bribing Forney. The majority report, written by Centrists Lyman Trumbull and Roscoe Conkling, held that although Bullock had done nothing unlawful, his efforts went beyond propriety. The minority report found Bullock innocent of any wrongful behavior, but it blamed Forney for charging "extravagant" prices for printing Bullock's articles. Certainly Bullock's efforts were heavy-handed. His agreement to pay Forney's prices indicated that he would do anything necessary to get his views before the Senate. Bullock probably thought the prices extravagant and guessed that by paying them he was paying bribe money. Historian T. Harry Williams's observation that "there is some terrible sense of urgency in the psychology of politicians who are driven by a sense of mission, a gnawing fear that time may be running out on them," seems particularly applicable to Bullock in 1870. If he did engage in questionable acts, something yet unproven by the evidence, Bullock believed he was losing the fight to Democrats and their Centrist allies.[16]

Bullock understood that Centrists were trying to take control and if successful would end Radical Reconstruction, and he accused them of using the "most atrocious lies and insinuations." He blamed Joshua Hill for starting a rumor that he had offered $10,000 in railroad bonds for one vote against the Bingham amendment. Clearly disheartened by the charges against him, Bullock scolded "pretend" Republicans: "I have been deeply discouraged by Republican Senators and Representatives . . . [who are] repeating and giving credence to the vile slanders of rebels and renegade Republicans." He reasserted his belief that the Bingham amendment would kill the Republican party in Georgia and return the state to "the very men and the very party" who had always fought against Reconstruction. Playing off Grant's inaugural declaration, "Let us have peace," Bullock warned: "I will not deny that this result would bring peace to Georgia; but it would be a peace of death. Republican principles would be abandoned forever. . . . There is no 'relief from the disability' [of being Radical] except in death, submission, or in flight." Then he tried to shame Congress into action by citing its expenditures to protect frontier settlers from Indians while doing little for "white and black friends of the Union [who] are whipped and murdered in the South." [17]

Ultimately, Bullock told Republicans that defeat of the Bingham amendment would "give full force to the great living principles of universal freedom." If they failed to vote for prolongation, the "responsibility for the utter destruction of Republicanism in Georgia will be with yourselves and not with us." He had done all he could.[18]

His efforts failed. Critics of prolongation called the scheme undemocratic. They could not lift their heads from the sand long enough to admit that Georgia had never had a democratic government; now the white man's democracy would continue for another century. They refused to understand that Klan violence and intimidation would thrust Democrats back into power if elections took place as scheduled, and they did not seem to care. They were weary of fighting white Georgians.

On July 15, 1870, despite the efforts of Butler, Sumner, and Bullock, Congress voted to readmit Georgia under Bingham's plan. They also decided to seat the two senators elected by the illegal 1868 legislature over those elected after reorganization. Clearly tired of the whole matter of Georgia's Reconstruction, they capitulated to the Democrats. Grant provided little or no leadership, and his Southern program as described in one newspaper was an "incomprehensible muddle and mystery, a parable that cannot be understood, a riddle that defies all guesswork." In response to a plea from Butler's son-in-law Adelbert Ames, the carpetbag governor of Mississippi, Grant revealed his hand: "The whole public are tired out with these annual autumnal outbreaks in the South, and the great majority are now ready to condemn any interference on the part of the government." Sumner and Butler could not maintain the force of their appeals to higher law. Even black Mississippi senator Hiram Revels's speech in support of Bullock and "for the helpless loyal people of Georgia . . . in the hour when a reconstructed State most needs support" availed little. Bryant's assaults on Bullock's character and accusations of corruption, even though unsupported, added to the Radical defeat and slandered Bullock personally. Revels's admonition that "he who permits oppression shares the crime" made no impact because national Republicans would give no more help. Any chance for Georgia Radicals lay within their own state.[19]

Butler published an open letter in the *New York Times* advising Bullock that nothing enacted by Congress required the Georgia legislature to schedule an election until it "chooses to have one" as long as the election came within two years. Clearly, Butler's interpretation of the final Georgia bill was not what Congress had in mind when it provided "that nothing herein should be taken to extend the term of any member . . . beyond the time fixed by the Constitution." But Butler insisted that delaying the election would not "extend" the time; it would only ensure a full term. Bullock supported that idea and promoted measures to that effect in the state legislature. In August, the senate voted twenty-one to fourteen for prolongation. The struggle in the lower house was closer.[20]

Joe Brown worked actively to persuade legislators not to delay elections past 1870. Henry Farrow, a longtime Bullock supporter, broke with the governor over this issue even though United States circuit judge John Erskine implored: "Stand by him, for I know he stood by you." Farrow encouraged legislators to vote against prolongation. Reflecting Grant administration policy, U.S. attorney general Amos Akerman sided against prolongation and believed that in a "fair election" Republicans would do all right. He said that even if Democrats won, Bullock had two more years and thus could provide a constitutional check on any outrageous legislation.

While citing "the atrocities of November, 1868," Akerman nevertheless believed that the "Democratic frenzy . . . has subsided." Republicans had had
two years to bring Georgians "to reason," and, in a statement revealing a
real misunderstanding of white Democrats, he said: "We can at least try
the experiment of trusting them." [21]

On August 11, 1870, by the vote of Democrats and Centrists and with
the influence of Brown, Farrow, Grant, and Akerman, legislators in the
Georgia house voted seventy-three to sixty-three not to prolong their terms.
Centrists could claim responsibility for stopping Bullock because twelve
white Republicans voted with the Democrats; African-Americans voted for
prolongation. Those opposing Bullock celebrated, and Republicans most
prominent in orchestrating the defeat received congratulatory letters. Republican senator Matthew Carpenter of Wisconsin, a Centrist, wrote Farrow predicting a Republican victory in the next Georgia election. Carpenter foolishly believed that Georgians would not prove "that the 'lost cause'
though lost is still cherished, and that the authority of the government is
only submitted to, not cherished." [22]

The legislature set the election for December 20–22 and, in an attempt
to ensure its fairness, changed election procedures. Bullock would pick
three of the five election managers for each county; the county ordinary
picked the other two. The legislature restricted voting to county courthouses to prevent intimidation in the countryside. Only one voter at a time
could come within fifteen feet of the ballot box and, after voting, must
withdraw to no closer than fifty feet. That way, black voters would have a
chance to penetrate the barrier Democrats had raised in 1868 by physically
denying the vote to anyone holding a Republican ballot. Bullock supported
these measures. Throughout his term he tried to ensure voting rights. He
vetoed all General Assembly measures that attempted to limit the franchise to property owners. Bullock understood that those measures aimed at
black disfranchisement and said they violated "the principles of republican
government." [23]

In appointing election managers, Bullock sought recommendations from
Republican leaders in each county. As a result, most of his appointments
went to Republicans who followed the party line. Bullock made no racial
distinction in these appointments and named many blacks. Black election
managers were supposed to ensure a fair election while persuading more
freedmen to vote. As the election drew closer, Bullock reminded all election
managers that every twenty-one-year-old male who met the state's six-

month and county's thirty-day residency requirements would be allowed to vote. He asked them to speed the voting and not delay a voter with excessive questioning. Only those who could not take an oath that they voted without bribes, had committed treason, or were prisoners or mentally ill would be denied a vote. To allow more freedmen to vote, legislators suspended poll taxes, and Bullock offered rewards of $100 for the arrest and conviction of anyone interfering with voters. He asked General Terry to deploy soldiers in several Georgia cities where election day troubles were likely.[24]

Bullock also asked Representative Benjamin Butler and Senators Simon Cameron, Oliver Morton, and John Thayer not to seat Georgia's senators until after the election. He asked them to let it be known that they were watching closely to see if Georgians were committed to "the absolute preservation of the public peace during the election and the permission of Union men, white and colored, to vote freely." If Klansmen were active and did not allow a free vote, the Senate would refuse to seat Georgia's senators or restore the state to the Union. At the time, the Senate was pondering which two of Georgia's four elected senators, Hill, Miller, Farrow, and Whiteley, to seat. Beyond these measures and suggestions, Bullock referred all letters concerning the election to Blodgett and other members of the state central committee, who decided all "questions of political policy." Republicans hoped that these positive steps would allow their constituents to return them to power.[25]

They were wrong. There were several reasons for the Republican defeat. Allegations in the press of carpetbag and scalawag corruption focused on Bullock and helped unite opposition to him. The split in Republican ranks led to personal confrontations that damaged the united effort necessary to win an election. The failure of the military to provide a presence in past elections emboldened the Ku Klux Klan and undermined the determination of Republicans who were afraid of retaliation if they voted their consciences. Citizens who might have voted Republican could hardly help from looking back over three years in which the military failed to secure lives and property against Democratic violence. They no longer dared stand up to the Klan. And the Klan was very active before the election.

Republican George Clower wrote from Forsyth that "the Democrats is in company and going through the Country and shooting a[t] many the republican Every night and trying to skier them out againce the day of the Election." Clower accused Democrats of paying freedmen not to vote and

telling them that on election day, policemen would arrest anyone attempting to vote Republican. In Greene County, sixty-five Klansmen beat black
legislator Abram Colby for campaigning among the freedmen and for naming a son Foster Blodgett. Bullock received a letter from Sparta warning
him that his "life is at stake" and saying that the Democrats would control
the ballot box there.[26]

Democratic actions proved stronger than Republican election laws.
Democrats disregarded election procedure and formed in phalanxes around
the polls to keep Republicans from voting. Deputy Marshal Josiah Sherman of Columbia County described the "awful oaths" and threats of Klan
retaliation and murder against those who voted Republican in Appling:

> For an hour or more voting went off briskly without any apparent trouble
> or intimidation to speak of until, to appearance, the democrats had mostly
> voted; and when the republicans, or those who carried their votes in their
> pockets, preferring not to show their ticket, made an effort to get to the
> ballot-box, then threats began in good earnest; swearing and shoving, and
> slinging slung shot; exhibiting the bowie knife . . . and using other methods
> of intimidation; closing up the passage-way with white men that had voted,
> twenty, thirty, and perhaps fifty men at a time, so placed before the passage-
> way that it was impossible for a man who did not show the democratic vote
> to get through, and if one did, a cry would start up, "Mark him, d——n
> him, mark him."[27]

In Sparta, Democrats carried through their promise to control the election. Powerful planter-lawyer Linton Stephens used his influence to force
the sheriff to arrest the three Bullock-appointed election managers and replace them with Democrats. Then he insisted that no person would vote
who had not paid the poll tax. In small cities and towns throughout Georgia, the old leaders controlled the vote.[28]

As a result, Democrats won 71 of the 86 contests for house seats and 19
of 22 senate seats to take overwhelming control of the legislature. In the
next legislature, Democrats would control the senate with 29 members to
14 Republicans and 1 Independent; in the house, they enjoyed a 136 to 29
to 9 advantage. And the 10 so-called Independents were actually Democrats
who always supported the majority. Bullock realized what had transpired,
blamed the failure of Reconstruction on the "ruling clique" of prewar
leaders, and acknowledged defeat: "That the Klan finally overthrew me I
must admit."[29]

The Democratic victory emboldened the Klan. In Louisville, thirty disguised men entered the jailhouse, removed the black prisoners, sliced off one man's ear, killed another with a dozen bullets, told the others to leave town forever, and warned that no more freedmen who went against whites would find escape in jails. Bullock wrote one letter after another to law enforcement and judicial officers imploring them to do their duty. But civil officers were afraid of Klan retaliation; one admitted, "I know my duty, but *I dare not do it.*" Judge H. D. D. Twiggs responded: "No one dare express his opinion for fear he be 'visited.'" In Robert Toombs's neighborhood, Klansmen warned Bullock appointee B. D. Evans that "no damned Radical shall live in this County" and announced their intention to "cleanse the county" of Radicals. "You are aware that one of your town gentlemen received the leaden bullet as a reward for office seeking. We say to you again beware. Gov. Bullock may appoint you when you apply but vengeance is ours and we will have it. . . . [You have ten days to] leave this latitude."[30]

Realizing he had no control over the new legislature, Bullock refused to call it into session until November 1, 1871. In Washington, the Senate refused to acknowledge the petitions of Farrow and Whiteley, deciding, on grounds of equity, to seat Joshua Hill and H. V. M. Miller. The next year, over the formal protest of twenty-two Georgia legislators, the Senate refused to seat Foster Blodgett. Clearly, the federal government was in full retreat from its Reconstruction agenda. It would give no further aid to Georgia Radicals except to pass a series of so-called Enforcement Acts aimed at protecting voting rights under the Fifteenth Amendment and stopping Klan violence. Reflecting on the situation and his actions as governor, Bullock said: "I have no fault to find or regrets to express, except that gentlemen claiming high position in the Republican party North lack the moral courage to sustain the results of their own acts." Bullock was a lame duck extraordinaire. During 1871, without a federal or state government to support him, he could do little more than watch the railroads being built, pardon the worthy, and appoint Georgians to positions within his official patronage.[31]

Bullock appointed more than one hundred people to county boards of education to fill vacancies created when counties refused to hold elections for those posts, elected officials refused to serve, or incumbents died. He selected notaries, justices of the peace, and solicitors, provided information for federal appointments, and revoked some commissions after receiving further information on certain individuals. He continued to ask for advice from Radicals before he made selections, and he appointed blacks to many positions. His choice of James Simms as district judge for the Savannah circuit caused an enormous outburst of criticism.[32]

Savannah district attorney T. R. Mills resigned his commission and claimed that to serve under a black judge would be "monstrous." The attack by "Nemesis" in the *Augusta Chronicle* surpassed all others in its vituperation: "I learn that there were five other applicants, well endorsed for this office; that all, except Simms, were white men. . . . The spiritual miscegenation of your Excellency with this child of Ebo [repulses me]. . . . I leave you to suck the honied-dew from His Honor's responsive lips." As early as 1869, Bullock expressed "great confidence in the judgment" of Simms; in 1871 he defended Simms as "a very good man . . . [with a] fair education, his moral character is excellent, and possessed [of] far more than natural ability . . . a great credit to himself and his race." Bullock refused to reverse his appointment.[33]

Throughout 1871, Bullock pondered what to do as Redeemer control of the legislature stared him in the face. Most Georgia editors called for impeachment as they had done since 1868. But in earlier days, the national government backed Bullock and the state legislature dared not impeach him. But three years had passed and there was little hope that congressional Radicals could rally, return the party to its moral heights, and sustain the promise of equality. The revolution of Reconstruction encountered unpredictable opponents who continued the war in guerrilla fashion against a free labor system, against the notion that blacks were equal citizens.

Bullock feared for his life and his liberty. He believed that the incoming legislators were capable of anything. He recognized the probability of impeachment and knew that even if he escaped what certainly would be a criminal conviction, something not possible considering the temper of the times, he would be removed from any official duties while the investigation proceeded. It was not necessary to convict him; all the Democrats had to do was to begin impeachment hearings and they would effectively remove him. As the day approached for the Redeemer legislature to convene, Bullock made a difficult decision. He resolved to try to perpetuate Republican power by resigning from office, which he called "the last move to check and defeat . . . [my] political enemies." He was bitter and confused in this personal capitulation. On October 23, nine days before the legislators met, Bullock wrote his resignation, effective on October 30. He entrusted it, along with all the property of the governor's office, to his executive secretary, R. H. Atkinson, and, telling no newspaperman of his actions, boarded a train for the nation's capital.[34]

If anyone other than Atkinson knew of Bullock's decision, he or she never revealed it, although it seems reasonable that Conley and Blodgett were informed. On October 30, Atkinson handed Bullock's resignation to Georgia secretary of state David G. Cotting. Cotting accepted it, immediately notified Benjamin Conley, president of the senate, and informed him that he had ten days to take the oath of office as governor or the job would fall to the Speaker of the House. Conley took the oath of office that day. The news stunned most Georgians. The *Atlanta New Era*'s speculation that perhaps Bullock had acted to protect the state's business and material interests was the lone voice of support. Democratic editors statewide celebrated Bullock's departure, called the resignation "equivalent to a plea of *guilty*," and called for an investigation and trial.[35]

On October 31, newspapers printed Bullock's letter of resignation and his letter of explanation "To My Political Friends and the Public." Bullock contended that the rebellion of 1860 continued because Rebels planned to overturn the Northern victory by defeating Reconstruction. He cited "information, the truth of which cannot be doubted," that the incoming legislature planned to regain complete control of the state by quickly preferring impeachment charges against him "without previous investigation." Bullock said that the promotion of Conley to the executive chair would "defeat this nefarious scheme of these desperate political conspirators."[36]

Under Georgia law, the president of the senate became governor when the elected governor resigned, died, or was disabled. Knowing he could not wait for the new legislature to meet, for it would surely elect a Democrat as president of the senate, Bullock made the rational choice. He secured a tactical victory over the forces of the reactionary planter leadership of Robert Toombs and other "unrepentant Rebel leaders, who, though comparatively few in numbers, move the masses by the irresistible pressure of sectional hate and social proscription." Bullock said he had persevered for three long years "against the assaults of these people upon the cause of equal rights and Republican Government"; he could not continue the unequal contest. He predicted that the press would declare him guilty of many crimes, and he said he welcomed the chance for a fair trial, "not the result of political bias and prejudice." He warned Georgians that if they continued to follow the old leaders, who counseled ignoring the Fourteenth and Fifteenth Amendments and insisted on the rightness of the Lost Cause, they risked another rebellion and the reversal of progress toward incorporating the South into the national mainstream.[37]

Once in Washington, Bullock met with Simon Cameron, Columbus Delano, and others, all of whom advised him not to return to Georgia. Bullock took a train to New York City, arriving there the day the Georgia legislature convened. He told a reporter for the *New York Times* that he desired a fair investigation into his conduct as governor and he intended to return to Georgia as soon as he could. The *New York Standard* reported Bullock's resignation and flight as part of the continuing effort by old secessionists to retain power. The *Standard* concluded that Bullock's "crime was that he believed in Union." Knowing he could not soon return to Atlanta, Bullock confided that friends warned that he would be " 'Ku-Kluxed' by a mob." [38]

When the legislature met on November 1, Georgia returned to Democratic rule. White Democrats celebrated the boast of one Atlanta editor that the Radicals "are gone—gone so far into the past that fame, with the trumpet of a thousand Gabriels, will never be able to resurrect them." Newspapers wildly accused Bullock of stealing from one to five million dollars and of planning to leave the country. In Atlanta, senators elected Leander Newton Trammel of Whitfield County (Dalton) president of the senate. Members of the house put Muscogee County representative James Milton Smith into the Speaker's chair. Almost immediately came a resolution that Conley sat illegally and should be replaced by Trammel. Trammel rejected that notion from fear that it might provoke further intervention from Congress. On November 22, legislators passed an act, over Conley's veto, setting December 19 for an election for a new governor. On December 6, a Democratic caucus unanimously nominated outspoken Radical-hater James M. Smith for governor.[39]

Conley tried to assuage the Democrats, but he further antagonized them by announcing himself "a consistent and unyielding Republican." He believed that "republican institutions rest upon the virtue and intelligence of the people," supported liberal educational endowments for both races, encouraged a full payment of the state debt, and continued the humanitarian program of pardons. He vetoed an act repudiating some of the state's bonds. He pardoned Blodgett, who was under indictment for larceny of state railroad funds, because he believed the charges against Blodgett were false, that they were political in origin, and that the situation made it impossible for Blodgett to get a fair trial. Georgia Republicans praised Conley for the pardon; Democrats asserted that it proved Blodgett's guilt.[40]

Republicans hoped that Congress or President Grant would prevent any election until the regular one scheduled for November 1872. Bullock was confident that national Republicans would sustain Conley "against any usurpation on the part of the rebel element," but Conley had reliable information that Grant was "reticent and non-committal" and had adopted a wait-and-see attitude. Conley promoted a plan of nonparticipation in the upcoming election and asked supporters not to vote for anyone. Blodgett went to Washington, met with Akerman, Grant, and others, and dismally reported to Conley that although they all supported him, they "seemed at a loss to know how it could be done." Blodgett chastised them as "timid and weak kneed as they usually have been about our matters."[41]

In the end, Blodgett's assessment proved correct. Akerman wrote directly to Conley that Northern Republicans were tired of fighting the South. "Even such atrocities as KuKluxery do not hold their attention. . . . The Northern mind being active and full of what is called progress, runs away from the past." Akerman feared that Northerners failed to grasp that Southerners "are still untaught in the elements of the Republican creed."[42]

Akerman meant "republican creed" and was accurate in his appraisal of Southern intransigence on matters of racial equality. In Georgia, Reconstruction and the Republican party died quick deaths before fireworks brought in the New Year 1872.

On December 19, voters elected James Smith governor in an election without a Republican candidate. With the election of Smith preordained, few citizens bothered voting and newspapers did not print election returns; in fact, only 35,000 of the state's 225,000 registered voters cast ballots. Conley forwarded the returns to the legislature and cited the low voter turnout as proof that Georgians believed the election was illegal. Many Republicans implored Conley to refuse to yield, but without support from Washington, he could do little else. Bowing to defeat, Conley did not contest the election.[43]

By the time Smith became governor on January 12, the legislators had overturned much of the work of Reconstruction. They ordered the governor to withhold all endorsements of bonds issued by railroads incorporated since July 4, 1868. They then began to nullify black votes. Democrats quickly changed the charter of the city of Atlanta to provide for citywide elections to eliminate the election of Republicans by ward vote. They passed an act over Conley's veto which provided for the appointment of boards of commissioners for several counties in which blacks had a numerical majority. Redeemers overrode another Conley veto to affirm that poll taxes must be paid retroactively through 1868 before voters could vote in future elections. They changed the law for choosing county school board members from a system of county elections to grand jury appointments, and the grand juries were always white. By 1875, the state had defined sharecroppers as wage workers with no control of the land or crops until after shares had been divided. Further, the supreme court ruled that the homestead exemption could be waived and creditors could take everything a small farmer owned.[44]

In 1875, English visitor Edward King wrote that Reconstruction was "null and void in Georgia. . . . Out of the 90,000 colored voters in the State, scarcely 30,000 vote today; free schools are almost unknown outside the large cities. . . . The negroes are grossly intimidated; and the ku-klux faction still exists as a kind of invisible empire." Legislative committees, under the direction and control of Robert Toombs, who was neither a member of the legislature nor a citizen of the United States, investigated Bullock, and Smith sent special marshal John B. Cumming to New York to arrest him and return him to Georgia.[45]

Cumming spent over a month in New York State and Canada looking for Bullock but never found him. Cumming reported to Smith that the "fugitive from justice" was protected by New York governor John Hoffman, a Democrat, who "refused to grant my demands." Cumming hired three private detectives to locate Bullock. They searched New York City, Buffalo, Albany, Albion, and, on a false tip that Bullock was hiding in Canada, looked in Toronto, Montreal, St. Catharines, and Niagara City. Cumming hired other detectives who searched the towns between Buffalo and Rochester. Cumming returned to Georgia empty-handed. Smith waited four years before sending another marshal after Bullock.[46]

Bullock wisely avoided arrest. Political fervor remained too high for him to get a fair trial, and he little cherished the thought of languishing in jail or being murdered by Klan zealots. A committee of the Georgia legislature, along with adviser Robert Toombs, went to New York in April and asked Bullock to meet with them, even offering to pay him $100 a day. By this time, Governor Hoffman had issued an executive warrant allowing Bullock's arrest. Thus Bullock declined the offer, sent attorneys in his stead, and said that Toombs and company would use any pretext to have him "carried back to Georgia a prisoner, to be crucified . . . for my political sins against the Ku Klux Klan." After a meeting with Democrats in Atlanta, journalist Edward King affirmed Bullock's decision: "If they could lay hands on Bullock they would put him in the penitentiary." Not until 1876 did Bullock return to Georgia to face his accusers.[47]

Early in his exile, Bullock lived in Buffalo and his family stayed with his parents at the house on the corner of Liberty and Park streets in Albion. When he felt safe enough, Bullock joined them there. Unlike their stay in Atlanta, the Bullocks actively participated in life outside their home, undoubtedly because in Albion they did not have the besieged mentality they had had in Georgia. In 1874, Bullock's wife, Marie, gave birth to a son, Hugh. Their son Volkert, eleven, and daughter Cornelia, eight, attended Orleans County schools; Volkert graduated from his father's alma mater, the Albion Academy. The Bullocks actively supported community affairs and joined the social life in Albion. A lifelong advocate of education, Bullock subscribed to three shares of stock in the Albion Library Association and promoted the construction of a new library. Always active in church, he served for three years as a vestryman of Christ Episcopal Church. But beyond those activities, Bullock depended on his parents' graciousness for his living and was not gainfully employed. His financial situation was precarious. Late in 1872, he wrote Joe Brown: "I am *not* revelling in ill gotten (or other) gains at Paris, London, Egypt or other of the places named for me by the accommodating newspapers." As his money dwindled, he asked acquaintances to help him find a job.[48]

Brown tried. He wrote Simon Cameron, Columbus Delano, Thomas Scott, and others that Bullock was "very poor" and should be helped. Referring to the fifty-nine-page *Address of Rufus B. Bullock to the People of Georgia* (1872), in which Bullock challenged every charge against him, Brown exclaimed: "[He] repelled every assault which they made upon his integrity & met them with some crushing blows, showing that they had been governed by political prejudice & political motives." He believed that because Bullock had braved the storm of protest to award the lease of the state road to them, they should help him now. He praised Bullock as "an excellent business man . . . [of] enterprise, ability, promptness & industry."[49]

Still, Bullock found no job. He understood the reason, which was a presumption of guilt surrounding his resignation as governor: "because of those circumstances I have not been able to engage in business nor add otherwise to my limited means." He did persuade Brown to place three people, one of them his personal secretary, R. H. Atkinson, on the payroll of the Western and Atlantic Railroad. After six years of unemployment, Bullock asked Brown for a position with the railroad, but, even though Brown supported him, other lessees, particularly M. T. Walters, refused to hire him. Walters thought the public would misconstrue their hiring Bullock. Brown insisted that there was nothing "covert" about the decision. Bullock's failure to gain a position demonstrates his innocence in the lease negotiations back in 1870 because he surely could have forced the lessees to give him a position in 1877 by threatening to expose the "deal." Because there was never any deal, Bullock remained unemployed. Undoubtedly, poverty and frustration influenced his decision to return to Georgia.[50]

When Governor Smith, who had been reelected in 1872, resumed the effort to return Bullock to Georgia, Bullock did not resist. On May 10, 1876, Marshal O. P. Fitzsimmons went to New York. Upon his arrival at the Fifth Avenue Hotel, Fitzsimmons learned that Governor Bullock was staying in the same hotel. Fitzsimmons obtained a warrant from Governor Samuel Tilden, got two New York City policemen to watch the governor's room all night, and the next morning attempted to arrest Alexander Bullock, former governor of Massachusetts. The following day, Fitzsimmons went to Albion to find the other Governor Bullock, of Georgia. Fitzsimmons later testified that Bullock did not attempt to evade arrest and had gone "cheerfully." That night, they boarded a southbound train.[51]

Bullock's arrival in Atlanta after a fifty-five-month absence created a sensation. Fitzsimmons allowed him to take a room in the Kimball House before delivering him to the sheriff. Thomas Alexander, one of the lessors of state convicts in Grant, Alexander, and Company, immediately offered security for Bullock's bond, and Bullock did not spend any time in the Atlanta jail. Apparently not a superstitious man, he stayed in Room 13 at the Kimball House. Friends visited often, and rarely did Bullock spend any time alone. He took daily walks with Benjamin Conley and others and spoke freely to reporters. He was a curiosity whose every move was news. Reporters told of his habit of walking under an umbrella, carrying a nosegay, and even described his clothing: "He dresses neatly in greyish pants, black alapacca sack coat and wears a high crown black hat. His whiskers are greyer than when he left Georgia and are worn with the English chin-chop out of the center." Many Atlantans were shocked to find

Bullock walking around the city at will and wondered why, after all he had done, he was not under constant guard in jail.[52]

Eager to convict him, the *Atlanta Constitution* exclaimed: "Now let the laws be enforced." Seven days later, the same paper decried other papers for reporting that "there is no more chance of Bullock going to the penitentiary than there is of a bull eating a locomotive." The *Constitution* insisted he would be tried like any other criminal but wondered why some prominent Democrats were saying a trial would be a mistake. The answer is that Democratic leaders understood what had happened during Reconstruction and knew that the charges against Bullock were fluff, made to reassert dominance by the old leaders and force a one-party system on Georgia. Democrats forged careers from Bullock-hating and now feared that their elaborate slander might be exposed.[53]

Bullock stayed in Georgia nearly a month, but when his prosecutors were allowed more time to develop the case, he went back to New York. One year later he returned to Atlanta for trial. Again the prosecutors stalled, insisted they were not ready, and delayed even though Bullock's attorneys moved for an immediate trial. It is doubtful whether Bullock could have hired better attorneys; they were men of the highest caliber and they shared his interests. One Atlanta reporter described Bullock's lawyers, Lucius J. Gartrell, H. K. McCay, John L. Hopkins, and O. A. Lochrane, as a "brilliant and powerful . . . alliance of counsel." Gartrell led the defense. He was a fifty-five-year-old Atlanta attorney whom one contemporary called "a powerful, robust man, full of animal spirits." Gartrell studied law in the office of Robert Toombs, served in the U.S. Congress from 1857 to 1860 and the Confederate Congress from 1862 to 1864, and, as a brigadier general, organized and commanded four Georgia regiments. He was a lifelong supporter of railroad building in Atlanta and promoted establishment and improvement of the public school system. In 1882, Gartrell ran for governor on a campaign touting the laboring man, for "freedom and purity" of the ballot, for education, for equality, against convict lease, and against monopolies. McCay and Lochrane were former Georgia Supreme Court justices, appointed by Bullock; Lochrane became chief justice after Joe Brown resigned to lease the state railroad. Hopkins served as judge of the Fulton County Superior Court during Reconstruction.[54]

Finally, Judge George Hillyer called the trial for Thursday, January 3. Hillyer was a native Georgian who had studied law at Mercer University in Macon before being elected in 1857, at age twenty-two, to the General

Assembly. During the war, Hillyer raised a regiment and gained a captain's commission. At Gettysburg, his fifty-two-man company charged up Cemetery Ridge with General George Pickett; only thirteen of them survived to run back down. After Gettysburg, in 1863, Governor Joe Brown appointed Hillyer as the auditor of the Western and Atlantic Railroad. When the war ended, Hillyer practiced law in Atlanta and served on the three-man commission chosen by the legislature in 1865 to audit the state road. In the election of 1870, voters in Fulton, Clayton, and Cobb counties elected him to the Georgia Senate. In 1877, Governor Alfred Colquitt, perhaps the state's largest planter, appointed Hillyer judge of the Fulton County Superior Court. Clearly, he understood the state railroad, knew the inside story of the Redeemer victory in 1870, and had a thorough knowledge of the charges against Bullock.[55]

Georgia attorney general Robert N. Ely led the prosecution. Ely was a classmate of Hillyer's at Mercer University. He served in the 1860–61 Georgia House and gained a commission as a major during the war. In 1877, Governor Colquitt appointed him attorney general. Benjamin H. Hill, Willis A. Hawkins, D. Pike Hill, and William J. Spears aided Ely, prompting the *Atlanta Constitution* to remark: "The prosecution could not have been in better hands." On January 4, 1878, Bullock pled not guilty to all the charges against him and waived arraignment. Prosecutors tried him on two separate cases. In the first case, *State v. Bullock,* he was charged with "larceny after trust delegated" for having transferred $130,000 in Atlanta city bonds to H. I. Kimball even though he knew Kimball had a $60,000 mortgage outstanding. The second case was *State v. Bullock, Blodgett, and E. N. Kimball* for cheating and swindling the state out of $42,500 for fifty railroad cars bought from the Tennessee Car Company but never delivered. Blodgett died in 1877, but his name remained on the indictment. Edwin Kimball, Hannibal's brother, was business manager of the car company.[56]

To prove their cases, prosecutors cited the 1872 legislative committee investigations into the governor's conduct and called the same witnesses that committee had called. But now those witnesses claimed the committee's report misstated what they said, left out parts of their testimony, and made conclusions not based on evidence. Witness John Conley called the report "grossly garbled" and testified that "the report of the evidence given by me as published by the committee . . . is wholly inaccurate and puts words into my mouth I have never uttered and makes me say things which are

not true in fact." It became increasingly obvious, as one contemporary observed, "that the State could not convict and did not desire to acquit." So
the trial continued. After four days of testimony, the jury, composed of men
mainly from outside the city limits of Atlanta, deliberated thirty minutes
and, at 12:10 A.M., on January 8, found Bullock not guilty in the bonds
case. On January 17, a different jury found him not guilty of cheating the
state in the Tennessee Car Company case. Calling him "an honest man and
a gentleman," prosecutor Hill admitted that "the most searching investigation failed to disclose any evidence of his guilt, and he was promptly
acquitted by a Democratic jury." [57]

The *Atlanta Constitution* reported that the public and the prosecutors
had been "misled by the [1872 legislative] report, which could not be sustained on the stand." The *Augusta Chronicle* reported the cases "fairly
tried" and admitted that any prejudices among jurors had been in the state's
favor. Then, in an "I told you so" manner, the *Chronicle* admitted that during Reconstruction, it fought Bullock "with a zeal that never flagged and a
bitterness that never softened" until it helped destroy the Republican party
and remove the governor. The editor continued, "When the Governor fled
the State . . . [we] had no desire to make him a political martyr, and for
that reason . . . never saw the wisdom of bringing him to trial." [58]

Others refused to accept the verdict. Atlanta's *Daily Tribune* tried to
excuse the excesses of Reconstruction and explained to the world that "the
good name and fame of Georgia were vindicated in his acquittal." The *New
York Tribune* called Bullock "abominably careless, even if he was not a
criminal magistrate. . . . It was a good time for thieves." Bullock responded
to editor Horace Greeley that the 1872 committee report was a political
"campaign document," denied being in bad company, insisted he was not
careless, and ruled out any possibility of a swindle in either case. For years
thereafter, newspapers, orators, and historians would claim that Bullock
was guilty as charged even though the state had had ample time to find evidence of his guilt—ten years since the first charges against him surfaced,
six years since he resigned and left the state, and a year and a half since he
returned to stand trial. The various committees combed Bullock's private
bank books for evidence to use against him; they found nothing. Because
of the time involved, the rancor of partisan politics, and the state's failure
to produce any evidence of misdealings, any conclusion other than the one
the juries found is untenable. [59]

Bullock's acquittals confirmed his innocence. The state really never had a case. In Albion, townspeople held a huge celebration on Bullock's return, and the local newspaper correctly analyzed the case against one of its favorite sons as "one of political persecution, but such was the torrent of slander and abuse turned out by the Southern press . . . for political effect, that many were induced to believe that there must be something in the charges preferred." [60]

The *Atlanta Independent* echoed that analysis and blamed "party hounds" who sought their own aggrandizement by slandering Radical politicians. The *Independent* understood the power of rhetorical propaganda: "For years the partisan press and orators have repeated the lie until the people came firmly to believe it. . . . The ghastly farce is ended." [61]

Because people believed what they read and heard, especially if it conformed with their ideology—in this case an ideology based on white supremacy—many were misled by Georgia's Democratic press and politicians. Editors and orators invented and endorsed false charges against Republicans chosen by black majorities. The *New York Times* lamented: "No matter how faithfully a man performed the services required of him, no matter how hard he worked, no matter what reforms he might originate and carry out, he was, nevertheless, 'a Radical,' and consequently a thief." [62]

As white Southerners continued the fight for their way of life after the Civil War ended, lies and Klan violence seemed minor evils compared to the loss of sons in and the failure to win the war. Planters maintained their power by inventing an enemy for the people to hate. In focusing hatred on Bullock and his stance for black equality they found a powerful conjure to keep whites together and to bolster planter power.

Bullock faced insurmountable odds while governor, but he did not know it. With his ideology firmly rooted in the moral precepts of higher law doctrine expressed by the Radical wing of the Republican party, he believed that Southerners would realize the Civil War's mandate for change. The Reconstruction constitutional amendments attested to the nation's belief in the equality of all men to vote for their representatives. Bullock tried to push his program of progress into an area still trying to hang on to the ideology of chattel slavery and onto a people bitter over the outcome of the war and what they saw as "bayonet rule."

Historian Thomas Cochran has explained that "scapegoat factors" played a role in placing blame on those who challenged existing values. The loss of the "good old days" when whites ruled and blacks slaved had to be explained. Because Bullock promoted Congressional Reconstruction and represented the most drastic change in existing values, he became the object, the scapegoat, against whom white Democrats could rally. In his 1936 study *Alien Americans,* Bertram Shrieke's analysis of Reconstruction backed the scapegoat theory. Shrieke wrote of the power of the fait accompli in national histories: "If a revolution is successful, its promoters are heroes, their opponents tyrants; if a revolution is unsuccessful, the promoters are dishonest agitators or at least impractical but dangerous idealists." With the failure of Reconstruction, the "slogans of the struggle of the southern Democrats—'Negro domination,' 'carpet-bagger governments,' 'corruption, frauds, and maladministration because of Negro participation in politics,' and so on—have now become 'historical verities.'" When the North tired and wanted to unify the nation, it was necessary to allow for the Southern interpretation and the "*fait accompli* of the undoing of reconstruction" to become "historical truth."[63]

Had Bullock been able to weld lower-class whites with blacks into a united political party, the revolution of Reconstruction might have succeeded. But Bullock and his friends had instituted reforms that were centralizing, modernizing, and urban. As the nascent sharecrop and crop lien systems developed, the old planter class localized power to maintain as much of the status quo as possible. Bullock never really pondered rural Georgia and little understood or cared about the furnishing system or tenant farmers—except to try to protect their rights to vote freely, to vote Republican. Bullock had come to the conclusion that if his group could rule in Atlanta, the Democrats could have the countryside, at least temporarily. Bullock was under the pressure of time, and he focused on black officeholding and business development at the expense of other tasks. Psychologist William Kurtines has noted that the overload of working on hard tasks decreases the ability of a person efficiently to take on other jobs—no matter how important they may be.[64]

Still, Democratic leaders feared Bullock's plea for poor whites to vote with blacks of their class. Planters responded by race-baiting. Bullock's inability to overcome planter rule and the racism of Georgia whites branded him corrupt, made him the scapegoat, and led to the verdict of national historians that he was a dishonest agitator, "the embodiment of racial fanatacism."[65]

None of those brands is true. But though Bullock defended blacks' political rights, he never went far enough to help them secure land of their own and independence for themselves and their children. Once asked to protect black workers from employers' abuses, Bullock fretted over his inability to help but suggested that they "form a 'protective labor union' by which each should aid the other, and when a member is thrown out of employment, or from sickness is unable to work, he would be assisted from a general fund established by contributions from members of the Union."[66]

His suggestion was too far ahead of its time, but it does indicate his belief that labor should organize to help itself. He also advised the workers to contact Freedmen's Bureau superintendent O. O. Howard for help. Although he appointed many blacks to office and supported them in elective races and in national appointments, he could have done more. With more blacks in office, the Republican party might have gained a stronger constituency than it had among freedmen. But Bullock knew that if he appointed more blacks, white Republicans would desert the party en masse. John Bryant, Joe Brown, and other Centrists left the fold because of Bullock's efforts to protect black rights, but for Bullock to have done other than he did was impossible. Black leaders stood by him because he offered them a better program than did any other white man.[67]

Most black leaders failed to ask for or introduce legislation to redistribute land and, as neophytes in the political arena, most blacks also were content or reconciled to let whites lead for the moment. Bullock's efforts combined political expediency with ideological commitment; he was more a determined realist than a politician. He believed that justice for the freedmen would come simultaneously with the implementation of Northern political and economic free labor institutions. Bullock accepted the expansion of federal authority and intervention in state affairs. He naively believed in the "competitive ideal," an assumption that anyone could rise if given access to the ballot and education. Compared with the slavery that preceded and racism and disfranchisement that followed, Bullock's administration gave Georgia blacks the best state government they would get until 1970.[68]

Numan Bartley, speaking of James Earl Carter, made the comparison: "Not since Rufus Bullock had a Georgia governor openly endorsed equality before the law." That Bullock did so one hundred years before Carter shows the failed promise of Reconstruction and the strength of Bullock.[69]

Chapter 8 ❧ Outsider as Insider

It is hard to realize that there was ever a time when even
an allegation of malfeasance could have been made
against him.

—*Planter's Journal,* 1884

I am a Republican and have been ever since the war. But I
am not a politician. I never was a candidate for a political
office, but once, and never held but one political office,
and that seemed to be forced upon me by business and
social necessity. . . . While I am not a politician, I am a
businessman.

—Rufus Brown Bullock, 1889

IN MARCH 1874, Hannibal Kimball left his home in Newton, Massachusetts, and returned triumphantly to Atlanta. Many of the city's most
prominent citizens welcomed him back; in fact, they had invited him to
return. Third only to Bullock and Blodgett as recipient of intemperate in-
vectives slung by Democrats, Kimball defiantly challenged his accusers to
convict him of any wrongdoing. Henry Grady, who criticized Kimball's
every enterprise during Reconstruction, now encouraged Atlantans to embrace all businessmen regardless of their politics. He promoted Kimball for
the position of president of a new cotton factory to be built in Atlanta and
implored others to "give him a fair hearing." Grady and other Atlanta business interests remembered Kimball's amazing talents in getting things built
and in commanding capital. They agreed with the *Constitution*'s remi-
niscence that "the two years 1869 to 1871 were what may be called the

sunshining years in Atlanta's history. Buildings were put up then with a rapidity that looked almost like insanity." Boosters hoped Kimball could revive some of that construction craziness.[1]

Within weeks of his return, Kimball rebuked his detractors: "You know I think the policy of *Repudiation* has been a curse to the State, and just throttles every enterprise that requires outside capital. I have been and am still a believer in 'State Aid' and a liberal policy toward Rail Road enterprises." Asserting that "progress is the genius of our modern civilization, and the individual or city that does not keep pace with the march of current events is soon distanced in the race, and sinks into insignificance or oblivion," Kimball successfully disarmed his critics. No one had proof that he had committed any crime. Businessmen hosted a huge banquet for him and elected him president of the proposed cotton factory.[2]

The cotton mill era in the South began in 1880. The Atlanta factory helped lead the way and represented the change in location of mills from the countryside to city centers. Kimball declared himself "in favor of a central location" and explained: "Here we already have the necessary labor, properly housed, and are not compelled to build tenement or boarding houses." He promoted local investment in the mill and issued twenty-five hundred shares of stock at $100 each. But when investors left $150,000 in subscribed stock unpaid and placed the enterprise's future in jeopardy, Kimball resigned. Six months later, after Atlanta businessmen renewed support, Kimball resumed his position. Finally, on July 7, 1875, seventy-five workers of J. C. Peck's construction company broke ground for the new factory within the city limits on Marietta Street (now the site of the Omni). Four years later, the Atlanta Cotton Factory stood six stories high and covered an area of nearly one hundred square yards—280 by 316 feet. Factory promoters envisioned four to six hundred workers operating 10,240 spindles on 330 looms to turn 60 bales of cotton into nearly 75,000 yards of "standard brown goods" per day. Even though Kimball threw a party for employees during the first week and urged them to a "high standard," it would be two years before the visions materialized.[3]

After Bullock's acquittal in January 1878, Kimball offered him a position as treasurer with the factory. Bullock readily accepted. Not only did he need the job, but he saw that Atlanta was booming. The city's population exploded from 21,789 in 1870 to 37,409 in 1880. Two decades later, Atlanta bulged with nearly 100,000 people. Initially, Bullock leased a room in the Kimball House hotel. His family remained in Albion at his parents' home and joined him in Atlanta sometime in 1879—probably after Volkert graduated from high school. His daughter, Cornelia, remained in New York to finish her education.[4]

Once he was financially stable, Bullock moved Marie and their children into a house at 320 Peachtree Street, only three blocks from their old residence, the governor's mansion. After twenty-one years of marriage, the Bullocks had their first real home. In keeping with his habits, when Bullock had money, he quickly spent it. He lived as high as or higher than his income allowed; by 1888, he had an unpaid debt of $25,000. There is no evidence that he or Marie ever saved any money. In 1882, when Bullock replaced Kimball as president of the cotton factory, they moved into a large four-story brick house at 173 Peachtree Street—one block closer to the mansion. Their neighbors were all middle- or upper-class businessmen. Poor people lived at the city's periphery.[5]

Their new home sat on a lot with a 50-foot frontage and a depth of 150 feet to a 10-foot-wide alley, where it narrowed to 55 feet and stretched back another 40 feet. On two occasions they purchased adjoining land to expand the lot. The house had four rooms on each of the bottom two floors and two rooms on each of the upper floors. Modern conveniences included hot and cold running water, gas lighting, and gas and coal heating. The rooms on the ground floor consisted of a servants' bathroom, kitchen, pantry, dining room, and billiard parlor. The second floor contained a large foyer and drawing room for receiving visitors, who entered up a flight of stairs from Peachtree, a well-stocked library, and a large bath with dressing rooms. The four bedrooms were located two each on the upper floors; an inventory of furnishings indicates that the children slept on the fourth floor. The Bullocks furnished the house with European and Oriental carpets; French clocks; local, English, and Mexican artwork and oil paintings; and walnut, mahogany, and rosewood furniture. Avid readers, they located books and bookcases on every floor.[6]

Marie and Rufus had a strong marriage that got stronger when they were subjected to controversy. He had brought her south from Rhode Island the year the Civil War began. Their second child, Rufie, died at the age of eight months. Bullock's life as governor was full of tension and misery. Certainly the taunts and threats thrown at him through the years did not miss Marie or the children, even if just in sneers, stares, and slights in stores and on streets or by the accidental insensitivity of other children on playgrounds or in classrooms. To move in with one's parents and in-laws is certainly a trial even in the best of times, but to be supported by them while under a cloud of controversy surely would strain the strongest bonds. After Bullock's mother died in 1882, his seventy-six-year-old father lived with them in Atlanta for a year before his death.[7]

After the relocation to Atlanta, Marie never participated in women's clubs and rarely engaged in social activities. Either the past slights were too much for her to forgive or Atlanta women refused to show the same "forgetfulness" their husbands did. Marie focused her attention on church activities and family. Certainly Bullock's activities made life for her and the children extremely difficult. Other than that obvious deduction, little else can be gleaned because of a lack of surviving information about her. Marie probably shared Bullock's convictions and gave him political advice, but mostly she stayed in the background of community social and political life. Volkert worked as a clerk for Wylly and Green grocers before obtaining a position as clerk with his father's mill. In 1894, he joined with publisher Henry Saunders to edit the *Southern Architect,* a monthly magazine that failed in 1895. The firm of Saunders and Bullock contracted for printing jobs and for five years published the *Atlanta City Directory.* Volkert also held a paid position as secretary of the Atlanta Chamber of Commerce for four years before working as an assistant postmaster from 1903 to 1910. Hugh was six years old in 1880 and went to school in Atlanta before finishing his education in the North. He returned to Atlanta in 1898 and became a regular player on Atlanta's first golf course, Brookstone Links.[8]

Cornelia finished school, returned to Atlanta by 1886, and, in 1888, married Leonard Treadwell Kendall of New York. For her wedding, the Bullocks spared no expense in decorating St. Luke's Episcopal Church with South American ferns, twelve-foot-tall banana plants, one thousand white roses, palm trees, and Canadian smilax. They hired an orchestra and forty choristers. When the couple returned from a "swing" through the North, the Bullocks gave a reception for them and invited nearly five hundred guests. The *Constitution* reported the party as "one of the most brilliant entertainments noted here for years. . . . In the hall Wurm's full orchestra played during the entire evening."[9]

The Bullocks joined Benjamin Conley and his wife as active members of St. Philip's Episcopal Church. St. Philip's was Atlanta's "society church," and a few blacks worshiped there. Those who did probably belonged to Atlanta's black bourgeoisie and resembled communicant John Pinkney, a store owner, described as "an especially worthy colored citizen, industrious, courteous and respectful." The Bullocks supported the parish by donating a window in honor of Rufie. In testament to Bullock's dedication to the church, the 508 members of the congregation elected him to the vestry in 1882. He served as junior and senior warden for many years. He represented the church in at least eight Georgia diocesan conventions between 1885 and 1900 and attended the national Episcopal triennial convention in Minneapolis in 1895. One member referred to him as a "tower of strength in the councils of the church," but clearly Bullock needed the church as much as it needed him.[10]

Marie had one or two close friends in Atlanta and liked to entertain them at home or to invite them to sojourn to the shores of Rhode Island, where she owned a beach house. She was very close to her sister, Mehitabel Sisson, who lived in Charlestown, Rhode Island. Every summer, beginning in 1868, Rufus took Marie and the children for a three-month visit with Mehitabel and her family. Bullock never stayed the entire summer, but he spent as much time there as business allowed. In 1887 the Bullocks bought a small cottage and land near the Sissons; by 1899, the Bullocks owned three houses and 120 acres of land worth $8,500. In 1870, Mehitabel purchased a large house at Cross's Mill on the north shore of Charlestown Pond; twenty-six years later, after her husband's death, she sold it to Marie for $2,000. This large two-story house boasted a cupola from which one could see the saltwater pond, Long Island Sound, and distant Block Island. Until 1904, the Bullocks sought the solace and beauty of this place, which they called Ocean House or Cold Brook Farm. It was a welcome change of pace from the business world of the New South.[11]

The Atlanta Cotton Factory had multiple problems. Financed by local capital, it never had adequate backing. Additionally, Kimball experienced labor problems and had difficulty hiring enough workers. His suggestion to employ blacks alongside whites met so much resistance from white leaders and workers that he was forced to abandon the idea. The factory needed to hire at least two hundred women so that payrolls could be reduced. Kimball could not get them. An editorial in the *Atlanta Constitution* tried to help Kimball find workers by condemning the Southern attitude that women should not work. The editor said it was not "ignoble" for women to help their husbands work. Calling unaided male support of the home a "burden," the writer used a free labor trumpet to claim: "This prejudice against having our women go to work is one of the false sentiments that grew out of our old system of slave labor. It should be allowed to perish. . . .

All labor is honorable, that is honest." Just six weeks later, the *Constitution* mixed Old South paternalism with the free labor gospel to advance a solution to the labor problem. The writer suggested that providing company houses for employees "insures steady and reliable labor, and enforces that necessary discipline. . . . In this way the managers of the factory come to be in some sort the guardians and protectors of those in their employ, and these relations are of vast mutual benefit." [12]

Kimball threatened to bring in Northern workers if his problems persisted, but he never did. Instead, he hired workers from Tennessee and, despite white resistance, employed a few black Georgians. Kimball also considered building tenements, as the *Constitution* suggested, but decided against that. There is some evidence that Thomas G. Healey built a few brick houses near the factory to rent to employees, but whether he did so with Kimball's approval is unknown. [13]

In 1879, workers received daily wages of only twenty-five cents. Despite that starvation pay, the factory's financial condition was so bad that Kimball had difficulty paying the 238 females, 136 males, and 120 children, the latter under the age of sixteen. He was also unable to make the payments on the modern steam machinery necessary to make the cloth. By 1880, Kimball turned his attention to politics. He ran for mayor on the Republican ticket against Democratic city councilman James W. English, future founder of two Atlanta banks and president of the Chattahoochee Brick Company. The election was close; Kimball lost by fifty-four votes. English's margin of victory may have been related to the *Constitution*'s labeling Kimball "communist" because he supported social programs, reminding whites of his "past crimes" as a "carpetbagger" and insisting that only "niggers and Republicans" supported him. Soon after the election, Kimball left the cotton factory. He remained in Atlanta one more year to promote a cotton exposition before moving to Chicago to work once more for George Pullman. [14]

The 1881 International Cotton Exposition marked Atlanta as a leader among New South cities and vanguard in the Southern cotton mill era. Boston capitalist Edward Atkinson originated the idea for a cotton exposition in August 1880 and suggested Atlanta as the most likely place to hold it. Atkinson called Atlanta "the railroad as well as the manufacturing center of a section." Not surprisingly, Kimball became the prime mover and served as director-general. His friend Bullock worked on the board of commissioners. Bullock was one of the four original organizers; others

included Governor Alfred Colquitt, Atlanta mayor James Calhoun, and
J. W. Ryckman. The exposition opened on October 5, 1881, with speeches
by leading Atlantans and Atkinson. A choir of eight hundred persons sang
Handel's "Hallelujah Chorus," and U.S. representative from Georgia N. J.
Hammond read Paul Hamilton Hayne's "Exposition Ode":

> Feeling her veins so full of lusty blood,
> That pulsed within them, like a rhythmic flood
>
> . . . .
>
> Atlanta, from a night of splendid dreams,
> Roused by soft kisses of the morning beams,
> Decreed a glorious festival
> Of art and commerce in her brave domain.[15]

The exposition drew together Southern industrialists and Northern investors and stimulated construction of Southern mills. Planters and farmers
became acquainted with the best and newest agricultural tools and techniques. In all, nearly three hundred thousand people visited the 1,113 ex-
hibits before the exposition closed on New Year's Eve. At the closing
ceremonies, Kimball stressed that the key word for the South was "improvement." Appropriately, the fair's buildings were sold and transformed
into a cotton factory, the Exposition Cotton Mills.[16]

But even with the exposition touting the profitability of "King Cotton"
and spurring growth, the Atlanta Cotton Factory's woes continued. Creditors sued for their money. United States District Court judge D. Pike Hill
seized the factory and appointed Bullock as receiver to administer the
factory's business. Atlanta lawyer and future governor Hoke Smith represented creditors and worked with Bullock to obtain a settlement. For three
years, Bullock ran the factory and paid debts. He installed electric lights
and hired workers to operate a night shift. Extolling Bullock's abilities
as manager, Henry Grady wrote: "He has lessened the expenses, system-
atized the work and very materially increased the profits. . . . If he is left in
control of affairs . . . he will work the mill out of its trouble and make it
a prosperous and independent property." But when the factory remained
plagued with money problems, Bullock found an old solution and turned
to Northern friends to fund the enterprise and bail out local investors.[17]

In 1883, Bullock convinced New York banker, newspaperman, and railroad entrepreneur Freeman Clarke and transportation magnate Henry
Plant, both old friends, to purchase the factory. Clarke provided most of

the funds, made Bullock president, and sent his son Edward to Atlanta as secretary-treasurer for the newly renamed Atlanta Cotton Mills. Edward had graduated from Yale and studied law in Heidelberg, Germany, and New York City before practicing in Rochester. In Atlanta, Edward and his wife, Saida, became close friends of the Bullocks, attended operas and baseball games with them, and dined frequently in their home. Saida and Marie became best friends and visited daily. Baseball fever swept Atlanta in 1885 when the city's first professional team opened its season at the Athletic Field on North Avenue. Edward wrote his mother: "The whole town is excited over base ball, and all *the* people attend with great regularity. The Bullocks . . . attend every game." [18]

Freeman Clarke had heard stories of Bullock's extravagance and remembered that when Bullock worked for him in 1855, the young man sometimes authorized expenditures without making proper bookkeeping entries. Careless bookkeeping had made it easier for Democrats to charge Bullock with corruption. Clarke wanted no such speculation and kept a close eye on his cotton mill. Clarke's wife, Henrietta, told Edward in very strong terms to make sure Bullock did not spend money or contract debts beyond what Clarke had authorized. If the factory needed money, Clarke would furnish it. [19]

Edward followed his mother's instructions, but he did not find Bullock extravagant. Edward reported to his mother a conversation he had had with Samuel Stocking, who was the factory's secretary before Edward took that position. After Edward told Stocking that "the bondsholders up in our part of the country had the notion that Gov. Bullock was very extravagant," Stocking agreed that that was true in his personal affairs "but not in running the factory." Stocking reported that extravagance had occurred but blamed Kimball, who "was the acknowledged head of it all and had his own way which no one was allowed to dispute. . . . The factory never did make a dollar of money until Bullock took hold of it. . . . And if any man can make the factory pay," that man would be Bullock. Edward believed Stocking's evaluation was accurate. He told his mother, "I can see myself that Gov Bullock is extremely popular here & there is a great deal of respect shown him." [20]

As a capitalist, Bullock was a competent manager, but he exploited laborers. For several years he and mill superintendent C. F. Coleman operated the factory around the clock six days a week in two shifts of eleven and one-half hours each. Later, claiming that double shifts did not double production, they reduced the operation to one eleven-hour shift. Workers produced mightily. During the last week of August 1883, they made 118,000 yards of cloth, leading Edward to exclaim to his mother: "I feel quite like a capitalist." In 1883, the weekly payroll of $1,200 included more than 400 workers. Wages varied with experience, position, sex, age, and race. The plant engineer and four overseers were paid weekly. Rough laborers—sweepers, coal heavers, roustabouts, and the like—were paid by the day; all others were paid weekly according to the amount of work completed. Many children under twelve years old worked the long shifts and earned less than a nickel an hour. By 1900, with no night shift operating, the mill employed 275 workers, of whom approximately 70 percent were women and children. Those workers made a total weekly salary of $1,175. The highest paid workers made around $6.50 for a sixty-six-hour week; the average worker received $4.00 a week. Bullock undoubtedly shared the belief of one of his competitors, Jacob Elsas, vice-president of Fulton Bag and Cotton Mill, who said: "It is not the custom to pay more than you have to pay." [21]

Bullock resigned as president in 1891 but continued to sit on the board of directors. In 1900, the federal government studied labor conditions in the United States and sent a commission to Atlanta to investigate conditions in the city's four cotton mills. On March 19, Bullock and mill vice-president H. E. Fisher testified before the committee. Bullock admitted that he never tried to have blacks and whites work together because of white workers' "race prejudice, and social prejudice." Bullock believed blacks were competent enough to operate the machinery and, comparing the races, said, "Some of them are more intelligent, some are less so; the same as white people." Bullock believed that in educational and material growth, "There is no history of any race that has made the improvement in 30 years that these negroes have." He believed that whites might be forced to accept black operatives, but in the interest of order, the races should be separated by operation—spinning, weaving, or carding. Fisher mentioned one black woman, Carrie Hall, who had worked in the cloth room for over twenty years and was accepted by white co-workers. At one time, Bullock employed an African-American to help prepare weekly pay envelopes for the employees. Perhaps there were other exceptions. Bullock commented ironically that although white workers believed blacks inferior, "when the white help goes out to get a can of snuff the colored sweepers run the loom." [22]

Bullock told the committee he supported national legislation to bring "uniformity, harmony, and fairness" to all sections, but his "fairness" favored capitalists, not workers. He favored legislation to prevent employers from hiring children under age twelve not because he thought it hurt the child to work long hours but because young children were too small and not worth their pay. Attempting to cover for the sordid practice of working children, Bullock testified that employers hired them only when their parents insisted on it. Fisher added that the mill directors once attempted to educate the children by hiring a teacher, Miss Brittain, and providing a room for her use until parents objected that they would lose control of the children if they were educated. Bullock supported legislation to set a maximum workday of ten hours nationwide and said that those opposing uniform laws had "fool notions about States' rights." Business interests still came first with Bullock. Echoing a policy he had promoted as chairman of the 1881 National Tariff Convention in Chicago, he favored protective legislation for mechanical industries and maintained that states should allow each new factory a ten-year tax exemption. He argued against a graduated income tax that took more from the rich. Bullock claimed that capitalists simply raised prices to cover the "expense" of higher taxes. Protesting against British ships carrying U.S. products to China, he wanted the federal government to mandate that American goods could be carried only by American ships. He thought a canal should be built across Florida to facilitate trade. He did not believe trusts or monopolies were necessarily objectionable; in fact, he said that large economies of scale brought cheaper goods to consumers. Still, he supported national regulation and open inspection of a company's books, similar to the powers the Interstate Commerce Commission had in reviewing railroad combines.[23]

As president and director of Atlanta's first cotton mill—and as the former governor who wanted growth—Bullock came to associate increasingly with promoters of the New South. Two of the sturdiest planks in the New South program were industrial development and Northern investment. Bullock's role in helping the Atlanta Cotton Mills to solvency through his courtship of Northern capital showed how he could help Atlanta become the foremost city in the South, one of his aims since 1868. As governor, he ran the state like a corporation of which he was president. He drummed up business, extolled Georgia as a land of unlimited natural resources, looked for ways to expand and promote, and became the chief cheerleader of Georgia's free labor future. His persistent appeal for rapid development readied Georgians for industrial progress. When Democratic leaders in Atlanta no longer feared Republican ascendancy with its insistence on racial equality, they supported Bullock's revitalization program.[24]

One of Bullock's most vociferous tormentors during Reconstruction became the primary spokesman for the New South. Henry Woodfin Grady was born in Athens, Georgia, in 1850, and graduated from the University of Georgia in 1868. After studying law for one year at the University of Virginia, Grady accepted a position as associate editor with the *Rome Courier* and joined the Ku Klux Klan. His first editorial, on September 7, 1869, attacked Bullock for "political filthiness" and described him as "the Accident that now occupies the Gubernatorial chair." Grady deprecated Bullock's disposition: "The sweetness of his countenance is absolutely appalling . . . [with] infinite smiles . . . [and] soft laughter . . . his face is tremendously delusive. . . . How deep and how effectively does this man hide his rascality!!" Yet, after Bullock's acquittal, Grady welcomed him into the social circle of promoters which included Kimball, Brown, Gordon, and others; undoubtedly, Grady needed men with Northern connections. Still, he had misread Bullock's manner.[25]

Bullock had a natural affability. Centrist Republican John H. Caldwell, who bitterly opposed Bullock during Reconstruction, wrote that through it all, he "bore me no malice, was a gentleman of charming urbanity and amiable disposition. I never knew him to lose his temper or treat an adversary with discourtesy." In his 1881 *History of Georgia*, editor and Klansman Isaac W. Avery called Bullock's administration "frightfully bad" and "unbrokenly evil" but described Bullock as "naturally a clever, amiable, correctly disposed person." Decidedly Democratic publications, including the *Planter's Journal* and *Southron*, attested that no man had been more hated than Bullock, but they acknowledged that his Reconstruction activities were based on moral convictions. By 1884, the *Southron* touted him as "emphatically a progressive man in every respect," and the *Planter's Journal* proclaimed him the "heart and soul in the cause of enterprise and progress." Perhaps Bullock should have lost his temper more often.[26]

Grady moved to Atlanta in 1872 to become editor of the *Atlanta Herald*. After the *Herald* folded four years later, editor Evan P. Howell of the *Atlanta Constitution* hired the young wordsmith. By 1880, Grady owned a one-fourth interest in that newspaper and was managing editor. Even though he courted Northern investors and insisted that the New South was really new, Grady revered the Old South and its Democratic stance that "the supremacy of the white race of the South must be maintained forever, and the domination of the negro race resisted at all points and at all hazards." [27]

Historians generally give Grady credit as the supreme promoter of the New South, but Bullock and Kimball were the true architects. Grady took Bullock's Reconstruction program, tore out the planks on free labor and black equality, hammered in white supremacy, and called it his own. Grady soaked up Bullock's ideas, replaced Bullock as the state's chief cheerleader, and used his talents as editor and orator to build on the gospel of prosperity. New South compatriot Alexander McClure described Bullock as one of "a small circle of Grady's prominent personal friends" who debated "without reserve" on politics and industrial development. McClure said that Bullock had confidence in Grady's ability to advance Georgia's material interests. In Henry Grady, Bullock found an ally and "front man" for Atlanta's growth. Once Bullock turned his back on state politics, his influence among Southern businessmen soared. [28]

The state's Republican party limped along after Bullock's resignation. In 1872 black leader Tunis Campbell unrealistically hoped that Radicals could rally and wrote Conley: "Let the White men of the Republican Party come up to the principals of the Party and there will be no trouble now to bring every colored Man to the front in solid Phalnxe true to our country & the fundamental Law." A former ally of Bullock's, Campbell campaigned against Bryant, Joshua Hill, and others of "that 'sore head class' who are seeking to make the Republican party 'respectable' by putting white men in office." A white Radical prayed that Conley might again be governor and appoint him warden of the penitentiary so that he might "have the *sweet pleasure* of hiring *Bryant & his syncophantic proseletes out to the State to drain the Okifinokee Swamp.*" [29]

Another factor in the party's weakness was the lack of a Radical newspaper after Governor Smith stopped official patronage to the *Atlanta Daily New Era* and *Savannah Republican*. Thomas Robinson, editor of the now defunct *Republican*, praised Bullock but damned Bryant's faction and the Redeemers: "Between that vile set and the KuKlux Democracy, as the upper and nether millstones, the good seed has gradually been ground, till there's hardly a ghost of a grist for an honest Republican left." [30]

After 1872 the Republican party in Georgia existed mainly to fill federal positions made available by Republican presidents. As leaders fought for control and patronage plums, the weak party got weaker and lost credibility as factional disputes split members into the Liberal Republican movement of Horace Greeley and later into "lily white" or "black and tan" groups. Old animosities between Radicals and Centrists remained. With Centrists on top, the *Atlanta Constitution* in 1882 correctly commented: "The negroes no longer have any confidence in the whites." With the loss of its black constituency, the party had little strength.[31]

On his return to Georgia, Bullock was careful not to become involved in local or state politics. To have done so would have jeopardized his position among New South promoters, hurt his business interests, and further damaged a Republican party already nagged by most Georgians' belief in the myths of "carpetbag, nigger, scalawag, military" rule. Bullock believed that further agitation over black rights actually hurt blacks more than helping them because it renewed old prejudices. These predilections notwithstanding, Bullock briefly entered the political fray in 1892 and 1896. During that time the Populist party attempted to unite black and white voters into a coalition to defeat the Democrats. The Republican party did not enter a candidate and split its support. In 1892, black leaders divided between Populist candidate William L. Peek and Democratic governor William J. Northen, a former president of the Georgia State Agricultural Society and educator. Henry Turner, Bullock, and others supported Northen because of his support for black education, for the establishment of a technical college for blacks in Savannah, and for a lynch law to stop vigilante killings. Bullock also liked Northen's urban orientation; both of them wanted political power to revolve around Atlanta and not around county courthouses. Knowing that Populists could not overcome Democratic rule, Bullock tried to raise his position by supporting Northen, who easily won the election.[32]

In 1896, black Republican leader William Pledger, who also supported Northen, correctly accused Bullock of being a national Republican only. Republican state chairman Alfred E. Buck, who was white, far more Centrist than Pledger, and supported Peek, added that it did not suit Bullock's "social environment" to help state Republicans. Buck was right, but he failed to understand Bullock's position. With Reconstruction always on his mind, Bullock believed that agitation and state party rivalry accomplished nothing. He said that when the lower classes attempted "political independence by organizing 'alliances,' 'third parties,' etc," Democrats returned to or used tactics similar to those that had proved effective in the past. And he was right. The Populist threat to Democratic control revived fraud at the ballot box. Democrats responded to the Populist appeal to blacks by raising the specter of Reconstruction, calling for white supremacy, controlling the ballot box, and using legislation effectively to disfranchise the lower classes.[33]

Realizing that the Georgia Republican party had no chance to change state policies, Bullock eschewed participation. He continued to support the national party. In 1888, he attended the Republican nominating convention to work for Benjamin Harrison. That year, some Northern newspapers even suggested that Harrison select him as the vice-presidential candidate on the Republican ticket. The *Utica Morning Herald* in New York State supported him as "intellectually abler than the several who have been proposed." But Bullock's notoriety and the political reality that a Southerner added no votes for the ticket made Bullock's candidacy unlikely. Harrison picked New Yorker Levi P. Morton.[34]

After the election, some Georgia Republicans backed Bullock for a cabinet position. Atticus Haygood, president of Emory College at Oxford, Georgia, and author of the remarkable *Our Brother in Black* (1881), wrote a glowing recommendation: "Bullock . . . has brains—business habits—business training—knowledge of men & of public affairs. He is moreover—a gentleman. . . . He has been an unflinchingly consistent Republican all the way. Everybody knows this—he has not made offerings to our Democratic sentiments. He has been a steadfast Republican & is in Georgia, easily, its foremost and best man." [35]

But the cabinet position was not to be. Instead, Harrison appointed Bullock, at the latter's request, to a four-year term as a government director of the Union Pacific Railroad. Bullock did not have influence with Harrison on Georgia patronage matters, and the one person he promoted for a position, Ephraim Tweedy for Augusta postmaster, did not get it. Beyond that, Bullock's only involvement in national politics was his consistent support for national "high tariff" Republicans who would protect nascent Southern industry. Even after Southern "infant" industries were twenty years old, Bullock continued to insist on protective tariffs; once a Henry Clay Whig, he never believed in free trade.[36] After this brief foray into national politics, Bullock concentrated on business, and he was aided by a new device. In 1880, the Atlanta Telephone Exchange began installing telephones in the city. Of the 132 telephones in Atlanta by 1881, only 16 were in private residences. Even before Grady had a phone, Bullock, Kimball, Brown, and thirteen others led the way. By 1884, 77 residences and 487 other buildings had phones and the New South circle had instant communication to coordinate their activities. At a per-outlet cost of $104 per year, the business rich were the only ones who could afford the convenience.[37]

Bullock joined and directed organizations that promoted development, including the Atlanta Manufacturers' Association, Atlanta Chamber of Commerce, Commercial Club, and Capital City Club. The Manufacturers' Association opened its membership to all merchants, mechanics, and industrialists, collected statistics, held hearings on future manufacturing ventures, and kept pressure on the city council to reduce taxes on manufactures. In 1887, the association reorganized, opened to black members, and elected Bullock, Grady, Hoke Smith, J. C. Peck, Evan Howell, and nineteen other prominent Atlanta businessmen to its board of directors. Smith was a lawyer, owner and editor of the *Atlanta Journal,* and future secretary of the interior and governor. Peck manufactured the infamous "Joe Brown Pikes" during the Civil War and thereafter became one of the leading builder-architects in Atlanta; he built the Kimball House hotel. Howell was a lawyer, state senator from 1875 to 1879, editor in chief and major stockholder in the *Atlanta Constitution,* and future mayor (1902). With so many newspapermen in its ranks, the association knew the power of the pen and was an active publisher of booster pamphlets, such as *Some Facts Showing the Commercial, Manufacturing, and Other Advantages of Atlanta.*[38]

On July 3, 1883, 113 members of the Atlanta Board of Trade reorganized as the Atlanta Chamber of Commerce and welcomed all city residents to join. Membership was regulated by a $100 admission fee and $20 annual dues along with recommendation and vote by an eleven-man board of directors. Bullock was active from the time of this meeting, when he and four others counted the votes for directors, until he left Atlanta in 1901. Each year he sat on the chamber's committees on arbitration, transportation, and national affairs and served as chairman of the committee on manufacturing and business enterprises. Among others, he represented the chamber at the 1885 National Commercial Convention in Atlanta, 1887 Interstate Commerce Commission hearing in Atlanta, 1888 Savannah River Convention in Augusta, 1889 opening of the Cincinnati Chamber of Commerce, 1890 and 1898 National Board of Trade and American Shipping League Conventions in Washington, D.C., 1890 Pan-American Conference, 1894 Industrial Meeting in New York, and 1898 Indianapolis Monetary Convention. From 1888 to 1899, members elected him to the board of directors and for three consecutive years, 1890–93, unanimously chose him as president of the organization. Bullock was personally involved in asking the Interstate Commerce Commission to eliminate disparities in shipping rates over different distances (sometimes short distances cost much more than long) and to reduce freight rates through distribution centers like Atlanta. At Atlanta city council meetings, he argued for reduced taxes on manufacturers. To facilitate trade and communication, he supported a Nicaraguan Canal and sent a resolution to Congress requesting faster mail service through Atlanta. Always the promoter, Bullock subscribed $1,000 to the Chamber of Commerce Investment Association, a $100,000 fund designed to contribute a subsidy of up to 20 percent of the cost involved in locating new corporations to Atlanta. It was state aid once more on a smaller scale.[39]

Bullock busily devoted himself to a wide range of projects designed to enhance the city's development. In 1883, the Kimball House burned and a call went up immediately to rebuild it. Kimball returned to Atlanta to oversee the project, even though he did not own the hotel that carried his name. Bullock and others solicited funds for the project and appealed for contributors to show Atlanta's spirit. The new Kimball House opened in 1885. In 1884 Bullock joined with Kimball, Jacob Elsas, and twenty-four other businessmen to buy for $45 an acre and incorporate the Westview Cemetery, a 577-acre tract on the city's outskirts. The cemetery was lavishly landscaped with more than ten thousand ornamental shrubs, and its five and one-half miles of drives became a favorite area for outings of the Gentleman's Driving Club. Later, many of the city's prominent residents were buried there, including Grady, Joel Chandler Harris, and Coca-Cola founder Asa Candler. In 1885, when Atlanta vied with Macon to gain legislative sanction as the site for a state technological school, Bullock joined the twenty largest contributors and campaigned for his city. After Atlanta boosters convinced the state legislature to approve its plan, the Georgia Institute of Technology opened its doors in the state's most progressive city.[40]

Bullock also belonged to the Commercial Club, an exclusive spin-off of leading Chamber of Commerce members, and in 1893 and 1894 he was the club's president. Corresponding with the reorganization of the chamber in 1883, leaders established the Capital City Club, limited membership to four hundred, exacted a $50 initiation fee and $50 annual dues, and, emphasizing its business and social orientation, built a new clubhouse at 168 Peachtree Street downtown. Bullock had sufficient status to be elected six times as vice-president.[41]

For more social activity, the businessmen formed the Gentleman's Driving Club in 1887 and, after the purchase of Piedmont Park, changed the name to the Piedmont Driving Club. When the city of Atlanta campaigned to buy Piedmont Park, Bullock supported the project and matched the largest contribution by any individual, $2,500. Clearly he sat in the inner circle of "polite society." He had come from being an outsider—carpet-bagger, scalawag, Republican governor—to be a prominent member of the New South club. If Democrats had only allowed him to participate without accepting him socially, they would not have elected him to high offices within their business and social organizations. Still, Bullock sometimes found himself in peculiar positions, once attending a banquet in honor of John B. Gordon. Another ironic event happened when Alexander Stephens died in 1883; the pallbearers were James M. Smith, Alfred H. Colquitt, John B. Gordon, Robert Toombs, Joseph Brown, Emory Speer, and Rufus Bullock. That Democrats allowed him this honor demonstrates his bonding with their economic group.[42]

Of course, New South promoters gained much by having Bullock among them. His presence fairly shouted to Northern investors that the South was changing. And with the predominance of Republicans in the White House during the Gilded Age, Bullock was useful at gatherings to welcome to Atlanta national Republicans such as Presidents Benjamin Harrison and William McKinley and financier Jay Gould. That Bullock participated in nearly every Northern commercial convention to which the Chamber of Commerce sent representatives and that he accompanied Grady to Boston and New York in 1889 when Grady's power was at its height indicated Atlantans' faith in his abilities. In 1898, they named him to the committee charged with coordinating the Atlanta Peace Jubilee, which celebrated victory in the Spanish-American War. President McKinley and other national leaders came to Atlanta for that event.[43]

Even though they had denigrated his actions during Reconstruction, Democrats now hailed his efforts in Atlanta. In his 1889 *History of Atlanta*, Wallace Reed wrote of Bullock's "steady support" of Atlanta: "In every measure for her promotion he has been foremost . . . and much of her progress and prosperity is due to his personal efforts and encouragement." *Dixie* magazine printed the following praise: "Henry W. Grady, J. C. Peck [architect], H. I. Kimball, and R. B. Bullock are responsible more than any other men for the splendid position Atlanta occupies today among the manufacturing cities of the United States." Benjamin H. Hill, Jr., commented in 1893 on Bullock's transition: "Governor Bullock is now one of the most honored citizens of Atlanta and a welcome guest at any Southern home." Clearly, as contemporary historian Lucian Knight observed, Bullock "converted obloquy into esteem." [44]

Although he grew in prestige and position among New South Atlantans, Bullock did not surrender his belief in equality. That is not to say that he was a true egalitarian; he was color-blind, not class-blind. Although he did not accept Grady's position on racial caste, he did believe in social class. When Grady spoke of "the right of character, intelligence, and property to rule," Bullock added: "The color or nativity of the ignorant and vicious voter is not material. The only safety is the united vote of intelligence and virtue." Grady wanted to exclude all blacks and lower-class whites. Bullock did not exclude upper-class blacks. Bullock implored Grady "to teach the people that the negro is with us as a citizen to stay. That the franchise cannot be regulated along a color line. That there is no 'problem' about it, except our own ability as white men and citizens to lift ourselves above our prejudices of 'caste.' " [45]

Grady refused that suggestion, and most Southerners were unable to agree that races have different pigmentation, not different capabilities. Both Grady and Bullock held elitist concepts that the upper class should rule. Both believed that society had superiors and subordinates; but Grady defined "superiors" in terms of race and class while Bullock defined them by class only. They differed in Bullock's belief in the impersonal free labor system over the old paternalistic dependency based on racial caste. From an upper-class viewpoint, Grady's model was more effective because it split white from black workers and limited the possibility that the lower class would develop class consciousness. [46]

Because of their different views on race and their prominence in Atlanta affairs, Bullock and Grady sometimes tangled in the press. Neither wanted this, of course—it went against their promotion of the New South as a tranquil place and belied their rhetoric of change; yet sometimes local politics interfered. Grady probably published Bullock's printed responses because he knew whites held to beliefs about the Lost Cause and the corruption of Reconstruction. Their December 1888 newspaper debate best illustrated their differences. On December 1, Grady editorialized: "It is not the democratic party of the south that is solid, but the white people. Everybody . . . knows that the solidity of the south hurts and cripples this section politically; everybody knows that it prevents a full and fair discussion of important issues. And yet—it is better to be politically crippled—

it is better to smother discussion, than to renew the experience of reconstruction times." [47] The next day, Bullock answered that "the 'experience
of reconstruction times' . . . was not hurtful of our material interests but
only to our prejudices of caste." He stressed that the section's material dis-
advantage was "the fault of our white people who refused to accept the
citizenship and enfranchisement of the negro." [48]

The next week, Grady wrote that one of the delegates at the Southern Forestry Conference convention in Atlanta had "African blood in his
veins." The convention met to discuss the depletion of American forests
and suggested legislation to promote conservation. The meeting was over
and the delegate was gone but, Grady fumed, a black man had stayed in the
Markham House and even roomed with a white man. Bullock, who was
president of the conference, acknowledged that Ohio delegate James Poin-
dexter was black. Bullock's rejoinder recalled abolitionist higher-law doctrine and the American creed:

> Is it not of vital importance for us white people to know, to admit and to
> act upon the fundamental fact that a man takes rank as an American citizen
> in all public affairs according to his intelligence and his personal character,
> neither advanced nor retarded by his nativity or by his blood? The great
> boast of Atlanta is her superiority to provincialism. Shall we keep this boast
> good and move on with the world into the new order of things, or shall we
> hedge ourselves within *the narrow lines of prejudice and arrogance* and be
> left behind? [49]

Grady refused to incorporate equality of opportunity into his New South
agenda. He not only parried Bullock's thrusts; he deflected attacks from
George Washington Cable, the most eloquent Southern voice for black
equality. Cable chided Southerners who saw the wrongs done to blacks and
stood silent "because their belief is unfortunately stronger in the futility
of their counsel than in the power of a just cause." Although he took up
the Radical position on civil and economic rights under law, Cable called
social equality "a fool's dream." Grady responded by insisting on white
supremacy and said that no friction existed between whites and blacks.
Grady adhered to the position he articulated in the 1886 speech that made
him famous and continued to insist that the Old South of slavery and secession had been replaced with a New South of freedom and union. Cable
knew that Grady was a racist who lied to promote the New South as a

region of "industrial and commercial expansion." In response to Grady's 1886 "New South" speech, Cable cleverly rhymed:

> He was eloquent, also, was Grady;
> Patriotic and bright as a lady.
> But on MEN'S EQUAL RIGHTS,
> The darkest of nights
> Compared with him wouldn't seem shady.
> There wasn't a line, good sirs, bless ye,
> Of all that he chose to address ye,
> That touched the one point
> Where the South's out of joint
> For it wasn't his wish to distress ye.

Cable explained this New South as one dominated by class rule, where promoters "set aside questions of right and wrong for questions of expediency."[50]

Because Bullock often helped defend Gilded Age Atlanta as a place where blacks progressed materially and educationally, he was part of the problem Cable defined. By 1891, as chief Atlanta booster through his office as president of the city's Chamber of Commerce, Bullock claimed that blacks had full political rights and good educational opportunities and credited the "master class" for that condition. Because he stood with his class and still placed confidence in the gospel of prosperity, Bullock found his voice for racial equality only when he felt the stings of verbal darts against his character. He failed to condemn lynchings and ignored the fact that sharecropping, crop lien, and convict lease were slavery refashioned. But when editors wrote about the evils of Reconstruction or criticized, in racist terms, a person or project with which he was associated, Bullock quickly responded.[51]

He did little else. He would not jeopardize his social position to fight a battle he could not win. Although he often appealed for racial justice, he placed business first and continued to hope that prosperity would bring change. In the main, he stood silent, remembered the failure of Reconstruction, and knew that even though society became increasingly divided, segregation was better than exclusion. Howard Rabinowitz concluded that white and black Radicals bowed to segregation when they realized integration was impossible and feared that exclusion might be forced if segregation failed. Cable was right; Bullock and others sought expediency. Yet, in the final analysis, because of men like Grady, neither Cable nor Bullock had much impact on the beliefs and behavior of white Southerners.[52]

On December 12, 1889, eleven days before pneumonia killed him, Grady delivered a speech before four hundred businessmen, including Andrew Carnegie, at the Boston Merchants' Association. Bullock joined the cadre of fifteen New South supporters who traveled with Grady. Responding to the protest of Northern editors that blacks still could not vote in the South, Grady opposed the passage of any federal enforcement act to supervise Southern elections. Grady admitted that the South had a "race problem" and claimed that there were "two utterly dissimilar races on the same soil—with equal political and civil rights—almost equal in numbers, but terribly unequal in intelligence and responsibility." The following day, Grady and Bullock had breakfast with leaders of the Boston association and exchanged views on business.[53]

In New York City the next day, Bullock, with a Confederate Survivor's Association button on his lapel, spoke against national interference in Southern elections. He suggested that if Congress refused to seat those elected when there was evidence of intimidation or fraud, the people of the unrepresented district would ensure their next vote was "full, free and fair." Bullock blamed communities and their "better elements" for allowing assaults against blacks and said that if they took the responsibility for protecting their people, "a better condition would soon be apparent." That night, Grady was too ill to attend the banquet at Delmonico's. The Georgia delegation went in his stead; again Bullock spoke against any new federal enforcement act to oversee elections.[54]

Actually, Bullock repeated a position he had expressed during the presidential campaign season in 1888. He called for an end to the Republican party's strategy of appealing to the "bloody shirt" to entice Northern voters to vote as they had fought during the Civil War. Bullock explained that Republicans should do nothing that might "arouse any of the old animosities or do anything to solidify the [Southern] whites." He believed that noninterference was the best policy for business and for the national Republican party. Instead of using federal supervisors to oversee elections, Bullock suggested that for a congressman's election to be valid, he should be required to win a certain percentage of the registered vote, not just of the vote cast. Bullock obviously supported noninterference at the state level to keep peace in Georgia while he advocated interference at the national level to help ensure voting rights. Bullock recited his compromise that the "South is prospering now as never before. The people are interested in manufactures and the development of the country. Any disturbance which would set the races by the ears and divert the general attention from business pursuits would be disastrous." [55]

In response, the *New York Times* editorialized that Bullock presented a "rose-colored view of the conditions of things in the South, but his conclusions . . . are perfectly sound." Misunderstanding Bullock's object, longtime black advocate Republican senator William E. Chandler of New Hampshire criticized: "Outcast, ex-Governor Rufus B. Bullock, has purchased his peace and a safe return to Georgia by publicly advocating, while yet claiming to be a republican, the deliberate abandonment by the north of the fifteenth amendment." [56]

Bullock called Chandler a willful liar and reaffirmed his full support for the Fifteenth Amendment. Bullock proved his dedication in an article he had already published in the most recent copy of the *Criterion*. Bullock had written that as quickly as racial prejudices could be outgrown, "we will give to those amendments [Fourteenth and Fifteenth] full force and effect." Bullock challenged readers to review the gains blacks had won in the South. In the immediate aftermath of the war, Bullock remembered, "Like children afraid of Spooks did we not fill our minds with imaginary fears of the dangers" as the Southern states shamefully enacted the black codes. He tried to shame whites who "assume title to superior political rights and duties, when, in fact under the law, there is absolutely no distinction. We are not responsible for what the negro may fail to become as a citizen, and we ought to guard carefully against the danger of being responsible for retarding him in any honest effort he may make to take his legal place as a citizen." [57]

In refuting Chandler's charge, Bullock could not resist casting blame for the failure of Reconstruction—and he remembered that during those years Chandler was Republican party chairman. Bullock recited the evaluation of a Radical leader of Chandler and others who failed to ensure Reconstruction's success as the " 'truckling cowardice of leading Republicans.' " Because both men remained friends of the freed people and supporters of equal rights, their newspaper feud was unfortunate. [58]

If Bullock was blind to and inconsistent on the need for more federal legislation to guarantee the black franchise, he was not alone. Many prosperous Atlanta blacks joined Booker T. Washington in successfully opposing passage of the 1890 Lodge Force Bill, which would have provided federal supervision of elections. Then, in 1899 and 1900, the Georgia legislature tightened voting requirements. Through the new "white primary," white Democrats selected the winning candidate before blacks were allowed to vote in the general election. Additionally, not only did voters have to pay a cumulative poll tax, they had to pass a literacy test to prove an "ability to read a clause in the Constitution and ability to understand that clause." If they were illiterate but white, the legislature allowed them to vote under a "grandfather" clause, which granted the franchise to those who had it before 1867.[59]

Bullock protested and, in several interviews in 1902, insisted that the Fifteenth Amendment already was "clear and distinct" about voting rights; if the Supreme Court and Congress would enforce that amendment, the South would comply. Bullock called the Republican party "pusillanimous" and "cowardly." He wanted the party to return to its "principles" and queried: "If the Republican Party is not responsible [for black disfranchisement in the South] who is?" He explained that Republicans let the South violate the conditions of its reentry to the Union by not enforcing the Fifteenth Amendment. He made a suggestion: "In defense of the black race and of the integrity of the Constitution, strike from the rolls of the Senate and House the names of Senators and members from states that have violated the conditions of franchise on which they were admitted." He steadfastly believed that the "Republican party cannot do less and command for itself respect."[60]

He derided the Compromise of 1877 by which Rutherford B. Hayes was elected as proof that non-Radical Republicans had defended black rights only to strengthen their Northern constituency. Citing recent Southern constitutions that excluded blacks through grandfather clauses, Bullock asked, "What has the Republican party done to protect the civil and political rights of the black race?" Bullock called Republican support of black rights a "plain duty."[61]

Yet he believed that new legislation beyond the enforcement of an amendment already on the books would only stir up old issues. His claim that "the colored vote has disfranchised itself by a failure to pay even the poll tax of $1.00 per year" showed him to be out of touch with poor people. Bullock clearly indicated his class orientation when he concluded: "The safety of every community is assured by the ballot being limited to the intelligent citizen, white and black." Educated black Georgians protested the grandfather clause, but even they supported the literacy tests. Bullock reemphasized that the electorate should "be composed of the more intelligent, thrifty property holders, white and black. . . . The intelligent, well-educated negro is as capable of exercising the franchise properly as a white man—much more entitled to it than a whiskey-drinking white loafer. It would be much better to have fewer voters than we have now."[62]

Bullock said the primary system "works exceedingly well in Georgia and makes it a white man's election, although there is no reason why colored men who are worthy [wealthy] of the franchise should be excluded." Bullock explained that under a primary system, "the tax-paying people" united to elect representatives and "unseemly party contests about local affairs have been avoided." Clearly Bullock supported class rule and the New South rhetoric of a peaceful South. By 1900, only nine hundred Atlanta blacks even bothered to register. There was almost no black voter participation in the elections, but that is hardly surprising considering the political milieu. In all the years since 1868, only two of twenty-three black candidates ever won city office, and that was in 1870.[63]

In 1894 and 1895 Atlanta leaders prepared to promote the city and entertain the nation by holding the Cotton States and International Exposition. New South leaders believed in the efficacy of expositions to promote the section. After the success of the 1881 International and Cotton Exposition, Atlanta hosted the 1887 Piedmont and 1889 Cotton expositions. As usual, Bullock was very active in organizing and promoting these fairs. He sat on the executive committee and board of directors of each exposition.[64]

While promoters planned, news swept the city that Bright's disease had claimed the life of H. I. Kimball at his brother's home in Boston. The *Atlanta Constitution* pronounced Kimball "a developer in the truest sense. . . . Impatient for the future, Kimball took time by the forelock and proceeded to organize, and put into operation various plans calculated to add to the importance of Atlanta." Cotton merchandiser and exporter Samuel M. Inman eulogized Kimball as having been "several years ahead of the people among whom he lived in his ideas of great enterprises. . . . Kimball was thoroughly honest in every one of his undertakings. With him money was a secondary consideration. He was a developing genius."[65]

A Chamber of Commerce committee of three, which included Inman and Bullock, met to consider erecting a monument to Kimball but concluded that the city already was full of "memorials" to him. Although praise for the developer abounded, only Bullock took a train north to attend the funeral.[66]

Patterned after the 1893 Chicago World's Fair, the Cotton States and

International Exposition was expected to inspire confidence and stimulate trade after the Panic of 1893. Working from the suggestion of W. A. Hemphill, business manager of the *Constitution,* Chamber of Commerce president Stewart Woodson and Commercial Club president Bullock called a joint meeting of over three hundred businessmen to promote the idea. Bullock enjoined the members to ensure that the exposition demonstrated the South's resources so it would draw immigrants and investors. He proposed an international scope to foster trade with South and Central America and the West Indies. He called for assistance from other chambers of commerce and a federal appropriation to ensure the success of the project. Bullock served conspicuously on the committees for colored exhibit, awards, reception for President Cleveland, government appropriations, legislation, ceremonial days, and entertainment.[67]

Bullock was perhaps most active on the committee that worked to promote the Colored Exhibit. This exhibit was designed and built entirely by blacks, who organized a committee of their own because no black sat on the board of directors. When the white committee met with the black committee, Bullock exchanged ideas with prominent black leaders, among them Bishop William J. Gaines of Atlanta, Booker T. Washington of Tuskegee Institute, and Virginian I. Garland Penn, who headed the committee. In April 1894, Bullock joined these men and twenty-five others before the House Appropriations Committee to ask for government support for the exposition. Success was theirs when Congress appropriated $200,000. The Colored Exhibit was the first of its kind at any American exposition. New South promoters hoped it would demonstrate to the world their commitment to black progress.[68]

Still, there was an argument over whether to include a black speaker in the opening ceremonies. Exposition president Charles A. Collier, a lawyer, banker, president of the Atlanta Gas Light Company, and major shareholder in a Columbus cotton mill, wanted a separate ceremony to open the Colored Exhibit. But Garland Penn asked Bullock to use his influence to give Booker T. Washington a place in the main ceremony. As chairman of the Committee on Ceremonial Days and member of the Committee on the Colored Exhibit as well as his position in Atlanta's business and social circles, Bullock persuaded others to acquiesce to Penn's request.[69]

The fair opened on September 18 to great fanfare despite some unfinished buildings, uncleared construction debris, and several wareless exhibitors. From Gray Gables, Massachusetts, President Grover Cleveland pressed a telegraphic key that started the machinery. As master of ceremonies, Bullock directed the day's events and introduced each speaker. He was proud of the advances of thirty years, as his opening remarks attest: "This is the greatest hour in the history of Atlanta and the South. We have assembled to officially open the greatest achievement that has been a result of Southern enterprise." Other speakers echoed the New South story.[70]

Then Bullock introduced the fair's most memorable moment: "We shall now be favored with an address by a great Southern educator." The crowd applauded loudly until Washington rose. Upon seeing the black man, the audience quickly fell silent. Bullock continued, "We have with us today a representative of Negro enterprise and Negro civilization." Blacks in the crowd cheered enthusiastically; most whites stared in silence. Washington walked to the podium, and his speech quickly gained wide approval with the crowd. He did not ask whites to accept blacks as social equals: "The wisest among my race understand that the agitation of questions of social equality is the extremest folly, and that progress in the enjoyment of all the privileges that will come to us must be the result of severe and constant struggle rather than of artificial forcing."[71]

When Washington finished his ten-minute address, Bullock rushed to congratulate him. They stood together hand in hand for a moment; both understood that although Washington wanted equality for blacks, he spoke the reality of turn-of-the-century America. The promise and ideals of Reconstruction seemed far away. Acknowledgment of gradualism replaced demands for immediate equality. Washington's biographer concluded that he was "not an intellectual, but a man of action" who wore different masks and played different roles to secure the best possible terms from a racist society. Bullock was much the same. Washington recognized their similarities, knew Bullock as a friend, and praised him as an honorable man of "high character and usefulness."[72]

Both men supported industrial training for blacks. Washington founded Tuskegee Institute for just that purpose. Bullock continued to support Atlanta University with financial contributions, attendance at graduation exercises, and as a member of its board of trustees from 1892 to 1896. With its pledge "to receive all students of either sex without regard to race or color," Atlanta University was the most progressive college in Georgia. Its faculty trained many teachers and skilled workers. The men's curriculum focused on industrial education in carpentry, blacksmithing, farming, drafting, and printing; women learned nursing, dressmaking, printing, sewing, and cooking. In 1887, after defying the state legislature's demand that it exclude white students, Atlanta University lost its $8,000 yearly state appropriation. Bullock's continued affiliation with the university shows him out of step with white lawmakers, and he conceded: "The great need of higher or university education to prepare competent colored leaders for the race is not so well understood by our people as it will be later."[73]

In 1893, J. L. M. Curry, chairman of the Slater Fund, a $1 million endowment to provide assistance to black education, asked Bullock his opinion on changing fund recipients from institutions that taught classical education to those teaching industrial vocations. Bullock answered in favor of vocational training "to provide our colored friends with such knowledge as will enable them by honest energy and intelligent application to earn good livelihoods . . . and at the same time benefit our community by having in our midst educated artisans."[74]

Washington and Bullock believed that economic opportunity and prosperity were touchstones for change; they asked that blacks have a fair chance to help themselves. Atlanta's black leaders were in general agreement. African-American Atlanta editor Benjamin Davis supported that idea and stated: "Our growth, if permanent and substantial, must like the white man's issue from material development." Black historian E. R. Carter called for blacks "to reconcile" with white Democrats: "We have tried politics . . . and still we are in our graves." Black Atlanta educator J. W. E. Bowen of the Gammon School of Theology explained: "There is no such thing as perfect equality . . . The negro must be a worker." These men witnessed the increasing numbers of Southern lynchings, heard white politicians defend them, and adjusted their positions to keep their people alive.[75]

In 1898, the outspoken Rebecca Latimer Felton, who became America's first woman senator, roared: "If it requires lynching to protect woman's dearest possession from ravening, drunken human beasts, then I say lynch a thousand a week." In 1899, Governor Allen D. Candler concurred that rape was "the crime which nine times out of ten is the cause . . . of lynching." Felton, Candler, and others readily conjured the image of the black beast to further their political aspirations. Historians now understand that rape was the excuse, not the cause. But with Southern lynchings averaging over one hundred a year during the 1890s, many black leaders feared further to infuriate whites by "demanding" equality. Henry Turner became so disillusioned that he called for a return to Africa and said: "Talk about

dying in Africa! My God! Can we die any faster than we are being murdered here?" Later, he added: "Hell is an improvement upon the United
States where the negro is involved."[76]

In 1898 Booker T. Washington spoke at the Chicago Peace Jubilee and
called on whites to overcome their prejudices concerning civil relations
with blacks. The *Atlanta Constitution* immediately denounced Washington and responded that social relations included travel restrictions: "It is
not a part of the civil rights of the negro that in order to travel, he must sit
by a white person. . . . Were there two passenger cars exactly alike attached
to the same train with the simple difference that the whites were to ride in
one and the blacks in the other, the latter would still claim that they were
being discriminated against." The *Constitution* contended that the races
were different, people understood the rule against social mixing, "and that
rule was written by God Almighty Himself."[77]

Bullock criticized that editorial and argued that it was wrong to put
blacks in "Jim Crow" cars if they paid equal fares or traveled with a white
companion. Bullock admitted that although no legislation could assure
social equality, "We must lift ourselves above our 'prejudices' and see to
it that every black American citizen has his equal civil and public rights."
He insisted that Washington told the "exact truth": "We have succeeded
in every contest except to conquer ourselves in the blotting out of racial
prejudices. . . . Until we thus conquer ourselves I say we shall have, especially in the southern part of our country, a cancer gnawing at the heart of
this republic."[78]

But as discrimination and de jure segregation increased in the early
1900s, it was apparent that few political power brokers listened to Bullock.
White Southerners brushed aside his admonitions and demonstrated the
basic difference between them and him. By appearances, Bullock seemed
to be an Atlanta insider, but his principles exposed him as an outsider.

Epilogue

Few Georgians, whether by birth or adoption,
did more real good for the state than he.
—*Atlanta Constitution*, April 28, 1907

He did not loot the state nor benefit by it,
but was sincere in his efforts.
—*Augusta Chronicle*, April 30, 1907

THE 1895 COTTON STATES AND INTERNATIONAL EXPOSITION
gave Bullock great satisfaction. He not only sat onstage with the most
prominent members of the New South, he was master of ceremonies. That
role fit him well, and he reveled in it; after all, he had long helped direct
Atlanta's industrialization. Now he orchestrated the preeminent display of
Southern manufacture, agriculture, and commerce. He was proud of his
role in getting Booker T. Washington on the program and in aiding the
coordination and completion of the first black exhibit at any exposition in
the United States. After the fair closed, Bullock remained active in Atlanta,
but with less and less energy.

The Bullocks never really felt at home in the city. Their kinship ties
to New York and Rhode Island were stronger than any friendships they
cultivated in Atlanta. Even their closest acquaintances were transplanted
Northerners. After thirty years in Georgia, they still did not fit; the Reconstruction struggle made that impossible. Certainly, it would be difficult
to forget and forgive the massive assault made against Bullock's personal
and official character during those postwar days. The rhetoric of the Lost

Cause and continual snipes about Reconstruction bond issues and corruption kept the issues alive and gave the Bullocks little rest. They never understood the absolute refusal of most white Southerners to judge people by accomplishments instead of skin color.

The same year of the great exposition, Bullock resigned his position as president of the Atlanta Cotton Mills to become president of the English-American Loan and Trust Company, a firm capitalized at $100,000. By 1899, business was good enough for the company to build Atlanta's first skyscraper, the English-American Building. Twelve stories high, the building rose in the triangular block of Peachtree and Broad streets, where it still stands and is known popularly as the flatiron building. It is appropriate that Bullock led the way in changing the Atlanta skyline to a more suitable image for the South's preeminent city, the "Chicago of the South." [1]

In 1901, Bullock left the English-American Company. His personal finances were in shambles, probably because he always spent more than he made. His twenty-seven-year-old son Hugh, a lieutenant in the army, had died of pneumonia on April 22 while visiting Rhode Island. Marie was ill. He withdrew from the Chamber of Commerce and completed his plans for retirement. Marie held title to their house at 233 Peachtree Street, and she had mortgaged it for $11,000 in 1898. With that loan, she repaid a note for the same amount made in 1895; perhaps the money helped back the establishment of the English-American Loan Company. When the latter loan came due in 1901, the Bullocks were unable to repay it and the bank foreclosed. At a courthouse sale on February 4, 1902, the land, house, and total contents brought $14,500. [2]

The Bullocks took a room in the Peachtree Inn before moving to their summer home, Cold Brook Farm, in Charlestown, Rhode Island. Sometime earlier, their daughter, Cornelia, moved north with her husband, Leonard Kendall, and spent several summers abroad. She visited her parents after they resettled in Rhode Island and enjoyed a comfortable life, with children and maids to care for them. [3]

Volkert, who was thirty-nine years old and still at home, rented an apartment in Atlanta. After his publishing house failed, he got a paid position as secretary of the Chamber of Commerce before obtaining a job as assistant Atlanta postmaster. In 1903, he was jilted after a five-year love affair with an Atlanta woman; he never married. Marie confided to a friend that he had "lost all faith in humankind." An extremely sensitive man, Volkert wrote a book of poems in 1904 titled *Some Fairy Fancies Here You See as They Crossed the Mind of V. V. B.* This collection of thirteen page-length poems shows a man lost in another world and coping with reality by escapism:

> Did the fairies ever whisper in your ear?
> When they do, you must surely stop to hear . . .
>
> . . . .
>
> They're ghostlike and invisible,
>   To those that rule by force;
> They only show their beauties to
>   Their loving friends, of course.

In 1911, Volkert committed suicide in Anniston, Alabama.[4]

In his final political statements, Bullock still maintained that blacks should be given equal opportunity and that whites should fulfill the promise of the American creed. Of course, he still spoke in terms of class even when he belittled white racism. Bullock's 1903 letter to the editor of the *Churchman* chided him for criticizing Theodore Roosevelt's appointments of blacks to federal offices. Bullock wrote that it was high time to erase the "color line" and accept the constitutional changes of "thirty-five years ago." He spoke of "large numbers of colored people in the south [who] have become educated men and women of most excellent character and capacity." He asked sardonically, "Is there now any reason except the jealous and envious hate of a few low class white people found in many communities, why the black skin should be a bar to favorable action by the federal appointing power?"[5]

The next year, at the Georgia Republican convention in Atlanta, Bullock watched his old friend Henry Turner declare that today's Republicans only sought patronage positions and had no principles. Therefore, Turner announced, he was out of the party. A feeble seventy-year-old Bullock, already wracked from the illness that would slowly kill him, had to be helped to the podium. There, for the umpteenth time, he demanded that the government enforce the Fifteenth Amendment. He presented a resolution calling on Congress to refuse to seat any representatives from states whose laws disfranchised blacks. The resolution passed, but Congress did not heed it. Noting Bullock's continued insistence on equal rights, one Georgia editor remarked: "He was an ardent friend of the colored race."[6]

Soon after that appearance, Bullock's health worsened and he remained bedridden for over a month in the Peachtree Inn. As the dogwoods blossomed toward the end of April 1904, he and Marie left Atlanta for the last time. Later that year, a few days before Christmas, Marie died of heart disease. Bullock moved back into his childhood home in Albion, where a nurse cared for him.[7]

While Bullock lingered in Albion, conditions grew worse for blacks in Georgia. Henry Turner became so upset with the worsening inequality around him and with the lie that is the American creed that he exclaimed: "To the negro in this country the American flag is a dirty and contemptible rag. Not a star on it can the colored man claim, for it is no longer the symbol of our manhood and rights." In a private letter to Booker T. Washington, Turner seethed: "Hundreds of the most barbarous and inhuman so-called laws have been enacted under this same flag, and nothing has been said or done about it." In reality, the flag and the creed it claimed to represent had never covered the black man. Bullock and Turner fought for years to gain something that had been corrupt in the beginning.[8]

In 1906, white Atlantans flocked to see a dramatic adaptation of Thomas Dixon's *Clansmen,* a novel that portrayed the myth of Reconstruction and upheld the Lost Cause. Following Dixon's lead, Atlanta editors called for whites to reactivate the Ku Klux Klan to keep blacks in their place. In this climate, Hoke Smith campaigned for governor on a platform of white supremacy and black disfranchisement. Smith told large audiences, who twice voted him into the governor's chair, "The Negro is in no respect the equal of the white man, and . . . cannot in the future in this state occupy a position of equality." In September, with feelings at fever pitch, Atlanta's largest race riot ever erupted and rocked the city for five days. Hundreds were injured. Twenty-five blacks and one white lay dead in the streets before it was over.[9]

Bullock died in Albion on April 27, 1907, of locomotor ataxia, a form of syphilis. In Georgia, Governor Joseph M. Terrell proclaimed him "a man of prominence in industrial upbuilding" and ordered all flags on public buildings lowered to half-mast. Later that year, the Georgia legislature completed a dream most whites had shared since Reconstruction and disfranchised blacks. Politically, it was a senseless gesture because de facto disfranchisement had already been obtained. At the time only one black, Amos Rogers of McIntosh County, sat in the General Assembly. It is sadly coincidental that blacks gained the right to vote and hold office in the year of Bullock's ascendancy to the governor's chair and lost those rights the year he died. It would be sixty years—until 1970—before another liberal Georgia governor, James Earl Carter, would stand up for the constitutional guarantees of one man, one vote.[10]

Notes

CHAPTER 1. Yankee Schoolboy to Confederate Lieutenant Colonel

1. Booker T. Washington, *Up from Slavery: An Autobiography* (1901; rpt. New York: Bantam Books, 1967), p. 156.

2. *United States City Directories on Microfilm, Atlanta, 1894*, pp. 78–79; Lionel D. Wyld, ed., *40' × 28' × 4': The Erie Canal, 150 Years* (Rome, N.Y.: Oneida County Commission, 1967), p. 14.

3. *Contemporary American Biography*, 3 vols. (New York: Atlantic, 1895), 2:67; James F. Cook, *Governors of Georgia* (Huntsville, Ala: Strode Publishers, 1979), p. 167; "Bullock, Rufus B.," source unknown, Vertical Files, University of Georgia, Athens; *Orleans American* (Albion, N.Y.), April [?], 1883, in scrapbook in Office of Orleans County Historian, Albion, N.Y.; *Census of the United States, 1800*, Albany County, N.Y., p. 143, and 1810, p. 101.

4. In New York State there are three geographical divisions of land: counties, towns, and villages. Towns are subdivisions within a county; villages are population points within a town. The town of Albion did not exist until 1870, when it was created from the town of Barre. The village of Albion dates from 1811, when William McCollister settled there. See Bernard Lynch, Irene Gibson, and Howard Pratt, eds., *Orleans County History: Past to Present* (Albion, N.Y.: Eddy Printing, 1976), pp. 48–49; Grantee Index, Book 2, p. 534, and Grantor Index, Book 2, pp. 534–35; Records of Deeds, Deed Book 19, p. 196; Book 20, pp. 118, 249, 394; Book 21, p. 122; Book 34, p. 413; Book 36, p. 634; Book 37, p. 177; Book 43, p. 25; Book 44, p. 425; Book 56, pp. 296, 462; Book 61, p. 189; Book 63, p. 258; Book 93, p. 487, Office of the Clerk of Orleans County, Albion, N.Y.

5. Under an act of May 1835, workers widened the canal to seventy feet wide, fifty-two feet six inches deep, and straightened it to a reduced 350 miles. See Isaac S. Signor, *Landmarks of Orleans County, New York* (Syracuse, N.Y.: D. Mason, 1894), pp. 64–66; Eric Foner, *Reconstruction: America's Unfinished Revolution, 1863–1877* (New York: Harper & Row, 1988), p. 32; Philip Freneau, "The Great Western Canal," quoted in Wyld, ed., *40' × 28' × 4'*, pp. 29–30;

Arad Thomas, *Pioneer History of Orleans County, New York* (Albion, N.Y.: Orleans American Steam Print, 1871), p. 55; Lynch, Gibson, and Pratt, eds., *Orleans County History,* p. 49.

6. Arad Thomas, *Sketches of the Village of Albion* (Albion, N.Y.: Willsea and Beach, 1853), pp. 8–9, 35–43; Hamilton Child, comp., *Gazetteer and Business Directory of Orleans County, New York, for 1869* (Syracuse, N.Y.: Journal Office, 1869), pp. 77, 81; J. H. French, *Gazetteer of the State of New York* (Syracuse, N.Y.: R. P. Smith, 1860), p. 512.

7. "Introduction" and Rufus Brown to Freeman Clarke, August 26, September 6, 1840, Freeman Clarke Family Papers, University of Rochester, Rochester, N.Y.; *Hoffman's Albany Directory and City Register, 1840–1* (Albany, N.Y.: L. G. Hoffman, 1840), p. 58; *Albany Citizen's Advertiser, 1834–5* (Albany, N.Y.: N.p., 1835), p. 217; *Albany City Directory for the Year 1814* (Albany, N.Y.: N.p., 1814), p. 31; Child, comp., *Gazetteer,* p. 118; *Orleans American,* April [?], 1883, in Rufus Brown Bullock File, Office of the Orleans County Historian; *Rochester Daily Democrat,* June 13, 1851, p. 2, col. 5 (hereafter page and column are in parentheses); *Rochester Daily Union,* June 13, 1856 (3, 3); U.S. Census, 1850, Orleans County, Albion, manuscript, p. 163, New York State Census, Orleans County, 1855, manuscript (no page listed), and New York State Census, Orleans County, 1865, manuscript, p. 89, Office of the Clerk of Orleans County; Thomas, *Sketches,* pp. 23, 38; Signor, *Landmarks,* p. 269.

8. *Orleans American,* April [?], 1883, and *Orleans Republican,* March 15, 1882, in Rufus Bullock File, Office of the Orleans County Historian; *One Hundred Twenty-Fifth Anniversary of the First Presbyterian Church of Albion, New York* (Albion, N.Y.: N.p., 1949), First Presbyterian Church file, Swan Library, Albion, N.Y.; Annette L. Noble, *A History of the Presbyterian Church of Albion, New York, for One Hundred Years, 1824–1924* (Albion, N.Y.: N.p., 1924), p. 20; *Orleans Republican,* March 1, 1848 (1, 7), March 8, 1847 (1, 7).

9. Eric Foner, *Free Soil, Free Labor, Free Men: The Ideology of the Republican Party Before the Civil War* (New York: Oxford University Press, 1970), pp. 9–39; Thomas, *Sketches,* pp. 23–24; *Rochester Daily Union,* April 16, 1883 (2, 2). During the 1840s and 1850s in Albion the Whigs (later Republicans) held a slight majority over the Democrats.

10. "Death of Mrs. Volkert V. Bullock," newspaper clipping, scrapbook, Office of the Orleans County Historian.

11. It is possible but unlikely that Rufus entered Albion Academy in 1840. The common school dated from 1835, and students probably went there first. Also, the "full course" at the academy usually lasted six years. Rufus graduated in 1850 and so probably entered in 1844. The dates are confused by his own statements that he graduated in 1850, a listing of him taking the "full course" from 1840 to 1846, and his 1890 letter stating that he attended the academy from 1840 to 1852. See

Thomas, *Sketches,* pp. 30–34, and *A Memorial of the Albion Academy* (Albion, N.Y.: Orleans American Steam Print, 1891), pp. 23, 45; Franklin B. Hough, *Historical Record of the University of the State of New York* (Albany, N.Y.: Weed, Parsons & Co., 1885), p. 578; *Catalogue of the Officers and Students of Albion Academy, Spring and Summer Terms, 1838* (Albion, N.Y.: T. C. Strong, 1838), pp. 9–12; *Orleans Republican,* November 29, 1843 (3, 3).

12. *Memorial of Albion Academy,* pp. 8–13, 42, 46; Signor, *Landmarks,* pp. 116–17.

13. *Memorial of Albion Academy,* pp. 10, 12, 19, 43, 45; *Orleans Republican,* November 25, 1846 (4, 2); Thomas, *Sketches,* p. 33.

14. *Orleans Republican,* November 29, 1843 (3, 3), March 5, 1862 (2, 3); *Orleans American,* July 27, 1899 (3, 5); *Memorial of Albion Academy,* pp. 18–19, 37, 39, 41. Stilson served in the 1860 New York Assembly and later became a grocer in Albion.

15. *Memorial of Albion Academy,* pp. 18, 45. In 1850, Fanning relocated to Brooklyn and actively participated in Henry Ward Beecher's Congregational church before his death in 1873. See *Orleans Republican,* November 26, 1873 (3, 3).

16. *Atlas of Niagara and Orleans Counties, New York, 1875* (Philadelphia: Beers, Upton & Co., 1875), pp. 76–85; Thomas, *Sketches,* p. 10; Thomas, *Pioneer History,* p. 180.

17. Edward Magdol, *The Anti-Slavery Rank and File: A Social Profile of the Abolitionists' Constituency* (Westport, Conn.: Greenwood Press, 1986), pp. 24–50; *Memorial of Albion Academy,* p. 8.

18. *Rochester Daily Democrat,* July 11, 1843 (2, 7); New York State Census, Orleans County, 1855, manuscript in Office of the Clerk of Orleans County; "Bullock, Rufus," Vertical Files, University of Georgia; *Augusta Chronicle,* March 16, 1884 (3, 2); John S. Wilson, *Atlanta as It Is* (New York: Little, Rennie, & Co., 1871), p. 20; Rufus B. Bullock Collection, Swan Library, Albion, N.Y.; U.S. Census, 1850, Orleans County, Albion, manuscript, p. 163, Office of the Clerk of Orleans County; *Augusta Chronicle,* March 16, 1884 (3, 2); Alexander Jones, *Historical Sketches of the Electric Telegraph Including Its Rise and Progress in the United States* (New York: George P. Putnam, 1852), p. 77; T. S. Texton to Freeman Clarke, December 3, 1845, Freeman Clarke Papers, Margaret Woodbury Strong Museum, Rochester, N.Y.; James D. Reid, *The Telegraph in America: Its Founders, Promoters, and Noted Men* (New York: Derby Brothers, 1879), pp. 289, 456–62; V. V. Bullock to Freeman Clarke, August 8, 1854, Clarke Family Papers, University of Rochester. Clarke's entrepreneurial activities stretched in many directions. In 1850, he was influential in organizing the Rochester, Lockport, and Niagara Falls Railroad. Complete from Albion to Rochester by 1852, this railroad passed east-west through Albion, about three blocks south of Bul-

lock's house (*Historical Atlas of Orleans County, New York* [New York: Sanford & Co., 1879], pp. 78–79; Thomas, *Pioneer History,* p. 63). In 1855, Clarke helped form the Western Union Telegraph Company. See Reid, *Telegraph in America,* pp. 280–81; George B. Prescott, *History, Theory, and Practice of the Electric Telegraph* (Boston: Ticknor & Fields, 1866), p. 125; Rufus Brown Bullock File, Office of the Orleans County Historian.

19. V. V. Bullock to Freeman Clarke, August 8, 1854, Clarke Family Papers, University of Rochester.

20. Ibid., August 4, 1855.

21. V. V. Bullock to Freeman Clarke, August 8, 1854, August 4, 1855, and Rufus Bullock to Freeman Clarke, July 31, 1855, ibid.

22. *Augusta Chronicle,* March 16, 1884 (3, 2), and *Providence Journal,* July [?], 1904, Rufus Brown Bullock File, Office of the Orleans County Historian; Reid, *Telegraph in America,* pp. 141, 414, 417, 455, 457, 462, 640; Wallace P. Reed, ed., *History of Atlanta, Georgia: With Illustrations and Biographical Sketches of Some of Its Prominent Men and Pioneers* (Syracuse, N.Y.: D. Mason, 1889), p. 12; *Memoirs of Georgia,* 2 vols. (Atlanta: Southern Historical Association, 1895), 2:730; Prescott, *Electric Telegraph,* p. 139.

23. Reid, *Telegraph in America,* pp. 456–57; *Augusta Chronicle,* March 16, 1884 (3, 2); *Atlanta Constitution,* April 28, 1907 (1, 4–5).

24. John R. DeTreville, "Reconstruction in Augusta, Georgia, 1865–1868" (M.A. thesis, University of North Carolina, 1979), pp. 1–7; Florence F. Corley, *Confederate City: Augusta, Georgia, 1860–1865* (Columbia, S.C.: University of South Carolina Press, 1960), pp. 8, 14; *Pictorial History of Augusta, Georgia* (Augusta, Ga.: Fleming, 1962), p. 15; U.S. Census, Eighth Census, 1860, Population Schedules, Richmond County, Ga., microfilm, roll 135, p. 767.

25. DeTreville, "Reconstruction in Augusta," p. 16; *Directory for the City of Augusta and Business Advertiser for 1859* (Augusta, Ga.: R. A. Watkins, 1859), p. 160.

26. *Tutler's Augusta Directory for 1861* (Augusta, Ga.: Steam Power Press, 1861), p. 45; *Pughe's Augusta City Directory, 1865–66* (Augusta, Ga.: E. H. Pughe, 1866), p. 11; William K. Miller, *History of St. Paul's Episcopal Church, Augusta, Georgia* (Augusta, Ga.: Tidwell Printing, 1945), p. 73; Index to Marriages, Burials, Confirmations, 1820–1913, Richmond County, St. Paul's Episcopal Church, Georgia Department of Archives and History (hereafter GDAH), microfilm, pp. 10, 12, 15. Rufie died May 9, 1865. See Parish Register of Communicants, Baptisms, Confirmations, Marriages, Burials, 1820–1868, ibid., pp. 118, 120, 122, 124, 185, 204, 289.

27. G. Hutchinson Smyth, *The Life of Henry B. Plant: Founder and President of the Plant System of Railroads and Steamships and Also of the Southern Express Company* (New York: G. P. Putnam's Sons, 1898), pp. 1, 54, 62, 99, 233;

S. Walter Martin, "Henry Bradley Plant," in *Georgians in Profile: Historical Essays in Honor of Ellis Merton Coulter*, ed. Horace Montgomery (Athens: University of Georgia Press, 1958), p. 261; *Directory for the City of Augusta and Business Advertiser for 1859*, pp. 33, 113; *Tutler's Augusta Directory for 1861*, pp. 25, 93; Edward J. Cashin, *The Story of Augusta* (Augusta, Ga.: Richmond County Board of Education, 1980), p. 205; Georgia Vol. 1B, p. 155, R. G. Dun & Company Collection, Baker Library, Harvard University, Cambridge, Mass.

28. Russell Duncan, "The Southern Express Company," in Richard N. Current, ed., *Encyclopedia of the Confederacy* (New York: Simon & Schuster, forthcoming).

29. Smyth, *Life of Plant*, p. 58; Martin, "Henry Bradley Plant," p. 270; *Rochester Mail and Express*, March 17, 1888, in Rufus Brown Bullock Papers, Huntington Library, San Marino, Calif.; Corley, *Confederate City*, pp. 30–32; Eleanore E. Weeks, "Chest Found in Wall Links Albion to Civil War South," *Rochester Democrat and Chronicle*, undated [1939], in Rufus Bullock file, Records of Mt. Albion Cemetery, Albion, N.Y.

30. *Augusta Daily Chronicle and Sentinel*, January 25 (2, 1), February 28 (3, 5), 1861; *Atlanta Daily New Era*, April 10, 1868 (2, 4), quoting the *Augusta Chronicle*. For amplification of the history of the Augusta Arsenal see Ruby M. Pfadenhauer, "History of the Augusta Arsenal," *Richmond County History* 2 (Summer 1970): 1–40.

31. Martin, "Henry Bradley Plant," pp. 266–67; E. Merton Coulter, *The Confederate States of America* (Baton Rouge: Louisiana State University Press, 1950), pp. 128–30, 281; *Augusta Chronicle*, April 10, 1861 (2, 4); *Augusta Constitutionalist*, April 17, 1868 (1, 1); Smyth, *Life of Plant*, p. 233.

32. C. G. Memminger to H. B. Plant, September 2, 1861, Plant to Memminger, September 24, 1861, and C.S.A. to Plant, August 18, 1862, January 31, September 30, December 31, 1864, in Confederate Papers Relating to Citizens or Business Firms, Microcopy 346, Roll 965, and Microcopy 345, Roll 805, National Archives (hereafter NA); Rufus B. Bullock to C. G. Memminger, December 2, 1861, Letters Received by the Confederate Secretary of War, 1861–1865, Microcopy 437, Roll 17, NA.

33. Bullock to Memminger, January 1, 1863, Letters Received by the Confederate Secretary of War, Microcopy 437, Roll 17, NA; [unknown] to General S. Cooper, November 10, 1864, Letters Received by the Confederate Adjutant and Inspector General, 1861–1865, Microcopy 474, Roll 145, p. 114, NA.

34. Corley, *Confederate City*, p. 49; *Augusta Chronicle*, January 15, 1865 (3, 2); *Contemporary American Biography* 2:68.

35. Mary A. DeCredico, "Georgia's Entrepreneurs and Confederate Mobilization, 1847–1873" (Ph.D. dissertation, Vanderbilt University, 1986), pp. 128, 189–90, 194, 217.

36. Martin, "Henry Bradley Plant," p. 268; *Augusta Chronicle*, August 4 (2, 1), 13 (3, 1), 16 (3, 2), May 17 (3, 1), July 11 (3, 1), 1861, August 7, 1863 (2, 2), March 4 (2, 2), May 24 (1, 1), 1864.

37. *Augusta Chronicle*, March 16, 1884 (3, 2), August 26, 1895 (2, 3); Cashin, *Story of Augusta*, p. 127.

38. Tax Digests for Richmond County, 1859–64, 1866–68, microfilm, GDAH; Smyth, *Life of Plant*, pp. 58, 99–100. H. B. Plant returned to America at war's end and developed his business in railroads, steamships, and telegraph and express services. He invested a great deal of money in Southern enterprises after 1879, controlling over two thousand miles of rail and twelve hundred miles of steamship lines. His total worth approached $19 million. In 1895 he employed more than two thousand blacks and contributed to black churches, schools, and enterprises. See ibid., pp. 242, 257–60.

39. *U.S. City Directories, Atlanta, 1894,* pp. 78–79; Rufus B. Bullock to Mrs. Achilles, February 17, 1902, Bullock Collection, Swan Library; Edwin M. Stanton to Maj.-Gen. Henry W. Halleck, May 4, 1865, and Halleck to Stanton, May 4, 1865, U.S. War Department, *The War of the Rebellion: A Compilation of the Official Records of the Union and Confederate Armies,* 128 vols. (Washington, D.C.: U.S. Government Printing Office, 1880–1901), Ser. 2, vol. 8, pp. 530–31.

40. *Savannah Morning News*, April 17, 1868 (2, 1); *Augusta Chronicle*, August 13, 1868 (3, 4); *Columbus Sun*, April 5, 1868, quoted in Alan Conway, *The Reconstruction of Georgia* (Minneapolis: University of Minnesota Press, 1966), p. 158.

CHAPTER 2. Augusta Entrepreneur

1. Larry N. Powell, *New Masters: Northern Planters During the Civil War and Reconstruction* (New Haven: Yale University Press, 1980).

2. Robert Somers, *The Southern States Since the War, 1870–71* (London: Macmillan, 1871), pp. 62–65; John Richard Dennett, *The South as It Is, 1865–1866* (1866; rpt. Athens: University of Georgia Press, 1986), p. 264.

3. *Pughe's Augusta City Directory, 1865–66* (Augusta, Ga.: E. H. Pughe, 1866), p. 11 and appendix, and ibid., *1867* (Augusta, Ga.: E. H. Pughe, 1867), pp. 12, 21, 52, 54; *Calvin's Augusta and Business Directory for 1865–66* (Augusta, Ga.: Constitutionalist Job Office, 1865), p. 10; *Augusta Chronicle*, July 7 (1, 1), August 18 (3, 1), 25 (3, 1), 1865, January 16 (2, 2), 20 (3, 2), 27 (3, 2), December 21 (3, 2), 1866.

4. Rufus B. Bullock to Freeman Clarke, May 4, December 6, 1865, Clarke Family Papers, University of Rochester; *Augusta Chronicle*, March 16, 1884 (3, 2). Through 1867, Bullock and Clarke stayed in contact concerning Southern in-

vestments and Bullock advised him on stock purchases. In 1881, Bullock became president of a company owned by Clarke in Atlanta. See Bullock to Freeman Clarke, March 23, 1867, Clarke Family Papers, University of Rochester.

5. *Augusta Chronicle*, October 15, 1864 (3, 1), September 1, 1866 (3, 2); Stock Certificate, Southern Porcelain Manufacturing Company, September 16, 1866, Charles Colcock Jones, Jr., Collection, University of Georgia, Athens; DeTreville, "Reconstruction in Augusta," p. 73; U.S. Department of Commerce, Bureau of the Census, *Eighth Census, 1860, Population Schedule*, Richmond County, Ga., p. 1037.

6. *Augusta Chronicle*, March 28, April 4, 1888, in Bullock Papers, Huntington Library; *Atlanta Daily New Era*, May 14, 1867 (2, 2); Kenneth Coleman and Charles Stephen Gurr, eds., *Dictionary of Georgia Biography*, 2 vols. (Athens: University of Georgia Press, 1983), 1:491–92; *Pughe's Augusta Directory, 1865–66*, appendix.

7. Rufus B. Bullock, "Reconstruction in Georgia, 1865–1870," *Independent* 55 (March 19, 1903): 671.

8. Bullock to Joshua Hill, March 7, 1867, Georgia Miscellany, Emory University, Atlanta, Ga.

9. George B. Tindall, *The Disruption of the Solid South* (Athens: University of Georgia Press, 1972), p. 6; Lochrane quoted in Dan T. Carter, *When the War Was Over: The Failure of Self-Reconstruction in the South, 1865–1867* (Baton Rouge: Louisiana State University Press, 1985), pp. 105–6.

10. Augusta City Council Minutes, 1857–68, 1: 1, 196–97, Office of the Clerk, Municipal Building, Augusta, Ga.; Tunis G. Campbell to John Pope, June 1, 1867, Bureau of Civil Affairs, Letters Received, 3rd Military District, Record Group 393 (hereafter RG), Records of the United States Army Continental Commands, Box 1, NA.

11. Jacob T. Davis to Capt. George R. Walbridge, April 4, 1867, William Hale to John Pope, April 5, 1867, John P. King to Gen. Pope, April 25, 1867, Bureau of Civil Affairs, Letters Received, 3rd Military District, RG 393, Box 1, NA.

12. J. S. Beane to William Markham, April 18, 1867, H. P. Farrow, E. Hulbert, M. G. Dobbins, et al. to Maj.-Gen. Pope, April 19, 1867, list of Augusta City Council Members, 1867, Bureau of Civil Affairs, Letters Received, and Special Order No. 12, April 30, 1867, Special Orders, 1867, 3rd Military District, RG 393, Box 1, NA; DeTreville, "Reconstruction in Augusta," p. 38; Alexander St. Clair-Abrams, *Manual and Biographical Register of the State of Georgia for 1871–72* (Atlanta: Plantation Publishing Co., 1872), p. 1; Georgia Vol. 1B, p. 142, R. G. Dun Collection.

13. *Trial of Andrew Johnson, President of the United States, Before the Senate of the United States, on Impeachment by the House of Representatives for High*

Crimes and Misdemeanors, 3 vols. (Washington, D.C.: U.S. Government Printing Office, 1868), 1: 375, 708–25; *Pughe's Directory of Augusta, 1867,* p. 16; Coleman and Gurr, eds., *Dictionary of Georgia Biography,* 1: 91, 215–16; *Augusta Chronicle,* April 19, 1861 (3, 1), August 1, 1867 (2, 1).

14. Augusta City Council Minutes, 1857–68, 3: 226–29.

15. Ibid., pp. 248, 257–58, 260, 273; Foster Blodgett to Maj.-Gen. John Pope, May 28, 1867, Bureau of Civil Affairs, Letters Received, 3rd Military District, RG 393, Box 1, NA; DeTreville, "Reconstruction in Augusta," p. 68.

16. *Augusta Chronicle,* May 4 (3, 2–3), 15 (2, 2), 1869, March 16, 1884 (3, 2); J. H. Nisbet to Joseph E. Brown, October 28, 1867, Brown Family Papers, University of Georgia, Athens; *Atlanta Constitution,* 1905, Bullock Papers, Huntington Library; *Savannah Morning News,* November 9, 1867 (2, 1).

17. *Augusta Chronicle,* March 16, 1884 (3, 2); *Atlanta Constitution,* 1905, Bullock Papers, Huntington Library.

18. Augusta City Council Minutes, 1857–68, 3: 349–50; John Hope Franklin, *Reconstruction: After the Civil War* (Chicago: University of Chicago Press, 1961), p. 96.

19. Foster Blodgett to Maj. Gen. John Pope, August 3, 1867, Bureau of Civil Affairs, Letters Received, 3rd Military District, RG 393, Box 2, NA.

20. *Augusta Chronicle,* August 1, 1867 (3, 1).

21. Bullock to E. Hulbert, July 30, 1867, Bureau of Civil Affairs, Letters Received, 3rd Military District, RG 393, Box 5, NA.

22. Ibid., September 24, 1867, Box 6.

23. Ibid.; Edwin C. Wooley, *The Reconstruction of Georgia* (1901; rpt. New York: AMS Press, 1970), p. 13.

24. Ruth Currie-McDaniel, *Carpetbagger of Conscience: A Biography of John Emory Bryant* (Athens: University of Georgia Press, 1987), is the only full study of Bryant; see also Edmund L. Drago, *Black Politicians and Reconstruction in Georgia: A Splendid Failure* (Baton Rouge: Louisiana State University Press, 1982), pp. 22, 166.

25. Edward Hulbert to Maj.-Gen. John Pope, November 19, 1867, Bureau of Civil Affairs, Letters Received, 3rd Military District, RG 393, Box 5, NA; Foster Blodgett, *Speech of Hon. Foster Blodgett, Before the Union Club of Augusta, Ga, on Monday Evening, August 12, 1867* (N.p.: N.p., 1867), p. 25.

26. *Augusta Chronicle,* October 9, 1867, enclosed in letter, Foster Blodgett to General [Pope?], October 9, 1867, Edward Hulbert to Maj.-Gen. John Pope, November 19, 1867, and E. Hulbert to J. F. Meline, January 20, 1868, Bureau of Civil Affairs, Letters Received, 3rd Military District, RG 393, Box 4, NA; Albert B. Saye, *A Constitutional History of Georgia, 1732–1945* (Athens: University of Georgia Press, 1948), pp. 253–63; Clark Howell, *History of Geor-*

gia, 4 vols. (Chicago: S. J. Clarke, 1926), 1: 583–86; Wooley, *Reconstruction of Georgia*, pp. 32–37. Hill articulated his strategy and opinions in "Notes on the Situation" published beginning June 19, 1867, in the *Augusta Chronicle*.

27. Hulbert quoted in C. Mildred Thompson, *Reconstruction in Georgia: Economic, Social, Political, 1865–1872* (1915; rpt. Savannah, Ga.: Beehive Press, 1972), p. 177; E. Hulbert to S. D. Dickson, November 1, 1867, Hulbert to Election Managers, Ft. Gaines, Ga., November 1, 1867, Hulbert to A. B. Clarke, November 1, 1867, Hulbert to A. N. Wilson, November 1, 1867, Bureau of Civil Affairs, Miscellaneous Letters Received, 1868, re: Fla, Ala, Ga, RG 393, Box 1, NA; Richard H. Abbott, *The Republican Party and the South, 1855–1877: The First Southern Strategy* (Chapel Hill: University of North Carolina Press, 1986), p. 98. For an excellent examination of Bradley see Joseph P. Reidy, "Aaron A. Bradley: Voice of Black Labor in the Georgia Lowcountry," in *Southern Black Leaders of the Reconstruction Era*, ed. Howard N. Rabinowitz (Urbana: University of Illinois Press, 1982), pp. 281–308.

28. *Journal of the Proceedings of the Constitutional Convention of the People of Georgia, Held in the City of Atlanta in the Months of December, 1867, and January, February, and March 1868* (Augusta: E. H. Pughe, 1868), p. 6; E. Hulbert to J. F. Meline, January 27, 1868, Bureau of Civil Affairs, Letters Received, 3rd Military District, RG 393, Box 5, NA. Hulbert's January 20, 1868, letter to J. F. Meline, ibid., lists different numbers: total registered, 191,501; votes for, 106,410; majority over half of registered vote, 10,660; estimated white vote, 36,000. Another official source also differs: total registered, 200,918; votes for, 101,739 (Georgia, Comptroller General's Office, *Report of Madison Bell, Comptroller General of the State of Georgia: From August 11, 1868, to January 1, 1869* [Atlanta: Samuel Bard, 1869], Table A).

29. Conway, *Reconstruction of Georgia*, p. 146; Olive Hall Shadgett, *The Republican Party in Georgia: From Reconstruction Through 1900* (Athens: University of Georgia Press, 1964), pp. 3–4.

30. Henry Keating et al. to Gen. Pope, November 3, 1867, Affidavit of Munday Johnson, November 4, 1867, Affidavit of Tom Turner, et al., November 4, 1867, Bureau of Civil Affairs, Letters Received, 3rd Military District, RG 393, Box 5, NA.

31. *Milledgeville Southern Recorder*, November 26 (3, 2), December 3 (2, 5–6), 1867; Allen D. Candler, comp., *The Confederate Records of the State of Georgia*, 6 vols. (Atlanta: Charles Byrd, 1911), 6:200–205; Elizabeth S. Nathans, *Losing the Peace: Georgia Republicans and Reconstruction* (Baton Rouge: Louisiana State University Press, 1968), pp. 55–57; *Journal of the Constitutional Convention*, pp. 611–13; Numan V. Bartley, *The Creation of Modern Georgia* (Athens: University of Georgia Press, 1983), p. 55.

32. *Journal of the Constitutional Convention,* pp. 10–13; Leslie Paul Rowan, "The Rise and Development of the Republican Party in Georgia" (M.A. thesis, Emory University, 1948), pp. 12–13.

33. *Journal of the Constitutional Convention,* p. 15; *Rome Weekly Courier,* February 28, 1868, quoted in Conway, *Reconstruction of Georgia,* p. 153.

34. Speech of J. E. Brown, March 4, 1867, Brown Family Papers, University of Georgia; Thompson, *Reconstruction in Georgia,* p. 204.

35. W. G. Brownlow to J. E. Brown, March 22, 1867, Brown Family Papers, quoted in Steven Hahn, *The Roots of Southern Populism: Yeoman Farmers and the Transformation of the Georgia Upcountry* (New York: Oxford University Press, 1983), p. 204.

36. *Atlanta Opinion* quoted in the *Atlanta New Era,* February 1, 1868 (2, 4); *Journal of the Constitutional Convention,* pp. 20, 23–24, 29, 40–41.

37. Jack B. Scroggs, "Carpetbagger Constitutional Reform in the South Atlantic States, 1867–1868," *Journal of Southern History* 27 (November 1961): 479–80; Goodwin quoted in Hahn, *Roots of Southern Populism,* p. 157.

38. *Journal of the Constitutional Convention,* pp. 89–90, 132–37, 203–6, 226–54, 556–57. On June 25, 1868, the U.S. Congress nullified the provision denying court jurisdiction over debts contracted before May 1865. Thus no real relief existed. See Henri Freeman, "Some Aspects of Debtor Relief in Georgia During Reconstruction" (M.A. thesis, Emory University, 1951), pp. 44–45, 103–4.

39. *Journal of the Constitutional Convention,* pp. 357, 390, 398–402; Nathans, *Losing the Peace,* pp. 60–66. The homestead exemption changed over the years. In 1869 crops produced on homestead land were exempted. In 1875, the General Assembly allowed owners to waive their rights to a homestead. The 1877 constitutional convention reduced the exemption to $1,600 total, all but $300 of which could be waived. Thus, after Reconstruction the Redeemer legislatures and delegates took from the poor and gave to the rich. See Freeman, "Some Aspects of Debtor Relief," pp. 52–64.

40. P. Reynolds to Maj.-Gen. Meade, January 12, 1868, Bureau of Civil Affairs, Letters Received, 3rd Military District, RG 393, Box 5, NA; John Durdin to Benjamin Conley, March 3, 1868, Benjamin Conley Papers, University of Georgia, Athens.

41. Conway, *Reconstruction of Georgia,* pp. 46–49; Freeman, "Some Aspects of Debtor Relief," pp. 4–8, 37; *Milledgeville Southern Recorder,* May 5, 1868, as quoted ibid., p. 44.

42. *Journal of the Constitutional Convention,* pp. 266, 279; Currie-McDaniel, *Carpetbagger of Conscience,* p. 84; Drago, *Black Politicians,* p. 35.

43. *Journal of the Constitutional Convention,* pp. 437, 504, 534–35; *Atlanta Constitution,* December 2, 1888 (5, 2); Saye, *Constitutional History of Georgia,* pp. 267–70; Nathans, *Losing the Peace,* p. 69.

44. *Journal of the Constitutional Convention,* pp. 549, 559.

45. Foster Blodgett to Gen. John Pope, November 5, 1867, Bureau of Civil Affairs, Letters Received, 3rd Military District, RG 393, Box 5, NA.

46. Saye, *Constitutional History of Georgia,* pp. 266–67; "Report of Maj-Gen. G. G. Meade," U.S. Congress, House of Representatives, *Annual Report of the Secretary of War, 1868,* Executive Documents, 40th Cong. 3d sess., pp. 74–82; *The American Annual Cyclopedia and Register of Important Events of the Year 1867* (New York: D. Appleton, 1869), p. 365; *Journal of the Constitutional Convention,* p. 131.

47. *Journal of the Constitutional Convention,* p. 53.

48. Ibid., pp. 56–61; Wilson, *Atlanta as It Is,* p. 21.

49. *Atlanta Constitution,* January 2, 1868, in Henry W. Grady Papers, Scrapbook 4, pp. 9–10, Emory University, Atlanta.

50. *Albany Tri-Weekly News,* January 31, 1868, in Henry Patillo Farrow Papers, University of Georgia, Athens.

51. Thompson, *Reconstruction in Georgia,* p. 184.

52. Shadgett, *Republican Party in Georgia,* pp. 7–9; *Atlanta Daily New Era,* March 11, 1868, in Joseph E. and Elizabeth G. Brown Collection, University of Georgia, Athens.

53. *Atlanta Daily New Era,* March 1 (2, 2), 3 (2, 3), 1868; Wallace C. Smith, "Rufus Brown Bullock and the Third Reconstruction of Georgia, 1867–1871" (M.A. thesis, University of North Carolina, 1964), p. 19.

54. *Atlanta Daily New Era,* March 8 (2, 2–7), 11 (2, 2–8), 12 (2, 1), 14 (2, 4), 1868; *Atlanta Daily New Era,* March 11, 1868, in Joseph E. and Elizabeth G. Brown Collection, University of Georgia; Allen Candler Smith, "The Republican Party in Georgia, 1867–1871" (M.A. thesis, Duke University, 1937), pp. 96–97; unidentified newspaper clipping, March 12, 1868, Farrow Papers.

CHAPTER 3. Bullock Is Our Man

1. A. L. Harris to Sen. John Sherman, November 29, 1867, John Sherman Papers, Library of Congress. For almost a year a rumor circulated among the freedmen that at Christmas 1867, Congress would grant each black family forty acres and a mule. White planters also knew of the rumor and feared it was true. Precedent for such a belief came from the 1862 Confiscation Acts, General William T. Sherman's Order No. 15 which established all of coastal South Carolina, Georgia, and Florida between Charleston and the St. Johns River for black settlement, and Freedmen's Bureau attempts to nurture black families on land of their own. All these efforts were meant to compensate former slaves for the valid claims each had to an equity in the land worked out through generations of unrequited toil. White Northerners could not keep such a revolutionary promise of

land redistribution. Not only would doing so go against beliefs about the sanctity of property, but, as Eric Foner concludes, it clashed with free labor ideology based on contracts and capitalism—which allowed for buying and selling and negotiating but not for giving away—and work ethics. See Claude Oubre, *Forty Acres and a Mule: The Freedmen's Bureau and Black Land Ownership* (Baton Rouge: Louisiana State University Press, 1978); William S. McFeely, *Yankee Stepfather: General O. O. Howard and the Freedmen* (New Haven: Yale University Press, 1968); and Foner, *Reconstruction*.

2. *Atlanta Intelligencer,* March 14, 1868, as quoted in Spencer B. King, *Georgia Voices: A Documentary History to 1872* (Athens: University of Georgia Press, 1966), p. 328.

3. Bartley, *Creation of Modern Georgia,* pp. 57–58; James F. Cook, "John B. Gordon," in *Dictionary of Georgia Biography,* ed. Coleman and Gurr, 1:354–55.

4. Ibid.

5. Ibid.

6. Bullock, "Reconstruction in Georgia," p. 673; Speech of Joseph E. Brown at Marietta, March 18, 1868, Joseph Emerson Brown Papers, Atlanta Historical Society, Atlanta.

7. *Atlanta Daily New Era,* April 14, 1868 (2, 4–5).

8. Rufus Bullock to Joseph E. Brown, March 25, 1868, and Joseph E. Brown to Dear Sir, March 26, 1868, Brown Family Papers, University of Georgia.

9. 1868 ballot and flyer, Reconstruction file, GDAH; List of Documents, Farrow Papers.

10. *Atlanta Daily New Era,* March [?] 1868, as quoted in Mark W. Summers, *Railroads, Reconstruction, and the Gospel of Prosperity: Aid Under the Radical Republicans, 1865–1877* (Princeton: Princeton University Press, 1984), p. 26; handbill in Joseph E. and Elizabeth G. Brown Collection, University of Georgia.

11. *Augusta Loyal Georgian,* February 15, 1868 (1, 2).

12. Foster Blodgett to John Sherman, December 30, 1867, Sherman Papers; Blodgett, *Speech, August 12, 1867,* p. 29.

13. Laurence Shore, *Southern Capitalists: The Ideological Leadership of an Elite, 1832–1885* (Chapel Hill: University of North Carolina Press, 1986), pp. 140–41; Jessie Pearl Rice, "Governor Rufus B. Bullock and Reconstruction in Georgia" (M.A. thesis, Emory University, 1931), p. 31; Rufus Bullock to Joseph E. Brown, March 27, 1868, Brown Family Papers, University of Georgia; Foner, *Reconstruction,* p. 326; Hahn, *Roots of Southern Populism,* pp. 211–16.

14. *Atlanta Daily New Era,* March 29 (2, 2), April 10 (2, 3), 12 (2, 2–3), 14 (2, 1–2), 1868.

15. Ibid., April 14, 1868 (2, 1–2); *New York Times,* April 5, 1868 (1, 7).

16. Summers, *Railroads, Reconstruction, and the Gospel of Prosperity,* p. 14.

17. *Atlanta Daily New Era,* March 1 (2, 1), April 29 (2, 3), 1868; Lucian L.

Knight, *The Standard History of Georgia and Georgians,* 6 vols. (Chicago: Lewis Publishing Co., 1917), 2:836; Wilson, *Atlanta as It Is,* pp. 20–21.

18. *Atlanta Daily New Era,* March 27 (2, 1), 28 (2, 3), 1868, October 18, 1870 (3, 1); *Augusta Chronicle,* April 4, 1868, Joseph E. and Elizabeth G. Brown Collection, University of Georgia.

19. Margaret Mitchell, *Gone with the Wind* (New York: Macmillan, 1936), pp. 873–74.

20. Ibid.; Smith, "Republican Party in Georgia," p. 125, lists pro-Republican papers: *Atlanta New Era, Augusta Republican, Griffin American Union,* and *Savannah Freedmen's Standard.*

21. *Augusta Chronicle,* April 16, 1868, and *Albany News,* April 11, 1868, in Joseph E. and Elizabeth G. Brown Collection, University of Georgia; *Augusta Chronicle,* March 29, 1868 (1, 6–7).

22. *Augusta Constitutionalist,* February 19, 1868, as quoted in Jack B. Scroggs, "Carpetbagger Influence in the Political Reconstruction of the South Atlantic States, 1865–1876" (Ph.D. dissertation, University of North Carolina, 1951), p. 150.

23. U. S. Grant to G. G. Meade, April 2, 1868, Telegrams Received, 1868, 3rd Military District, RG 393, NA; Elizabeth O. Daniell, "The Ashburn Murder Case in Georgia Reconstruction, 1868," *Georgia Historical Quarterly* 59 (Fall 1975): 296–312; *Columbus Sun,* April 1, 1868, quoted in Charles G. Bloom, "The Georgia Election of April, 1868: A Re-Examination of the Politics of Georgia Reconstruction" (M.A. thesis, University of Chicago, 1963), p. 55; Allen W. Trelease, *White Terror: The Ku Klux Klan Conspiracy and Southern Reconstruction* (New York: Harper & Row, 1971), pp. 75–78; Fred C. Rathbun, ed., *Names from Georgia, 1865–1866: Freedmen's Bureau Letters, Roll 13* (microfilm; N.p.: By the author, 1986), frames 518, 528.

24. Theodore B. FitzSimons, "The Ku Klux Klan in Georgia, 1868–1871" (M.A. thesis, University of Georgia, 1957), p. 14; Testimony of J. H. Caldwell, U.S. Congress, *Report of the Joint Select Committee to Inquire into the Condition of Affairs in the Late Insurrectionary States,* 13 vols. (Washington, D.C.: U.S. Government Printing Office, 1872), 7:431; John H. Caldwell, *Reminiscences of the Reconstruction of Church and State in Georgia* (Wilmington, Del.: J. Miller Thomas, 1895), pp. 12–13; Raphael J. Moses, Autobiography, p. 81, Southern Historical Collection, University of North Carolina, Chapel Hill.

25. U. S. Grant to G. G. Meade, April 2, 1868, Telegrams Received, 1868, 3rd Military District, RG 393, NA; Rufus Bullock to Joseph Brown, April 1, 1868, Brown Family Papers, University of Georgia; William H. Smythe to R. C. Drum, November 1, 1868, Military Affairs, Letters Received, 3rd Military District, RG 393, NA; Derrell C. Roberts, *Joseph E. Brown and the Politics of Reconstruction* (University, Ala.: University of Alabama Press, 1973), p. 63. For the Democratic

claim that Radicals had killed Ashburn to create a martyr and for the testimony taken by the military see the biased but informative 1868 Democratic presidential campaign document *Radical Rule: Military Outrage in Georgia. Arrest of the Columbus Prisoners* (Louisville, Ky.: Morton and Co., 1868).

26. E. Hulbert to Col. J. F. Meline, February 28, March 12, 17, April 2, 1868, Charles S. Evans to E. Hulbert, April 1, 1868, F. Blodgett to Col. J. F. Meline, April 27, 1868, Bureau of Civil Affairs, Letters Received, 3rd Military District, RG 393, Box 6, NA.

27. E. Hulbert to Col. J. F. Meline, February 28, March 12, 17, April 2, 1868, Charles S. Evans to E. Hulbert, April 1, 1868, F. Blodgett to Col. J. F. Meline, April 27, 1868, Bureau of Civil Affairs, Letters Received, 3rd Military District, RG 93, Box 6, NA; E. Hulbert to HQ 3rd District, Georgia, undated, Hulbert to A. S. Wilson, April 21, 1868, Hulbert to Thomas S. King, April 24, 1868, Bureau of Civil Affairs, Miscellaneous Letters Received, 1868, re: Florida, Alabama, Georgia, RG 393, Box 1, NA; Georgia, Comptroller General's Office, Table A.

28. *Augusta Constitutionalist,* April 19, 1868 (2, 1); G. G. Meade to U. S. Grant, April 29, 1868, U.S. Congress, House of Representatives, *Annual Report of the Secretary of War, 1868,* Executive Documents, 40th Cong. 3d sess., pt. 1, p. 102; Rufus Bullock to George G. Meade, April 29, 1868, Rufus Brown Bullock, Oversize, File II, Names, GDAH.

29. W. B. Dixon to James A. Jackson, April 26, 1868, Reconstruction file, GDAH; Amos T. Akerman to Foster Blodgett, April 23, 1868, Amos T. Akerman file, File II, Names, GDAH.

30. Letters to B.-Gen. C. C. Sibley, Registers of Letters Received, 1867, 1868, RG 393, vol. 1, NA; Bloom, "Georgia Election of April, 1868," pp. 51–53, 60–61.

31. D. G. Cotting file, File II, Names, GDAH.

32. Bloom, "Georgia Election of April, 1868," pp. 70–72; Meade to Grant, April 29, July 6, 1868, U.S. Congress, House of Representatives, *Annual Report of the Secretary of War, 1868,* pt. 1, pp. 82–83; *Savannah Morning News,* April 30, 1868 (2, 3).

33. W. E. B. Du Bois, *Black Reconstruction: An Essay Toward a History of the Part Which Black Folk Played in the Attempt to Reconstruct Democracy in America, 1860–1880* (New York: Russell and Russell, 1935), p. 500; Thompson, *Reconstruction in Georgia,* p. 190; John H. Caldwell to William Claflin, July 4, 1868, William E. Chandler Papers, Book 6, Library of Congress; R. B. Bullock, *Remarks of Gov. Bullock to the Judiciary Committee of the Senate in re. Reconstruction of Georgia, March 2, 1870* (Washington, D.C.: Chronicle Print, 1870), pp. 5–6; *New York Times,* July 18, 1868 (3, 7); Bartley, *Creation of Modern Georgia,* p. 61; Act of June 25, 1868, *Acts and Resolutions,* 40th Cong., 2d sess., p. 3, in Walter L. Fleming, ed., *Documentary History of Reconstruction: Political,*

Military, Social, Religious, Educational and Industrial, 1865–1906, 2 vols. (1907; rpt. New York: McGraw-Hill, 1966), 1:476–79. Even though Congress made Georgia nullify its sections on debt relief, Joe Brown received letters from John Sherman of the Senate Finance Committee and soon to be vice-president Schuyler Colfax advising him that the Georgia legislature could still achieve relief by passing statutes of limitations on debt collection or simply striking it from the constitution as Congress required, then passing legislation, which "would not probably come under review here" (John Sherman to Joseph E. Brown, June 10, 1868, and Schuyler Colfax to Brown, June 13, 1868, Brown Family Papers, University of Georgia).

34. General Order No. 91, Third Military District, June 28, 1868, Rufus Bullock, File II, Names, GDAH; Rufus B. Bullock, *Letter from Rufus B. Bullock, of Georgia, to the Republican Senators and Representatives in Congress Who Sustain the Reconstruction Acts. Dated Williard's Hotel, May 21, 1870* (Washington, D.C.: Chronicle Print, 1870), p. 4; Bullock to General Meade, July 8, 17, 18, 1868, Miscellaneous Records, 1867–68, RG 393, NA.

35. George G. Meade to Bullock, July 20, 1868, Miscellaneous Records, 1867–68, RG 393, NA; Meade to RBB, July 8, 1868, Letters Sent, 1868, HQ 3rd Military District, RG 393, NA; Georgia, General Assembly, Senate, *Journal of the Senate of the State of Georgia, 1868* (Atlanta: J. W. Burke, 1868), pp. 24, 31, 43; Meade to U. S. Grant, July 18, 21, 22, 1868, U. S. Grant to John A. Rawlins, July 23, 1868, Telegrams Received, 1868, RG 393, NA.

36. Bullock, *Remarks to the Judiciary Committee*, pp. 31–33.

37. Bullock, "Reconstruction in Georgia," p. 672.

38. Records of the Fourteenth Amendment, Georgia, Rejection and Ratification, RG 11, General Records of the United States Government, NA; *New York Times*, July 23 (5, 2), 27 (5, 5–6), 29 (1, 6), 1868.

39. *New York Times*, July 23 (5, 2), 27 (5, 5–6), 1868; Conley quoted in Reed, ed., *History of Atlanta*, p. 240.

40. *Georgia Senate Journal, 1868*, pp. 52–69; Bullock to Senators and Representatives, July 24, 1868, Georgia Executive Department, Minutes, 1866–70, microfilm, p. 153, GDAH.

41. *Georgia Senate Journal, 1868*, pp. 52–69; Bullock to Senators and Representatives, July 24, 1868, Georgia Executive Department, Minutes, 1866–74, microfilm, p. 153, GDAH.

42. *Georgia Senate Journal, 1868*, pp. 52–69; Bullock to Senators and Representatives, July 24, 1868, Georgia Executive Department, Minutes, 1866–74, microfilm, p. 153, GDAH.

43. *Atlanta Constitution*, July 23 (1, 7; 3, 2), 24 (1, 2; 2, 1–4), 1868; Toombs quoted in Du Bois, *Black Reconstruction*, p. 496; *New York Times*, July 27, 1868

(5, 6); Cobb quoted in Conway, *Reconstruction of Georgia*, p. 119; Benjamin H. Hill, Jr., comp., *Senator Benjamin H. Hill of Georgia: His Life, Speeches and Writings* (Atlanta: T. H. P. Bloodworth, 1893), p. 277.

44. *Atlanta Constitution*, July 24, 1868 (2, 2–4); Conway, *Reconstruction of Georgia*, p. 164; Hill, comp., *Senator Benjamin H. Hill*, pp. 308–19.

CHAPTER 4. A Vital Question

1. *Journal of the Constitutional Convention*, p. 559; Atlanta City Council Minutes, February 26, 1868, Georgia Executive Department, Incoming Correspondence, Rufus Brown Bullock, 1868–71, GDAH; Royce Shingleton, *Richard Peters: Champion of the New South* (Macon, Ga.: Mercer University Press, 1985), pp. 148–64.

2. Alice E. Reagan, *H. I. Kimball, Entrepreneur* (Atlanta: Cherokee Publishing, 1983), pp. 1–9, 18–20; Reagan, "Promoting the New South: Hannibal I. Kimball and Henry W. Grady," *Atlanta Historical Journal* 27 (September 1983): 5–8; Georgia Vol. 13, p. 212, Dun Collection.

3. James M. Russell, "Atlanta, Gate City of the South, 1847–1885" (Ph.D. dissertation, Princeton University, 1972), p. 5; quote from E. Y. Clarke, *Illustrated History of Atlanta* (Atlanta: James P. Harrison, 1878), p. 49; Somers, *Southern States Since the War*, p. 96.

4. William Bailey Williford, *Peachtree Street, Atlanta* (Athens: University of Georgia Press, 1962), pp. 31–33.

5. Grigsby H. Wotton, "New City of the South: Atlanta, 1843–1873" (Ph.D. dissertation, Johns Hopkins University, 1973), pp. ii–v, 39–41, 55, 65–67, 77, 165, 222; James C. Bonner, "Richard Peters," and John W. Patillo, "William Markham," in *Dictionary of Georgia Biography*, ed. Coleman and Gurr, 2:684–85, 792–93.

6. Bartley, *Creation of Modern Georgia*, pp. 110–26.

7. F. Barham Zincke, *Last Winter in the United States* (London: John Murray, 1868), p. 128; Massey's recollections quoted from *Atlanta Constitution*, October 4, 1987 (12S, 3); Sterchi quote in Conway, *Reconstruction of Georgia*, p. 133.

8. Wotton, "New City of the South," pp. 210–12, 405.

9. Jerry J. Thornberry, "The Development of Black Atlanta, 1865–1885" (Ph.D. dissertation, University of Maryland, 1977), pp. 86, 268–72; Eula T. Kuchler, "Charitable and Philanthropic Activities in Atlanta During Reconstruction" (M.A. thesis, Emory University, 1942), pp. 12, 24, 37, 43–46, 52; Kuchler, "Charitable and Philanthropic Activities in Atlanta During Reconstruction," *Atlanta Historical Bulletin* 40 (December 1965): 28, 35; *Atlanta Herald*, February 28, 1871, quoted in Wotton, "New City of the South," p. 406; Henry K. Newman,

"The Vision of Order: White Protestant Christianity in Atlanta, 1865–1906" (Ph.D. dissertation, Emory University, 1977), pp. 4–5, 16–17, 41.

10. *Journal of the Constitutional Convention*, pp. 151–54, 558; R. R. Hollingsworth, "Education and Reconstruction in Georgia," *Georgia Historical Quarterly* 19 (June 1935): 112–33, and 19 (September 1935): 229–50; *Georgia Senate Journal, 1868*, pp. 162, 169, 178, 183; Eugene Davis to John C. McCall, August 2, 1869, and H. C. Corson to E. Hubbard, August 22, 1870, Georgia Executive Department, Executive Secretary's Letter Books, GDAH.

11. Bullock, Message to General Assembly, August 15, 1870, Georgia Executive Department, Minutes, 1866–74, microfilm, GDAH; *Savannah Morning News,* September 30, 1870 (2, 1).

12. Turner quoted in Peter Wallenstein, *From Slave South to New South: Public Policy in Nineteenth-Century Georgia* (Chapel Hill: University of North Carolina Press, 1987), p. 163.

13. E. A. Ware to Rufus Bullock, July 21, 1868, *Georgia Senate Journal, 1868,* pp. 78–79; John A. Rockwell to Alfred, January 28, 1869, John A. Rockwell Letters, University of Georgia, Athens.

14. Arthur R. Taylor, "From the Ashes: Atlanta During Reconstruction, 1865–1876" (Ph.D. dissertation, Emory University, 1973), pp. 206, 230; Newman, "Vision of Order," p. 65; Wotton, "New City of the South," pp. 285–309; "Letter from Georgia," *American Missionary* 23 (July 1869): 160–62; Clarence A. Bacote, *The Story of Atlanta University: A Century of Service, 1865–1965* (Atlanta: Atlanta University Press, 1969), pp. 21–22, 46–47.

15. Martin Luther King, Jr., *Letter from Birmingham City Jail* (Philadelphia: American Friends Service Committee, 1963), p. 6; Jacqueline Jones, *Soldiers of Light and Love: Northern Teachers and Georgia Blacks, 1865–1873* (Chapel Hill: University of North Carolina Press, 1980), p. 89; *Bulletin of Atlanta University,* June 1891, pp. 1–2, January 1892, pp. 2–3, June 1895, p. 2, June 1896, p. 2.

16. J. W. Alvord, *Letters from the South Relating to the Condition of the Freedmen* (Washington, D.C.: Howard University Press, 1870), pp. 21–22; Horace C. Wingo, "Race Relations in Georgia, 1872–1908" (Ph.D. dissertation, University of Georgia, 1969), pp. 191–99; Harris quoted in Robert Perdue, "The Negro as Reflected in the Atlanta Constitution, Atlanta Intelligencer, and Atlanta Daily New Era from 1868–1880" (M.A. thesis, Atlanta University, 1963), p. 23.

17. *Georgia Senate Journal, 1868,* pp. 91–93, 96; Georgia General Assembly, House, *Journal of the House of the State of Georgia, 1868* (Macon, Ga.: J. W. Burke, 1868), pp. 100–108.

18. *Georgia Senate Journal, 1868,* pp. 84–86.

19. *Georgia House Journal, 1868,* pp. 222, 229, 242–43. Strangely not using

the "rule" that one drop of black blood makes a person black, the house allowed four mulattoes to keep their seats (*Georgia House Journal, 1868,* pp. 121-30, 138, 243-44, 272-73, 277-80); Testimony of Governor Bullock, "Condition of Affairs in Georgia," U.S. Congress, House, *House Miscellaneous Document No. 52,* 40th Cong., 3d sess., p. 6). Earlier, Senator Aaron A. Bradley resigned his seat in the face of certain ejection over charges that he had committed a crime in New York State; there was no conclusive evidence of Bradley's guilt, and his real "crime" was being a vocal advocate of black rights.

20. *Georgia Senate Journal, 1868,* pp. 277-81; Turner quoted in Du Bois, *Black Reconstruction,* pp. 501-2.

21. Russell Duncan, *Freedom's Shore: Tunis Campbell and the Georgia Freedmen* (Athens: University of Georgia Press, 1986), pp. 53-55; Benjamin Conley et al. to the Congress of the United States, September 18, 1868, "Condition of Affairs in Georgia," *House Miscellaneous Document No. 52,* pp. 86-87.

22. *New York Times,* September 14, 1868 (2, 3-4); *Georgia Senate Journal, 1868,* pp. 324-27; Bullock to Georgia House of Representatives, September 9, 1868, Georgia Executive Department, Minutes, 1866-70, microfilm, pp. 179-83, GDAH.

23. *New York Times,* September 14, 1868 (2, 3-4); *Georgia Senate Journal, 1868,* pp. 324-27; Bullock to Georgia House of Representatives, September 9, 1868, Georgia Executive Department, Minutes, 1866-74, microfilm, pp. 179-83, GDAH; Volney Spalding to William E. Chandler, September 1, 1868, and John H. Caldwell to William Claflin, September 1, 1868, Chandler Papers.

24. C. H. Hopkins to Bullock, August 24, 1868, Georgia Executive Department, Incoming Correspondence, Bullock, 1868-71, GDAH; *Augusta Chronicle,* September 11, 1868 (2, 1).

25. Bullock, *Letter to the Republican Senators and Representatives,* p. 4; unidentified newspaper clipping, January 2, 1878, Grady Papers.

26. Bullock, *Letter to the Republican Senators and Representatives,* p. 4; unidentified newspaper clipping, January 2, 1878, Grady Papers.

27. Richard L. Zuber, "The Role of Rufus Brown Bullock in Georgia Politics" (M.A. thesis, Emory University, 1957), pp. 109-10; Howell, *History of Georgia,* 1:600; Robert Kegan, *The Evolving Self: Problem and Process in Human Development* (Cambridge, Mass.: Harvard University Press, 1982), pp. 8, 11, 19, 60-63, 70-71, 142, 214.

28. Bartley, *Creation of Modern Georgia,* pp. 65-66; *Contemporary American Biography,* pp. 68-69.

29. Conway, *Reconstruction of Georgia,* pp. 168-70; George C. Rable, *But There Was No Peace: The Role of Violence in the Politics of Reconstruction* (Athens: University of Georgia Press, 1984), pp. 73-74; O. H. Howard to J. R. Lewis, September 20, 1868, in *Rochester Democrat and Chronicle,* Septem-

ber 19, 1868 (1, 4). For an interpretation favoring the townsmen see Theodore B. FitzSimons, "The Camilla Riot," *Georgia Historical Quarterly* 35 (June 1951): 116–25.

30. *Georgia Senate Journal, 1868,* pp. 353–57, 364–69; *Augusta Chronicle,* September 12 (1, 4–5), 23 (2, 1–2) 1868; Rable, *But There Was No Peace,* p. 74, Clemenceau quoted ibid., p. 189.

31. George Meade to Bullock, October 3, 1868, and E. J. Higbee to Bullock, October 25, 1868, Georgia Executive Department, Incoming Correspondence, Bullock, 1868–71, GDAH.

32. James E. Sefton, *The United States Army and Reconstruction, 1865–1877* (Baton Rouge: Louisiana State University Press, 1967), pp. 261–62; Willard E. Wight, ed., "Reconstruction in Georgia: Three Letters by Edwin G. Higbee," *Georgia Historical Quarterly* 41 (March 1957): 83–89. Clearly, many soldiers disliked blacks, Republicans, or both; incidents like the ones in Atlanta in 1866 and 1867 when drunken soldiers fired on a black group celebrating the Fourth of July and entered black houses, stealing and beating, led one observer to say: "There is a very bitter feeling between the Negroes and the Yankees." See Wotton, "New City of the South," pp. 278–81.

33. Foster Blodgett to John Sherman, December 30, 1867, Sherman Papers; Bullock to Joseph E. Brown, March 27, 1868, and John Pope to Joseph E. Brown, March 29, 1868, Brown Family Papers, University of Georgia; V. A. Gaskill to George Meade, March 6, 1868, Bureau of Civil Affairs, 3rd Military District, Letters Received, RG 393, Box 6, NA; *Atlanta Constitution,* April 4, 1888, in Bullock Papers, Huntington Library; Memorial to Congress [Crumley and Joiner], December 4, 1868, "Condition of Affairs in Georgia," *House Miscellaneous Document No. 52,* pp. 91–98, quote from p. 96. For Meade's defense of his actions during Reconstruction see George G. Meade to John A. Rawlins [chief of staff], October 31, 1868, Bureau of Civil Affairs, 3rd Military District, Letters Received, RG 393, Box 5, NA.

34. G. G. Meade to Bullock, November 18, 1868, and Bullock to J. M. Schofield, November 13, 1868, Georgia Executive Department, Incoming Correspondence, Bullock, 1868–71, GDAH.

35. Ibid.

36. On September 14, 1868, Bullock issued a proclamation calling for all militia units then organizing to disband because Congress had prohibited them. Bullock added that militia units threatened "the peace and good order of the State." See Bullock, File II, Names, GDAH; J. F. Wilson to Bullock, August 13, 1868, Reconstruction file, GDAH. In an interview for the *Cincinnati Commercial* in 1868, Nathan Bedford Forrest warned: "If the militia are called out, we can only look upon it as a declaration of war. In all the Southern states there are about 555,000 Klansmen. I think I could raise 40,000 men in five days, ready for the field. If the

militia goes to hunting down and shooting these men, there will be war, and a bloodier one than we have ever witnessed" (quoted in Stetson Kennedy, *Southern Exposure* [New York: Doubleday, 1946], p. 31).

37. *Atlanta Constitution,* July 24, 1868 (1, 2).

38. Jack B. Scroggs, "Southern Reconstruction: A Radical View," *Journal of Southern History* 24 (November 1958): 420; Bartley, *Creation of Modern Georgia,* pp. 35, 62–63; "Memoirs of Edgar A. Ross," Hermione Ross Walker Collection, Southern Historical Collection, University of North Carolina, Chapel Hill. For further mention of the Democrat/Klan connection, see Testimony of Amos T. Akerman, Isaac Seeley, and A. W. Stone, "Condition of Affairs in Georgia," *House Miscellaneous Document No. 52,* pp. 13, 40, 47, 50; Testimony of John B. Gordon, U.S. Congress, *Report of the Condition of Affairs in the Late Insurrectionary States,* 7:308–24. For the best discussion of ties between the Klan and the Democratic party, see Stanley K. Deaton, "Violent Redemption: The Democratic Party and the Ku Klux Klan in Georgia, 1868–1871" (M.A. thesis, University of Georgia, 1988). For analyses of Klan violence perceived by contemporaries as expressions of popular will instead of as crimes, see Bertram Wyatt-Brown, *Southern Honor: Ethics and Behavior in the Old South* (New York: Oxford University Press, 1982), esp. pp. 364–400; Albert C. Smith, "Down Freedom's Road: The Contours of Race, Class, and Property Crime in Black-Belt Georgia, 1866–1910" (Ph.D. dissertation, University of Georgia, 1982), pp. 8–12; and Rable, *But There Was No Peace,* pp. 93–101.

39. Thomas E. Watson, "Some Aftermath of the Civil War," *Watson Magazine,* August 1907, pp. 781–83.

40. George Ormond to N. Sellers Hill, July 21, 1868, D. C. Carvart to E. Hulbert, August 18, 1868, William Heal to Bullock, August 19, 1868, Joel R. Griffin to Bullock, August 24, 1868, Affidavit of Dennis Lewis and Worrel Jackson, August 17, 1868, Daniel Losey to C. C. Sibley, September 8, 1868, Shep Rogers to Daniel Losey, September 4, 1868, Georgia Executive Department, Incoming Correspondence, Bullock, 1868–71, GDAH.

41. L. P. Gudger to W. E. Chandler, September 7, 1868, Chandler Papers. The National Union Republican party sent $5,000 to aid the Georgia campaign. See T. L. Tullock to Benjamin Conley, August 24, September 23, 1868, Conley Papers, University of Georgia.

42. Foster Blodgett to W. E. Chandler, September 13, 16, 1868, Joseph E. Brown to Chandler, October 8, 1868, J. H. Caldwell and J. E. Bryant to Chandler, September 16, 1868, and J. H. Caldwell to Chandler, September 30, 1868, Chandler Papers.

43. H. H. Waters to Bullock, October 16, 1868, Georgia Executive Department, Executive Secretary's Letter Books, GDAH; Proclamations suspending poll tax and ordering peace, Rufus Bullock, File II, Names, GDAH; *Augusta Chronicle,*

October 13, 1868 (4, 2); Georgia Executive Department, Minutes, 1866–74, microfilm, GDAH; Drago, *Black Politicians and Reconstruction*, pp. 148–49. For testimony on the numbers of freedmen who were denied the vote for nonpayment of taxes, see "Condition of Affairs in Georgia," *House Miscellaneous Document No. 52*, pp. 45, 49, 51–52, 56–58, 65, 71–74, 76.

44. Francis A. Kirby to Bullock, July 9, 1868, Georgia Executive Department, Incoming Correspondence, Bullock, 1868–71, GDAH; Rufus B. Bullock, *Have the Reconstruction Acts Been Fully Executed in Georgia?* (Washington, D.C.: Chronicle Printers, 1868), pp. 1–3.

45. Bullock, *Reconstruction Acts*, pp. 1–3.

46. H. F. Young to Frank Gallagher, October 16, 1868, H. L. Haskell to Frank Gallagher, October 5, 1868, Howell C. Flourney to C. C. Sibley, October 5, 1868, Daniel Losey to C. C. Sibley, July 6, 1868, A. McIntyre to James Ulio, July 23, 1868, John J. Knox to Bullock, October 6, 1868, N. Sellers Hill to C. C. Sibley, July 13, 1868, W. F. White to Frank Gallagher, August 4, 1868, A. N. See to Bullock, September 23, 1868, L. S. Powell to Bullock, September 27, 1868, Georgia Executive Department, Incoming Correspondence, Bullock, 1868–71, GDAH.

47. F. J. Robinson to Bullock, September 28, 1868, and Frank Gallagher to Bullock, October 2, 1868, ibid.

48. "Report of Outrages Committed Upon Freedmen in the State of Georgia, Jan. 1–Nov. 15, 1868," and "Additional Report of Outrages Since Nov. 1868," ibid.; see "Condition of Affairs in Georgia," *House Miscellaneous Document No. 52*, pp. 55–139, for documents, affidavits, and letters concerning abuses and murders in Georgia in 1868; D. G. Cotting to Bullock, December 8, 1869, Bullock Papers, Huntington Library; Trelease, *White Terror*, pp. 236, 241, 333.

49. "Condition of Affairs in Georgia," *House Miscellaneous Document No. 52*, pp. 7–9, 14–16, 39–40; Malcolm Moos, *The Republicans: A History of Their Party* (New York: Random House, 1956), p. 128.

50. Testimony of Romulus Moore, U.S. Congress, *Report of the Condition of Affairs in the Late Insurrectionary States*, 7:738; J. M. Hoag to J. R. Lewis, November 9, 1868, James A. Jackson Memorandum, and newsclipping from Athens, Georgia Executive Department, Incoming Correspondence, Bullock, 1868–71, GDAH.

CHAPTER 5. An Expressive Sense of Justice

1. Reconstruction Act of March 23, 1867, "Iron Clad" Test Oath, and Fourteenth Amendment, in Fleming, ed., *Documentary History of Reconstruction*, 1:191–92, 407–11, 479.

2. Drago, *Black Politicians and Reconstruction*, pp. 53–56. Of Georgia's black leaders, only A. A. Bradley of Savannah broke openly with Bullock. Their feud

reached back to the 1868 constitutional convention when Bullock led the move to expel Bradley for insulting other convention members. See ibid., pp. 62–63; Foner, *Reconstruction*, p. 342.

3. Joseph E. Brown to Bullock, December 3, 1868, Brown Papers, Atlanta Historical Society.

4. *Contemporary American Biography*, 2:69.

5. Michael Perman, *The Road to Redemption: Southern Politics, 1869–1879* (Chapel Hill: University of North Carolina Press, 1984), pp. 5–30, 42–50.

6. Joseph E. Brown to Ulysses S. Grant, May 10, 1869, Brown Family Papers, University of Georgia; Joseph E. Brown to Henry Wilson, December 19, 1868, Bullock Papers, Huntington Library.

7. Bullock to the Editor, *Atlanta Constitution*, May 4, 1896 (4, 4).

8. Volney Spalding to W. E. Chandler, August 14, 1868, Chandler Papers; Caldwell, *Reminiscences*, p. 14.

9. Shadgett, *Republican Party in Georgia*, pp. 49–51; Nathans, *Losing the Peace*, pp. vii, 147; Currie-McDaniel, *Carpetbagger of Conscience*, pp. 89–91; Pomeroy quoted in Michael Les Benedict, *A Compromise of Principle: Congressional Republicans and Reconstruction, 1865–1869* (New York: Norton, 1974), p. 326.

10. Drago, *Black Politicians and Reconstruction*, pp. 54–56; Currie-McDaniel, *Carpetbagger of Conscience*, pp. 89–91; Nathans, *Losing the Peace*, pp. 130–31; Smith, "Republican Party in Georgia," p. 166; J. W. O'Neal to John A. Wimpy, February 20, 1869, and Foster Blodgett to Benjamin F. Butler, June 12, 1869, Benjamin F. Butler Papers, Library of Congress; Carter, *When the War Was Over*, p. 90; Alvord, *Letters from the South*, pp. 20–21; Bullock to L. P. Gudger, January 25, 1870, Georgia Executive Department, Executive Secretary's Letter Books, p. 96, GDAH.

11. *New York Times*, December 8, 1868 (5, 2); *Congressional Globe*, 40th Cong., 3d sess., pt. 1, pp. 1–5, 43, 568; U.S. Congress, Senate, *Journal of the Senate of the United States*, 40th Cong., 3d sess., pp. 5–6, 18, 141–42; William A. Russ, Jr., "Radical Disfranchisement in Georgia, 1867–1871," *Georgia Historical Quarterly* 19 (September 1935): 196–98.

12. Joseph E. Brown to Joshua Hill, December 7, 1868, Brown Family Papers, University of Georgia.

13. Testimony of Governor Bullock, "Condition of Affairs in Georgia," *House Miscellaneous Document No. 52*, pp. 1–6, quotes from pp. 2, 3; *Congressional Globe*, 40th Cong., 3d sess., pt. 1, p. 10. For an excellent discussion of Reconstruction loyalty oaths see Harold M. Hyman, *Era of the Oath: Northern Loyalty Tests During the Civil War and Reconstruction* (Philadelphia: University of Pennsylvania Press, 1954), esp. pp. 82–155.

14. Testimony of Governor Bullock, "Condition of Affairs in Georgia," *House Miscellaneous Document No. 52*, pp. 2–3.

15. Testimony of James M. Simms, Henry M. Turner, Amos T. Akerman, V. A. Gaskill, John E. Bryant, James A. Madden, S. P. Powell, and A. W. Stone, "Condition of Affairs in Georgia," ibid., pp. 6–48, documentary evidence, pp. 48–139; *Congressional Globe,* 40th Cong., 3d sess., pt. 1, pp. 3–4; U.S. Congress, Senate, *Journal,* 40th Cong., 3d sess., pp. 192, 334.

16. Alexander Stephens to James Brooks, July 24, 1868, Felix Hargrett Collection, University of Georgia, Athens; Georgia, Comptroller General's Office, *Report of Madison Bell,* Table A; "Condition of Affairs in Georgia," *House Miscellaneous Document No. 52,* pp. 140–237; *Augusta Chronicle,* September 9, 1869 (2, 1).

17. Zuber, "Bullock in Georgia Politics," pp. 49–52; Nelson Tift to Mother, April 24, 1869, Nelson Tift letter, University of Georgia, Athens; Early "Lost Cause" historians of Georgia helped perpetuate the myth of a "slander mill"; see Howell, *History of Georgia,* 1:601–2.

18. Joseph E. Brown to Nelson Tift, January 2, 1868 [1869], "Condition of Affairs in Georgia," *House Miscellaneous Document No. 52,* pp. 141–46.

19. "Letter from Governor Bullock, of Georgia, in Reply to the Statement of Hon. Nelson Tift to the Reconstruction Committee of Congress," February 26, 1869, in *House Miscellaneous Document No. 52,* pt. 2, pp. 1–4.

20. Ibid.

21. *Congressional Globe,* 41st Cong., 2d sess., pp. 27, 38, 74, 171, 1506; "A Bill to Enable the People of Georgia to Form a State Government Republican in Form," January 5, 1869, Butler Papers.

22. Bullock Annual Message, January 13, 1869, Georgia Executive Department, Minutes, 1866–74, microfilm, GDAH; Franklin, *Reconstruction,* pp. 63–64.

23. Bullock to Benjamin F. Butler, February 7, 1869, J. L. Dunning to Butler, February 3, 1869, Butler Papers.

24. Bullock to Benjamin F. Butler, February 7, 1869, J. L. Dunning to Butler, February 3, 1869, C. H. Hopkins to Butler, February 14, 1869, Henry M. Turner to Butler, February 19, 1869, ibid.

25. Bullock to General Assembly and Senate, February 15, 1869, Georgia Executive Department, Minutes, 1866–74, GDAH.

26. Ibid.; "Letter from Governor Bullock, of Georgia, in Reply to the Statement of Hon. Nelson Tift," in *House Miscellaneous Document No. 52,* pt. 2, p. 3; *New York Times,* February 15 (5, 3), 16 (5, 2), 1869.

27. "Letter from Governor Bullock, of Georgia, in Reply to the Statement of Hon. Nelson Tift," in *House Miscellaneous Document No. 52,* pt. 2, p. 3; *New York Times,* February 15 (5, 3), 16 (5, 2), 1869.

28. Nathans, *Losing the Peace,* p. 154; Bullock to General Assembly, March 10, 1869, Georgia Executive Department, Executive Secretary's Letter Books; *New York Times,* March 11 (1, 6), 20 (11, 1) 1869.

29. *New York Times,* March 10, 1869 (5, 4–5). For a lucid explanation of

congressional support of the Fifteenth Amendment as a way to consolidate Republican party power in the North, see William Gillette, *The Right to Vote: Politics and the Passage of the Fifteenth Amendment* (Baltimore: Johns Hopkins University Press, 1969).

30. Eugene Davis to Edward McPherson, July 26, 1869, Georgia Executive Department, Executive Secretary's Letter Books, GDAH; Georgia, House, *Journal of the House of the State of Georgia, 1869* (Atlanta: Public Printer, 1869), pp. 575–80; Georgia, Senate, *Journal of the Senate of the State of Georgia, 1869* (Atlanta: Public Printer, 1869), pp. 652–58. In the house vote, three members voted to ratify but stipulated that they interpreted the proposed amendment as not granting officeholding rights to blacks.

31. Gillette, *Right to Vote*, pp. 98–101; Howell, *History of Georgia*, 1:611–12.

32. F. J. Robinson to Bullock, April 9, September 18, 1869, Georgia Executive Department, Incoming Correspondence, Bullock, 1868–71, GDAH.

33. Adam Palmer to Bullock, August 24, 1869, ibid.

34. J. Spilman to Bullock, August 23, 1869, Eli Barnes to W. H. Harrison, August 22, 1869, and William Wilson to Bullock, August 22, 1869, ibid.

35. Affidavit of Martha Spencer, August 25, 1869, John W. Oneil, et al., to Senate and House of Representatives, January 1, 1869, and Bullock to General Commanding, undated (two letters, in September 22 and November 20, 1869, folders), ibid.; Reward for outrages, November 29, 1869, Georgia Executive Department, Minutes, 1866–74, microfilm, GDAH; Joshua Hill to President Grant, May 24, 1869, Joshua Hill letter, University of Georgia, Athens; Trelease, *White Terror*, pp. 232–34; *New York Times*, May 17, 1869 (1, 2).

36. A. L. Harris to Benjamin Conley, May 11, 1869, Benjamin Conley Letters and Papers, Atlanta Historical Society, Atlanta.

37. William S. McFeely, "Amos T. Akerman: The Lawyer and Racial Justice," in *Region, Race, and Reconstruction: Essays in Honor of C. Vann Woodward*, ed. J. Morgan Kousser and James M. McPherson (New York: Oxford University Press, 1982), pp. 395–415, Akerman quote on p. 402.

38. *Can a Negro Hold Office in Georgia? Decided in the Supreme Court of Georgia, June Term, 1869* (Atlanta: Daily Intelligencer, 1869), pp. 18–19, 65–79; Henry R. Goetchius, "Litigation in Georgia During the Reconstruction Period, 1865 to 1872," *Report of the Georgia Bar Association* (N.p.: N.p., 1897), pp. 34–35. For a full description of proceedings of the case see *White v. Clements*, Georgia, Supreme Court, *Reports of Cases in Law and Equity Decided Before the Supreme Court of Georgia . . . 1869* (Macon, Ga.: Burke, 1870), pp. 232–85.

39. Appointment of Hiram Warner, August 14, 1868, Georgia Executive Department, Minutes, 1866–74, p. 164, GDAH.

40. Appointment of H. K. McCay, ibid.; Alexander A. Lawrence, "Henry Kent McCay: Forgotten Jurist," *Georgia Bar Journal*, undated, pp. 6–10, in Henry K.

McCay, File II, Names, GDAH; *White* v. *Clements*, Georgia, Supreme Court, *Reports of Cases in Law and Equity, 1869,* pp. 232–85.

41. Zuber, "Role of Rufus Brown Bullock," p. 58; Eugene Davis to J. M. Bishop, July 9, 1869, Georgia Executive Department, Executive Secretary's Letter Books, p. 286, GDAH; *Augusta Chronicle,* June 30, 1869; W. Calvin Smith, "The Reconstruction 'Triumph' of Rufus B. Bullock," *Georgia Historical Quarterly* 52 (December 1968): 416.

42. Henry Wilson to U. S. Grant, May 14, 1869, U.S. Congress, House of Representatives, *Report of the Secretary of War,* Executive Documents, 41st Cong., 2d sess., 2:89.

43. Bullock to Benjamin F. Butler, July 8, August 2, 1869, Butler Papers.

44. Foster Blodgett to Benjamin F. Butler, November 6, 1869, ibid.; Bullock to the Editor, *New York Times,* December 4, 1869 (1, 7).

45. A. H. Terry to William T. Sherman, August 14, 1869, U.S. Congress, House of Representatives, *Report of the Secretary of War,* Executive Documents, 41st Cong., 2d sess., 2:89–95. The last quote from Terry is in Sefton, *United States Army and Reconstruction,* pp. 200–201.

46. Bullock to Wesley Shropshire, November 24, 1869, Georgia Executive Department, Executive Secretary's Letter Books, p. 367, GDAH.

47. *Congressional Globe,* 41st Cong., 2d sess., p. 4; William Gillette, *Retreat from Reconstruction, 1869–1879* (Baton Rouge: Louisiana State University Press, 1979), pp. 86–89.

48. Gillette, *Right to Vote,* esp. pp. 48–50; Smith, "Reconstruction 'Triumph,' " pp. 414–23.

49. Tunis G. Campbell, *Sufferings of the Rev. T. G. Campbell and His Family in Georgia* (Washington, D.C.: Enterprise Publishing Co., 1877), p. 10; *Congressional Globe,* 41st Cong., 2d sess., pp. 165–66, 201–6, 209–18, 222, 224–25, 232, 246–47, 275–93, 325. In debate, some feared that Bullock might delay in calling the legislature and thereby gain unprecedented power, a fear Bullock alleviated by pledging to convene the legislature the moment the bill became law.

50. The *Augusta Chronicle,* January 29, 1870 (3, 1), claimed that Bullock spent $5,000 on the feast and that he took champagne baths costing $75 each. For an adverse view of Bullock's triumph and the dinner, see Claude G. Bowers, *The Tragic Era: The Revolution After Lincoln* (Cambridge, Mass.: Houghton Mifflin, 1929), pp. 302–3; Howell, *History of Georgia,* 1:612; Isaac W. Avery, *The History of the State of Georgia from 1850 to 1881 . . .* (New York: Brown and Derby, 1881), p. 423; *Washington Chronicle,* December 24 (1, 6), 25 (1, 4), 1869.

51. C. H. Prince to Benjamin Conley, December 18, 1869, Conley Letters and Papers, Atlanta Historical Society.

52. Avery, *History of Georgia,* p. 421.

53. Bullock Proclamation of December 22, 1869, Georgia Executive Depart-

ment, Minutes, 1866–74, microfilm, p. 448, GDAH; Sefton, *United States Army,* pp. 201–2; William T. Sherman to General A. H. Terry, December 24, 1869, Records of the Adjutant General's Office, 1780s–1917, RG 94, Microcopy 565, Roll 38, NA.

54. Appointment of J. G. W. Mills and A. L. Harris, January 8, 1870, Georgia Executive Department, Minutes, 1866–74, microfilm, p. 455, GDAH; Georgia, House, *Journal of the House of the State of Georgia, 1870,* 3 vols. (Atlanta: W. A. Hemphill, 1870), 1:3; General A. H. Terry to Bullock, January 8, 1870, Georgia Executive Department, Incoming Correspondence, Bullock, 1868–71, GDAH; *Atlanta Daily New Era,* January 11, 1870 (2, 2–3); Campbell, *Sufferings,* pp. 10–12; Zuber, "Role of Rufus Brown Bullock," pp. 65–69.

55. Military District of Georgia, General Order No. 3, January 13, 1870, in N. L. Angier, *The Georgia Legislature, Legally Organized in 1868* (Washington, D.C.: Gibson Brothers, 1870), p. 13; Bullock to General Terry, January 15, 1870 (two letters), January 19, 1870, Rufus Bullock, File II, Names, GDAH; Bullock to William Lawrence, January 20, 1870, Hamilton Fish Collection, Library of Congress; W. C. Morrill to Simon Cameron, January 15, 1870, Simon Cameron Papers, microfilm, Library of Congress; *Augusta Chronicle,* January 14 (2, 1), 15 (2, 2), 19 (1, 1), 1870; Avery, *History of Georgia,* pp. 430–32.

56. Military District of Georgia, General Orders No. 9, 10, 11, and 13, January 25, 28, and 31, 1870, in Angier, *Georgia Legislature,* pp. 15–16; *Georgia House Journal, 1870,* 1:3–72; Bullock to Senators Trumbull, Stewart, Edmonds, Conkling, Carpenter, and Rice, January 28, 1870, and Bullock to J. M. Thayer, January 28, 1870, Georgia Executive Department, Executive Secretary's Letter Books, pp. 101–3, 105–7, GDAH; Bullock to General Terry, February 1, 1870, Rufus Bullock, File II, Names, GDAH; *Congressional Globe,* 41st Cong., 2d sess., pp. 576, 1029, 1128; Smith, "Bullock and the Third Reconstruction," pp. 100–101; Russ, "Radical Disfranchisement," pp. 201–3.

57. *New York Times,* February 17, 1870 (1, 4); Bullock to General Assembly, February 2, 1870, and Amendment Ratification, February 2, 1870, Georgia Executive Department, Minutes, 1866–74, microfilm, pp. 488, 490–98, GDAH; Russ, "Radical Disfranchisement," pp. 202–4.

58. *Georgia House Journal, 1870,* 1:72–78, 81.

CHAPTER 6. Development and Scandal

1. William C. Harris, "The Creed of the Carpetbagger: The Case of Mississippi," *Journal of Southern History* 40 (May 1974): 202–3, 219; Richard N. Current, *Northernizing the South* (Athens: University of Georgia Press, 1983), p. 13; James S. Allen, *The Negro Question in the United States* (New York: Interna-

tional Publishers, 1936), p. 35. For definition and discussion of core and periphery see Immanuel Wallerstein, *The Modern World-System: Capitalist Agriculture and the Origins of the European World-Economy in the Sixteenth Century* (New York: Academic Press, 1974), esp. pp. 347–57.

2. Powell, *New Masters,* pp. xiii, 8; Foner, *Free Soil, Free Labor, Free Men,* p. 39; Abbott, *The Republican Party and the South,* p. 233.

3. Bullock Address to General Assembly, July 24, 1868, Georgia Executive Department, Minutes, 1866–74, microfilm, p. 144, GDAH.

4. *Atlanta Daily New Era,* October 18, 1870 (2, 3); Shore, *Southern Capitalists,* pp. 127–34, 142. For the fullest exposition on the gospel of prosperity, see Summers, *Railroads, Reconstruction, and the Gospel of Prosperity;* "Bullock of Georgia," June 14, 1877, Grady Papers, Scrapbook 4, p. 6, Emory University; *Atlanta Independent,* January 20, 1878, in Joseph E. and Elizabeth G. Brown Collection, University of Georgia; Affidavit of William E. Armstrong, in Rufus B. Bullock, *Address of Rufus B. Bullock to the People of Georgia: A Review of the Revolutionary Proceedings of the Late Repudiating Legislature* (Atlanta: New Era Printing, 1872), p. 6.

5. Reagan, *Kimball,* pp. 15, 28, 39–45, 60, 109–10, 134; Wotton, "New City of the South," p. 187; Georgia Vol. 13, p. 424, Dun Collection; John F. Stover, "Northern Financial Interests in Southern Railroads, 1865–1900," *Georgia Historical Quarterly* 39 (September 1955): 209; Raymond B. Nixon, *Henry W. Grady: Spokesman of the New South* (New York: Knopf, 1943), p. 109; Kimball quoted in *Atlanta Journal,* February 22, 1874, in Scrapbooks of John Calvin Peck, Peck Family Collection, GDAH.

6. Linton Stephens to Joseph E. Brown, January 26, 1871, Brown Papers, Atlanta Historical Society; H. I. Kimball, *An Open Letter from H. I. Kimball to the Augusta Chronicle and Sentinel* (Atlanta: Atlanta Herald, 1874), p. 15.

7. Adverse views of the Bullock-Kimball relationship abound. Most influential have been Thompson, *Reconstruction in Georgia,* p. 202; E. Merton Coulter, *Georgia: A Short History* (Chapel Hill: University of North Carolina Press, 1935), p. 353; and Georgia Vol. 13, p. 485, Dun Collection. That Kimball and Bullock were only two years apart in age, that both knew George Pullman, and that they were Northerners who came south to promote business surely influenced their friendship although the key factor was a shared vision of internal improvements and free labor.

8. Bullock, *Address to the People of Georgia,* pp. 19, 25–29; *Georgia Senate Journal, 1869,* pp. 524–30; Bullock to General Assembly, March 1, 1869; Georgia Executive Department, Minutes, 1866–74, microfilm, p. 311, GDAH. For Kimball's account of how he spent the $54,500 and a complete inventory of costs by item, including labor, freight, forty spittoons, five hundred inkstands, forty dozen

chairs, and more, see Testimony of H. I. Kimball, in Georgia, General Assembly, *Joint Committee to Investigate Charges Against Governor Bullock* (Atlanta: State Printer, 1870); Farrow quoted in *New York Times,* February 10, 1869 (3, 3).

9. Reagan, *Kimball,* pp. 19–23; Executive Department Order, August 23, 1870, William Ezzard to Bullock, July 20, 1870, Georgia Executive Department, Incoming Correspondence, Bullock, 1868–71, GDAH; Bullock to General Assembly, July 23, 1870, Georgia Executive Department Minutes, 1866–74, microfilm, GDAH.

10. *Kimball's Opera House* (N.p., n.d.), Joseph E. and Elizabeth G. Brown Collection, University of Georgia; B. W. Froebel, File II, Names, GDAH; *New York Tribune,* February 9, 1878 (3, 3); *Atlanta Constitution,* February 10, 1985 (1H, 1).

11. Carole E. Scott, "Coping with Inflation: Atlanta, 1860–1865," *Georgia Historical Quarterly* 69 (Winter 1985): 538–39; Ulrich B. Phillips, "An American State-Owned Railroad," *Yale Review* 15 (November 1906): 259–82; Wallenstein, *From Slave South to New South,* pp. 29–38, 177; Roberts, *Brown and the Politics of Reconstruction,* pp. 5–7.

12. Perman, *Road to Redemption,* pp. 33, 70; Thomas C. Cochran and William Miller, *The Age of Enterprise: A Social History of Industrial America* (New York: Harper & Row, 1961), pp. 78–81; Coulter, *Georgia,* p. 331; Wallenstein, *From Slave South to New South,* pp. 176–77; Summers, *Railroads, Reconstruction, and the Gospel of Prosperity,* pp. 9, 75–76; quote from Carter, *When the War Was Over,* pp. 124–25.

13. A. Elizabeth Taylor, "The Abolition of the Convict Lease System in Georgia," *Georgia Historical Quarterly* 26 (September 1942): 273; Wallenstein, *From Slave South to New South,* pp. 80, 202–3; A. Elizabeth Taylor, "The Convict Lease System in Georgia, 1866–1908" (M.A. thesis, University of North Carolina, 1940), pp. 6–8.

14. Bullock to Robert K. Scott, June 28, 1869, Georgia Executive Department, Executive Secretary's Letter Books, p. 178, GDAH; Bullock to General Assembly, September 4, 1868, Georgia Executive Department, Minutes, 1866–74, microfilm, pp. 176–77, GDAH; B. B. DeGraffenried to John L. Conley, September 26, 1868, Georgia Executive Department, Executive Secretary's Letter Books, p. 203, GDAH; Blake McKelvey, "Penal Slavery and Southern Reconstruction," *Journal of Negro History* 20 (April 1935): 154–56. Aaron Bradley was the only black leader openly to oppose convict lease at its inception. See Joseph P. Reidy, "Aaron A. Bradley: Voice of Black Labor in the Georgia Lowcountry," in *Southern Black Leaders of the Reconstruction Era,* ed. Howard N. Rabinowitz (Urbana: University of Illinois Press, 1982), p. 297.

15. James M. Russell, "John Thomas Grant," in *Dictionary of Georgia Biography,* ed. Coleman and Gurr, 1:362–64; Taylor, "Convict Lease System in Geor-

gia," pp. 9–11. The abuses of the convict-lease system were little publicized in the middle of the nineteenth century. Massachusetts inaugurated the system as early as 1798; Kentucky followed in 1825. See Fletcher M. Green, "Some Aspects of the Convict Lease System in the Southern States," in *Essays in Southern History,* ed. Green (Chapel Hill: University of North Carolina Press, 1949), pp. 115–17; Eugene Davis to Messrs. Grant, Alexander, & Company, October 10, 1868, Bullock to O. H. Walton, November 3, 1868, Eugene Davis to Grant, Alexander, and Company, June 24, 1869, Eugene Davis to Overton H. Walton, June 28, 1869, Georgia Executive Department, Executive Secretary's Letter Books, pp. 102–3, 154–55, 333–34, 386–87, GDAH; Bullock to Principal Keeper Overton Walton, March 13, 1869, Bullock to Grant, Alexander, and Company, June 28, 1869, Georgia Executive Department, Minutes, 1866–74, microfilm, pp. 317, 372–73, GDAH; Georgia, General Assembly, *Proceedings of the Joint Committee Appointed to Investigate the Condition of the Georgia Penitentiary* (Atlanta: N.p., 1870), p. 5.

16. Robert L. Humphreys, ed., *The Journal of Archibald C. McKinley* (Athens: University of Georgia Press, 1991), pp. 5–6; Georgia, General Assembly, *Testimony Taken by the Committee Appointed to Investigate the Official Conduct of Rufus B. Bullock, Late Governor of Georgia* (Atlanta: W. A. Hemphill, 1872), pp. 151–52.

17. Bullock letter for John Christopher, July 7, 1869, H. C. Corson to Rev. Francis A. Peck, October 29, 1870, H. C. Corson to Rev. James Porter, October 29, 1870, H. C. Corson to Grant, Alexander, and Company, October 29, 1870, and Bullock to Grant, Alexander, and Company, August 27, 1870, July 8, 1871, Georgia Executive Department, Executive Secretary's Letter Books, pp. 96, 232–34, 236, 239, 274–75, GDAH; Georgia, Penitentiary, *Annual Report of the Principal Keeper of the Georgia Penitentiary, 1869* (Atlanta: Samuel Bard, 1870), pp. 6–10; *Proceedings of the Joint Committee Appointed to Investigate the Condition of the Georgia Penitentiary,* pp. 1, 195–99; Georgia, Penitentiary, *Annual Report of the Principal Keeper of the Georgia Penitentiary, 1870* (Atlanta: Samuel Bard, 1871), pp. 6–8; Bullock, *Address to the People of Georgia,* p. 30; Taylor, "Convict Lease System in Georgia," pp. 11–15.

18. Benjamin Conley to W. I. Dagrath, June 24, 1868, Conley Papers, University of Georgia; James A. Nisbet to Benjamin Conley, June 10, 1868, Conley Letters and Papers, Atlanta Historical Society.

19. Bullock to C. D. Phillips, July 8, 1871, Georgia Executive Department, Executive Secretary's Letter Books, p. 104, GDAH; *Daily Financial News,* undated, in Daniel L. Russell Papers, Southern Historical Collection, University of North Carolina, Chapel Hill.

20. *Augusta Chronicle,* September 4, 1869 (2, 1); Nixon, *Grady,* pp. 69–70; *Memoirs of Georgia,* 2:731; *Atlanta Daily New Era,* January 27, 1870 (3, 1).

21. Henry Clews to the Editor, *New York Times*, March 18, 1871 (2, 3); Georgia, General Assembly, *Committee to Investigate the Bonds of the State of Georgia, Issued or Negotiated Since July 4, 1868*, 5 vols. (Atlanta: W. A. Hemphill, 1872), 5:126; Bullock, *Address to the People of Georgia*, pp. 8, 39; Summers, *Railroads, Reconstruction, and the Gospel of Prosperity*, p. 68.

22. Reagan, *Kimball*, pp. 59, 66; Willard Range, "Hannibal I. Kimball," *Georgia Historical Quarterly* 29 (June 1945): 52–53; Thompson, *Reconstruction in Georgia*, p. 288, puts Kimball's completed rail mileage at three hundred miles; *New York Tribune*, February 9, 1878 (3, 3–4); Georgia Vol. 13, p. 485, Dun Collection.

23. *Atlanta Journal*, February 22, 1874, and *Atlanta Constitution*, February 23, 1874, Scrapbook, Peck Family Collection, GDAH; *Atlanta Constitution*, February 10, 1874 (2, 4); Kimball, *Open Letter*, p. 20.

24. Bullock, *Address to the People of Georgia*, p. 29.

25. Bullock to A. S. Buford, June 16, 1870, Georgia Executive Department, Executive Secretary's Letter Books, p. 339, GDAH.

26. Russell, "Atlanta," p. 200; Benjamin Conley to W. I. Dagrath, December 1, 1868, and W. I. Dagrath to Benjamin Conley, December 4, 1868, Conley Papers, University of Georgia; Reagan, *Kimball*, p. 8.

27. Bullock veto of Lookout Mountain Railroad, October 19, 1870, Georgia Executive Department, Minutes, 1866–74, microfilm, GDAH; *Atlanta Daily New Era*, October 18, 1870 (2, 3).

28. Bullock to C. D. Forsyth, August 20, 1870, Georgia Executive Department, Executive Secretary's Letter Books, pp. 270–72, GDAH; Summers, *Railroads, Reconstruction, and the Gospel of Prosperity*, pp. 137–38.

29. Bullock to H. I. Kimball, July 20, 1869, and Bullock to W. L. Avery, July 18, 1870, Georgia Executive Department, Executive Secretary's Letter Books, pp. 14, 371, GDAH; *New York Times*, March 18, 1871 (2, 2); Order Seizing Alabama and Chattanooga Railroad, August 2, 1871, and Order Seizing Brunswick and Albany Railroad, October 23, 1871, Georgia Executive Department, Minutes, 1866–74, microfilm, GDAH.

30. *The Invalid Bonds of Georgia: Arguments of Pat Calhoun, Esq., and Hon. N. J. Hammond Before the Attorney-General of New York, June 1885* (New York: N.p., 1885), pp. 5–7; Georgia, General Assembly, *Committee to Investigate the Bonds, 1868*, 5:183; *New York Times*, March 14, 1871 (2, 2); Smith, "Bullock and the Third Reconstruction of Georgia," p. 103; Bartley, *Creation of Modern Georgia*, pp. 71–72.

31. Henry Clews, *Twenty-Eight Years in Wall Street* (New York: Irving Publishing Co., 1888), pp. 257–87; *The Claim of Henry Clews and Company Against the State of Georgia* (Macon, Ga.: R. A. Alston, 1876), pp. 9–10, 27; Henry Clews to the Editor, *New York Times*, June 3, 1879 (2, 7); Henry Clews to

Benjamin Conley, July 23, 25, 1872, Conley Letters and Papers, Atlanta Historical Society.

32. Clews, *Wall Street*, p. 268; Bullock, *Address to the People of Georgia*, pp. 7–8, 12, 17–18, 20; *New York Times*, May 9, 1870 (5, 4).

33. Bullock, *Address to the People of Georgia*, pp. 17–18, 20; W. C. Morrill to Simon Cameron, November 22, 1871, Cameron Papers, Library of Congress; Bullock to Henry Clews, September 7, 1870, Bullock to N. L. Angier, November 30, 1870, Bullock to Russell Sage, May 25, 1871, and Bullock to Henry Clews, February 24, 1871, Georgia Executive Department, Executive Secretary's Letter Books, pp. 85, 124–26, 146–47, 204, GDAH; Bullock to Benjamin Conley, December 1, 2, 18, 1871, and J. B. Johnston to Benjamin Conley, January 8, 1872, Georgia Executive Department, Governor's Letter Books, Benjamin Conley, GDAH; D. G. Cotting to Bullock, August 25, 1870, Reconstruction file, GDAH. For more on Bullock's defense of the bonds, see Rufus B. Bullock, *Georgia's Repudiated Bonds. Letters from Ex-Governor Bullock to the Constitution Newspaper . . . Editorials . . . 1882 & 1885* (Atlanta: Harrison Printers, 1886), and *Atlanta Constitution*, February 19, 1900 (4, 5).

34. Bullock to the Editor, *Atlanta Post-Appeal*, November 24, 1881, and *Buffalo Express*, undated, in Bullock Papers, Huntington Library; Bullock to Joseph E. Brown, March 30, 1874, and Joseph E. Brown to H. I. Kimball, April 21, 1874, Brown Papers, Atlanta Historical Society; *New York Times*, November 30 (2, 7), December 10 (8, 6), 1882. As late as 1904, Bullock responded to newspaper articles that called repudiation just; but after thirty-five years, no one listened to Bullock when he said it was "a financial, not a political issue." See Bullock to the Editor, *Atlanta Constitution*, July 12, 1904, Bullock Papers, Huntington Library.

35. Joseph E. Brown to U. S. Grant, May 5, 1868, Hargrett Collection, University of Georgia.

36. E. Hulbert to Bullock, August 21, September 28, December 1, 1868, January 14, February 10, March 22, April 10, May 25, June 17, July 20, August 20, September 23, October 23, 1869, Foster Blodgett to Bullock, January [?], March 24, 1870, and Bullock to William W. Clayton, July 19, 1869, Georgia Executive Department, Executive Secretary's Letter Books, pp. 1, 2–3, 7, 10, 12, 13, 15–17, 19, 20, 25, 26, 29, 30, GDAH; *Atlanta Constitution*, April 4, 1888, in Bullock Papers, Huntington Library; Georgia, Comptroller-General's Office, *Report of the Comptroller-General and Insurance Commissioner* (Atlanta: N.p., 1870), pp. 9–10.

37. Foster Blodgett to Bullock, January [?], 1870, Georgia Executive Department, Executive Secretary's Letter Books, p. 30, GDAH; Walter G. Cooper, *The Story of Georgia*, 3 vols. (New York: American Historical Society, 1938), 3:193; Georgia, General Assembly, *Joint Committee to Investigate the Condition*,

Finances, and Management of the Western and Atlantic Railroad (Atlanta: J. J. Toon, 1870), p. 3; Georgia, General Assembly, House, Finance Committee, *Remarks and Statements of the Superintendent on the Condition of the Road . . . September 23, 1870* (Atlanta: State Printer, 1870), pp. 5, 12.

38. Georgia, General Assembly, *Joint Committee to Investigate the Western and Atlantic Railroad,* pp. 55, 100–103.

39. *Georgia House Journal, 1869,* pp. 54–57; Bullock to General Assembly, March 1, 1869, Georgia Executive Department, Minutes, 1866–74, microfilm, pp. 300–301, GDAH; *New York Times,* February 17 (1, 2), 18 (5, 1), 1869, July 20, 1870 (5, 2).

40. Georgia, General Assembly, *Joint Committee to Investigate Charges Against Governor Bullock,* pp. 5, 134, 138, 140. Angier's resentment may have hinged in part on his losing a $1,000 investment when Kimball bought the unfinished Opera House. See Testimony of Nedom L. Angier, U.S. Congress, *Report of the Condition of Affairs in the Late Insurrectionary States,* 6:162.

41. Bullock to W. C. Calhoun, June 3, 19, 1869, Georgia Executive Department, Executive Secretary's Letter Books, pp. 55, 529–36, GDAH; Testimony of Nedom L. Angier, U.S. Congress, *Report of the Condition of Affairs in the Late Insurrectionary States,* 6:156, 174.

42. Bullock to Henry Clews, April 22, 1871, Bullock to Foster Blodgett, November 23, 1869, January 20, 1870, Bullock to I. W. Avery, April 7, 1871, Georgia Executive Department, Executive Secretary's Letter Books, pp. 78–80, 87–88, 176, 322, GDAH; Testimony of Nedom L. Angier, U.S. Congress, *Report of the Condition of Affairs in the Late Insurrectionary States,* 6:152–56; Executive Order, August 19, 1871, Georgia Executive Department, Minutes, 1865–80, p. 172, GDAH; Bullock, *Address to the People of Georgia,* pp. 36–37.

43. For the fullest testimony concerning Blodgett's management of the Western and Atlantic, see Georgia, General Assembly, *Joint Committee to Investigate the Indebtedness of Foster Blodgett, Treasurer and Superintendent of the Western and Atlantic Railroad* (Atlanta: W. A. Hemphill, 1873).

44. Phillips, "American State-Owned Railroad," p. 281; H. C. Corson to F. Wyatt, October 11, 1870, Georgia Executive Department, Executive Secretary's Letter Books, pp. 66–67, GDAH; Summers, *Railroads, Reconstruction, and the Gospel of Prosperity,* pp. 263–65.

45. Georgia, General Assembly, *Acts and Resolutions of the General Assembly of the State of Georgia, 1870* (Atlanta: Public Printer, 1871), pp. 423–27; Georgia, Senate, *Journal of the Senate of the State of Georgia, 1870* (Atlanta: W. A. Hemphill, 1870), 3:569–71; *Georgia House Journal, 1870,* 2:1024–25; Bullock, *Address to the People of Georgia,* pp. 22–24.

46. Thompson, *Reconstruction in Georgia,* pp. 226–31.

47. Ibid.; C. A. Nutting to Simon Cameron, December 18, 1870, and W. C.

Morrill to Cameron, December 29, 1870, Cameron Papers; Conway, *Reconstruction of Georgia*, p. 192. Stephens resigned from the company on January 4, 1871, citing poor health and press complaints against Bullock's award of the lease (Alexander H. Stephens to Joseph E. Brown, January 4, 7, 1871, Brown Papers, Atlanta Historical Society). For evidence that Hill was never satisfied to be associated with his former enemies, see B. H. Hill to Simon Cameron, January 27, 1871, Cameron Papers; *Atlanta Daily New Era*, December 29, 1870 (2, 1).

48. Lease of Western and Atlantic Railroad, December 27, 1870, Georgia Executive Department, Minutes, 1866–70, microfilm, pp. 2–6, GDAH. For a list of lessees, securities, and complete inventory of the state road at time of lease, see *Commissioners' Report: Western and Atlantic Railroad to His Excellency Rufus B. Bullock, Governor, January, 1871* (Atlanta: George W. Harrison, 1891), pp. 1–2, 39; Bullock to A. G. Dobbins, December 28, 1870, Georgia Executive Department, Minutes, p. 12, GDAH.

49. Bullock to Joseph E. Brown, December 24, 1870, Brown Family Papers, University of Georgia.

50. Testimony of Benjamin H. Hill and Foster Blodgett and Majority and Minority Reports, Georgia, General Assembly, *Joint Committee to Investigate the Western and Atlantic Railroad, 1872* (Atlanta: W. A. Hemphill, 1872), pp. 127–33, 226–33, 4, 14, 26, 37; Joseph E. Brown to Linton Stephens, January 30, 1871, Brown Papers, Atlanta Historical Society; B. H. Hill to Joseph E. Brown, March 23, 1871, Brown Family Papers, University of Georgia. Blodgett's company, not Blodgett, offered Bullock stock if he would give it the lease. Blodgett said, "I did not have any influence over Governor Bullock. He was a man that influenced himself." Testimony about the Seago attempt to bribe Bullock can be found in Georgia, General Assembly, *Joint Committee to Investigate the Western and Atlantic Railroad, 1872*, pp. 96–97, 102–3, 154, 217, 227–28. Several witnesses testified that Bullock had no interest in the lease (ibid., pp. 21, 39, 48–49, 76, 150–51). In 1871, Brown's company published a pamphlet detailing the lease and the merit of Bullock's action: *The Lease of the Western and Atlantic Railroad with Correspondence and Other Papers in Relation Thereto* (Atlanta: Constitution Publishing, 1871). For the 1872 investigation into the lease see Georgia, General Assembly, *Reports of Legislative Committees, Submitted in July 1872* (Atlanta: W. A. Hemphill, 1872), vols. 1–3, 5; Georgia Vol. 13, p. 447, Dun Collection.

51. Hodding Carter, *Their Words Were Bullets: The Southern Press in War, Reconstruction, and Peace* (Athens: University of Georgia Press, 1969), pp. 1, 3, 11, 40–41, 45; Wilson, *Atlanta as It Is*, p. 22; Ellen Weldon, "The *Atlanta Constitution* Views the Ku Klux Klan: 1868–1872" (M.A. thesis, University of Missouri, 1964), pp. 20, 40.

52. Editor, *Augusta Chronicle*, to Nemesis, undated, in Thomas Manson Nor-

wood Papers, University of Georgia, Athens. Complete copies of the "Nemesis" articles used in this chapter are located in the Thomas Manson Norwood Papers, Southern Historical Collection, University of North Carolina, Chapel Hill.

53. Bullock, *Address to the People of Georgia*, p. 48.

54. Ibid., pp. 14, 31–32; *Savannah Morning News*, September 6, 1869 (2, 2); *Augusta Chronicle*, September 9, 1869 (2, 1); Testimony of B. H. Hill and Nedom Angier, U.S. Congress, *Report of the Condition of Affairs in the Late Insurrectionary States*, 7:172, 780.

55. Bullock, *Address to the People of Georgia*, pp. 14, 33; Bullock to R. Brewer, January 14, 1870, R. Paul Lester to Noel B. Knight, September 2, 1869, Eugene Davis to J. Clarke Swayze, June 28, 1869, and Bullock to Judge R. D. Harvey, March 14, 1871, Georgia Executive Department, Executive Secretary's Letter Books, pp. 81–82, 129, 175–76, 574, GDAH.

56. R. H. Atkinson to Bullock, July 4, 1871, and Testimony of Henry M. Turner, U.S. Congress, *Report of the Condition of Affairs in the Late Insurrectionary States*, 7:809–10, 1040; *Journal of the Constitutional Convention*, pp. 491, 494. The records of the Executive Department, 1868–71, in the Georgia Department of Archives and History are filled with letters and petitions for pardons, along with correspondence by Bullock asking for more information on questionable cases. See especially the Executive Secretary's Letter Book for September 3, 1868–January 30, 1869. In contrast to Bullock's leniency, in 1872 Democratic Governor James M. Smith pardoned only three inmates. See Georgia, Penitentiary, *Annual Report of the Principal Keeper of the Georgia Penitentiary, 1873* (Atlanta: W. A. Hemphill, 1873), p. 7.

57. Pardons for Robert Garvin, Jinsey Rawson, Jane McMasters, Daniel Newton, R. W. Chaffin, Henry Jasper, Samuel Gray, A. O. Garrard, Martha Mullins, Jim Jones, Georgia Executive Department, Minutes, 1866–74, microfilm, pp. 137, 164, 173, 175, 177, 224, 227, 235, 273, 411, GDAH; R. H. Atkinson to John Darnell, October 7, 1870, Georgia Executive Department, Executive Secretary's Letter Books, p. 25, GDAH; Testimony of R. H. Atkinson, U.S. Congress, *Report of the Condition of Affairs in the Late Insurrectionary States*, 7:109–10.

58. Bullock, *Address to the People of Georgia*, p. 12; Carter, *Their Words Were Bullets*, pp. 42, 45; *Statutes at Large*, 18 Stat., pt. 3, p. 115, in General Records of the United States Government, RG 11, NA; Perdue, "Negro as Reflected in the Atlanta Constitution," p. 58.

59. Bullock to J. S. Peterson, June 1, 1869, and H. C. Corson to Dr. Thomas Foster, February 23, 1870, Georgia Executive Department, Executive Secretary's Letter Books, pp. 317, 471, GDAH.

60. Bullock, *Address to the People of Georgia*, pp. 30, 42; Testimony of Joseph E. Brown, U.S. Congress, *Report of the Condition of Affairs in the Late Insurrectionary States*, 7:824, 827.

CHAPTER 7. Failure and Vindication

1. Thornberry, "Development of Black Atlanta," pp. 230–31; Russell, "Atlanta," pp. 271–72; Edward B. Young, "The Negro in Georgia Politics, 1867–1877" (M.A. thesis, Emory University, 1955), pp. 46–49, 62, 110; Bullock, *Letter to the Senators and Representatives in Congress*, p. 7.

2. *Georgia House Journal, 1870*, 3:90–98.

3. Bartley, *Creation of Modern Georgia*, p. 69.

4. *Augusta Chronicle*, January 14 (3, 3), February 4, 1870 (3, 4); Caldwell, *Reminiscences*, p. 15; *Georgia House Journal, 1870*, pp. 33–34; John M. Matthews, "Negro Republicans in the Reconstruction of Georgia," *Georgia Historical Quarterly* 60 (Summer 1976): 150, 156. One year earlier, the *New York Times*, March 7, 1869 (8, 1), reported that the party split between Radicals and moderates was "bitter and venomous" and noted that the "politician negroes like Turner, Sims, Costin, Beard, and the excluded members . . . all side with Blodgett." Toombs quote in letter to Alexander H. Stephens, February 8, 1870, Alexander H. Stephens Collection, Emory University, Atlanta, Ga.

5. Sumner quoted in David H. Donald, *Charles Sumner and the Rights of Man* (New York: Knopf, 1970), p. 448; *Macon Telegraph* quoted in *Washington Chronicle*, March 11, 1870 (1, 6–7).

6. Bullock, *Remarks to the Judiciary Committee*, pp. 13–16, 19, 21; *Washington Chronicle*, March 5, 1870 (1, 3–6).

7. Bullock, *Remarks to the Judiciary Committee*, pp. 22–23, 25–26; Bullock, *Letter to the Senators and Representatives in Congress*, pp. 5, 7; *New York Times*, May 23, 1870 (1, 3–4).

8. Bullock, *Remarks to the Judiciary Committee*, pp. 43–44.

9. John E. Bryant, *A Letter to Hon. Charles Sumner of the United States Senate, Exposing the Bullock-Blodgett Ring in Their Attempt to Defeat the Bingham Amendment* (Washington, D.C.: Gibson Brothers, 1870), p. 6.

10. Bullock to House of Representatives, March 4, 1869, Rufus Bullock, File II, Names, GDAH; H. L. Carroll to Henry P. Farrow, July 20, 1870, Farrow Papers, University of Georgia.

11. Bryant, *Letter to Sumner*, pp. 6, 18–20.

12. *New York Times*, March 17, 1870 (5, 2); *Washington Chronicle*, April 11, 1870 (1, 7).

13. John E. Bryant, *Gov. Bullock's Dispatches from Georgia: Why They Are Sent* (Washington, D.C.: Gibson Brothers, 1870), pp. 6, 8; Nathans, *Losing the Peace*, pp. 186–89; John E. Bryant and John Bowles, *Governor Bullock and the Democratic Press of Georgia* (Washington, D.C.: Gibson Brothers, 1870), p. 4.

14. *Atlanta Constitution*, April 23, 1870 (2, 1). Democrats used the "Outrages Wanted" approach before Bryant incorporated it; see *Augusta Chronicle*, January 14, 1870 (3, 3).

15. *New York World,* March 18, 1870, quoted in Bowers, *Tragic Era,* p. 304; J. E. Bryant to James M. Thompson, March 11, 1870, Thompson to Bryant, March 11, 1870, and Thompson to Bullock, March 11, 1870, Bullock Papers, Huntington Library.

16. T. Harry Williams, *Romance and Realism in Southern Politics* (Athens: University of Georgia Press, 1961), p. 75; U.S. Congress, Senate, *Judiciary Report 175,* 41st Cong., 2d sess., pp. i–xii, 1–150. By 1872 most Centrists had joined either the Democratic party or the Liberal Republican party of Horace Greeley. That Greeley was the Democratic nominee for president in 1872 demonstrates the absolute ties of the two groups. After Greeley used Bullock as an example of Radical corruption, Bullock responded that he had a "proud" record, said, "I have done no wrong," and rebuked Greeley, Trumbull, and others by saying, "You lie, you villain." See *New York Times,* August 22, 1872 (2, 4–6), and Michael Les Benedict, *The Fruits of Victory: Alternatives in Restoring the Union, 1865–1877* (Philadelphia: J. B. Lippincott, 1975), pp. 53–55.

17. Bullock to Hon. John Harris, May 28, 1870, Georgia Executive Department, Executive Secretary's Letter Books, pp. 180–81, GDAH; Bullock, *Letter to the Senators and Representatives in Congress,* pp. 5–7, 9.

18. Bullock, *Letter to the Senators and Representatives in Congress,* p. 10.

19. Debate on the Georgia bill can be found in the *Congressional Globe,* 41st Cong. 2d sess., esp. pp. 1570, 1701–23, 1743–51, 1765–71, 1924–30, 2061, 5623; *New Orleans Daily Picayune,* March 25, 1871, quoted in Gillette, *Retreat from Reconstruction,* p. 166; Grant quoted in Richard N. Current, *Three Carpetbag Governors* (Baton Rouge: Louisiana State University Press, 1967), p. 88; *Washington Chronicle,* March 17, 1870 (1, 1–2).

20. *New York Times,* August 12, 1870 (6, 2); Avery, *History of Georgia,* pp. 439–40.

21. *New York Times,* August 12, 1870 (5, 4); *Georgia House Journal, 1870,* 3:340–43; John Erskine to H. P. Farrow, February 28, 1870, Farrow Papers, University of Georgia.

22. *Georgia House Journal, 1870,* 3:343; Matt H. Carpenter to Henry P. Farrow, August 30, 1870, Farrow Papers, University of Georgia. For other letters in the Farrow Papers from Republican senators supporting Farrow's role in defeating prolongation, see Roscoe Conkling to Farrow, September 27, 1870, Orris S. Ferry to Farrow, August 31, 1870, and Joseph S. Fowler to Farrow, September 2, 1870; Shadgett, *Republican Party in Georgia,* pp. 21–22.

23. Conway, *Reconstruction of Georgia,* p. 176; *Savannah Morning News,* March 9, 1869 (1, 1); *The American Annual Cyclopedia and Register of Important Events of the Year 1869* (New York: D. Appleton, 1870), 9:303; Bullock to General Assembly, February 26, 1869, Georgia Executive Department, Minutes, 1866–74, microfilm, p. 296, GDAH; Frank W. Prescott, "A Footnote on Georgia's

Constitutional History: The Item Veto of the Governors," *Georgia Historical Quarterly* 42 (December 1958): 5–13.

24. Bullock to Election Managers, December 7, 1870, Georgia Executive Department, Minutes, 1865–80, pp. 732–33, GDAH; W. L. Clark to Bullock, December 12, 1870, and D. G. Cotting to Bullock, December 14, 1870, Reconstruction file, GDAH; Executive Department Proclamation, December 13, 1870, Rufus Bullock, File II, Names, GDAH; Bullock to General A. H. Terry, October 5, 1870, Georgia Executive Department, Executive Secretary's Letter Books, p. 131, GDAH. Beginning in May 1870, Congress enacted a series of four Enforcement Acts to protect voters against force, bribery, and intimidation. Federal supervisors first oversaw elections in cities with over twenty thousand people, then in rural areas. The act of April 20, 1872, commonly referred to as the Ku Klux Act, outlawed the Klan and other conspiratorial groups. Unfortunately, none of these "Force Acts" slowed election abuses. Few were prosecuted. Bullock understood that Klan juries and judges held down convictions in all sorts of cases. On August 15, 1870, Bullock asked the General Assembly to "revise the jury box, as will place therein the name of every 'upright and intelligent' colored man in each county, and exclude [every Klan member]. . . . Let the ballot box be fairly represented in the jury box. . . . Prevent men from sitting on the jury, who are bound to a secret oath, to violate their official oaths as jurors, and to find as innocent, the guilty members of their 'Klan.' " See Bullock to General Assembly, August 15, 1870, Georgia Executive Department, Minutes, 1866–74, microfilm, p. 581, GDAH.

25. Bullock to Simon Cameron, December 1, 1870, Cameron Papers; H. C. Corson to W. T. Loften, October 19, 1870, Georgia Executive Department, Executive Secretary's Letter Books, p. 273, GDAH.

26. George H. Clower to Bullock, December 14, 18, 1870, and Benjamin Clements to Bullock, November 29, 1870, Reconstruction file, GDAH.

27. *Augusta Chronicle*, December 21, 1870 (2, 2); Affidavit of Josiah Sherman, January 10, 1871, Georgia Executive Department, Incoming Correspondence, Bullock, 1868–71, GDAH; Testimony of Josiah Sherman, U.S. Congress, *Report of the Condition of Affairs in the Late Insurrectionary States*, 7:1148.

28. Testimony of Linton Stephens and Eli Barnes, U.S. Congress, *Report of the Condition of Affairs in the Late Insurrectionary States*, 7:954–57, 974–77; James D. Waddell, *Biographical Sketch of Linton Stephens* (Atlanta: Dodson & Scott, 1877), pp. 322–28, 341–43.

29. Thompson, *Reconstruction in Georgia*, p. 250; St. Clair-Abrams, *Manual and Biographical Register of the State of Georgia*, pp. 111–12; Bullock, *Address to the People of Georgia*, pp. 29–30, 32. Historians continue to debate the Klan's role in the overthrow of Georgia's government. For contrasting arguments see Rable, *But There Was No Peace*, which asserts that the Klan "failed to overthrow

a single Republican state government" (p. 110), and Deaton, "Violent Redemption," which concludes that it did.

30. KKK to B. D. Evans, January 29, 1871, and KKK to Col. Evans, undated, Ku Klux Klan Collection, University of Georgia, Athens; Unknown to H. D. D. Twiggs, February 16, 1871, Georgia Executive Department, Incoming Correspondence, Bullock, 1868–71, GDAH.

31. *Congressional Globe,* 41st Cong., 3d sess., pp. 527, 530, 663, 678, 703–7, 816–30, 848–51, 871, 1086, 1163–84, 1632; Protest of Members of Georgia Legislature, November 14, 1871, Foster Blodgett, File II, Names, GDAH; Fleming, ed., *Documentary History of Reconstruction,* pp. 102–28; Rufus B. Bullock, "Letter from His Excellency Governor Bullock, of Georgia, in Reply to the Honorable John Scott, United States Senator, Chairman of Joint Select Committee to Inquire into the Condition of the Late Insurrectionary States," *Commercial and Financial Chronicle,* July 22, 1871, p. 109. Bullock's letter to Scott also can be found in *New York Times,* July 20, 1871 (2, 4).

32. Bullock's appointments to county boards of education can be found in Georgia Executive Department, Minutes, 1866–74, microfilm, pp. 30–196 passim; R. H. Atkinson to George Wallace, Atkinson to T. G. Campbell, October 10, 1870, and Eugene Davis to Richard Goodman, July 23, 1869, Georgia Executive Department, Executive Secretary's Letter Books, pp. 44–46, 398, GDAH; Appointment of James Simms, January 16, 1871, Georgia Executive Department, Minutes, 1866–1874, microfilm, p. 16, GDAH.

33. Perdue, "The Negro as Reflected in the Atlanta Constitution," p. 34; Nemesis Letters 3 and 4, Norwood Papers, Southern Historical Collection, University of North Carolina.

34. "Governor Bullock's Trial," unidentified newspaper clipping, January 2, 1878, Grady Papers, Scrapbook 4, pp. 9–10, Emory University; Bullock to Whom It May Concern, October 23, 1871, Reconstruction file, GDAH; "The Georgia Troubles," undated newspaper clipping, Bullock Papers, Huntington Library.

35. R. H. Atkinson to D. G. Cotting, October 30, 1871, R. H. Atkinson file, File II, Names, GDAH; D. G. Cotting to Benjamin Conley, October 30, 1871, Reconstruction file, GDAH; *Atlanta Daily Sun,* October 31, 1871 (2, 1).

36. Bullock, "To My Political Friends and the Public," *Atlanta Constitution,* October 31, 1871 (3, 2).

37. Ibid.; John L. Conley, ed., *The Constitution of the State of Georgia with Full Marginal Notes* (N.p.; 1868), p. 27.

38. *Atlanta Daily Sun,* November 2, 1871 (2, 2); R. H. Brown to Benjamin Conley, November 1, 1871, Conley Papers, University of Georgia; Columbus Delano to Bullock, November 7, 1871, Bullock Papers, Huntington Library; *New York Times,* November 2, 1871 (1, 3); *New York Standard,* November 2, 1871, in Bullock Papers, Huntington Library.

39. *Atlanta Daily Sun,* November 2 (3, 1), 3 (2, 2), 5 (3, 3), December 7 (2, 3), 1871; Georgia, House, *Journal of the House of the State of Georgia, 1871* (Atlanta: W. A. Hemphill, 1872), pp. 7, 9, 18, 189–91, 398; Shadgett, *Republican Party in Georgia,* pp. 26–29.

40. Benjamin Conley to the General Assembly, November 4, 1871, Georgia Executive Department, Minutes, 1866–74, microfilm, pp. 200–204, GDAH; *Georgia House Journal, 1871,* pp. 25–35; Veto message of Benjamin Conley, in *Benjamin Conley: Messages, 1871–1872* (Atlanta: New Era, 1872), pp. 5–11; T. R. Rhodes to Benjamin Conley, January 8, 1872, P. M. Sheibley to Ex-Gov. Conley, January 19, 1872, Conley Papers, University of Georgia; *Augusta Chronicle,* January 16 (2, 4), 18 (4, 1), 1872.

41. *Atlanta Constitution,* January 2, 1878, Grady Papers, Scrapbook 4, pp. 9–10, Emory University; R. H. Brown to Benjamin Conley, November 1, 1871, Foster Blodgett to Conley, December 4, 13, 1871, W. S. Mayfield to Conley, November 5, 1871, and Thomas J. Speer to Conley, December 9, 1871, Conley Papers, University of Georgia.

42. Amos T. Akerman to Benjamin Conley, December 28, 1871, Conley Papers, University of Georgia.

43. *New York Times,* August 22, 1872 (2, 4–6); Message of Benjamin Conley, January 11, 1872, in *Conley: Messages,* pp. 4–5; D. H. Denning to Benjamin Conley, November 2, 1871, and F. J. Robinson to Conley, January 9, 1872, Conley Papers, University of Georgia; Georgia, Senate, *Journal of the Senate of the State of Georgia, 1872* (Atlanta: W. A. Hemphill, 1872), pp. 13, 25–26.

44. *Augusta Chronicle,* January 13, 1872 (2, 2); Wotton, "New City of the South," pp. 310–11; *Atlanta Constitution,* December 5, 1871 (3, 2); *Atlanta Daily New Era,* December 5, 1871 (1, 4); Georgia, House, *Journal of the House of the State of Georgia, 1872* (Atlanta: W. A. Hemphill, 1872), pp. 341–44, 347–48, 353, 357, 398; Young, "Negro in Georgia Politics," pp. 64–69; Zuber, "Role of Bullock in Georgia Politics," pp. 89, 101; James M. Smith to Governor of New York, March 13, 1872, Georgia Executive Department, Minutes, 1866–74, microfilm, p. 311, GDAH.

45. Edward King, *The Southern States of North America: A Record of Journeys,* 4 vols. (London: Blackie & Son, 1875), 2:354; Testimony of W. E. B. Du Bois, *Report of the Industrial Commission on the Relations and Conditions of Capital and Labor Employed in Manufactures and General Business,* 19 vols. (Washington, D.C.: U.S. Government Printing Office, 1901), 15:168.

46. E. B. Cumming to James M. Smith, April 23, 1872, Reconstruction file, GDAH; *Atlanta Constitution,* January 8, 1878 (2, 4–7; 3, 1–5).

47. Bullock to the Editor of the Times, April 25, 1872, manuscript, Bullock Papers, Huntington Library; E. B. Cumming to James M. Smith, April 23, 1872, Reconstruction file, GDAH; King, *Southern States,* 2:355.

48. *Memorial of the Albion Academy,* p. 23; New York State Census, 1875, Orleans County, p. 67, in Office of the Clerk of Orleans County, Albion, N.Y.; *Orleans Republican,* December 13, 1871 (3, 3); *The Story of the Organization and First Fifty Years, 1844–1894, of Christ Church, Albion, N.Y.* (Albion, N.Y.: A. M. Eddy, 1894), p. 28; *Centennial Anniversary, Christ Episcopal Church, Albion, N.Y., 1844–1894* (N.p.: N.p., n.d.), p. 45, Swan Library, Albion, N.Y.; Bullock to Joseph E. Brown, November 21, 1872, Brown Papers, Atlanta Historical Society.

49. Joseph E. Brown to Simon Cameron, October 24, 1874, Columbus Delano to Brown, October 31, 1874, Thomas Scott to Brown, November 3, 1874, Brown Papers, Atlanta Historical Society.

50. Bullock to M. T. Walters, March 28, 1877, Bullock to Joseph E. Brown, March 31, 1872, March 29, April 20, May 25, 1877, M. T. Walters to Brown, March 31, 1877, Brown to M. T. Walters, April 4, 18, 1877, Brown to Bullock, April 5, 1872, April 14, May 2, 1877, ibid.

51. *New York Times,* May 24, 1876 (2, 2); *Atlanta Constitution,* January 8, 1878 (2, 4–7; 3, 1–5).

52. *Atlanta Constitution,* May 19 (1, 2), 21 (3, 2–4), 1876.

53. Ibid., May 19 (4, 2), 26 (2, 2), 30 (2, 2), 1876.

54. Ibid., June 14, 1877, Grady Papers, Scrapbook 4, p. 6, Emory University; ibid., June 13, 1877 (3, 4); *New York Times,* June 18, 1877 (3, 5); *Orleans American,* January 31, 1878 (2, 2), Bullock Papers, Huntington Library; Willard E. Wight, "Gartrell, Lucius Jeremiah," in *Dictionary of Georgia Biography,* ed. Coleman and Gurr, 1:338; *Atlanta Southern Advance,* August [?], 1888 (2, 1, 3, 3–6), in Joseph E. and Elizabeth G. Brown Collection, University of Georgia.

55. George Hillyer file, File II, Names, GDAH; Wright Bryan, "Hillyer, George," in *Dictionary of Georgia Biography,* ed. Coleman and Gurr, 1:457–58; *The Atlanta Centennial Year Book: 1837–1937* (Atlanta: Franklin Printing Co., 1937), p. 107; Clarke, *Illustrated History of Atlanta,* pp. 68, 78; Samuel A. Echols, *Georgia's General Assembly of 1878: Biographical Sketches of Senators, Representatives, the Governor and Heads of Departments* (Atlanta: J. P. Harrison, 1878), p. 5.

56. Echols, *Georgia's General Assembly of 1878,* p. 11; *Orleans American,* January 31, 1878 (2, 3), quoting *Atlanta Constitution,* January 23, 1878; Fulton County Superior Court, Minutes, 1877–79, microfilm, pp. 261–63, 273, GDAH.

57. For an in-depth look at the testimony recorded by the 1872 committee and an exposé of its falseness, see *Testimony Taken by the Committee Appointed to Investigate the Official Conduct of Rufus B. Bullock; Atlanta Constitution,* January 3 (4, 2–5), 4 (4, 2–5), 8 (1, 1–2; 2, 4–7; 3, 1–5), 9 (1, 1), 1878; Bullock, *Address to the People of Georgia,* p. 14; *Atlanta Republican,* January 11, 1878, quoted in *Orleans American,* January 24, 1878 (2, 2); undated newspaper clipping, Grady Papers, Emory University; Hill, *Senator Benjamin H. Hill,* p. 61.

58. *Atlanta Constitution,* January 23, 1878 (3, 1–7; 4, 2–5); *Augusta Chronicle,* January 18, 1878 (1, 2).

59. *Orleans American,* January 17, 1878 (2, 4), quoting the *Atlanta Daily Tribune; New York Tribune,* January 18 (4, 3–4), February 9 (3, 3–4), 1878; R. H. Brown to J. B. Campbell, July 16, 1872, and R. H. Brown to J. M. Smith, July 16, 1872, J. B. Campbell file, File II, Names, GDAH.

60. *Orleans American,* January 10, 1878 (2, 2).

61. *Atlanta Independent,* January 20, 1878, Joseph E. and Elizabeth G. Brown Collection, University of Georgia; *Atlanta Independent,* undated (1878), Bullock Papers, Huntington Library.

62. *New York Times,* March 10 (1, 2), November 18 (4, 3–4), 1878.

63. Thomas C. Cochran, *Challenges to American Values: Society, Business, and Religion* (New York: Oxford University Press, 1985), p. 109; Bertram Shrieke quoted in Gunnar Myrdal, *An American Dilemma: The Negro Problem and Modern Democracy,* 2 vols. (New York: Harper & Brothers, 1944), 2:1314–15.

64. William M. Kurtines and Jacob L. GeWirtz, *Morality, Moral Behavior, and Moral Development* (New York: Wiley, 1984), pp. 34, 110.

65. James L. Roark, *Masters Without Slaves: Southern Planters in the Civil War and Reconstruction* (New York: Norton, 1977), pp. 186–93; Candler, comp., *Confederate Records of the State of Georgia,* 6:49.

66. Bullock to Revs. Mr. Johnson and Mr. Beale, July 10, 1869, Georgia Executive Department, Executive Secretary's Letter Books, pp. 295–96, GDAH.

67. Ibid.

68. Perman, *Road to Redemption,* pp. 39–40; Rufus Bullock file, Vertical Files, University of Georgia; Francis B. Simkins, "New Viewpoints of Southern Reconstruction," *Journal of Negro History* 5 (February 1939): 56–58. For a discussion of the belief in equal opportunity, which he calls the "competitive ideal," see George M. Fredrickson, *The Black Image in the White Mind: The Debate on Afro-American Character and Destiny, 1817–1914* (New York: Harper & Row, 1971), esp. pp. 165–86.

69. Bartley, *Creation of Modern Georgia,* p. 207. Edward King aptly summarized Bullock's struggles: "It is evident that he required the shrewdness of an archangel to march without stumbling. It was for the interest of the Democratic party in the State to make reconstruction unsuccessful, and toward that end they unceasingly toiled" (*Southern States,* 2:352).

CHAPTER 8. Outsider as Insider

1. H. I. Kimball to R. A. Alston, *Atlanta Herald,* March 7, 1874, in Brown Papers, Atlanta Historical Society; Reagan, *Kimball,* pp. 71–74; *Atlanta Constitution,* September 5, 1878, in Ackerman Scrapbook, Atlanta Historical Society. Atlanta's first cotton factory was promoted in 1873 with E. E. Rawson as presi-

dent, but the financial panic of that year delayed plans and opened the door for a more experienced promoter—Kimball. See *Atlanta Journal*, February 26, 1873, in Scrapbook of John Calvin Peck, Peck Family Collection, GDAH.

2. H. I. Kimball to R. A. Alston, *Atlanta Herald*, March 7, 1874, in Brown Papers, Atlanta Historical Society; Reagan, *Kimball*, pp. 71–74; H. I. Kimball, *An Address by H. I. Kimball Before the Mechanics' Institute of Atlanta, December 29, 1874, on the Manufacture of Cotton in Atlanta* (Atlanta: Atlanta Herald Job Office, 1875), p. 3; Reagan, "Promoting the New South," pp. 10–12; *Atlanta Daily Herald*, July 7, 1875 (3, 2); *Handbook of the City of Atlanta: A Comprehensive Review of the City's Commercial, Industrial, and Residential Conditions* (Atlanta: Southern Industrial Publishing Co., 1896), pp. 40, 44.

3. Broadus Mitchell, *The Rise of the Cotton Mills in the South* (Baltimore: Johns Hopkins University Press, 1921), pp. 60, 233; G. W. Adair to the Stockholders of the Atlanta Cotton Factory Co., January 12, 1877, Atlanta Cotton Factory file, Atlanta Historical Society; Kimball, *Address*, p. 9; *Atlanta Daily Herald*, July 7, 1875 (3, 2); *Atlanta Constitution*, July 5 (4, 1), 8 (2, 3), 1879; Reed, ed., *History of Atlanta*, p. 462; *Atlanta Constitution*, September 5, 1878, in Ackerman Scrapbook, Atlanta Historical Society. "Standard brown goods" was a term used for unbleached, coarse cloth sold mainly to export markets in China and Africa and thus not in competition with the finer grade of cloth made by New England mills for home and European consumption. See Testimony of Rufus B. Bullock, *Report of the Industrial Commission*, 7:523–24.

4. *U.S. City Directories, Atlanta, 1878,* microfilm, pp. 53, 137, 401; ibid., *1879,* p. 135. H. I. Kimball no longer owned the hotel that bore his name; upon his bankruptcy in 1871, he sold it to Scoville, Seldon, and Company. See ibid., *1880,* p. 258.

5. Ibid., *1881,* pp. 36, 183; ibid., *1884,* pp. 16, 137. In 1892 the city renumbered houses along Peachtree, and Bullock's address changed from 173 to 233. See ibid., *1892,* pp. 82, 449; Richard J. Hopkins, "Occupational and Geographic Mobility in Atlanta, 1870–1896," *Journal of Southern History* 34 (May 1968): 200; James M. Russell, "Politics, Municipal Services, and the Working Class in Atlanta, 1865–1890," *Georgia Historical Quarterly* 66 (Winter 1982): 469–71; Fulton County Tax Digest, 1888, p. 31, Tax Digests, GDAH; *Atlanta Journal*, February 5, 1902 (3, 2).

6. Inventory of Bullock household, Consent Decree, Joseph Francis Burke Papers, Emory University, Atlanta, Ga.

7. *Atlanta Constitution*, October 11, 1888, April 2, 23, 1901, in Bullock file, Office of the Orleans County Historian, Albion, N.Y.

8. *Orleans Republican*, March 15, 1882, and *Orleans American*, undated, in Bullock file, Office of the Orleans County Historian, Albion, N.Y.; *Rochester Daily Union*, April 13, 1883 (3, 7). Marie is conspicuous by her absence from

Dau's Society Blue Book and Ladies Address Book (New York: Dau Publishing Co., 1901), Atlanta's Women Club Collection, Atlanta Historical Society, and Mrs. Henry L. Wilson, *The Atlanta Exposition Cookbook, 1895* (Athens: University of Georgia Press, 1984). She seems to have confined her social activities to receptions where Rufus was prominent such as those for Presidents Harrison and McKinley. See *Atlanta Constitution*, April 16, 1891 (1, 4), December 15, 1898 (2, 4–6); *U.S. City Directories, Atlanta, 1884,* p. 137; ibid., *1886,* p. 138; ibid., *1887,* p. 132; ibid., *1894,* p. 491; ibid., *1895,* pp. 483, 1089, 1129; ibid., *1896,* p. 1117; ibid., *1897,* p. 1479; ibid., *1898,* p. 489; ibid., *1899,* p. 495; ibid., *1901,* p. 543; *Atlanta City Directory, 1903* (Atlanta: Foote and Davies, 1903), pp. 501, 561; Augusta King Wylie, "Golf as First Played in Atlanta," *Atlanta Historical Bulletin* 32 (December 1947): 9–10; G. B. Cortelyou to Bullock, February 21, March 23, April 11, May 31, 1901, William McKinley Papers, microfilm, University of Georgia, Athens.

9. *Atlanta Constitution,* October 11, 1888, and undated [1888], in Bullock file, Office of the Orleans County Historian, Albion, N.Y.

10. *Atlanta Constitution,* November 23, 1884 (9, 1); *St. Philip's Parish, Atlanta, Georgia: Historical Notes, 1847–1897* (Atlanta: V. P. Sisson, 1897), pp. 3, 13, 18, 32, 43; Alex Hitz, *A History of the Cathedral of St. Philip* (Atlanta: Conger Printing Co., 1947), pp. 34, 38, 40, 55, 56, 58, 59; Parish Register, 1870–84, St. Philip's Episcopal Church of Atlanta, microfilm, pp. 267–88 passim, GDAH; Bullock to H. B. Thurber, October 14, 1895, Grover Cleveland Papers, microfilm, University of Georgia, Athens.

11. *Providence* (R.I.) *Journal,* July 1904, in Bullock file, Office of the Orleans County Historian, Albion, N.Y.; Edward Clarke to Mother, September 16, 1883, Clarke Family Papers, University of Rochester; "Bullock, Marie E. and Rufus B.," Tax Books and Treasurer's Report, 1887–1906, Charlestown Town Hall, Charlestown, R.I.; Land Evidence, Town Hall, Charlestown, R.I., vol. 11, p. 449, vol. 12, pp. 52, 313–14, vol. 13, pp. 239–40, 243–45, 264, 285, 386–87, vol. 14, pp. 60–63, 83, 87–92, 368, 430, 458–66, vol. 15, p. 110.

12. Resolutions of Stockholders of Atlanta Cotton Factory, July 21, 1880, Peck Collection, GDAH; *Atlanta Constitution,* November 20, 1879 (2, 1), January 2 (2, 1), March 31 (4, 2), July 20 (3, 1), 1880.

13. *Atlanta Constitution,* January 2, 1880 (2, 1); Reagan, *Kimball,* pp. 74, 89–92; Thornberry, "Development of Black Atlanta," p. 194; Testimony of Bullock, *Report of the Industrial Commission,* 7:522.

14. Russell, "Atlanta," p. 243; U.S. Department of Commerce, Bureau of the Census, *Tenth Census of the United States, 1880: Statistics of Manufactures* (Washington, D.C.: U.S. Government Printing Office, 1880), p. 208; John W. Patillo, "English, James Warren," in *Dictionary of Georgia Biography,* ed. Coleman and Gurr, 1:293; Reagan, *Kimball,* pp. 108, 112. Kimball returned to Atlanta

in 1883 to help rebuild the hotel bearing his name, in 1885 to promote a national commercial convention, and at various times for short visits with friends. See ibid., pp. 113, 119, 127.

15. Mitchell, *Rise of the Cotton Mills*, pp. 71–72, 122; H. I. Kimball, *International Cotton Exposition: Atlanta, Georgia, 1881, Report of the Director-General, H. I. Kimball* (New York: D. Appleton, 1882), pp. 9, 13, 27, 39, 93–94, 165–68; Reed, ed., *History of Atlanta*, pp. 472–76; Matthew B. Hammond, *The Cotton Industry* (New York: Macmillan, 1897), p. 139; Autobiography of John Calvin Peck, pp. 91–93, Peck Collection, GDAH.

16. Reed, ed., *History of Atlanta*, pp. 475–76.

17. *Atlanta Constitution*, October 5, 1881 (18, 4–5; 19, 6); Hoke Smith to Bullock, May 6, 1880, March 13, 1883, Hoke Smith Papers, University of Georgia, Athens; *U.S. City Directories, Atlanta, 1882*, pp. 38, 113, 198.

18. Edward to Mother, November 16, 1884, June 14, November 22, December 20, 1885, Clarke Family Papers, University of Rochester.

19. Bullock to Freeman Clarke, July 31, 1855, Henrietta Clarke to Edward S. Clarke, February 24, 1883, ibid.

20. Edward Clarke to Mother, September 2, 1883, ibid.

21. Edward Clarke to Mother, September 2, 8, 11, 1883, ibid.; Testimony of Bullock, Testimony of H. E. Fisher, and Testimony of Oscar Elsas, *Report of the Industrial Commission*, 7:522–23, 528–30, 570, 574.

22. Testimony of Bullock, *Report of the Industrial Commission*, 7:521–27, 529.

23. Testimony of Bullock and Testimony of Fisher, ibid., pp. 522–26, 530; newspaper clipping (1895) entitled "Proof of the Pudding," Peck Collection, GDAH; newspaper clipping, November 15, 1881, in Bullock Papers, Huntington Library. The *Report of the Industrial Commission* contains a wealth of valuable information about conditions in nineteenth-century mills and turn-of-the-century education. Although the commissioners did not interview factory workers, they did interview mill owners, governors, labor leaders, and editors of labor journals, as well as black educators W. E. B. Du Bois, Richard R. Wright, and W. J. Gaines. For Georgia testimony, see ibid., 7:511–74, and 15:139–210.

24. *Mail and Express*, March 17, 1888, in Bullock Papers, Huntington Library; Mitchell, *Rise of the Cotton Mills*, p. 56; *Memoirs of Georgia*, 2:731. Bullock's efforts planted seeds for industrial development during Reconstruction—a time described by one business historian as "a germinal period for manufactures" (Victor S. Clark, *The South in the Building of the Nation*, 12 vols. [Richmond, Va.: Southern Publication Society, 1909], 6:254–66).

25. *Rome Tri-Weekly Courier*, September 7, 1869, in Grady Papers, Scrapbook 1, Emory University.

26. Caldwell, *Reminiscences*, p. 16; Avery, *History of Georgia*, p. 462; *Planter's Journal*, April 1884, pp. 116–18; *Southron*, undated, in Bullock Papers, Huntington Library.

NOTES TO PAGES 159–161

27. *Atlanta Centennial Year Book,* pp. 105, 136; Bartley, *Creation of Modern Georgia,* pp. 84–85; Grady quoted in Edwin D. Shurter, ed., *The Complete Orations and Speeches of Henry W. Grady* (New York: Hinds, Noble & Eldredge, 1910), p. 33.

28. Alexander McClure, *Colonel Alexander McClure's Recollections of Half a Century* (Salem, Mass.: By the author, 1902), pp. 401–2. For a full exposition of McClure's views on the New South, see his *The South: Its Industrial, Financial, and Political Condition* (Philadelphia: J. B. Lippincott, 1886), esp. pp. 58–71. Grady credited B. H. Hill with influencing him the most. Hill was the leader of the Democratic resistance to Bullock before being converted to the program of industrial growth and leasing the state railroad. In an 1871 address at the University of Georgia, Hill called for a New South and waxed poetic: "We have given up the dusky Helen. Pity we kept the Harlot for so long." Grady would use Hill's reference to slavery to proclaim an end to the Old South. Hill's program, now Grady's program, sans racial equality, was taken from Bullock and the Radicals. See Shore, *Southern Capitalists,* pp. 12, 149–70, Hill quote on p. 150. Bullock first used the expression "New South" before the National Tariff Convention in Chicago in 1881 (newspaper clipping, November 15, 1881, Bullock Papers, Huntington Library).

29. Tunis G. Campbell to Benjamin Conley, February 22, July 25, 1872, Jesse Wimberley to Conley, July 6, 1874, February 25, 1875, Conley Papers, University of Georgia.

30. Thomas Robinson to Benjamin Conley, May 27, June 11, 1873, ibid.

31. Thomas B. Alexander, "Persistent Whiggery in the Confederate South, 1860–1877," *Journal of Southern History* 27 (August 1961): 320–22; Cecil T. Greer, "Georgia in the Presidential Campaign and Election of 1872" (M.A. thesis, University of Georgia, 1953), pp. i, 9; Judson C. Ward, Jr., "The Republican Party in Bourbon Georgia, 1872–1890," *Journal of Southern History* 9 (May 1943): 201–6; John E. Talmadge, "The Death Blow to Independentism in Georgia," *Georgia Historical Quarterly* 39 (March 1955): 38; Hanes Walton, *Black Republicans: The Politics of the Black and Tans* (Metuchen, N.J.: Scarecrow Press, 1975), pp. 45–55; *Atlanta Constitution,* August 5, 1882 (4, 3); Shadgett, *Republican Party in Georgia,* pp. 91–158.

32. *Atlanta Constitution,* September 27, 1892 (2, 2; 8, 2). For the best explanations on the complexities of Georgia Populism, see Bartley, *Creation of Modern Georgia,* pp. 92–112; C. Vann Woodward, *Origins of the New South, 1877–1913* (Baton Rouge: Louisiana State University Press, 1951), pp. 175–290; Woodward, *Tom Watson: Agrarian Rebel* (1938; rpt. New York: Oxford University Press, 1978); Hahn, *Roots of Southern Populism;* Gerald H. Gaither, *Blacks and the Populist Revolt: Ballots and Bigotry in the "New South"* (University, Ala.: University of Alabama Press, 1977). Northen later changed his stance on lynching.

33. *Atlanta Constitution,* September 27, 1892 (8, 2), May 1 (4, 5), 2 (5, 1–2),

4 (4, 4), 1896; *New York Times,* March 30, 1893 (4, 5); Shadgett, *Republican Party in Georgia,* p. 159; Shyam K. Bhurtel, "Alfred Eliab Buck: Carpetbagger in Alabama and Georgia" (Ph.D. dissertation, Auburn University, 1981), pp. 77, 82–101, 160.

34. *Columbus Enquirer-Sun,* March 19, 1888, *Rochester Democrat and Chronicle,* March 14, 1888, *Utica Morning Herald,* March 12, 1888, *Augusta Chronicle,* March 21, 1888, and *New York Tribune,* December 11, 1888, in Bullock Papers, Huntington Library.

35. Curtis W. Garrison, "Slater Fund Beginnings: Letters from General Agent Atticus G. Haygood to Rutherford B. Hayes," *Journal of Negro History* 5 (May 1939): 243.

36. "Annual Report of the Government Directors of the Union Pacific Railroad, 1889," *Senate Executive Documents,* No. 48, 51st Cong., 1st sess., pp. 1–3; "Report of Union Pacific, 1890," ibid., No. 233, 51st Cong., 2d sess. pp. 1–6; "Report of Union Pacific, 1891," ibid., No. 6, 52d Cong., 1st sess., pp. 1–5; "Report of Union Pacific, 1892," ibid., No. 4, 52d Cong., 2d sess., pp. 1–4; Bullock to E. W. Halford, June 4, 5, 1889, March 15, 20, April 1, 5, 9, 10, 11, 12, 19, 20, 23, 24, May 23, 29, June 18, July 3, 5, 1890, November 11, 1892, and Bullock to Benjamin Harrison, January 15, 1889, March 1, 1890, Benjamin Harrison Papers, microfilm, University of Georgia, Athens; *Contemporary American Biography,* 2:70.

37. *U.S. City Directories, Atlanta, 1880–1881,* pp. 53, 131; Jack Adair Papers, Atlanta Historical Society; *Atlanta Constitution,* August 6, 1884 (3, 3–6).

38. *Atlanta Constitution,* December 12 (4, 4), 23 (18, 5), 1888; Norman Shavin and Bruce Galphin, *Atlanta: Triumph of a People* (Atlanta: Capricorn, 1982), p. 138; Russell, "Atlanta," p. 157; Atlanta Manufacturers' Association Papers, Atlanta Historical Society; Reed, *History of Atlanta,* p. 471; *Atlanta Journal,* May 1, 1889 (2, 1).

39. Minutes, May 14, 1883–June 12, 1900, pp. 11–15, 23, 43, 80–83, 105, 144, 157, 273, 287–90, 322, 337, 338, 343, 353, 376, 379, 382, 398, 411, 416, 425, 429, 447, 468, 472–73, 491, 514, 523, 527, 529, 553, 558, 560, Atlanta Chamber of Commerce; *Atlanta Constitution,* February 2 (4, 5), 3 (20, 2–3), 1889, April 16, 1890 (7, 1); *Augusta Chronicle,* November 15, 1888 (1, 1; 4, 1); *Dedicatory Exercises at the Opening of the New Building of the Cincinnati Chamber of Commerce at Merchant's Exchange, January 29 and 30, 1889* (Cincinnati: Commercial Gazette, 1889), pp. 11, 15, 120–24, 223; "Report of the Interstate Commerce Commission, *Senate Executive Documents,* No. 48, 51st Cong., 1st sess., p. 54.

40. Kimball House Collection, Atlanta Historical Society; Shingleton, *Richard Peters,* pp. 191–92; Shavin and Galphin, *Atlanta,* pp. 142–43; Franklin Garrett, *Atlanta and Environs: A Chronicle of Its People and Events,* 3 vols. (New York: Lewis Historical Publishing Co., 1954), 1:50; *Atlanta in 1890: The Gate City* (Neenah, Wisc.: Pratt, 1890), pp. xxiv, 52; *Atlanta Constitution,* October 3, 1886

(3, 5); Robert C. McMath, Ronald H. Bayor, James E. Brittain, Lawrence Foster, August W. Griebelhaus, and Germaine M. Reed, *Engineering the New South: Georgia Tech, 1885–1985* (Athens: University of Georgia Press, 1985), p. 15.

41. Minutes, p. 464, Atlanta Chamber of Commerce; Shingleton, *Richard Peters*, p. 193; *Officers, Members, Constitution and Rules of the Capital City Club of Atlanta, Georgia* (Atlanta: C. P. Byrd Printer, 1896), pp. 3–18, 42; Capital City Club file, Atlanta Historical Society; *Officers, Members, Constitution and Rules of the Capital City Club, 1912* (Atlanta: Foote & Davies, 1912), pp. 1–6.

42. *Atlanta Constitution*, June 8, 1881 (1, 1), September 14, 1887 (3, 2); *U.S. City Directories, Atlanta, 1888*, p. 19; *By-laws and Rules of the Piedmont Driving Club of Atlanta, Georgia* (Atlanta: Franklin Printing, 1899), p. 26; Scrapbook, Peck Collection, GDAH; Garrett, *Atlanta and Environs*, pp. 21, 50.

43. *Atlanta Constitution*, April 15 (1, 1), 16 (1, 1–6), 1891; *Atlanta Journal*, December 14 (1, 4; 1, 7), 15 (5, 2), 1898; Garrett, *Atlanta and Environs*, p. 240; "Atlanta Peace Jubilee, 1898," Atlanta Chronology, 1845–99, Atlanta Historical Society; Elizabeth Marshall, "Atlanta Peace Jubilee," *Georgia Historical Quarterly* 50 (September 1966): 276–82.

44. Reed, *History of Atlanta*, p. 16; *Dixie* magazine clipping, undated, Scrapbook, Peck Collection, GDAH; Hill, *Senator Benjamin H. Hill*, p. 62; Lucian L. Knight, *Reminiscences of Famous Georgians*, 2 vols. (Atlanta: Franklin-Turner, 1908), 2:298.

45. Fredrickson, *Black Image in the White Mind*, pp. 198–227, Grady quote on p. 203; *Atlanta Constitution*, December 2, 1888 (5, 2); *Contemporary American Biography*, 2:71.

46. James C. Cobb, *The Selling of the South: The Southern Crusade for Industrial Development, 1936–1980* (Baton Rouge: Louisiana State University Press, 1982), pp. 2, 96; Lawrence H. Larsen, *The Rise of the Urban South* (Lexington: University Press of Kentucky, 1985), pp. x, 28, 92–93; C. Vann Woodward, *The Strange Career of Jim Crow* (New York: Oxford University Press, 1955), p. 49.

47. *Atlanta Constitution*, December 1, 1888 (4, 2).

48. *Atlanta Constitution*, December 2, 1888, in Bullock Papers, Huntington Library.

49. *Atlanta Constitution*, December 5 (4, 5–6), 9 (14, 6), 10 (10, 4), 1888.

50. George Washington Cable, *The Negro Question: A Selection of Writings on Civil Rights in the South* (1890; rpt. New York: Doubleday, 1958), pp. 63, 76, 83, 148; *New York Times*, December 23, 1886 (2, 2); Paul M. Gaston, *The New South Creed: A Study in Southern Mythmaking* (New York: Vintage Books, 1973), esp. pp. 17, 131, 153, 194, 208, Cable quote on p. 94. Gaston divides New Southers into the Grady wing and a more "liberal minority wing" that emphasized character and training over race. Because both groups cultivated the myth of black rule during Reconstruction and venerated the Lost Cause, Bullock does not fit into either.

Gaston's contention that Booker T. Washington was a New South spokesman is valid, but Washington would not ascribe to the Lost Cause. Therefore, there is a third wing, which has been overlooked by historians and may best be described as the free labor wing, which included Bullock, Washington, Cable, and Kimball. See ibid., pp. 144, 209.

51. Rufus B. Bullock, *Address of Rufus B. Bullock, Ex-Governor of Georgia, Delivered August 22, 1891, Before the Alumni Association of the Albion Academy at Albion, Orleans County, N.Y.* (Albion, N.Y.: Orleans American Steam Print, 1891), p. 6.

52. Rabinowitz, *Race Relations in the Urban South*, pp. 127, 331–32.

53. Nixon, *Grady*, pp. 317–19; Henry W. Grady, *The Race Problem* (Chicago: George L. Shuman, 1900), p. 1.

54. *Atlanta Constitution*, December 13 (4, 3–6), 15 (15, 1), 1889.

55. *New York Times*, January 8 (1, 3; 4, 1), 11 (4, 1–2), 1889; clipping from the *Criterion*, July 6, 1888, in Bullock Papers, Huntington Library; *Atlanta Constitution*, February 6 (2, 1), 21 (2, 1–2), 1889.

56. William E. Chandler, "Our Southern Masters," *Forum*, July 1888, p. 509.

57. *Atlanta Constitution*, undated, three clippings in Bullock Papers, Huntington Library.

58. Ibid.

59. Gaither, *Blacks and the Populist Revolt*, pp. 29–31.

60. *Atlanta Constitution*, March 24, 1902, and *Rochester Democrat and Chronicle*, October 31, November 5, 7, 8, 1902, and undated clipping, "A Yell of Thirty Years Ago," in Bullock Papers, Huntington Library.

61. *Rochester Democrat and Chronicle*, October 31, 1902, Bullock Papers, Huntington Library.

62. *Atlanta Constitution*, March 24, 1902, and undated newspaper clipping, "A Talk with Ex-Governor Bullock of Georgia," Bullock Papers, Huntington Library.

63. *Atlanta Constitution*, March 24, 1902, and undated newspaper clipping, "A Talk with Ex-Governor Bullock of Georgia," Bullock Papers, Huntington Library; *New York Times*, December 1, 1899 (6, 2–3); *Augusta Chronicle*, June 30, 1904 (6, 4–5); Eugene J. Watts, "Black Political Progress in Atlanta, 1868–1895," *Journal of Negro History* 59 (July 1974): 284–85; *Atlanta Journal*, October 17, 1899 (?), in Joseph E. and Elizabeth G. Brown Collection, University of Georgia.

64. Reed, ed., *History of Atlanta*, p. 476; Bullock to General Harrison, January 27, 1889, Harrison Papers.

65. *Atlanta Constitution*, April 29 (4, 1–2; 5, 1–6), 1895.

66. Ibid., April 30 (4, 7), May 3 (10, 2), 1895.

67. Walter G. Cooper, *The Cotton States and International Exposition and South, Illustrated Including the Official History of the Exposition* (Atlanta: Illus-

trator Co., 1896), pp. 5, 14–17, 85, 118; Minutes, p. 468, Atlanta Chamber of Commerce; *The Official Catalogue of the Cotton States and International Exposition, Atlanta, Georgia, September 18 to December 31, 1895* (Atlanta: Claflin & Mellichamp, 1895), pp. 10–14; *Charter and By-Laws of the Cotton States and International Exposition Company, Atlanta, Ga.* (Atlanta: Franklin Printing, 1894), pp. 5–9.

68. Cooper, *Cotton States and International Exposition*, pp. 18, 23–25, 59, 63. For U.S. government participation in the exposition, see Records Relating to the Cotton States and International Exposition at Atlanta, 1895, RG 43, NA, and The Cotton States and International Exposition, RG 70, Series II, Smithsonian Institute Archives, Washington, D.C.

69. Washington, *Up from Slavery*, pp. 206–9; I. Garland Penn to Booker T. Washington, August 19, 1895, in Louis R. Harlan, John W. Blassingame, et al., eds., *The Booker T. Washington Papers*, 14 vols. (Urbana: University of Illinois Press, 1972–84), 3:568.

70. Cooper, *Cotton States and International Exposition*, pp. 93–94; Russell Duncan, "Cotton States and International Exposition, Atlanta, 1895," in *Historical Dictionary of World's Fairs and Expositions*, ed. John E. Findling (Westport, Conn.: Greenwood Press, 1991), pp. 139–41.

71. Cooper, *Cotton States and International Exposition*, pp. 98–99; Bullock quoted in Louis R. Harlan, *Booker T. Washington: The Making of a Black Leader, 1856–1901* (New York: Oxford University Press, 1972), pp. viii, ix, 216–17.

72. Harlan, Blassingame, et al., eds., *Washington Papers*, 1:79, 4:54; Washington, *Up from Slavery*, pp. 86, 153–67, 225; W. E. B. Du Bois lauded Washington's speech as "a word fitly spoken"; only later would he denounce the orator's position. See W. E. B. Du Bois, *Writings* (New York: Viking Press, 1986), p. 1286.

73. *Bulletin of Atlanta University*, October 1891, January 1892, June 1893, October 1893; *Atlanta Constitution*, May 4, 1896 (4, 4); Bullock, "Reconstruction in Georgia," p. 674.

74. George Washington Cable to Booker T. Washington, March 21, 1890, in Harlan, Blassingame, et al., eds., *Washington Papers*, 3:40–41. Perhaps Bullock decided not to attend the conference because of local pressure. For an editorial against the conference, see *Atlanta Constitution*, June 11, 1890 (4, 2–3); newspaper clipping, in Minutes, p. 445, Atlanta Chamber of Commerce.

75. Davis and Turner quoted in Bartley, *Creation of Modern Georgia*, p. 141; E. R. Carter, *The Black Side: A Partial History of Business, Religions, and Educational Side of the Negro in Atlanta* (Atlanta: N.p., 1894), p. 290; *New York Times*, October 22, 1895 (3, 4).

76. *Atlanta Journal*, November 15, 1898 (1, 7). For a discussion of rape as a false issue for lynchings, see Laurence E. Baughman, *Southern Rape Complex:*

Hundred Year Psychosis (Atlanta: Pendulum Books, 1966), and Michael J. Cassity, *Chains of Fear: American Race Relations Since Reconstruction* (Westport, Conn.: Greenwood Press, 1984), pp. 49–57; Turner quote in Wingo, "Race Relations in Georgia," p. 175.

77. *Atlanta Constitution*, October 18, 1898 (4, 2).

78. Ibid., October 19, 1898 (4, 2–4).

EPILOGUE

1. *U.S. City Directories, Atlanta, 1895*, p. 593; *Handbook of the City of Atlanta*, p. 68; *Historical Sketches of Atlanta, 1895* (Atlanta: N.p., 1895), frontispiece.

2. *Atlanta City Directory, 1901: Revised Edition* (Atlanta: J. Maloney Publishers, 1901), pp. 614, 739; "Abstract of Title," February 2, 1898, "Bond to Reconvey Title," February 2, 1898, and "City Court of Atlanta," August 13, 1901, December 18, 1901, and July 21, 1902, Burke Papers, Emory University; *Atlanta Constitution*, February 5, 1902 (3, 2, 12, 3); Grantor Index, 1889–1901, microfilm, vol. 127, p. 768, and Grantor Index, 1901–1910, vol. 159, p. 608, Fulton County, Superior Court, Deeds and Mortgages, GDAH. J. W. English, president of the American Trust and Banking Company, purchased Bullock's house at the sale. English held the house for two years and offered it to Bullock at cost, but Bullock could not or would not buy it back. After acquiring the property in 1903, J. F. Burke sold it in 1909 for $28,000. See Bullock to J. W. English, December 2, 1902, Deed conveyance, January 14, 1909, Burke Papers. For a full listing of the contents of Bullock's house, see "Consent Decree," ibid.

3. *Atlanta Constitution*, April 23, 1901, in Scrapbook, Office of the Orleans County Historian, Albion, N.Y.; *U.S. City Directories, Atlanta, 1897*, p. 518.

4. *Atlanta City Directory, 1903*, p. 501; ibid., *1910*, p. 561; Bullock to J. W. English, December 2, 1902, Marie E. Bullock to Mrs. J. F. Burke, June 16, 23, 1903, Burke Papers; Volkert V. Bullock, *Some Fairy Fancies Here You See as They Crossed the Mind of V. V. B.* (Atlanta: Franklin Publishing, 1904), no page numbers.

5. Bullock to Editor of the *Churchman*, January 20, 1903, Theodore Roosevelt to Bullock, February 2, 1903, Theodore Roosevelt Papers, microfilm, University of Georgia, Athens; *Atlanta Constitution*, March 24, 1904 (7, 3–4).

6. Newspaper clipping, April [?], 1904, in Bullock Papers, Huntington Library.

7. Ibid., Register of Interments, Mount Albion Cemetery, Albion, N.Y.; New York State Census, 1905, p. 14, in Office of the Clerk of Orleans County, Albion, N.Y.

8. Turner quoted from Edwin S. Redkey, ed., *Respect Black: The Writings and Speeches of Henry McNeil Turner* (New York: Arno Press, 1971), pp. 196–98.

Turner denied that he had so called the flag, but his letter to Washington seems to uphold the historical conclusion that he did.

9. Marion L. Scott, "The Atlanta Race Riot of 1906 and Press Coverage of Race-Related Crimes" (M.A. thesis, University of Georgia, 1979), pp. 1–8; Ray Stannard Baker, *Following the Color Line: An Account of Negro Citizenship in the American Democracy* (1908; rpt. Williamstown, Mass.: Corner House Publishers, 1973), pp. 3–4, Smith quote on p. 267; Dewey Grantham, *Hoke Smith and the Politics of the New South* (Baton Rouge: Louisiana State University Press, 1958), esp. pp. 25, 54, 147–48. In 1915, filmmaker D. W. Griffith turned Dixon's novel into an epic motion picture, *Birth of a Nation,* and thereby aided the immediate revival of the Ku Klux Klan.

10. *Rochester Democrat and Chronicle,* April 28, 1907 (2, 3); *Atlanta Constitution,* April 28, 1907 (1, 4–5); Minutes of the Executive Department of the State of Georgia, 1906–7, microfilm, p. 117, GDAH.

Bibliography

Primary Sources

NEWSPAPERS

Atlanta Constitution	*New York Times*
Atlanta Daily Herald	*Orleans American* (Albion, N.Y.)
Atlanta Daily New Era	*Orleans Democrat* (Albion, N.Y.)
Atlanta Daily Sun	*Orleans Republican* (Albion, N.Y.)
Augusta Constitutionalist	*Rochester Daily Union*
Augusta Chronicle	*Rochester Democrat and Chronicle*
Augusta Loyal Georgian	*Savannah Morning News*
Augusta Republican	*Washington Chronicle*
Milledgeville Southern Recorder	

MANUSCRIPT COLLECTIONS

Albion, New York

  Mount Albion Cemetery

    Rufus Bullock file.

    Register of Interments.

  Office of the Clerk of Orleans County

    Grantee and Grantor indexes.

    New York State Census: 1850, 1855, 1865, 1875, 1892, 1905. Manuscript.

    Records of Deeds.

    U.S. Census, Orleans County, N.Y.: 1850, 1870. Microfilm.

  Office of the Orleans County Historian

    Famous People file.

    Rufus Brown Bullock file.

    Scrapbooks.

Orleans County Courthouse
  Office of the Surrogate
    Index to Wills and Administration Prior to 1897.
    Index to Wills and Administration, 1897–1926.
    Will Books 9 and 12.
Swan Library
  Rufus B. Bullock Collection.
  Scrapbooks, 1865–1915. 8 vols.
  Subject file.
Athens, Georgia
  University of Georgia
    Nellie Peters Black Collection.
    Foster Blodgett Papers.
    Broadside Collection, 1868–1900.
    Joseph Emerson Brown Papers.
    Joseph E. and Elizabeth G. Brown Collection.
    Brown Family Papers.
    Rufus B. Bullock letter.
    Grover Cleveland Papers. Microfilm.
    Benjamin Conley Papers.
    E. Merton Coulter. Historical Collection.
    Telamon Cuyler Collection.
    DeRenne Collection.
    Henry Patillo Farrow Papers.
    Rebecca Latimer Felton Collection.
    James A. Garfield Papers. Microfilm.
    Ulysses S. Grant Papers. Microfilm.
    Felix Hargrett Collection.
    Benjamin Harrison Papers. Microfilm.
    Joshua Hill letter.
    Charles Colcock Jones, Jr., Collection.
    Ku Klux Klan Collection.
    William McKinley Papers. Microfilm.

Thomas Manson Norwood Papers.

Proceedings of the Republican National Convention, 1868, 1872, 1876.

Keith Read Collection.

John A. Rockwell Letters.

Theodore Roosevelt Papers. Microfilm.

Hoke Smith Papers.

Nelson Tift letter.

Robert Toombs Collection.

Vertical Files.

Atlanta, Georgia

Atlanta Chamber of Commerce

Minutes, 1883–1900.

Atlanta Historical Society

A. K. Ackerman Scrapbook.

Jack Adair Papers.

Atlanta Chronology, 1845–99.

Atlanta City Directories, 1867–1906.

Atlanta Cotton Factory file.

Atlanta Cotton Factory, Visual Arts Collection.

Atlanta Manufacturers' Association Papers.

Atlanta Women's Club Collection.

Abbie M. Brooks Diaries, 1865 and 1870.

Joseph Emerson Brown Papers.

Rufus Brown Bullock file.

Capital City Club file.

Benjamin Conley Letters and Papers.

Hannibal I. Kimball file.

Kimball House Collection.

Mayor of Atlanta file.

Mary Connally Spalding Scrapbooks.

Emory University

Joseph Francis Burke Papers.

Henry W. Grady Papers and Scrapbooks.

Georgia Miscellany.

Alexander H. Stephens Collection.

Georgia Department of Archives and History

Samuel Bard/J. W. Burke. Printer's Account Book, 1870.

Civil War Records: Georgia.

Confederate Pensions and Records Department. Pensions. Applications and Index. Microfilm.

County Records. Microfilm.

Fulton County.

Index to Wills, 1848–1909.

St. Philip's Episcopal Church. Parish Register, 1870–84.

Superior Court.

Deeds and Mortgages.

Minutes, 1877–79.

File II. Names.

Amos T. Akerman.

Alton Angier.

R. H. Atkinson.

Marion Bellups.

Foster Blodgett.

John E. Bryant.

Rufus B. Bullock. Oversize.

J. B. Campbell.

Benjamin Conley.

D. G. Cotting.

J. W. English.

B. W. Frobel.

John Harris.

William A. Hemphill.

George Hillyer.

Henry K. McCay.

Josiah R. Parrott.

Hiram Warner.

Georgia Executive Department.

    Bound and Unbound Proclamations, 1854–69.

    Executive Secretary's Letter Books, August 21, 1868–January 13, 1872.
    26 vols.

    Governor's Letter Books. Conley, Smith.

    Incoming Correspondence. Rufus Brown Bullock, 1868–71.

    Military Rosters, Index, 1869.

    Minutes, 1866–74 and 1865–80. Microfilm.

    Registration Oath Books. Richmond County. District 18.

John B. Gordon Papers.

Negroes file.

William J. Northen Scrapbooks.

Autobiography and Scrapbooks of John Calvin Peck, Peck Family Collection.

Reconstruction file.

Surveyor's General Office.

    Atlanta City Maps, 1878, 1893.

    Bird's Eye View of Atlanta, 1871, 1878.

Tax Digests for Richmond, Dekalb, and Fulton counties.

Vanishing Georgia Photographic Collection. Fulton and Richmond counties.

Western and Atlantic Railroad. Auditor. Bound Bonds of Lessees and
Inventory of 1871.

National Archives Branch (East Point, Georgia)

Records of the Adjutant General's Office. Record Group 94. Microcopy 619
and 725. Letters Received by the Office of the Adjutant General, Georgia.

Records of the Bureau of Refugees, Freedmen, and Abandoned Lands.
Record Group 105.

Records of the Secretary of War. Telegrams Received. Record Group 107.

Augusta, Georgia

Augusta College

Augusta Chronicle. Typescript, 1861–73.

Augusta City Directories, 1859, 1861, 1865–67.

Augusta Newspaper Digest. WPA Index.

St. Paul's Episcopal Church Records.

Municipal Building, Office of the Clerk

City Council Minutes, 1857–68. 3 vols.

Index to Deeds. Corporations, 1842–88.

Index to Deeds, 1850–70.

Richmond County Marriage Licenses. Book C, 1856–63.

Richmond County Will Book C, 1853–57.

Cambridge, Massachusetts

Harvard University, Baker Library

R. G. Dun and Company Collection.

Chapel Hill, North Carolina

University of North Carolina

Southern Historical Collection

Autobiography of Raphael J. Moses.

Thomas Manson Norwood Papers.

Daniel L. Russell Papers.

Thomas Settle Papers.

Hermione Ross Walker Collection.

Charlestown, Rhode Island

Town Hall

Land Evidence. Vols. 11–15.

Tax Books and Treasurer's Report, 1887–1906.

Jackson, Mississippi

Mississippi Department of Archives and History

Adelbert Ames Papers.

Samuel Gibbs French Papers.

Rochester, New York

Rochester Public Library

Diaries Collection, 1799–1918. M. Elizabeth Stewart.

Local Rochester Newspaper Index.

Margaret Woodbury Strong Museum

Freeman Clarke Papers.

University of Rochester

Freeman Clarke Family Papers.

Jackson Hadley Records and Accounts, 1847–50. 5 vols.

MSS Collection. Undated letter. Rufus Bullock to E. T. Coann.

San Marino, California

Henry E. Huntington Library

Rufus Brown Bullock Papers.

Washington, D.C.

Library of Congress

Benjamin F. Butler Papers.

Simon Cameron Papers. Microfilm.

William E. Chandler Papers.

Hamilton Fish Collection.

Andrew Johnson Papers.

John Sherman Papers.

Alexander H. Stephens Collection. Microfilm.

National Archives

Confederate Papers Relating to Citizens or Business Firms. Microcopy 345, Rolls 18, 805, Microcopy 346, Roll 965.

General Records of the United States Government. Record Group 11. Records of the 14th and 15th Amendments, Georgia, Rejection and Ratification. Letters Received by the Confederate Adjutant and Inspector General, 1861–65. Microcopy 474. Rolls 95, 121, 145.

Letters Received by the Confederate Secretary of War, 1861–65. Microcopy 437, Roll 17.

Records of the Adjutant General's Office, 1780s–1917. Record Group 94. Microcopy 565.

Records of the Secretary of War. Record Group 107.

Records of the United States Army Continental Commands. Record Group 393. Different titles. Multiple boxes.

PUBLISHED SOURCES

Albany Citizen's Advertiser, 1834–5. Albany, N.Y.: N.p., 1835.
Albany City Directory, 1814–42. Albany, N.Y.: Publishers and dates vary.
Alvord, J. W. *Letters from the South Relating to the Condition of the Freedmen.* Washington, D.C.: Howard University Press, 1870.

The American Annual Cyclopedia and Register of Important Events of the Year. 41 vols. New York: D. Appleton, 1869–73.

Anderson, J. A., comp. *Code of the City of Atlanta.* Atlanta: N.p., 1899.

Andrews, Sidney. *The South Since the War.* Boston: Ticknor & Fields, 1866.

Angier, N. L. *The Georgia Legislature, Legally Organized in 1868.* Washington, D.C.: Gibson Brothers, 1870.

————. *N. L. Angier, Treasurer of Georgia, to the Reconstruction Committee, in Reply to Governor Bullock, and Further Comments on the Affairs in Georgia.* Atlanta: N.p., 1870.

Annual Reports of the Officers of the Western and Atlantic Railroad to . . . Rufus B. Bullock . . . for the Fiscal Year Ending Sept. 30, 1869. Atlanta: Samuel Bard, 1870.

Appleton's Cyclopedia of American Biography. 6 vols. New York: D. Appleton, 1888.

Atlanta: A Twentieth-Century City. Atlanta: Atlanta Chamber of Commerce, Byrd Printers. 1903.

The Atlanta Exposition and the South Illustrated. Chicago: Adler Art Publishing, 1895.

Atlanta in 1890: The Gate City. Neenah, Wisc.: Pratt, 1890.

Atlas of Niagara and Orleans Counties, New York, 1875. Philadelphia: Beers, Upton & Co., 1875.

Baker, Ray Stannard. *Following the Color Line: An Account of Negro Citizenship in the American Democracy.* 1908. Reprint. Williamstown, Mass.: Corner House Publishers, 1973.

Bard, Samuel. *A Letter from Samuel Bard to President Grant, on the Political Situation in Georgia and the South.* Atlanta: Daily True Georgian, 1870.

Barnwell's Atlanta City Directory, 1867. Atlanta: Intelligencer Book Office, 1867.

Ben-Ansel, Rabbi [pen name of B. F. Sawyer, editor of the *Rome Courier*]. *The Books of the Chronicles of the Land of Georgia as Written in the Archives of the State.* Rome, Ga.: Rome Courier Office, 1872.

Benjamin Conley: Messages, 1871–1872. Atlanta: New Era Printing, 1872.

Blodgett, Foster. *The Campaign Speech of Hon. Foster Blodgett on the Issues Involved in the Georgia Campaign, at Augusta, November 3, 1870.* Atlanta: New Era Printing, 1870.

————. *Speech of Hon. Foster Blodgett, Before the Union Club of Augusta, Ga., on Monday Evening, August 12, 1867.* N.p.: N.p., 1867.

Brock, R. A., ed. *The Appomattox Roster: A List of Paroles of the Army of Northern Virginia Issued at Appomattox Courthouse on April 9, 1865.* New York: Antiquarian Press, 1962.

Brown, Joseph E. *A Statement of Facts Connected with the Compromise Between*

the State and the Heirs of Samuel Mitchell for the Park Property in Atlanta.
Atlanta: W. R. Barrow, 1872.

Bryant, John E. *A Letter to Hon. Charles Sumner of the United States Senate,
Exposing the Bullock-Blodgett Ring in Their Attempt to Defeat the Bingham
Amendment.* Washington, D.C.: Gibson Brothers, 1870.

Bryant, John E., and John Bowles. *Governor Bullock and the Democratic Press of
Georgia.* Washington, D.C.: Gibson Brothers, 1870.

———. *Gov. Bullock's Dispatches from Georgia: Why They Are Sent.* Washington, D.C.: Gibson Brothers, 1870.

The Bulletin of Atlanta University. Atlanta: Atlanta University Printing Office,
1891–1900.

Bullock, Rufus B. *Address of Rufus B. Bullock, Ex-Governor of Georgia, Delivered August 22, 1891, Before the Alumni Association of the Albion Academy
at Albion, Orleans County, N.Y.* Albion, N.Y.: Orleans American Steam
Print, 1891.

———. *Address of Rufus B. Bullock to the People of Georgia: A Review of the
Revolutionary Proceedings of the Late Repudiating Legislature.* Atlanta: New
Era Printing, 1872.

———. *Georgia's Repudiated Bonds. Letters from Ex-Governor Bullock to the
Constitution Newspaper . . . Editorials . . . 1882 & 1885.* Atlanta: Harrison
Printers, 1886.

———. *Have the Reconstruction Acts Been Fully Executed in Georgia?*
Washington, D.C.: Chronicle Printers, 1868.

———. "Letter from His Excellency Governor Bullock, of Georgia, in Reply to
the Honorable John Scott, United States Senator, Chairman of Joint Select
Committee to Inquire into the Condition of Affairs in the Late Insurrectionary
States." *Commercial and Financial Chronicle,* July 22, 1871.

———. *Letter from Rufus B. Bullock, of Georgia, to the Republican Senators
and Representatives in Congress Who Sustain the Reconstruction Acts. Dated
Williard's Hotel, May 21, 1870.* Washington, D.C.: Chronicle Print, 1870.

———. "Reconstruction in Georgia, 1865–1870." *Independent* 55 (March 19,
1903): 670–74.

———. *Remarks of Governor Bullock to the Judiciary Committee of the Senate in re. Reconstruction of Georgia, March 2, 1870.* Washington, D.C.:
Chronicle Print, 1870.

Bullock, Volkert V. *Some Fairy Fancies Here You See as They Crossed the Mind
of V. V. B.* Atlanta: Franklin Publishing, 1904.

Butler, Benjamin F. *Butler's Book: A Review of His Legal, Political, and Military
Career.* Boston: A. M. Thayer, 1892.

By-Laws and Rules of the Piedmont Driving Club of Atlanta, Georgia. Atlanta:
Franklin Printing, 1899.

Cable, George Washington. *The Negro Question: A Selection of Writings on Civil Rights in the South.* 1890. Reprint. New York: Doubleday, 1958.

————. *The Silent South.* New York: Scribners, 1885.

Caldwell, John H. *Reminiscences of the Reconstruction of Church and State in Georgia.* Wilmington, Del.: J. Miller Thomas, 1895.

Campbell, Tunis G. *Sufferings of the Rev. T. G. Campbell and His Family in Georgia.* Washington, D.C.: Enterprise Publishing Company, 1877.

Can a Negro Hold Office in Georgia? Decided in the Supreme Court of Georgia, June Term, 1869. Atlanta: Daily Intelligencer, 1869.

Candler, Allen D., comp. *The Confederate Records of the State of Georgia.* 6 vols. Atlanta: Charles Byrd, 1911.

Catalogue of the Officers and Students of Albion Academy, Spring and Summer Terms, 1838. Albion, N.Y.: T. C. Strong, 1838.

Charter and By-Laws of the Cotton States and International Exposition Company, Atlanta, Ga. Atlanta: Franklin Printing, 1894.

Child, Hamilton, comp. *Gazetteer and Business Directory of Orleans County, New York, for 1869.* Syracuse, N.Y.: Journal Office, 1869.

City of Atlanta: A Descriptive, Historical and Industrial Review of the Gateway City of the South, Being the World's Fair Series on Great American Cities. Louisville, Ky.: Interstate Publishing Co., 1891.

The Claim of Henry Clews and Company Against the State of Georgia. Macon, Ga.: R. A. Alston, 1876.

Clarke, E. Y. *Illustrated History of Atlanta.* Atlanta: James P. Harrison, 1878.

Clews, Henry. *Twenty-Eight Years in Wall Street.* New York: Irving Publishing Co., 1888.

The Code of the State of Georgia. Macon, Ga.: J. W. Burke, 1873.

Commissioners' Report: Western and Atlantic Railroad to His Excellency Rufus B. Bullock, Governor, January, 1871. Atlanta: George W. Harrison, 1891.

Congressional Globe. 1867–1872.

Conley, John L. *Analysis of the Constitution of Georgia, as in Force Since July 21st, 1868.* Atlanta: N.p., 1870.

————., ed. *The Constitution of the State of Georgia with Full Marginal Notes.* N.p.: N.p., 1868.

Constitution, Ordinances and Resolutions of the Georgia Convention, Assembled in Pursuance of the Reconstruction Acts of Congress, and Held, by Order of General Pope, in the City of Atlanta, in 1867 and 1868. . . . Atlanta: New Era Printing, 1870.

Contemporary American Biography. 3 vols. New York: Atlantic, 1895.

Cooper, Walter G. *The Cotton States and International Exposition and South,*

Illustrated Including the Official History of the Exposition. Atlanta: Illustrator
  Co., 1896.
Dau's Society Blue Book and Ladies Address Book. New York: Dau Publishing
  Co., 1901.
Dennett, John Richard. *The South as It Is, 1865–1866.* 1866. Reprint. Athens:
  University of Georgia Press, 1986.
Directory for the City of Augusta and Business Advertiser for 1859. Augusta, Ga.:
  R. A. Watkins, 1859.
Du Bois, W. E. B. *Writings.* New York: Viking Press, 1986.
Echols, Samuel A. *Georgia's General Assembly of 1878: Biographical Sketches of
  Senators, Representatives, the Governor and Heads of Departments.* Atlanta:
  J. P. Harrison, 1878.
Felton, Rebecca L. *My Memoirs of Georgia Politics.* Atlanta: Index Printing
  Co., 1911.
Fleming, Walter L., ed. *Documentary History of Reconstruction: Political, Mili-
  tary, Social, Religious, Educational and Industrial, 1865–1906.* 2 vols. 1907.
  Reprint. New York: McGraw-Hill, 1966.
French, J. H. *Gazetteer of the State of New York.* Syracuse, N.Y.: R. P.
  Smith, 1860.
Georgia. Comptroller General's Office. *Annual Report of the Comptroller
  General of Georgia, 1867–72.* Places and publishers vary.
————. *Report of the Comptroller General and Insurance Commissioner.* Places
  and dates vary.
Georgia. General Assembly. *Acts and Resolutions of the General Assembly of the
  State of Georgia, 1870.* Atlanta: Public Printer, 1871.
————. *Committee to Investigate the Bonds of the State of Georgia, Issued or
  Negotiated Since July 4, 1868.* 5 vols. Atlanta: W. A. Hemphill, 1872.
————. *Committee to Investigate the Official Conduct of Rufus B. Bullock.
  Testimony Taken by the Committee Appointed to Investigate the Official
  Conduct of Rufus B. Bullock, Late Governor of Georgia.* Atlanta: W. A.
  Hemphill, 1872.
————. *The Evidence Taken by the Joint Committee of the Legislature of the
  State of Georgia Appointed to Investigate the Management of the State Road,
  Under the Administration of R. B. Bullock and Foster Blodgett.* Atlanta: J. H.
  Smith, 1872.
————. *Joint Committee to Investigate the Charges Against Governor Bullock.*
  Atlanta: N.p., 1870.
————. *Joint Committee to Investigate the Charges Against N. L. Angier, State
  Treasurer.* Atlanta: N.p., 1870.
————. *Joint Committee to Investigate the Condition, Finances, and General*

Management of the Western and Atlantic Railroad. Atlanta: J. J. Toon, 1870.

————. *Joint Committee to Investigate the Indebtedness of Foster Blodgett, Treasurer and Superintendent of the Western and Atlantic Railroad.* Atlanta: W. A. Hemphill, 1873.

————. *Joint Committee to Investigate Macon and Brunswick Railroad Bonds, 1874.* Atlanta: N.p., 1875.

————. *Joint Committee to Investigate the Western and Atlantic Railroad, 1872.* Atlanta: W. A. Hemphill, 1872.

————. *Proceedings of the Joint Committee Appointed to Investigate the Condition of the Georgia Penitentiary.* Atlanta: N.p., 1870.

————. *The Relief Law of Georgia Passed by the General Assembly, October 1870.* Atlanta: Constitution Publishing, 1870.

————. *Report of the Majority of the Joint Committee Appointed by the General Assembly to Investigate the Fairness or Unfairness of the Contract Known as the Lease of the Western and Atlantic Railroad Made December 27, 1870 by Rufus B. Bullock, Late Governor, and to Investigate the Question of Fraud in Said Contract, if Any Exists.* Atlanta: W. A. Hemphill, 1872.

————. *Reports of Legislative Committees, Submitted in July 1872.* 5 vols. Atlanta: W. A. Hemphill, 1872.

————. *Testimony Taken by the Committee Appointed to Investigate the Official Conduct of Rufus B. Bullock, Late Governor of Georgia.* Atlanta: W. A. Hemphill, 1872.

————. House. *Journal of the House of the State of Georgia.* Atlanta: Public Printer, 1865–78.

————. House. Finance Committee. *Remarks and Statements of the Superintendent on the Condition of the Road . . . September 23, 1870.* Atlanta: State Printer, 1870.

————. Senate. *Journal of the Senate of the State of Georgia.* Atlanta: Public Printer, 1865–78.

Georgia. Governor. *Messages, 1868–1871.* Atlanta: Public Printer, 1872.

————. *Messages, 1871–1872.* Atlanta: New Era Printing, 1872.

————. *Messages, 1872–1877.* Atlanta: H. G. Wright, 1878.

————. James M. Smith. *The Claim of Henry Clews Against the State of Georgia.* Macon: R. A. Alston, 1876.

————. *Veto Message of His Excellency Benjamin Conley . . . November 21, 1871.* Atlanta: N.p., 1871.

Georgia. Penitentiary. *Annual Report of the Principal Keeper of the Georgia Penitentiary.* Places and publishers vary, 1868–78.

Georgia. Supreme Court. *Georgia Digest.* Atlanta: Publishers vary, 1865–1900.

————. *Reports of Cases in Law and Equity Decided Before the Supreme Court of Georgia . . . 1869.* Macon, Ga.: Burke, 1870.

Grady, Henry W. *The Race Problem*. Chicago: George L. Shuman, 1900.

Guide to Atlanta, 1889. With City Map. Atlanta: Constitution Job Office, 1889.

Handbook of the City of Atlanta: A Comprehensive Review of the City's Commercial, Industrial, and Residential Conditions. Atlanta: Southern Industrial Publishing Co., 1898.

Harlan, Louis R., John W. Blassingame, et al., eds. *The Booker T. Washington Papers*. 14 vols. Urbana: University of Illinois Press, 1972–84.

Hill, Benjamin H., Jr. *Senator Benjamin H. Hill of Georgia: His Life, Speeches and Writings*. Atlanta: T. H. P. Bloodworth, 1893.

Historical Sketches of Atlanta, 1895. Atlanta: N.p., 1895.

Hoffman's Albany Directory and City Register, 1840–1. Albany, N.Y.: L. G. Hoffman, 1840.

Hough, Franklin B. *Gazetteer of the State of New York*. Albany, N.Y.: Andrew Boyd, 1872.

———. *Historical Record of the University of the State of New York*. Albany, N.Y.: Weed, Parsons, & Co., 1885.

Humphreys, Robert L., ed. *The Journal of Archibald C. McKinley*. Athens: University of Georgia Press, 1991.

The Invalid Bonds of Georgia: Arguments of Pat Calhoun, Esq., and Hon. N. J. Hammond Before the Attorney-General of New York, June 1885. New York: N.p., 1885.

Journal of the Proceedings of the Constitutional Convention of the People of Georgia, Held in the City of Atlanta in the Months of December, 1867, and January, February and March 1868. Augusta, Ga.: E. H. Pughe, 1868.

Kendrick, Benjamin B., ed. *The Journal of the Joint Committee of Fifteen on Reconstruction: 39th Congress, 1865–1867*. New York: By the author, 1914.

Kimball, H. I. *An Address by H. I. Kimball Before the Mechanics' Institute of Atlanta, December 29, 1874, on the Manufacture of Cotton in Atlanta*. Atlanta: Atlanta Herald Job Office, 1875.

———. *International Cotton Exposition: Atlanta, Georgia, 1881, Report of the Director-General H. I. Kimball*. New York: D. Appleton, 1882.

———. *An Open Letter from H. I. Kimball to the Augusta Chronicle and Sentinel*. Atlanta: Atlanta Herald, 1874.

King, Edward. *The Southern States of North America: A Record of Journeys*. 4 vols. London: Blackie & Son, 1875.

King, Martin Luther, Jr. *Letter from Birmingham City Jail*. Philadelphia: American Friends Service Committee, 1963.

Kirwin's Directory of the County of Orleans for the Years 1879–1880. Lockport, N.Y.: Union Printing, 1879.

Knight, Lucian L. *Reminiscences of Famous Georgians*. 2 vols. Atlanta: Franklin-Turner, 1907–8.

The Lease of the Western and Atlantic Railroad with Correspondence and Other Papers in Relation Thereto. Atlanta: Constitution Publishing, 1871.

McClure, Alexander. *Colonel Alexander McClure's Recollections of Half a Century.* Salem, Mass.: By the author, 1902.

Memoirs of Georgia. 2 vols. Atlanta: Southern Historical Association, 1895.

A Memorial of the Albion Academy. Albion, N.Y.: Orleans American Steam Print, 1891.

Officers, Members, Constitution and Rules of the Capital City Club of Atlanta, Georgia. Atlanta: C. P. Byrd Printer, 1896.

Officers, Members, Constitution and Rules of the Capital City Club, 1912. Atlanta: Foote and Davies, 1912.

The Official Catalogue of the Cotton States and International Exposition, Atlanta, Georgia, September 18 to December 31, 1895. Atlanta: Claflin & Mellichamp, 1895.

Phillips, Ulrich B. "An American State-Owned Railroad." *Yale Review* 15 (November 1906): 259–82.

———, ed. *The Correspondence of Robert Toombs, Alexander H. Stephens and Howell Cobb.* 1913. Reprint. New York: Da Capo, 1970.

Proceedings of a Meeting of the State Central Committee of the Union Republican Party of Georgia, Held at Atlanta, Wednesday, November 24, 1869. Atlanta: New Era Printing, 1869.

Proceedings of the Provisional Legislature, Session Commencing April 25, 1870. Atlanta: New Era Printing, 1870.

Pughe's Augusta City Directory, 1865–66. Augusta, Ga.: E. H. Pughe, 1866.

Radical Rule: Military Outrage in Georgia. Arrest of the Columbus Prisoners. Louisville, Ky.: Morton & Co., 1868.

Rathbun, Fred C., ed. *Names from Georgia, 1865–1866: Freedmen's Bureau Letters, Roll 13.* Microfilm. N.p.: By the author, 1986.

Redkey, Edwin S., ed. *Respect Black: The Writings and Speeches of Henry McNeil Turner.* New York: Arno Press, 1971.

Reid, Whitelaw. *After the War: A Southern Tour, May 1, 1865 to May 1, 1866.* New York: Sampson, Low, Son, & Co., 1866.

Report of the Industrial Commission on the Relations and Conditions of Capital and Labor Employed in Manufactures and General Business. 19 vols. Washington, D.C.: U.S. Government Printing Office, 1901.

Resolution of the Legislature of Georgia Declaring the Assent of Said State to the Condition Imposed upon Said State by the Act of Congress of June 25, 1868. . . . Washington, D.C.: Chronicle Print, 1870.

St. Clair-Abrams, Alexander. *Manual and Biographical Register of the State of Georgia for 1871–72.* Atlanta: Plantation Publishing Co., 1872.

Shurter, Edwin D., ed. *The Complete Orations and Speeches of Henry W. Grady.* New York: Hinds, Noble & Eldredge, 1910.

Somers, Robert. *The Southern States Since the War, 1870–71*. London: Macmillan, 1871.

A Souvenir Book of the Village of Albion, Orleans County, New York. Albion, N.Y.: Chamber of Commerce, 1905.

A Stenographic Report of the Proceedings of the Constitutional Convention Held in Atlanta, Georgia, 1877. Atlanta: Constitution Job Office, 1877.

Taylor, Bayard. *Sketches of Men of Progress*. New York: New York and Hartford Publishing Co., 1871.

Thomas, Arad. *Sketches of the Village of Albion*. Albion, N.Y.: Willsea and Beach, 1853.

Trial of Andrew Johnson, President of the United States, Before the Senate of the United States, on Impeachment by the House of Representatives for High Crimes and Misdemeanors. 3 vols. Washington, D.C.: U.S. Government Printing Office, 1868.

Tutler's Augusta Directory for 1861. Augusta, Ga.: Steam Power Press, 1861.

U.S. City Directories on Microfilm, Atlanta, 1861–1901. New Haven, Conn.: Research Publications, 1980.

U.S. Department of Commerce. Bureau of the Census. *Fifth to Twelfth Censuses of the United States*. Washington, D.C.: U.S. Government Printing Office, 1830–1900.

———. *Negro Population, 1790–1915*. Washington, D.C.: Government Printing Office, 1871.

U.S. Congress. House. Executive Documents. 40th Cong., 3d sess., Nos. 1, 3; 41st Cong., 2d sess., Nos. 1, 41, 288.

———. Miscellaneous Documents. 40th Cong., 3d sess., No. 52; 41st Cong., 1st sess., No. 34.

———. Report of the Joint Committee on Reconstruction. 39th Cong., 1st sess., No. 30.

———. Report of the Joint Select Committee to Inquire into the Condition of Affairs in the Late Insurrectionary States. 42d Cong., 2d sess., No. 22. 13 vols. Washington, D.C.: U.S. Government Printing Office, 1872.

U.S. Congress. Senate. Executive Documents. 41st Cong., 2d sess., No. 41; 51st Cong., 1st sess., No. 48; 51st Cong., 2d sess., No. 233; 52d Cong. 1st sess., No. 6; 52d Cong., 2d sess., No. 4.

———. *Journal of the Senate of the United States*. 40th Cong., 3d sess.

———. Senate Reports. 40th Cong., 3d sess., No. 192; 41st Cong., 2d sess., No. 175.

U.S. War Department. *The War of the Rebellion: A Compilation of the Official Records of the Union and Confederate Armies*. 128 vols. Washington, D.C.: U.S. Government Printing Office, 1880–1901. Series 2. Vol. 8.

Washington, Booker T. *Up from Slavery: An Autobiography*. 1901. Reprint. New York: Bantam Books, 1967.

Webster, Emma Reed, ed. *Record of the Orleans County Pioneer Association: Original Minutes, 1858–1905.* Albion, N.Y.: D.A.R., 1939.

Wight, Willard E. "Reconstruction in Georgia: Three Letters by Edwin G. Higbee." *Georgia Historical Quarterly* 41 (March 1957): 81–90.

Wilson, John S. *Atlanta as It Is: Being a Sketch of Its Early Settlers.* New York: Little, Rennie & Co., 1871.

Zincke, F. Barham. *Last Winter in the United States.* London: John Murray, 1868.

Secondary Sources

Abbott, Richard H. *Cotton and Capital: Boston Businessmen and Antislavery Reform, 1854–1868.* Amherst: University of Massachusetts Press, 1991.

———. *The Republican Party and the South, 1855–1877: The First Southern Strategy.* Chapel Hill: University of North Carolina Press, 1986.

Adams, James T. "Our Lawless Heritage." *Atlantic Monthly* 142 (December 1928): 732–40.

Adams, Olin B. "The Negro and the Agrarian Movement in Georgia, 1874–1908." Ph.D. dissertation, Florida State University, 1973.

Ahern, Wilbert H. "Laissez Faire vs. Equal Rights: Liberal Republicans and Limits to Reconstruction." *Phylon* 40 (March 1979): 52–65.

Alexander, Hooper. *Some Observations as to the Western and Atlantic Railroad.* Atlanta: N.p., 1907.

Alexander, Thomas B. "Persistent Whiggery in the Confederate South, 1860–1877." *Journal of Southern History* 27 (August 1961): 305–29.

Allen, Ivan. *Atlanta: From the Ashes.* Atlanta: Ruralist Press, 1929.

Allen, James S. *The Negro Question in the United States.* New York: International Publishers, 1936.

Allen, Steve. *Ripoff: A Look at Corruption in America.* Secaucus, N.J.: L. Stuart, 1979.

Anderson, George L. "The South and Problems of Post–Civil War Finance." *Journal of Southern History* 9 (May 1943): 181–95.

Atlanta: A City of the Modern South. W. P. A. Writers' Program. St. Clair Shores, Mich.: Smith and Durrell, 1973.

The Atlanta Centennial Yearbook: 1837–1937. Atlanta: Franklin Printing Co., 1937.

The Atlanta Journal and Encyclopedia of Political and General Information, 1897. Atlanta: Atlanta Journal, 1897.

Avery, Isaac W. *The History of the State of Georgia from 1850 to 1881 . . . .* New York: Brown and Derby, 1881.

Ayers, Edward L. *The Promise of the New South: Life After Reconstruction.* New York: Oxford University Press, 1992.

————. *Vengeance and Justice: Crime and Punishment in the 19th-Century American South*. New York: Oxford University Press, 1984.

Bacote, Clarence A. *The Story of Atlanta University: A Century of Service, 1865–1965*. Atlanta: Atlanta University Press, 1969.

Bartley, Numan V. *The Creation of Modern Georgia*. Athens: University of Georgia Press, 1983.

————. "In Search of the New South: Southern Politics After Reconstruction." In *The Promise of American History: Progress and Prospects*, pp. 36–53. Edited by Stanley I. Kutler and Stanley N. Katz. Baltimore: Johns Hopkins University Press, 1982.

Bayor, Ronald H. "Ethnic Residential Patterns in Atlanta, 1880–1940," *Georgia Historical Quarterly* 63 (Winter 1979): 435–51.

Beale, Howard K. *The Critical Year: Andrew Johnson and Reconstruction*. Baton Rouge: Louisiana State University Press, 1947.

Beard, Charles A. *The Economic Basis of Politics*. New York: Knopf, 1922.

Bell, Earl L., and Kenneth C. Crabbe. *The Augusta Chronicle: Indomitable Voice of Dixie, 1785–1960*. Athens: University of Georgia Press, 1960.

Benedict, Michael Les. *A Compromise of Principle: Congressional Republicans and Reconstruction, 1865–1869*. New York: Norton, 1974.

————. *The Fruits of Victory: Alternatives in Restoring the Union, 1865–1877*. Philadelphia: J. B. Lippincott, 1975.

Bhurtel, Shyam K. "Alfred Eliab Buck: Carpetbagger in Alabama and Georgia." Ph.D. dissertation, Auburn University, 1981.

Billings, Dwight B. *Planters and the Making of a "New South": Class, Politics, and Development in North Carolina, 1865–1900*. Chapel Hill: University of North Carolina Press, 1979.

Black, Nellie, comp. *Richard Peters: His Ancestors and Descendants*. Atlanta: Foote and Davies, 1904.

Bloom, Charles G. "The Georgia Election of April, 1868: A Re-Examination of the Politics of Georgia Reconstruction." M. A. thesis, University of Chicago, 1963.

Bowers, Claude G. *The Tragic Era: The Revolution After Lincoln*. Cambridge, Mass.: Houghton Mifflin, 1929.

Brock, W. R. "The Waning of Radicalism." In *Reconstruction: An Anthology of Revisionist Writings*, pp. 496–515. Edited by Kenneth Stampp and Leon Litwack. Baton Rouge: Louisiana State University Press, 1969.

Brooks, Robert C. *Corruption in American Politics and Life*. New York: Dodd, Mead, and Co., 1910.

Bryce, James. *The American Commonwealth*. 2 vols. 1893. Reprint. New York: Macmillan, 1910.

Candler, Allen D., comp., *The Confederate Records of the State of Georgia*. 4 vols. Atlanta: C. P. Byrd, 1909–11.

Candler, Allen D., and Clement Evans, eds. *Georgia: Comprising Sketches of Counties, Towns, Events, Institutions, and Persons, Arranged in Cyclopedic Form.* . . . Atlanta: State Historical Association, 1906.

Carter, Dan T. *When the War Was Over: The Failure of Self-Reconstruction in the South, 1865–1867.* Baton Rouge: Louisiana State University Press, 1985.

Carter, E. R. *The Black Side: A Partial History of Business, Religions, and Educational Side of the Negro in Atlanta.* Atlanta: N.p., 1894.

Carter, Hodding. *Their Words Were Bullets: The Southern Press in War, Reconstruction, and Peace.* Athens: University of Georgia Press, 1969.

Cash, Wilbur J. *The Mind of the South.* New York: Knopf, 1941.

Cashin, Edward J. *The Story of Augusta.* Augusta, Ga.: Richmond County Board of Education, 1980.

Centennial Anniversary, Christ Episcopal Church, Albion, N.Y., 1844–1944. Albion, N.Y.: N.p., 1944.

Chambliss, William J. *On the Take: From Petty Crooks to Presidents.* Bloomington: Indiana University Press, 1978.

Chappel, Absalom H. *Miscellanies of Georgia: Historical, Biographical, Descriptive, Etc.* Columbus, Ga.: Gilbert Printing Company, 1874.

Clark, Thomas D., ed. *Travels in the New South: A Bibliography.* 2 vols. Norman: University of Oklahoma Press, 1961.

Clark, Victor S. *The History of Manufactures in the United States.* 3 vols. New York: McGraw-Hill, 1929.

———. *The South in the Building of the Nation.* 12 vols. Richmond, Va.: Southern Publication Society, 1909.

Clarke, Michael, ed. *Corruption: Causes, Consequences, and Control.* New York: St. Martin's Press, 1983.

Cobb, James C. *Industrialization and Southern Society, 1877–1984.* Lexington: University Press of Kentucky, 1984.

———. *The Selling of the South: The Southern Crusade for Industrial Development, 1936–1980.* Baton Rouge: Louisiana State University Press, 1982.

Cochran, Thomas C. *Challenges to American Values: Society, Business, and Religion.* New York: Oxford University Press, 1985.

Cochran, Thomas C., and William Miller. *The Age of Enterprise: A Social History of Industrial America.* New York: Harper & Row, 1961.

Cohen, Stanley A. "Northeastern Business and Radical Reconstruction: A Reexamination." In *Reconstruction: An Anthology of Revisionist Writings,* pp. 85–106. Edited by Kenneth Stampp and Leon Litwack. Baton Rouge: Louisiana State University Press, 1969.

Coleman, Kenneth. *A History of Georgia.* Athens: University of Georgia Press, 1977.

Coleman, Kenneth, and Stephen Gurr, eds., *Dictionary of Georgia Biography.* 2 vols. Athens: University of Georgia Press, 1983.

Conway, Alan. *The Reconstruction of Georgia*. Minneapolis: University of Minnesota Press, 1966.

Cook, James F. *Governors of Georgia*. Huntsville, Ala.: Strode Publishers, 1979.

Cooper, Walter G. *The Story of Georgia*. 3 vols. New York: American Historical Society, 1938.

Corley, Florence F. *Confederate City: Augusta, Georgia, 1860–1865*. Columbia: University of South Carolina Press, 1960.

Coulter, E. Merton. *The Confederate States of America*. Baton Rouge: Louisiana State University Press, 1950.

———. "Cudjo Fye's Insurrection." *Georgia Historical Quarterly* 38 (September 1954): 213–25.

———. *Georgia: A Short History*. Chapel Hill: University of North Carolina Press, 1935.

———. *The South During Reconstruction*. Baton Rouge: Louisiana State University Press, 1947.

Current, Richard N. *Northernizing the South*. Athens: University of Georgia Press, 1983.

———. *Those Terrible Carpetbaggers: A Reinterpretation*. New York: Oxford University Press, 1988.

———. *Three Carpetbag Governors*. Baton Rouge: Louisiana State University Press, 1967.

Currie-McDaniel, Ruth. *Carpetbagger of Conscience: A Biography of John Emory Bryant*. Athens: University of Georgia Press, 1987.

Daniell, Elizabeth O. "The Ashburn Murder Case in Georgia Reconstruction, 1868." *Georgia Historical Quarterly* 59 (Fall 1975): 296–312.

Davis, Harold E. "Henry W. Grady, Master of the Atlanta Ring, 1880–1886." *Georgia Historical Quarterly* 69 (Spring 1985): 1–38.

Deaton, Stanley K. "Violent Redemption: The Democratic Party and the Ku Klux Klan in Georgia, 1868–1871." M.A. thesis, University of Georgia, 1988.

DeCredico, Mary A. "Georgia's Entrepreneurs and Confederate Mobilization, 1847–1873." Ph.D. dissertation, Vanderbilt University, 1986.

———. *Patriotism for Profit: Georgia's Urban Entrepreneurs and the Confederate*. Chapel Hill: University of North Carolina Press, 1990.

Degler, Carl. *The Other South: Southern Dissenters in the Nineteenth Century*. New York: Harper & Row, 1974.

DeTreville, John R. "Reconstruction in Augusta, Georgia, 1865–1868." M.A. thesis, University of North Carolina, 1979.

Dixon, William H. *White Conquest*. 2 vols. London: Chatto and Windus, 1876.

Donald, David H. *Charles Sumner and the Rights of Man*. New York: Knopf, 1970.

Drago, Edmund L. *Black Politicians and Reconstruction in Georgia: A Splendid Failure*. Baton Rouge: Louisiana State University Press, 1982.

Drake, Richard B. "Freedmen's Aid Societies and Sectional Compromise." *Journal of Southern History* 29 (May 1963): 175–86.

Du Bois, W. E. B. *Black Reconstruction: An Essay Toward a History of the Part Which Black Folk Played in the Attempt to Reconstruct Democracy in America, 1860–1880.* New York: Russell and Russell, 1935.

———. "Reconstruction and Its Benefits." *American Historical Review* 15 (July 1910): 781–99.

Duncan, Russell. "Cotton States and International Exposition, Atlanta, 1895." In John E. Findling, ed., *Historical Dictionary of World's Fairs and Expositions.* Westport, Conn.: Greenwood Press, 1981.

———. *Freedom's Shore: Tunis Campbell and the Georgia Freedmen.* Athens: University of Georgia Press, 1986.

———. "The Southern Express Company." In Richard N. Current, ed., *Encyclopedia of the Confederacy.* New York: Simon and Schuster, forthcoming.

Dunning, William A. *Reconstruction: Political and Economic, 1865–1877.* New York: Harper & Brothers, 1907.

Fields, Barbara J. "The Advent of Capitalist Agriculture: The New South in the Bourgeois World." In *Essays on the Postbellum Southern Economy,* pp. 73–94. Edited by Thavolia Glymph. Arlington: University of Texas Press, 1985.

FitzSimons, Theodore B. "The Camilla Riot." *Georgia Historical Quarterly* 35 (June 1951): 116–25.

Flynn, Charles L. *White Land, Black Labor: Caste and Class in Late Nineteenth-Century Georgia.* Baton Rouge: Louisiana State University Press, 1983.

Foner, Eric. *Free Soil, Free Labor, Free Men: The Ideology of the Republican Party Before the Civil War.* New York: Oxford University Press, 1970.

———. *Nothing but Freedom: Emancipation and Its Legacy.* Baton Rouge: Louisiana State University Press, 1983.

———. *Reconstruction: America's Unfinished Revolution, 1865–1877.* New York: Harper & Row, 1988.

Formwalt, Lee W. "The Camilla Massacre of 1868: Racial Violence as Political Propaganda." *Georgia Historical Quarterly* 71 (Fall 1987): 399–426.

———, ed. "Petitioning Congress for Protection: A Black View of Reconstruction at the Local Level." *Georgia Historical Quarterly* 73 (Summer 1989): 305–22.

Foster, Gaines M. *Ghosts of the Confederacy: Defeat, the Lost Cause, and the Emergence of the New South, 1865–1913.* New York: Oxford University Press, 1987.

Franklin, John Hope. *Reconstruction: After the Civil War.* Chicago: University of Chicago Press, 1961.

Fredrickson, George M. *The Black Image in the White Mind: The Debate on Afro-American Character and Destiny, 1817–1914.* New York: Harper & Row, 1971.

Freeman, Henri H. "Some Aspects of Debtor Relief in Georgia During Reconstruction." M.A. thesis, Emory University, 1951.

Friedrich, Carl J. *The Pathology of Politics: Violence, Betrayal, Corruption,
Secrecy and Propaganda*. New York: Harper & Row, 1972.

Fries, Adelaide L. "The Elizabeth Sterchi Letters." *Atlanta Historical Bulletin* 5
(April 1940): 107–23, and 5 (July 1940): 197–208.

Gaede, Erwin A. *Politics and Ethics: Machiavelli to Neibuhr*. Lanham, Md.:
University Press of America, 1983.

Gaither, Gerald H. *Blacks and the Populist Revolt: Ballots and Bigotry in the
"New South."* University, Ala.: University of Alabama Press, 1977.

Garrett, Franklin. *Atlanta and Environs: A Chronicle of Its People and Events*.
3 vols. New York: Lewis Historical Publishing, 1954.

Garrison, Curtis W. "Slater Fund Beginnings: Letters from General Agent Atticus G. Haygood to Rutherford B. Hayes." *Journal of Negro History* 5 (May
1939): 223–45.

Garrison, Ellen B. "Old South or New?: Georgia and the Constitution of 1877."
Ph.D. dissertation, Stanford University, 1981.

Gaston, Edward A., Jr. "A History of the Negro Wage Earner in Georgia,
1890–1940." Ph.D. dissertation, Emory University, 1957.

Gaston, Paul M. *The New South Creed: A Study in Southern Mythmaking*. New
York: Vintage Books, 1973.

Gerster, Patrick, and Nicholas Cords, eds. *Myth and Southern History: The New
South*. Chicago: Rand McNally, 1974.

——— . *Myth and Southern History: The Old South*. Chicago: Rand McNally,
1974.

Gillette, William. *Retreat from Reconstruction, 1869–1879*. Baton Rouge:
Louisiana State University Press, 1979.

——— . *The Right to Vote: Politics and the Passage of the Fifteenth Amendment*.
Baltimore: Johns Hopkins University Press, 1969.

Goetchius, Henry R. "Litigation in Georgia During the Reconstruction Period,
1865 to 1872." *Report of the Georgia Bar Association*. Atlanta: N.p., 1897.

Goodrich, Carter. "Public Aid to Railroads in the Reconstruction South."
Political Science Quarterly 71 (September 1956): 418.

Goodwyn, Lawrence. "Heirarchy and Democracy: The Paradox of the Southern
Experience." In *From the Old South to the New: Essays on the Transitional
South*, pp. 227–40. Edited by Walter J. Fraser, Jr., and Winfred B. Moore, Jr.
Westport, Conn.: Greenwood Press, 1981.

Gould, David J. *The Effects of Corruption on Administrative Performance: Illustrations from Developing Countries*. Washington, D.C.: World Bank, 1983.

Grantham, Dewey. *The Democratic South*. Athens: University of Georgia
Press, 1963.

————. *Hoke Smith and the Politics of the New South*. Baton Rouge: Louisiana State University Press, 1958.

Greer, Cecil T. "Georgia in the Presidential Campaign and Election of 1872." M.A. thesis, University of Georgia, 1953.

Groover, Robert L. "Margaret Mitchell, the Lady from Atlanta." *Georgia Historical Quarterly* 52 (March 1968): 53–69.

Guide to Historical Resources in Orleans County, New York Repositories. Ithaca, N.Y.: Cornell University Press, 1982.

Hahn, Steven. *The Roots of Southern Populism: Yeoman Farmers and the Transformation of the Georgia Upcountry*. New York: Oxford University Press, 1983.

Hammond, Matthew B. *The Cotton Industry*. New York: Macmillan, 1897.

Harlan, Louis R. *Booker T. Washington: The Making of a Black Leader, 1856–1901*. New York: Oxford University Press, 1972.

Harris, Joel C. *Life of Henry W. Grady, Including His Writings and Speeches*. New York: Cassell Publishing Company, 1890.

Harris, William C. "The Creed of the Carpetbagger: The Case of Mississippi." *Journal of Southern History* 40 (May 1974): 199–220.

————. *William Woods Holden: Firebrand of North Carolina Politics*. Baton Rouge: Louisiana State University Press, 1987.

Heidenheimer, Arnold J., ed. *Political Corruption: Readings in Comparative Analysis*. New Brunswick, N.J.: Transaction Books, 1978.

Henderson, Lillian, comp. *Roster of the Confederate Soldiers of Georgia, 1861–1865*. 5 vols. Hapeville, Ga.: Longina & Porter, 1959–64.

Herbert, Hilary A., ed. *Why the Solid South?* 1890. Reprint. New York: Greenwood Press, 1969.

Hesseltine, William B., and Larry Gara. "Georgia's Confederate Leaders After Appomattox." *Georgia Historical Quarterly* 35 (December 1951): 1–15.

Hirshson, Stanley P. *Farewell to the Bloody Shirt: Northern Republicans and the Southern Negro, 1877–1893*. Bloomington: Indiana University Press, 1962.

Historical Atlas of Orleans County, New York. New York: Sanford & Co., 1879.

Hitz, Alex. *A History of the Cathedral of St. Philip*. Atlanta: Conger Printing Co., 1947.

Hollingsworth, R. R. "Education and Reconstruction in Georgia." *Georgia Historical Quarterly* 19 (June 1935): 112–33, and 19 (September 1935): 229–50.

Hopkins, Richard J. "Occupational and Geographic Mobility in Atlanta, 1870–1896." *Journal of Southern History* 34 (May 1968): 200–226.

————. "Patterns of Persistance and Occupational Mobility in a Southern City: Atlanta, 1870–1920." Ph.D. dissertation, Emory University, 1972.

Howell, Clark. *History of Georgia*. 4 vols. Chicago: S. J. Clark, 1926.

Hunter, Floyd. *Community Power Succession*. Chapel Hill: University of North Carolina Press, 1980.

Hyman, Harold M. *Era of the Oath: Northern Loyalty Tests During the Civil War and Reconstruction.* Philadelphia: University of Pennsylvania Press, 1954.

Johnston, James H. *The Western and Atlantic Railroad of the State of Georgia.* Atlanta: Stein Printing Co., 1931.

Jones, Alexander. *Historical Sketches of the Electric Telegraph Including Its Rise and Progress in the United States.* New York: George P. Putnam, 1852.

Jones, Jacqueline. *Soldiers of Light and Love: Northern Teachers and Georgia Blacks, 1865–1873.* Chapel Hill: University of North Carolina Press, 1980.

Kegan, Robert. *The Evolving Self: Problems and Process in Human Development.* Cambridge, Mass.: Harvard University Press, 1982.

Key, V. O. *Southern Politics in State and Nation.* New York: Knopf, 1949.

———. "The Techniques of Political Graft in the United States." Ph.D. dissertation, University of Chicago, 1936.

Kincaid, Larry. "Victims of Circumstance: An Interpretation of Changing Attitudes Toward Republican Policy Makers and Reconstruction." *Journal of American History* 57 (June 1970): 48–66.

King, Augusta Wylie. "Golf as First Played in Atlanta." *Atlanta Historical Bulletin* 32 (December 1947): 9–11.

King, Spencer B. *Georgia Voices: A Documentary History to 1872.* Athens: University of Georgia Press, 1966.

Knight, Lucian Lamar. *History of Fulton County, Georgia.* Atlanta: A. H. Cawston, 1930.

———. *The Standard History of Georgia and Georgians.* 6 vols. Chicago: Lewis Publishing Co., 1917.

Kousser, J. Morgan. *The Shaping of Southern Politics: Suffrage Restriction and the Establishment of the One-Party South, 1880–1910.* New Haven: Yale University Press, 1974.

Kousser, J. Morgan, and James M. McPherson, eds. *Region, Race, and Reconstruction: Essays in Honor of C. Vann Woodward.* New York: Oxford University Press, 1982.

Kuchler, Eula T. "Charitable and Philanthropic Activities in Atlanta During Reconstruction." M.A. thesis, Emory University, 1942.

———. "Charitable and Philanthropic Activities in Atlanta During Reconstruction." *Atlanta Historical Bulletin* 40 (December 1965): 12–54.

Kurtines, William M., and Jacob L. GeWirtz. *Morality, Moral Behavior, and Moral Development.* New York: Wiley, 1984.

Lane, Mills, comp. *The New South: Writings and Speeches of Henry Grady.* Savannah, Ga.: Beehive Press, 1971.

Larsen, Lawrence H. *The Rise of the Urban South.* Lexington: University Press of Kentucky, 1985.

Little, Robert D. "The Ideology of the New South: A Study in the Development of Ideas, 1865–1910." Ph.D. dissertation, University of Chicago, 1950.

Litwack, Leon, and August Meier, eds. *Black Leaders of the Nineteenth Century.* Urbana: University of Illinois Press, 1988.

Lynch, Bernard, Irene Gibson, and Howard Pratt, eds. *Orleans County History: Past to Present.* Albion, N.Y.: Eddy Printing, 1976.

Lynd, Staughton, ed. *Reconstruction.* New York: Harper & Row, 1967.

Lyon, Elizabeth. "Business Buildings in Atlanta: A Study in Urban Growth and Form." Ph.D. dissertation, Emory University, 1971.

Magdol, Edward. *The Anti-Slavery Rank and File: A Social Profile of the Abolitionists' Constituency.* Westport, Conn.: Greenwood Press, 1986.

Marshall, Elizabeth. "Atlanta Peace Jubilee." *Georgia Historical Quarterly* 50 (September 1966): 276–82.

Martin, S. Walter. "Henry Bradley Plant." In *Georgians in Profile: Historical Essays in Honor of Ellis Merton Coulter,* pp. 261–76. Edited by Horace Montgomery. Athens: University of Georgia Press, 1958.

Martin, Thomas H. *Atlanta and Its Builders.* 2 vols. Atlanta: Century Memorial Publishing Co., 1902.

Mathis, Roy. "Mythology and the Mind of the South." *Georgia Historical Quarterly* 60 (Fall 1976): 228–38.

Matthews, John M. "Negro Republicans in the Reconstruction of Georgia." *Georgia Historical Quarterly* 60 (Summer 1976): 145–64.

———. "Studies in Race Relations in Georgia, 1890–1930." Ph.D. dissertation, Duke University, 1970.

McCloskey, Robert G. *American Conservatism in the Age of Enterprise, 1865–1910.* Cambridge, Mass.: Harvard University Press, 1951.

McClure, Alexander K. *The South: Its Industrial, Financial and Political Condition.* Philadelphia: J. B. Lippincott, 1886.

McCoy, Carl L. "A Historical Sketch of Black Augusta, Georgia, from Emancipation to the *Brown* Decision: 1865–1984." M.A. thesis, University of Georgia, 1984.

McDougald, Louise B. "A Trip Down Peachtree Street in 1886." *Atlanta Historical Bulletin* 21 (April 1940): 134–45.

McFeely, William S. *Grant: A Biography.* New York: Norton, 1981.

———. *Yankee Stepfather: General O. O. Howard and the Freedmen.* New Haven: Yale University Press, 1968.

McGuiness, Colleen, and Maria J. Sayers, eds. *American Leaders, 1789–1987.* Washington, D.C.: Congressional Quarterly, Inc., 1987.

McKelvey, Blake. "Penal Slavery and Southern Reconstruction." *Journal of Negro History* 20 (April 1935): 153–79.

McKinley, Carlyle. *An Appeal to Pharoah: The Negro Problem and Its Radical Solution.* New York: Fords, Howard & Hulbert, 1889.

McLaurin, Melton A. *Paternalism and Protest: Southern Cotton Mills and Organized Labor, 1875–1905.* Westport, Conn.: Greenwood Press, 1971.

McLeod, Jonathon W. "Black and White Workers: Atlanta During Reconstruction." Ph.D. dissertation, University of California, Los Angeles, 1987.

McMath, Robert C., Jr., Ronald H. Bayor, James E. Brittain, Lawrence Foster, August W. Griebelhaus, and Germaine M. Reed. *Engineering the New South: Georgia Tech, 1885–1985.* Athens: University of Georgia Press, 1985.

McWilliams, Tennant S. *The New South Faces the World: Foreign Affairs and the Southern Sense of Self, 1877–1950.* Baton Rouge: Louisiana State University Press, 1988.

Meier, August. *Negro Thought in America, 1880–1915: Racial Ideologies in the Age of Booker T. Washington.* Ann Arbor: University of Michigan Press, 1963.

Miller, Kelly. *Out of the House of Bondage.* New York: Neale Publishing Co., 1914.

Miller, William H. "Congressional Reconstruction as a Means of Perpetuating Radical Republicanism." M.A. thesis, Emory University, 1959.

Miller, William K. *History of St. Paul's Episcopal Church, Augusta, Georgia.* Augusta, Ga.: Tidwell Printing, 1945.

Mitchell, Broadus. *The Rise of the Cotton Mills in the South.* Baltimore: Johns Hopkins University Press, 1921.

Mitchell, Margaret. *Gone with the Wind.* New York: Macmillan, 1936.

Montgomery, David. *Beyond Equality: Labor and the Radical Republicans, 1862–1872.* New York: Knopf, 1967.

Moore, A. B. "One Hundred Years of Reconstruction." *Journal of Southern History* 9 (May 1943): 153–80.

Moore, James T. "Redeemers Reconsidered: Change and Continuity in the Democratic South, 1870–1900." *Journal of Southern History* 44 (August 1978): 357–78.

Moos, Malcolm. *The Republicans: A History of Their Party.* New York: Random House, 1956.

Murphy, Gregory, ed. *Builders of Georgia.* Atlanta: Gregory Murphy, 1941.

Myrdal, Gunnar. *An American Dilemma: The Negro Problem and Modern Democracy.* 2 vols. New York: Harper and Brothers, 1944.

Nathans, Elizabeth S. *Losing the Peace: Georgia Republicans and Reconstruction.* Baton Rouge: Louisiana State University Press, 1968.

National Cyclopedia of American Biography. Vol. 1. New York: James T. White & Co., 1892.

Newby, I. A. *Plain Folk in the New South: Social Change and Cultural Persistence, 1880–1915.* Baton Rouge: Louisiana State University Press, 1988.

Newman, Henry K. "The Vision of Order: White Protestant Christianity in Atlanta, 1865–1906." Ph.D. dissertation, Emory University, 1977.

Nixon, Raymond B. *Henry W. Grady: Spokesman of the New South.* New York: Knopf, 1943.

Noble, Annette L. *A History of the Presbyterian Church of Albion, New York, for One Hundred Years, 1824–1924*. Albion, N.Y.: N.p., 1924.

Northen, William J., ed. *Men of Mark in Georgia*. 7 vols. Atlanta: A. B. Caldwell, 1911.

Olsen, Otto H., ed. *Reconstruction and Redemption in the South*. Baton Rouge: Louisiana State University Press, 1980.

One Hundred Twenty-Fifth Anniversary of the First Presbyterian Church of Albion, New York. Albion, N.Y.: N.p., 1949.

Oubre, Claude. *Forty Acres and a Mule: The Freedmen's Bureau and Black Land Ownership*. Baton Rouge: Louisiana State University Press, 1978.

Parks, Joseph. *Joseph E. Brown of Georgia*. Baton Rouge: Louisiana State University Press, 1977.

Perdue, Robert. "The Negro as Reflected in the Atlanta Constitution, Atlanta Intelligencer, and Atlanta Daily New Era from 1868–1880." M.A. thesis, Atlanta University, 1963.

Perman, Michael. *Emancipation and Reconstruction, 1862–1879*. Arlington Heights, Ill.: Harlan Davidson, 1987.

———. *Reunion Without Compromise: The South and Reconstruction, 1865–1868*. Cambridge: Cambridge University Press, 1973.

———. *The Road to Redemption: Southern Politics, 1869–1879*. Chapel Hill: University of North Carolina Press, 1984.

Pfadenhauer, Ruby M. "History of Augusta Arsenal." *Richmond County History* 2 (Summer 1970): 1–40.

Pictorial History of Augusta, Georgia. Augusta, Ga.: Fleming, 1962.

Potter, David M. *People of Plenty: Economic Abundance and the American Character*. Chicago: University of Chicago Press, 1954.

Powell, Larry N. *New Masters: Northern Planters During the Civil War and Reconstruction*. New Haven: Yale University Press, 1980.

Prescott, Frank W. "A Footnote on Georgia's Constitutional History: The Item Veto of the Governors." *Georgia Historical Quarterly* 42 (December 1958): 1–25.

Prescott, George B. *History, Theory, and Practice of the Electric Telegraph*. Boston: Ticknor & Fields, 1866.

Rabinowitz, Howard N. *Race Relations in the Urban South, 1865–1900*. New York: Oxford University Press, 1978.

Rable, George C. *But There Was No Peace: The Role of Violence in the Politics of Reconstruction*. Athens: University of Georgia Press, 1984.

Radical Rule: Military Outrage in Georgia. Louisville, Ky.: Morton and Co., 1868.

Raffel, Burton. *Politicians, Poets, and Con Men: Emotional History in Late Victorian America*. Hamden, Conn.: Archon Books, 1986.

Range, Willard. "Hannibal I. Kimball." *Georgia Historical Quarterly* 29 (June 1945): 47–70.

Ransom, Roger L., and Richard Sutch. *One Kind of Freedom: The Economic Consequences of Emancipation*. Cambridge: Cambridge University Press, 1977.

Reagan, Alice E. *H. I. Kimball, Entrepreneur*. Atlanta: Cherokee Publishing, 1983.

——— . "Promoting the New South: Hannibal I. Kimball and Henry W. Grady." *Atlanta Historical Journal* 27 (September 1983): 5–20.

——— . "The Reconstruction and Redemption of the Fundamental Law: Constitutional Revision in Georgia, 1865–1877." *Southern Historian* 6 (Spring 1985): 28–39.

Reed, Wallace P., ed. *History of Atlanta, Georgia: With Illustrations and Biographical Sketches of Some of Its Prominent Men and Pioneers*. Syracuse, N.Y.: D. Mason, 1889.

Reid, James D. *The Telegraph in America: Its Founders, Promoters, and Noted Men*. New York: Derby Brothers, 1879.

Reidy, Joseph P. "Aaron A. Bradley: Voice of Black Labor in the Georgia Lowcountry." In Howard N. Rabinowitz, ed., *Southern Black Leaders in the Reconstruction Era*. Urbana: University of Illinois Press, 1982.

——— . *From Slavery to Agrarian Capitalism in the Cotton Plantation South: Central Georgia, 1800–1880*. Chapel Hill: University of North Carolina Press, 1991.

——— . "Masters and Slaves, Planters and Freedmen: The Transition from Slavery to Freedom in Central Georgia, 1820–1880." Ph.D. dissertation, Northern Illinois University, 1982.

Rice, Jessie Pearl. "Governor Rufus B. Bullock and Reconstruction in Georgia." M.A. thesis, Emory University, 1931.

Roark, James L. *Masters Without Slaves: Southern Planters in the Civil War and Reconstruction*. New York: Norton, 1977.

Roberts, Derrell C. *Joseph E. Brown and the Politics of Reconstruction*. University, Ala.: University of Alabama Press, 1973.

Ross, Earle D. *The Liberal Republican Movement*. New York: Henry Holt, 1910.

Rowan, Leslie Paul. "The Rise and Development of the Republican Party in Georgia." M.A. thesis, Emory University, 1948.

Russ, William A., Jr. "Radical Disfranchisement in Georgia, 1867–1871." *Georgia Historical Quarterly* 19 (September 1935): 175–209.

Russell, James M. *Atlanta, 1847–1890: City Building in the Old South and the New*. Baton Rouge: Louisiana State University Press, 1988.

——— . "Atlanta, Gate City of the South, 1847–1885." Ph.D. dissertation, Princeton University, 1972.

————. "Politics, Municipal Services, and the Working Class in Atlanta, 1865–1890." *Georgia Historical Quarterly* 66 (Winter 1982): 467–91.

Russell, James M., and William Thornberry. "William Finch and Reconstruction Politics in Atlanta: The Black Politician as Civic Leader." In *Southern Black Leaders of the Reconstruction Era*, pp. 314–21. Edited by Howard N. Rabinowitz. Urbana: University of Illinois Press, 1982.

St. Philip's Parish, Atlanta, Georgia: Historical Notes, 1847–1897. Atlanta: V. P. Sisson, 1897.

Saye, Albert B. *A Constitutional History of Georgia, 1732–1945.* Athens: University of Georgia Press, 1948.

Schott, Thomas. *Alexander H. Stephens of Georgia: A Biography.* Baton Rouge: Louisiana State University Press, 1987.

Scott, Carole E. "Coping with Inflation: Atlanta, 1860–1865." *Georgia Historical Quarterly* 69 (Winter 1985): 536–56.

Scott, Marion L. "The Atlanta Race Riot of 1906 and Press Coverage of Race-Related Crimes." M.A. thesis, University of Georgia, 1979.

Scroggs, Jack B. "Carpetbagger Constitutional Reform in the South Atlantic States, 1867–1868." *Journal of Southern History* 27 (November 1961): 475–93.

————. "Carpetbagger Influence in the Political Reconstruction of the South Atlantic States, 1865–1876." Ph.D. dissertation, University of North Carolina, 1951.

————. "Southern Reconstruction: A Radical View." *Journal of Southern History* 24 (November 1958): 407–29.

Sefton, James E. *The United States Army and Reconstruction, 1865–1877.* Baton Rouge: Louisiana State University Press, 1967.

Shadgett, Olive Hall. *The Republican Party in Georgia: From Reconstruction Through 1900.* Athens: University of Georgia Press, 1964.

Shavin, Norman, and Bruce Galphin. *Atlanta: Triumph of a People.* Atlanta: Capricorn, 1982.

Shenton, James P., ed. *The Reconstruction: A Documentary History of the South After the Civil War, 1865–1877.* New York: Putnam and Co., 1963.

Shingleton, Royce. *Richard Peters: Champion of the New South.* Macon, Ga.: Mercer University Press, 1985.

Shore, Laurence. *Southern Capitalists: The Ideological Leadership of an Elite, 1832–1885.* Chapel Hill: University of North Carolina Press, 1986.

Shufelt, Marcia. "A Checklist of Atlanta, Georgia, Imprints: From 1846 to 1876, with a Historical Introduction." M.S. thesis, Catholic University of America, 1956.

Signor, Isaac S. *Landmarks of Orleans County, New York.* Syracuse, N.Y.: D. Mason, 1894.

Simkins, Francis B. "New Viewpoints of Southern Reconstruction." *Journal of Negro History* 5 (February 1939): 49–61.

Smith, Albert C. "Down Freedom's Road: The Contours of Race, Class, and Property Crime in Black-Belt Georgia, 1866–1910." Ph.D. dissertation, University of Georgia, 1982.

Smith, Allen Candler. "The Republican Party in Georgia, 1867–1871." M.A. thesis, Duke University, 1937.

Smith, John D. *An Old Creed for the New South: Proslavery Ideology and Historiography, 1865–1918*. Westport, Conn.: Greenwood Press, 1985.

Smith, W. Calvin. "The Reconstruction 'Triumph' of Rufus B. Bullock." *Georgia Historical Quarterly* 52 (December 1968): 414–25.

———. "Rufus Brown Bullock and the Third Reconstruction of Georgia, 1867–1871." M.A. thesis, University of North Carolina, 1964.

Smyth, G. Hutchinson. *The Life of Henry B. Plant: Founder and President of the Plant System of Railroads and Steamships and Also of the Southern Express Company*. New York: G. P. Putnam's Sons, 1898.

Stampp, Kenneth M., and Leon F. Litwack, eds. *Reconstruction: An Anthology of Revisionist Writings*. Baton Rouge: Louisiana State University Press, 1969.

Stevens, O. B., ed. *Georgia: Historical and Industrial*. Atlanta: Harrison, 1901.

The Story of the Organization and First Fifty Years, 1844–1894, of Christ Church, Albion, New York. Albion, N.Y.: A. M. Eddy, 1894.

Stovall, Pleasant A. *Robert Toombs: Statesman, Speaker, Soldier, Sage*. New York: Cassell Publishing Company, 1892.

Stover, John F. "Northern Financial Interests in Southern Railroads, 1865–1900." *Georgia Historical Quarterly* 39 (September 1955): 205–20.

Summers, Mark W. *The Plundering Generation: Corruption and the Crisis of the Union, 1849–1861*. New York: Oxford University Press, 1987.

———. *Railroads, Reconstruction, and the Gospel of Prosperity: Aid Under the Radical Republicans, 1865–1877*. Princeton: Princeton University Press, 1984.

Talmadge, John E. "The Death Blow to Independentism in Georgia." *Georgia Historical Quarterly* 39 (March 1955): 37–47.

Taylor, A. Elizabeth. "The Abolition of the Convict Lease System in Georgia." *Georgia Historical Quarterly* 26 (September 1942): 273–87.

———. "The Convict Lease System in Georgia, 1866–1908." M.A. thesis, University of North Carolina, 1940.

———. "The Origins and Development of the Convict Lease System in Georgia." *Georgia Historical Quarterly* 26 (June 1942): 113–28.

Taylor, Arthur R. "From the Ashes: Atlanta During Reconstruction, 1865–1876." Ph.D. dissertation, Emory University, 1973.

Tebeau, C. W. "Visitors' Views of Georgia Politics and Life, 1865–1880." *Georgia Historical Quarterly* 26 (March 1942): 1–15.

Terry, S. M. "Depiction of the Reconstruction Period in Georgia History Textbooks." *Georgia Social Science Journal* 14 (1983): 5–10.

Thomas, Arad. *Pioneer History of Orleans County, New York*. Albion, N.Y.: Orleans American Steam Print, 1871.

Thompson, C. Mildred. *Reconstruction in Georgia: Economic, Social, Political, 1865–1872*. 1915. Reprint. Savannah, Ga.: Beehive Press, 1972.

Thompson, Holland. *The New South*. New Haven: Yale University Press, 1919.

Thompson, Margaret Susan. *The "Spider Web": Congress and Lobbying in the Age of Grant*. Ithaca, N.Y.: Cornell University Press, 1986.

Thornberry, Jerry J. "The Development of Black Atlanta, 1865–1885." Ph.D. dissertation, University of Maryland, 1977.

Tindall, George B. *The Disruption of the Solid South*. Athens: University of Georgia Press, 1972.

Trelease, Allen W. *White Terror: The Ku Klux Klan Conspiracy and Southern Reconstruction*. New York: Harper & Row, 1971.

Tretten, Rudie W. *Morality in Government: Dream or Necessity?* Boston: Allyn and Bacon, 1977.

Waddell, James D. *Biographical Sketch of Linton Stephens*. Atlanta: Dodson & Scott, 1877.

Wallenstein, Peter. *From Slave South to New South: Public Policy in Nineteenth-Century Georgia*. Chapel Hill: University of North Carolina Press, 1987.

Wallerstein, Immanuel. *The Modern World-System: Capitalist Agriculture and the Origins of the European World-Economy in the Sixteenth Century*. New York: Academic Press, 1974.

Walton, Hanes. *Black Republicans: The Politics of the Black and Tans*. Metuchen, N.J.: Scarecrow Press, 1975.

Ward, Judson C., Jr. "Georgia Under the Bourbon Democrats, 1872–1890." M.A. thesis, University of North Carolina, 1947.

———. "The New Departure Democrats of Georgia: An Interpretation." *Georgia Historical Quarterly* 41 (September 1957): 227–36.

———. "The Republican Party in Bourbon Georgia." *Georgia Historical Quarterly* 39 (December 1955): 37–47.

———. "The Republican Party in Bourbon Georgia, 1872–1890." *Journal of Southern History* 9 (May 1943): 196–209.

Watson, Thomas E. "Some Aftermath of the Civil War." *Watson Magazine*, August 1907, pp. 781–92.

Watts, Eugene J. "Black Political Progress in Atlanta, 1868–1895." *Journal of Negro History* 59 (July 1974): 268–86.

———. *The Social Bases of City Politics: Atlanta, 1865–1903*. Westport, Conn.: Greenwood Press, 1978.

Weibe, Robert H. *The Search for Order, 1877–1920*. New York: Hill and Wang, 1967.

Weisberger, Bernard A. "The Dark and Bloody Ground of Reconstruction Historiography." *Journal of Southern History* 25 (November 1959): 427–47.

Weldon, Ellen. "The *Atlanta Constitution* Views the Ku Klux Klan: 1868–1872." M.A. thesis, University of Missouri, 1964.

Werner, Randolph D. "Hegemony and Conflict: The Political Economy of a Southern Region, Augusta, Georgia, 1865–1895." Ph.D. dissertation, University of Virginia, 1977.

Williams, T. Harry. *Romance and Realism in Southern Politics*. Athens: University of Georgia Press, 1961.

Williford, William Bailey. *Peachtree Street, Atlanta*. Athens: University of Georgia Press, 1962.

Wilson, Charles Reagan. *Baptized in Blood: The Religion of the Lost Cause, 1865–1920*. Athens: University of Georgia Press, 1980.

Wingo, Horace C. "Race Relations in Georgia, 1872–1908." Ph.D. dissertation, University of Georgia, 1969.

Woodward, C. Vann. *American Counterpoint: Slavery and Racism in North-South Dialogue*. Boston: Little, Brown, 1971.

———. *The Burden of Southern History*. Baton Rouge: Louisiana State University Press, 1960.

———. *Origins of the New South, 1877–1913*. Baton Rouge: Louisiana State University Press, 1951.

———. *Reunion and Reaction: The Compromise of 1877 and the End of Reconstruction*. Boston: Little, Brown, 1951.

———. *The Strange Career of Jim Crow*. New York: Oxford University Press, 1955.

Wooley, Edwin C. *The Reconstruction of Georgia*. 1901. Reprint. New York: AMS Press, 1970.

Wotton, Grigsby H. "New City of the South: Atlanta, 1843–1873." Ph.D. dissertation, Johns Hopkins University, 1973.

Wright, Gavin. *Old South, New South: Revolutions in the Southern Economy Since the Civil War*. New York: Basic Books, 1986.

Wyatt-Brown, Bertram. *Southern Honor: Ethics and Behavior in the Old South*. New York: Oxford University Press, 1982.

Wyld, Lionel D., ed. *40' × 28' × 4': The Erie Canal, 150 Years*. Rome, N.Y.: Oneida County Commission, 1967.

Wynne, Lewis N. *The Continuity of Cotton: Planter Politics in Georgia, 1865–1892*. Macon, Ga.: Mercer University Press, 1986.

Young, Edward B. "The Negro in Georgia Politics, 1867–1877." M.A. thesis, Emory University, 1955.

Young, T. M. *The American Cotton Industry: A Study of Work and Workers*. New York: Charles Scribner's Sons, 1903.

Zuber, Richard L. "The Role of Rufus Brown Bullock in Georgia Politics." M.A. thesis, Emory University, 1957.

Index